No Better Death

No Better Death

The Great War diaries and letters
of William G. Malone

Edited by John Crawford
with Peter Cooke

In association with the New Zealand Defence Force
to commemorate the centenary of the First World War

EXISLE
PUBLISHING

First published 2014.
This is an updated and corrected edition of a work
published by Reed Publishing in 2005.

Exisle Publishing Limited,
P.O. Box 60-490, Titirangi, Auckland 0642, New Zealand.
'Moonrising', Narone Creek Road, Wollombi, NSW 2325, Australia.
www.exislepublishing.com

A catalogue record for this book is available from
the National Library of New Zealand.

ISBN 978-1-77559-128-3

10 9 8 7 6 5 4 3 2 1

Text design and production by IslandBridge
Cover design by Nick Turzynski, redinc.
Printed in Shenzhen, China, by Ink Asia

Contents

Foreword

Lieutenant General Tim Keating

The centenary of the First World War is a time for us to reflect on the achievements and experiences of New Zealanders during that terrible conflict. One of the more than 18,000 New Zealanders to lose their lives in the war was Lieutenant-Colonel William Malone, who was killed on 8 August 1915 leading the epic defence of Chunuk Bair, the highest point seized by the Allies during the Gallipoli campaign. Before he set out on the operation to seize Chunuk Bair, Malone considered that he had little chance of surviving the battle. So it proved. Along with more than 300 of his men, Malone still lies in an unmarked grave on Chunuk Bair.

For many years after his death, Malone's achievements and qualities were not widely appreciated. Over the last 30 years, thanks to the work of his grandson, Edmond, and others he has justifiably become a national hero. This new edition of *No Better Death: The Great War Diaries and Letters of William G. Malone* will foster a greater understanding of this complex man, whose many fine qualities and love of New Zealand shine through his writings. *No Better Death* also tells us much about the loving relationship Malone had with his wife, Ida, and about the experiences of a family at war.

Like so many New Zealand families, the Malones have a proud record of serving the nation in wartime. William Malone and four of his sons served in the New Zealand Expeditionary Force. One, Lieutenant Edmond Malone MC, was killed, and a fifth son, Captain Barney Malone, was killed in action during the Second World War. Other descendants of William Malone fought in the Second World War. In 2012 his great-great-grandson, Lance Corporal Rory Malone, was mortally wounded in a fierce engagement in Afghanistan.

Malone was hard-working, intelligent and thoughtful, but was not an easy man to serve under. Throughout his military service he set exacting performance standards for himself and those under his command. He was intent on shaping his battalion into a fine fighting force, and did not seek popularity. Nonetheless, the officers and men of the Wellington Infantry

Battalion became devoted to Malone once they realised that he asked nothing of them that he was not prepared to do himself and had their best interests at heart.

Although it is almost a century since Malone was killed, a great deal of what he says about leadership and courage, both moral and physical, remains highly relevant to the men and women of the New Zealand Defence Force.

Finally, I am convinced that New Zealanders who read Malone's account of the heroism and endurance displayed by their countrymen at Gallipoli will be filled with pride, reminded of the debt we owe those who have freely given up their lives in defence of our homeland, and convinced that William Malone was a truly great New Zealander.

Tim Keating
Lieutenant General
Chief of Defence Force

February 2014

Acknowledgements

We would like to acknowledge again all those who assisted or supported the production of the first edition of this book, published in 2005. Members of the Malone family played a crucial role in the successful completion of the first edition of the diaries and letters of William George Malone. We would especially like to thank Judy Malone, Tessa Keegan, Clare Lyons and Anita Young for allowing us to make use of their valuable archival collections. We also acknowledge the work of the late Ted Malone who deposited the diaries and letters in the Alexander Turnbull Library and who did a great deal of research into his grandfather's life.

The Chief of the Defence Force in 2005, Air Marshal Bruce Ferguson, saw immediately when the proposal for the publication of an edition of Malone's diaries and letters was presented to him that it would be an appropriate way for the New Zealand Defence Force to mark the 90th anniversary of the Gallipoli campaign. He was an enthusiastic supporter of the project and maintained an active interest in its progress throughout. The project director, Warren Inkster, played a significant role in bringing the publication of the Malone diaries and letters to fruition. We especially thank Melissa Ford, Janet Krivan and Mata Parakoti for their many hours of hard work transcribing the diaries and letters.

We could not have delivered on our tight deadlines without the assistance of many people, including Lea Bellini, Ray Cleaver, Dennis Davidson, Ashley Gould, Boris Halliday, Joan Keate, Des Malone, Andrew Menken, Hilda McDonnell, Murray Moorhead, Anna Rogers, Philip Rankin, Sean Shadbolt, Debbie Sheehy, Mary Slatter, L.J. Smith, Carol Spragg, Gillian Tasker, Kevin Vincent, Derek Weber and Rosalie Whitmore.

The following institutions and their staff assisted us with our work on the book: Alexander Turnbull Library; National Library of New Zealand, Te Puna Matauranga O Aotearoa; Kippenberger Military Archive and Research Library, Queen Elizabeth II Army Memorial Museum; Archives New Zealand; Australian War Memorial; Auckland War Memorial Museum; Defence Library, Headquarters New Zealand Defence Force; New Zealand Defence Force Personnel Archives; Puke Ariki and District Libraries,

New Plymouth; St Patrick's College (Wellington); Stratford District Council; Te Papa Museum of New Zealand; Wairarapa Archive; Whanganui Regional Museum; Wanganui District Library; Ministry for Culture and Heritage. We thank especially Margaret Calder, who was in 2005 the Chief Librarian, Alexander Turnbull Library and David Colquhoun, Curator, Manuscripts and Archives, for providing permission for the New Zealand Defence Force to publish the diaries and their enthusiastic support for the project.

In addition to those thanked in the acknowledgements to the first edition, we would like to acknowledge the valuable assistance we have received during the preparation of this revised edition from Judy Malone. William and Ida Malone's three British-based granddaughters, Tessa Keegan, Anita Young and Clare Lyons have again been of great assistance. We also acknowledge the part their late sister, Phillida Bassett, had in preserving the Malone family archive in London. Denis Malone freely shared his memories of his late son Rory. Many other people have also been of assistance, including Matthew Buck, Melissa Ford, Penny and Zane Kidd, John McLeod, Ian Maxwell, Chris Pugsley and Major Craig Wilson. Ian Watt and his highly professional team at Exisle Publishing have done fine work to produce a first-rate book.

The Chief of Defence Force, Lieutenant General Tim Keating, and his predecessor, Lieutenant General Rhys Jones, could not have been more supportive of the project to mark the centenary of the outbreak of the First World War with a new edition of William Malone's diaries and letters.

Finally, we again thank our families for their support and assistance during our work on this book.

John Crawford   *Peter Cooke*
February 2014

Preface

During the last year of his life, August 1914 to August 1915, William George Malone wrote a substantial quantity of official, demi-official and private correspondence, kept a detailed diary and took many photographs. Like other soldiers in the Great War, Malone wanted to document his military service both to aid his own memory and to inform his family. The letters he wrote and received were highly important to him as the key way in which he could maintain contact with his family, friends and former life.[1] He went to some trouble to ensure that this material was preserved, periodically sending copies of his diary and letters to his wife Ida.[2] Malone's diaries and letters do not simply set out the work of a capable, hard-working officer. They tell us a great deal about his character, his relationship with his wife and children, his values, view of the world and his place in it. He regarded his service at Gallipoli as the high point of his life. On 27 May 1915, for example, he wrote that he was 'Living as I never lived before'. His wartime experiences led him to reassess his life and made him determined to be a better husband and father in the future.[3]

The diaries and letters reproduced in this edition are drawn from the W.G. Malone collection of the Alexander Turnbull Library in Wellington. This collection consists, with a few exceptions, of Malone's demi-official and private writings. The papers amount to more than 135,000 words, and in this edition it has been necessary to delete some diary entries and letters and sections of others that are repetitive or contain material of limited interest. The great bulk of the deleted material relates to the period before the start of the Gallipoli campaign. The letter books contain copies of correspondence with a large number of people. The correspondence ranges from highly personal letters to his wife to fairly routine correspondence about business or military matters. The books also include copies of a few pieces of official correspondence, but mainly contain material of a personal or demi-official nature. Malone usually wrote up his diary daily, except when he was particularly busy. In general he wrote substantial entries for the great majority of days.[4] He illustrated his diaries and letters with many small drawings and sketch maps, some of which are reproduced in this edition.

Malone's diaries and letters were deposited in the Alexander Turnbull Library in 1988 by a grandson, Edmond Penn (Ted) Malone. He had earlier received them from his uncle, Denis Malone, who had in turn received them from his mother, William Malone's widow, Ida. Earlier, in 1980, the New Zealand High Commission in London had given the library a copy of a typescript copy of the diary held by Mrs Massey-Stewart, the widow of Lieutenant-Colonel Hugh Stewart. She had no idea how her late husband, who was the author of the official history of the New Zealand Expeditionary Force [NZEF] on the Western Front, had come to have the document in his possession. This typescript is most probably a corrected version of a typescript prepared in the 1920s by Ida Malone with the assistance of Denis Malone. A copy of this earlier typescript was given, it appears, to Brian Malone, a son of William Malone, most probably during the 1920s.[5] As part of this project, a new complete transcript of the diaries and letters has been prepared and deposited at the Alexander Turnbull Library.

The diary and letters were written, in pencil, under often difficult circumstances on whatever paper Malone had available. The first group of diaries and letter books [Alexander Turnbull library references, MSX 2541, 42, 43, 48 and 49] are manifold books that Malone had purchased in New Zealand. These books were specially designed so that carbon copies of whatever was written in them could be easily produced. Malone purchased several similar books in Cairo that he used during his stay in Egypt and during the early part of his service at Gallipoli [MSX 2544, 45, 46 and 47]. He then resorted to using official NZEF field service correspondence books (Army Book 152), [MSX 2550, 51, 52 and 53]. When he first landed at Gallipoli [25 April to 14 May 1915] and towards the end of his life, Malone was obliged to use NZEF message and signal form pads (Army Form C2121) for his diaries [MS papers 4130]. These form books were not specifically designed for making copies of material written in them, so if Malone continued to make copies he must have used loose writing and carbon paper. The last few entries in Malone's diary [2 to 5 Aug 1915] are written in the correspondence book of Lieutenant Douglas Bryan who had earlier been wounded and evacuated from Gallipoli [MSX 2547]. This book and MSX 2546 [diary 10 Apr 1915–25 Apr 1915 and 29 May–1 Aug 1915] contain both the original and carbon copies of the diary, probably because Malone was killed before he had sent these parts of his diary to his wife. The collection at the Alexander Turnbull Library, therefore, consists of a mixture of original diaries and carbon copies.

On at least one occasion during the Gallipoli campaign Malone made use of paper from the haversack of a dead Turkish soldier that he had found while searching for material with intelligence value. We only know of the existence of this letter because it was published in New Zealand newspapers. It is quite possible that he did not make copies of all his letters or that the copies of some letters have been lost.[6] In particular, Malone seems to have written more condolence letters to the next of kin of men from his battalion than are included in the collection.[7]

After William Malone was killed, his effects were sent to his widow. It follows, therefore, that Ida Malone should have had both the original and carbon copies of the diaries, the letter books and at least some of the letters Malone received while on active service. The Malone family in London hold a few of the letters received by Malone between August 1914 and August 1915, but none of those sent by Ida. They do not hold the original diaries missing from the Alexander Turnbull's collection. The missing letters were destroyed by Denis Malone. On her deathbed Ida Malone instructed Denis, who was particularly close to his mother, to destroy her often intimate letters to William Malone and his letters to her. Denis did as his mother asked, but overlooked the carbon copies that William Malone had kept of his letters to Ida.[8] The fate of the missing original diaries is unknown.

The circumstances under which he wrote, Malone's handwriting, his extensive use of abbreviations and a number of idiosyncratic conventions, combine to make much of the manuscript material reproduced in this volume very difficult to read. Malone, for instance, attached the ampersand [&] he almost always used in place of 'and', to the word that followed it. He also often placed question marks in front of the word being referred to. Although considerable effort has gone into deciphering the original letters and diaries, some words are illegible and are marked as such. In cases where there is doubt about what Malone has written, this is indicated by: [?]. In order to make the text more readily understandable, it has been necessary to make a number of editorial decisions. The guiding principle in the editorial process has been to keep the published text as close as possible to what Malone actually wrote in his diaries and letters.

All material that appears in square brackets is editorial insertion. The most important editorial conventions concern the use of abbreviations, punctuation and spelling. The number of abbreviations used in the material, especially in the diaries, has been reduced. For instance, when Malone uses 'Sfd' to refer to the town of Stratford, this edition gives the town's name in full. Similarly 'about' and 'enough' are rendered in full, rather than as 'abt' and 'eno'. Malone was not consistent in his use of abbreviations, sometimes giving a word in full and on other occasions using two or three different abbreviations. In such cases, when a word appears in full it has been left in this form and when it has been abbreviated, the abbreviation most commonly used by Malone is generally used. For instance, the abbreviation Bn for Battalion is used throughout the published text. The list of abbreviations used in the book includes words that are generally abbreviated by Malone, but that appear in full in the published text.

In his diaries and letters, Malone rarely used apostrophes and where necessary these have been inserted into the text in the interests of clarity. Where Malone repeatedly mis-spelt a word, such as a person's surname, the mis-spelling is corrected in the first instance and the correct spelling used from then on. The names of ships are referred to in various ways in the letters and diaries, and in the interests of clarity and consistency they have all been rendered in italics in the published text. Italics are also used for non-English words and phrases and the titles of books and other publications. Malone made use of some obscure colloquial expressions, especially in his diaries, and whenever possible the most likely meaning has been noted. The diaries and letters include many short, unnecessary paragraphs and in some cases these have been combined in order to save space. Malone's idiosyncratic use of commas and capitalisation has not been corrected unless it makes the meaning unclear. The book includes endnotes that identify and give information about people mentioned by Malone and additional material relevant to the text. The biographical notes are set out in the following way: Rank at time of Malone's mention (highest rank achieved)–Christian name–other initials–surname, regiment or corps (if significant); awards (listed in order of precedence); date of birth–place of birth–date of death; marital status–occupation–place of enlistment; regimental number–subunit–unit; fate; service in South African War (if relevant); later significant details, including service in World War II. The biographical notes and many of the other endnotes were prepared by Peter Cooke, who also did a great deal of work on the transcription of the diaries and letters. In addition, Peter carried out the photographic research for the book and assisted with research on other matters.

John Crawford
February 2014

Glossary

A	Australian
a	acting
A/C	Account
abt	about, a contraction used by WGM
affect, affectly	affectionate, affectionately
AIB	Auckland Infantry Battalion
AIF	Australian Imperial Force
Ammn	Ammunition
AMR	Auckland Mounted Rifles Regiment
ann	annum
ANZ	Archives New Zealand, Wellington
ARRC	Associate (or 2nd Class) Royal Red Cross
ATL	Alexander Turnbull Library, National Library of New Zealand Te Puna Matauranga O Aotearoa
att	attached
Aust and Austn	Australian
aye	forever
BAC	Brigade Ammunition Column
Bde	Brigade. WGM often used Bgde
Bgadier	Brigadier, a contraction often used by WGM
Bn	Battalion
Brig	Brigadier
Bty	Battery
C	Celsius
Capt	Captain
CB	Companion of the Most Honourable Order of the Bath
CBE	Commander of the Most Excellent Order of the British Empire
CG	Croix de Guerre, awarded by France and Belgium
CIB	Canterbury Infantry Battalion

CMG	Companion of the Most Distinguished Order of St Michael and St George
CMR	Canterbury Mounted Rifles
Col	Colonel
Corp	Corporal
Cour	Ordre de Couronne, awarded by Belgium
Coy	Company
DAC	Division Ammunition Column
Dan	Ordre of Danilo, issued by Montenegro
DCM	Distinguished Conduct Medal
Div or Divn	Division
Divl, Divnl	Divisional, contractions used by WGM
do do	ditto
DOD	Died of Disease (sickness)
DOW	Died of Wounds
DSO	Distinguished Service Order (2 = '& Bar', a second DSO)
E	East
eno	enough
ere	before
FA	Field Artillery
Fd	Field
GCB	Knight Grand Cross of the Most Honourable Order of the Bath
Gen	General
Genl	General, WGM sometimes wrote the word in full
GOC	General Officer Commanding
HG	Home Guard
HQ	Headquarters. WGM also used HdQrs and Hdqrs
HQNZDF	Headquarters New Zealand Defence Force, Wellington
I	Infantry
IKM	Ida Katherine Jemima Malone
Inf	infantry
Inst	abbreviation of instant, meaning 'this month'
Kara	Star of Karageorge, issued by Serbia
KBE	Knight Commander of the Most Excellent Order of the British Empire
KCB	Knight Commander of the Most Honourable Order of the Bath

KCMG	Knight Commander of the Most Distinguished Order of St Michael and St George
KIA	Killed in Action
KMARL	Kippenberger Military Archive and Research Library, Queen Elizabeth II Army Memorial Museum, Waiouru
L/Cpl	Lance-Corporal
Leo	Ordre de Leopold, awarded by Belgium
LH	Légion d'Honneur, awarded by France
Lt	Lieutenant
Lt-Col	Lieutenant-Colonel
M/gun	machine gun
Maj	Major
MBE	Member of the Most Excellent Order of the British Empire
MC	Military Cross
MFCL	Malone Family Collection London
MIA	Missing in Action
mid	Mention in Despatches (number of times)
MM	Military Medal
MR	Mounted Rifles
N	North
NCO	Non-Commissioned Officer
nd	no date
NZ	New Zealand
Nzder	New Zealander
N Zealander	New Zealander
NZAOC	NZ Army Ordnance Corps
NZASC	NZ Army Service Corps
NZE	NZ Engineers
NZEF	NZ Expeditionary Force
NZFA	NZ Field Artillery
NZPS	NZ Permanent Staff
NZSC	NZ Staff Corps
OBE	Officer of the Most Excellent Order of the British Empire
OC	Officer Commanding, refers to all Commandant and Commanding Officer positions
OIB	Otago Infantry Battalion
OMR	Otago Mounted Rifles Regiment

Pdrs	Pounders
P/F	Personal File, files opened on every member of the New Zealand Military Forces
POW	Prisoner of War
Pte	Private
QM	Quartermaster, as in QM-Sgt
RA	Royal Artillery
Refts	Reinforcement drafts
Regt	Regiment
Reinfcts	Reinforcements, a contraction generally used by WGM
RFA	Royal Field Artillery
RND	Royal Naval Division
S	South
S A	Salvation Army
Sam	Samaritan Cross, awarded by Serbia
2i/c	Second In Command
2/Lt	2nd Lieutenant
Sfd	Stratford
Sgt	Sergeant
Sgt-Maj	Sergeant-Major
Sigs	Signals
SSWar	Brought to the notice of the Secretary of State for War (number of times)
Stan	Order of St Stanislav, awarded by Russia
TD	Territorial Decoration
Ulto	abbreviation of ultimo, meaning 'of last month'
VC	Victoria Cross
VD	Volunteer Decoration
W	West
WE	Order of the White Eagle, awarded by Serbia
WGM	William George Malone
Wgton, Wgtn	Wellington, contractions generally used by WGM
WIA	Wounded in Action
WIB	Wellington Infantry Battalion
WMR	Wellington Mounted Rifles Regiment
WO	Warrant-Officer
yd	yard
yday	yesterday, a contraction almost always used by WGM
Yr	your

Introduction

A full and varied life

Lieutenant-Colonel William George Malone lived and died by the doctrine he set out for his children in a letter he wrote before he sailed from New Zealand in 1914: 'work and duty – duty to themselves – their fellows and above all to their country!'[1] He would certainly have approved of the way in which he met his end: heroically leading his men in desperate fighting on Chunuk Bair at Gallipoli on 8 August 1915. In fact as Malone put it, he could imagine 'no better death'.[2]

During his 56 years he had achieved a great deal in farming and legal affairs, as well as being a devoted husband and father. There can, however, be no doubt that he regarded the last year of his life, from August 1914 to August 1915 as the year of his most significant accomplishments. This was the year in which Malone prepared and then led in battle the Wellington Infantry Battalion.

William George Malone has probably become the best-known New Zealander to serve at Gallipoli. His name is forever connected with the epic capture and defence of Chunuk Bair. It is perhaps less well known that it was he who introduced the 'lemon squeezer' hat that has become an icon of the New Zealand Army. His status as a representative of the generation of New Zealanders who fought in the Great War was emphasised when one of his last letters to his wife was read by the Governor-General Dame Silvia Cartwright at the memorial service honouring New Zealand's Unknown Warrior on 11 November 2004.

On 24 January 1859 William Malone was born in the village of Lewisham in Kent, which is now a suburb of London. Although his birth certificate refers to him as William Malone he was always known as William George Malone. Other members of the Malone family generally called him Willie.[3] He was the second child of Thomas Augustine Malone and Louisa Malone, née Childs.[4] Malone's grandfather had emigrated from Ireland to England and his father was born in England. Thomas Malone was an able chemist, who had since the mid-1840s been an assistant to the leading scientist and developer of the negative-positive system of photography, William Henry Fox Talbot. After working for Fox Talbot in Reading, where he had previously been employed in a shop that sold the scientist chemicals, Thomas Malone moved to London where he continued to work for Fox Talbot until his death. He became a Fellow of the Chemical Society and was acquainted with a number leading British scientists of the day.[5]

Thomas Malone, who was a staunch Roman Catholic, died in 1867 at the age of 44. His death left the family in reduced circumstances financially. His son William was educated at a succession of Catholic schools. He first attended St Joseph's College in the London suburb of Clapham. Later he went as a boarder to a Marist Brothers school in Plymouth, before spending two years at another Marist Brothers school in Lille, France. During his time in Lille, Malone became fluent in French.[6] He was a competent pianist with a strong interest in music, especially classical music.[7]

After completing his education in France, Malone started work in an office in London in 1876. The same year he demonstrated an early interest in military matters by joining the London and Westminster Rifle Volunteers. In 1877 he transferred to the Royal Naval Artillery Volunteers. He served in that unit as a Seaman Gunner until 1879, when he sailed for New Zealand on the *Western Monarch*.[8] Throughout the rest of his life Malone seems to have been interested in small boats and boating.[9]

Malone travelled as a steerage passenger [the cheapest type of passage], landing in New Zealand in January 1880. On arriving in the colony, Malone transferred to a smaller ship which took him to Opunake beach where he and his luggage were rowed ashore. The young immigrant tipped the lighterman sixpence, but he returned it saying: 'You'll be needing this yourself before long'.[10] The following month he enlisted in the Armed Constabulary. His older brother, Austin, had already emigrated to New Zealand and had been serving in the Armed Constabulary since May 1878. Both brothers apparently served at Opunake. Austin Malone left the Armed Constabulary in November 1880. A year later William Malone was part of the force that suppressed Te Whiti o Rongomai

William George Malone in 1879, as he prepared to set out for a new life in New Zealand.

Malone Family Collection Wellington (now in ATL)

and Tohu's community at Parihaka. In April 1882 he took his discharge from the Armed Constabulary. He worked for a short period on the surf-boats operating on the Opunake coast. William then went into partnership with Austin in a small block of 79 acres of bush country at Stratford in Taranaki. William Malone, it appears, first became acquainted with the Stratford area in 1881 when he was made Drill-Instructor Sergeant for a newly raised Volunteer Corps, the Stratford Rangers. Shortly after they began farming, the Malone brothers were joined by their mother and their two sisters, Louisa [known as Louie] and Agnes. They may well have provided some of the capital to purchase the block of land on the Opunake Road, Stratford, which was valued at £220.[11] In January 1886 the Malone brothers' farm suffered significant damage in a huge bush fire that devastated much of the Stratford area.[12] William Malone had a reputation for being a good neighbour, who would go out of his way to help others. On one occasion, Austin and William went, in the middle of the night, to assist a neighbour in the awkward and strenuous task of rescuing a horse or a cow that was stuck in a waterhole.[13]

William George Malone was a man of great energy and drive and in a few years succeeded through hard work in converting his bush-covered land into productive farmland.[14] He was also a keen rugby player who in 1889 and 1890 represented Taranaki.[15] The partnership between the Malone

Malone's first family house, near Stratford, in July 1902. Two of Malone's sons can be seen wearing distinctive lemon squeezer hats.

Malone Family Collection Wellington (now in ATL)

brothers was dissolved in 1889, after which Austin Malone farmed on his own account near Stratford.[16] Austin later fell on hard times. He moved away from Taranaki and was killed in an accident while working with a railway construction gang in South Auckland on 19 February 1915.[17]

In New Plymouth, on 27 November 1886, Malone married Elinor Lucy Penn aged 22, a member of a well-to-do Taranaki family.[18] They had five children: Edmond Leo born in September 1888, Terence Joseph in August 1890, Brian in May 1893, Maurice Patrick in May 1895 and Norah in October 1897.[19]

Malone's 'personality and ability speedily earned him the confidence and respect of his fellow settlers, whom he ably served on local bodies.'[20] During the 1880s he was as a member and for a time chairman of the Ngaire Road Board and a member of the Hawera County Council. In 1890 Malone set himself up as a land and commission agent in Stratford.[21]

In June 1890, Malone was a member of a delegation of local people who went to Wellington to lobby the government to open the East Road to facilitate settlement of the area from Stratford to Otorohanga. Some local people saw this initiative as being prompted, at least in part, by the self-interest of large landholders in the area and others who stood to benefit from the development of this district. Later in the year Malone was a key figure in the successful campaign to establish the Stratford County Council. At the public meeting to initiate steps to form the new local body, Malone attacked the Hawera County Council for failing to undertake essential public works in the area, in particular the East Road. The new local body took over the responsibilities of four roads boards and the Stratford Town Board and was an important step in the development of the area. The following year Malone was appointed the new county's first clerk-treasurer, a part-time position carrying a salary of £52 a year. Within a few years Malone was regarded as an expert on municipal law whose advice was 'eagerly sought' by and 'generously given' to other local body officials. He held the post until he resigned in 1900. For much of this time the council's office was in Malone's business premises, an arrangement for which he initially received five shillings a week in rent.[22] After the introduction of compulsory military training in 1910, Malone lent, then rented out, rooms in his premises to serve as the offices for the regular military personnel based in Stratford.[23]

Malone was made a Justice of the Peace in December 1892.[24] Even though he was busy with his farming, business and community affairs, Malone still found time for part-time legal studies. In April 1894 he was admitted as a solicitor and in September 1899 he qualified as a barrister.

He began to practise in Stratford by himself, before in 1903 going into partnership with James McVeagh and William Anderson. The opening of new land, its subdivision and the expansion of the dairy industry meant that it was an auspicious time to be a lawyer in Taranaki. Malone's firm acted for a range of clients including local farmers, businessmen, local bodies and dairy companies. Arranging for clients to take out mortgages or for clients to invest money in mortgages over property was an important part of the partnership's business. It was a highly successful firm and within a few years had branches at New Plymouth, Inglewood, Eltham and Kaponga. Malone moved to New Plymouth in 1903 to establish a branch of his firm.[25]

Malone's active involvement in military affairs was renewed in 1900 when he was instrumental in the formation of the Stratford Rifle Volunteers. This unit was one of nearly 100 new Volunteer Corps established between July 1899 and September 1901 as a result of the patriotic enthusiasm generated by the South African War. Malone was elected by the members of the corps to command it and was commissioned as a captain in the New Zealand Volunteer Force after passing the necessary examination. The Stratford Rifles was, like other Volunteer Corps, a small unit with three officers and 28 non-commissioned officers [NCOs] and other ranks. Malone, as a prominent local lawyer and farmer, was typical of the sort of men who dominated the leadership of the Volunteer Force. Although he already had substantial personal and business commitments, Malone proved to be a dedicated Volunteer.[26]

In 1900, it appears, Malone gave up alcohol and tobacco and embarked on a regime of physical fitness and toughening intended to prepare him for the challenge of war. Reportedly, he usually slept on a military stretcher instead of a soft bed. Malone also apparently later paced out the distance from his home to his office and marched between the two at the unique Rifle Brigade rate of 140 paces a minute.[27] He was, as his daughter Norah later wrote, 'an extremely disciplined and self-controlled man.'[28] Nonetheless, Malone was an outgoing man who enjoyed social events.[29]

Malone's move to New Plymouth in 1903 necessitated his resignation from command of the Stratford Rifle Volunteers in September 1903.[30] The commander of the local Volunteer battalion, however, did not want to lose the services of a man he regarded as 'a very capable officer' and successfully requested that he be appointed adjutant of the 4th Battalion Wellington (Taranaki) Rifle Volunteers.[31] Malone was clearly very well regarded by other Taranaki Volunteer officers and by regular officers in the Wellington military district. In 1904 he was made an additional member of the Wellington Local

Above

Malone and the Stratford Rifle
Volunteers outside the town's post
office.

Alexander Turnbull Library

Left

Malone in 1902, as seen on the
Stratford Rifle Volunteers shield
dedicated to Elinor Malone.

Malone Family Collection Wellington (now in ATL)

Opposite

This photograph, taken in 1908 at the
time of the Wellington district Easter
manoeuvres, shows a clean-shaven
and determined William Malone.

Malone Family Collection Wellington (now in ATL)

Four of William and Elinor Malone's children at their Opunake Road farm near Stratford in about 1902. From left: Terry, Edmond, Norah and Brian.

Malone Family Collection Wellington (now in ATL)

Board of Military Examination. The following year he was promoted to major and made second in command of his battalion.[32] Malone's military abilities were clearly evident during the 1908 Wellington district manoeuvres. The scenario for the manoeuvres involved a hostile 'Blue Force' that had landed at Paramata north of Wellington attempting to seize the capital, which was defended by a substantially larger 'Red Force'. The 'Blue Force' was made up principally of Volunteers from Taranaki, Wanganui and the Manawatu. Malone, who was the force's chief staff officer, carefully reconnoitred the hilly, rugged country north of the city and with his commanding officer devised an innovative plan to outflank the defending force by marching

Above left

Elinor Malone later
in life.

Malone Family Collection
Wellington (now in ATL)

Above right

Ida Malone in about
1906.

Malone Family Collection
Wellington (now in ATL)

across country at night. During the night of 18–19 April, Malone guided the
attacking troops through the screen of outposts maintained by the defending
'Red Force' in hills north of the city and into the capital. The 'Blue Force's'
attack was widely praised by senior New Zealand officers as an exemplary
model of sound planning, good tactics and disciplined hard work by the
troops involved. Malone was one of the officers singled out for particular
praise.[33]

Tragedy struck Malone's life on 18 June 1904 when his wife Elinor and
the baby boy she was giving birth to died at their home in New Plymouth.
At the time of his wife's death Malone was in Stratford.[34] He did not remain
a widower for long. On 11 September 1905, in Christchurch, Malone, who
one newspaper described as 'a highly esteemed Taranaki settler', married
Ida Katherine Jemima Withers, who had, it appears, for some years been
Elinor's companion and a tutor for the children. Ida, whom Malone generally
referred to as Mater [Latin for mother], was 16 years younger than her new
husband and was a strikingly attractive woman.[35] Their father's marriage
seems, at least initially, to have led to some friction between Ida and her
stepchildren, but later they became very fond of each other. Certainly before
the outbreak of war in 1914 the Malone household appears to have been a
generally happy one.[36]

Malone was utterly devoted to his wife, but near the end of his life realised that he had on occasion neglected her and his family because he was so busy with his business and military affairs. He also admitted that he could be 'hard, and unforgiving'.[37] William and Ida Malone had three children, Denis George Withers, who was born in July 1906, William Bernard, known as Barney, who was born in December 1907 and Elinor Mary, known as Mollie or Molly, who was born in March 1910. All three children were born in New Plymouth.[38] Malone was a loving, but strict father whose children were rather in awe of him.[39]

Through his farming and legal practice, Malone acquired significant assets. When he was living in New Plymouth he had a substantial house built called the 'The Farlands', and when he returned to Stratford he had another large house built, also called 'The Farlands'. The Stratford house included seven bedrooms, a dining room, drawing room, study and billiard room and was set in large attractive grounds that included a tennis court. Several domestic staff, including two maids and a gardener, were employed by Malone at 'The Farlands'. Malone was a keen gardener, who would often work in the grounds before changing into his business clothes and walking nearly five kilometres into his office in Stratford.[40] In 1905 his land holdings

Malone (2nd from left) at the head of the 'Blue Force' in Wellington 19 April 1908. Alongside him are other Taranaki officers, including Lieutenant Colonel E.N.L. Okey (left) and Lieutenant Felix Bellringer (2nd from right). The original caption for the postcard was: 'Easter Manoeuvres Wellington N.Z. 1908 Invading Forces led by Major Malone'.

ZAK Postcard, DONZ Coll

consisted of 445 acres of freehold rural land, 54 acres of freehold suburban land and approximately 3 acres of freehold town land. In partnership with H.B. Worthington he also held 1300 acres 'occupation with the right of purchase, and of 400 acres of lease in perpetuity' land.[41] By August 1914 Malone's assets, which included land, mortgages and other investments exceeded his liabilities by £33,450, the equivalent in today's terms of about $5,000,000.[42] In 1905, when he gave evidence to a royal commission on land tenure and settlement, he described himself as 'a working-man, and, by the way, a solicitor and also, by the way, a farmer.' Such multiple roles were common amongst the kind of hard-working and entrepreneurial settlers who made such a contribution to the development of New Zealand during the nineteenth and early twentieth centuries, and of whom Malone is a good example.[43]

Malone was a well-educated and well-read man who took an intelligent interest in the issues of the day. He was strongly committed to the development of New Zealand in general and of Taranaki, in particular. Malone considered himself a countryman and was convinced of the superiority, both moral and physical, of country-dwellers over those who lived in towns and cities. In 1905, he stated that 'I try to do my own thinking and I think our first duty is to see what we are doing in New Zealand in the way of building up a race and nation. Setting aside the individual for the people should be the real object in this colony. We must all agree that the people we want to build up here into a nation should be independent, free, thrifty, sturdy, and clean, both physically and morally.'[44] Malone considered 'the pioneers as being heroes – greater heroes than men who simply perform some single act of bravery. I say that those men who go into the forest and back country with their wives and families and hew out homes for themselves and live there their lifetime are true heroes. The men in the towns generation after generation are becoming less fit members of the nation. Life in town does not conduce to the sturdiness of mind, body, and even soul, which we desire to see in a nation.'[45] On Imbros during the Gallipoli campaign, Malone met a Greek peasant family, which he thought 'seemed an ideal family, natural, unsophisticated and absolutely united.'[46] Such idealised conceptions of country people and Social Darwinist concepts that emphasised the dangers the modern world posed to the physical, intellectual and moral well-being of Europeans in New Zealand and elsewhere were widely held at this time.

Malone set out his personal philosophy in a lecture on work delivered at the Technical School, New Plymouth on 18 September 1907. He stated that: 'Everyone should make up his or her mind to work with all his or her

might – work – whilst they worked, play whilst they played.' Malone then stated that the 'world was made up of conquerors and conquered.' He went on to claim that in New Zealand 'there were no very rich people and few poor people, and the really poor were very often poor from their own faults – habits of intemperance or indolence.' Malone was critical of those who lacked a commitment to hard work, stating that: 'Men who were not honest workmen, who kept an eye on the clock and did as little as possible, were fools, and would soon have no work to do. In time the men who put work first would find plenty of work and plenty of pay.' Although Malone took a very hard-nosed attitude towards the poor, essentially blaming them for their own condition, he was prepared to admit that many manual workers were underpaid. They should, he considered, receive a wage that would enable them to keep themselves, a wife and family in reasonable comfort and enjoy some recreation. In this lecture Malone expounded his commitment to the widely held Victorian ideals of self-help and self-improvement through hard work and education – habits that had helped make Malone a wealthy and successful member of the Taranaki community.[47] Malone's father had also held these beliefs, writing that 'incessant practice and step-by-step is the way but beware of decline after rising to height ... A review of progress in <u>all</u> departments is needed monthly or quarterly or yearly'.[48]

Questions related to land tenure were the subject of great debate in New Zealand during the nineteenth and early twentieth centuries.[49] Malone saw the extension of the freehold system of land tenure as being absolutely

Ida Malone with her family. From right: stepdaughter Norah, stepson Maurice (in the boater), and Barney and Denis in front, Mollie on her mother's lap (the older girl, left, is a visiting family friend).

NZ Freelance Coll, Alexander Turnbull Library

central to the future health and development of New Zealand. He strongly promoted these ideas to the royal commission on land tenure in 1905 and when he stood as an independent liberal in a by-election held in the Taranaki House of Representatives electorate in May 1907. Malone described himself as a 'Liberal of long standing of democratic tendencies who does most of his own thinking'.[50] His views on the extension of freehold title, and support for leaseholders being able to buy their land at its original valuation, mirrored those of the conservative candidate. During the campaign's many public meetings Malone demonstrated a quick wit. In a closely contested election, Malone split the Liberal vote, thereby ensuring the success of the conservative candidate.[51]

The following year, the Liberal leader Sir Joseph Ward, it seems, offered to make Malone his party's official candidate in the Taranaki electorate in that year's general election. Malone would not accept unless he was allowed to follow his conscience on the freehold issue, something Ward could not agree to. He again campaigned vigorously as an independent liberal, stressing 'the 'supremity' of New Zealand; of the New Zealander; of Taranaki; and of the Taranaki man, a platform 'calculated to appeal vaguely to patriotism and to parochialism.'[52] He cut a handsome and eloquent figure during the election campaign and was allegedly a particular favourite of female voters. In the election held on 17 November 1908 the sitting conservative, opposition member Henry Okey, obtained 2826 votes, Malone 1546 and the official Liberal candidate, Bellringer, 849. The strong backing received by Malone reflected support for his independent status, his policies, which appear to have been generally popular, and the fact that the official Liberal candidate was, in some respects, weak.[53] That Malone was a staunch Roman Catholic probably counted against him in the political arena during a period when relations between Catholics and non-Catholics were marked by a degree of suspicion and tension.[54] Malone and his family were active in the Stratford Catholic church and the four eldest boys, Edmond, Brian, Terry and Maurice, all attended St Patrick's College, Wellington and Norah the Sacred Heart Convent in Island Bay, Wellington.[55]

During this period Malone continued to serve

A studio portrait of William and Ida Malone taken by the well-known Taranaki photographer James McAllister. Malone took this print overseas with him in 1914, but tore it in half to excise himself from it.

Malone Family Collection Wellington (now in ATL)

as a Volunteer officer, and in May 1910 he was made an acting lieutenant-colonel and appointed commanding officer of the 4th Battalion Wellington (Taranaki) Rifle Volunteers.[56] At this time Malone seems to have reduced his involvement in legal work. He sold his share of his practice and returned to Stratford where he started a smaller firm, Malone and King. He then devoted more time to his other interests.[57] Malone's appointment took place at a time when the New Zealand armed forces were being radically restructured. Compulsory military training was introduced to provide manpower for a new Territorial Force, which could both defend New Zealand and provide an expeditionary force for service overseas in a major conflict.[58] Malone had for several years been a firm supporter of compulsory military training. He was also convinced that the British Empire was under threat, and was likely to be engaged in a major war within a few years. These views and his longstanding interest in military matters led him to devote much of his time to his military duties in what were to be the last years of his life.[59]

A British Army Officer, Major-General Alexander Godley, was appointed by the New Zealand government to command the local forces and implement the new defence arrangements. Godley was from an Anglo-Irish family and later wrote of his first meeting with Malone that 'the fact that we were fellow countrymen at once established a bond of sympathy and I was much impressed by his attractive personality and obvious keenness.' Godley's confidence in Malone meant that he was quickly confirmed in the rank of lieutenant-colonel and given command of one of the new Territorial Force battalions, the 11th Regiment (Taranaki Rifles).[60]

Malone read widely on military subjects, including military history, leadership, tactics and strategy. He annotated many of his books on the subject and wrote, at least, one very detailed notebook setting out key points from books and articles he had read.[61] It is clear that he thought carefully about the knowledge, qualities and habits required to lead men successfully in battle. The breadth and depth of Malone's study of military matters is clearly evident in the scope and content of a series of six lectures he gave on military topics in New Plymouth in mid-1910. The subjects

Malone at a Volunteer Force training camp. He is wearing an early model of a lemon squeezer hat.

Alexander Turnbull Library

covered in the lectures included, 'Mobilisation. Intercommunication and Orders', 'Billets, Camps and Bivouacs: Protection at Rest', 'Marches: Protection on the Move', 'The Battle. Attack' and 'The Battle. The Defence'.[62] The lectures encapsulated many of the principles and practices that guided Malone's conduct as a military officer in peacetime and in war. In his synopsis of the introduction to the lecture series, for instance, Malone wrote: 'War, dire necessity for, peace and vice. War and virtue.' He then went on to stress that the education of military officers 'must be more thorough than that of a Lawyer or Doctor' and that officers had a duty 'to acquire and perfect knowledge.' In his discussion of how a military commander should develop and set out his operational plans, Malone stressed the need to keep the object of an operation clearly in focus and the need for plans to be based on a sound appreciation of the position 'and not [an] appreciation made to fit [a] plan.' He also emphasised the need for military plans to be practical, with all relevant details worked out and to be set out in a logical manner.[63]

Malone at a training camp, probably in 1910 or 1911.

Puke Ariki

The commanding officers of Territorial Force units, especially initially, faced many difficulties. There was a significant level of popular opposition to compulsory training. Many men objected to compulsory training simply because of the way it disrupted their lives. A significant proportion of employers were also opposed to the new military training scheme, because it led to employees being called away for training at inconvenient times. In back-country areas, including much of Taranaki, roads were practically impassable after dark, making it very difficult for many men to attend drills.[64]

From the outset Malone's Regiment was one of the most effective units in the Territorial Force.[65] In his report for the 1913–14 year, the district commander Colonel [later Major-General] Sir Edward Chaytor wrote that the Taranaki Rifles was in 'a very satisfactory condition' and that Malone was 'very capable and is ably backed up by a number of excellent company commanders'. Chaytor went on to comment that the battalion's work in the field was 'good', but that discipline needed to be improved; something he thought would happen as officers gained more experience.[66] The commander of the Wellington Infantry Brigade, Colonel R.W. Tate, thought that Malone was hard-working but headstrong, and that he took great care to look after the men under his command.[67]

Malone was proud that his regiment was designated the Taranaki Rifles, and followed the British Rifle Brigade's practices in style of drill and other matters. He achieved something of a coup when the Governor, the Earl of Liverpool, a former Rifle Brigade officer, agreed to be the new regiment's honorary colonel.[68] Originally, like other infantry regiments in the new force, Malone's regiment wore felt, slouch hats with the left side of the brim turned up. The Wellington Infantry Brigade's 1911 annual camp at Takapau was marked by several days of heavy rain. Water collected in the dents in the top of the slouch heads and in response Malone decided that the men of his regiment should lower the left side of the brim and pinch the crown into a point, thereby converting them into 'lemon squeezer' hats that mirrored the shape of Mount Taranaki, a facsimile of which formed the central element in the 11th Regiment's badge.[69]

The 11th (Taranaki Rifles) Regiment in 1913, formed up with its commanding officer mounted in the foreground. Many of these men willingly followed him to war.

Malone Family Collection Wellington (now in ATL)

Incidents at Territorial Force camps before the First World War provide a useful insight into Malone's style of command. At the Wellington District camp at Oringi near Dannevirke in April 1913, several men from B Company 11th Regiment, decided to mete out some unofficial punishment to one of their comrades whom they considered had shown disloyalty to the regiment by writing, in his civilian capacity as a reporter for a New Plymouth newspaper, a less than complimentary article about some aspects of the camp. When they discovered that other members of the regiment were intent on joining in the affair they defended their comrade and prevented any assault from taking place. Officers and NCOs of the Taranaki Rifles moved quickly to end to the disturbance. Later Malone was informed that Godley considered that his regiment had shown a lack of discipline and, in particular, that its NCOs had failed in their duty to keep a close eye on their men. Malone considered

Wm G. Malone
New Plymouth. NZ.
17. 3. 09.

Albuera. ALBUERA.   A.D. 1811.

English. 7000 Spanish Portuguese 25000 + 38 Guns
(Infantry 30000 Cavalry 2000. Artillery - - - -

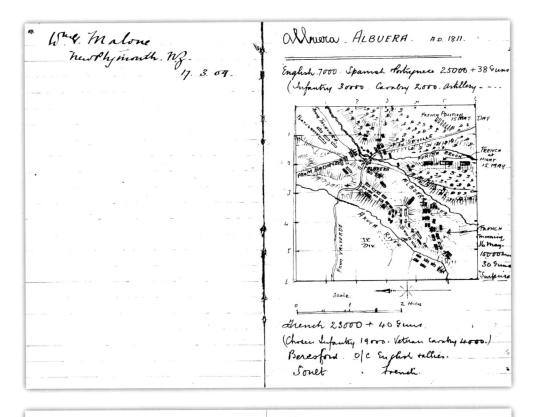

French 23000 + 40 Guns.
(Chosen Infantry 19000. Veteran Cavalry 4000.)
Beresford   O/C English rallies.
Soult   . French.

The pioneers carry axes & shovels. and
know how to make small bridges, remove
obstacles in the way of the troops.
When the Battalion goes into action the Bandsmen
& officers servants are usually divided among
the companies.
If Battalion carries tents. 7 wagons extra.
An English Company = 116 strong.
a NZ.   "   63   "

BATTALION.
INFANTRY.

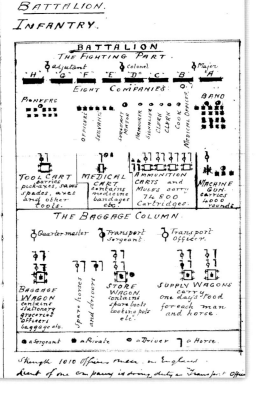

Strength 1010 Officers men. in England.
Lieut of one company is doing duty as Transport Officer

Opposite

Typical pages from
Malone's 1909
military notebook.
The top page
shows the Battle
of Albuera, a costly
engagement fought
between an Anglo-
Portuguese army
and a French Army
on 16 May 1811. The
bottom page sets
out the organisation
of an infantry
battalion.

Malone Family Collection
Wellington (now in ATL)

this criticism to be unwarranted, and in a well-argued response stressed the practical difficulties Territorial Force NCOs and officers faced when it came to disciplining their men. Throughout the affair Malone exhibited good sense and a desire to act reasonably and fairly.[70] A year later a fairly serious disturbance developed at the divisional camp at Takapau. The disturbance mainly involved men from the 7th (Wellington West Coast) Regiment, although men from Malone's regiment were also involved. Through his calm and sensible approach, Malone played a significant role in defusing the situation.[71]

When the First World War broke out in August 1914, New Zealand raised the New Zealand Expeditionary Force (NZEF) for service overseas in accordance with Imperial defence plans. On 6 August, Malone was one of the first officers to offer to serve in the new force, which was raised from volunteers drawn from throughout New Zealand. His reputation as an extremely capable officer led to him being offered command of the Wellington Infantry Battalion of the NZEF even though he was 55 years of age. The other NZEF infantry battalion commanders were 36, 37 and 45 years of age. Malone received the telegram notifying him of his appointment on 8 August 1914, exactly a year before his death, and only three days after the outbreak of war between the British Empire and Germany.[72] Mobilisation camps for the expeditionary force were established in each of the four military districts. The Wellington district's camp was set up at the Awapuni Racecourse near Palmerston North. It was the largest of the four camps, as it included not only the Wellington Mounted Rifles Regiment and Wellington Infantry Battalion, but also the force's artillery and other divisional units.[73]

On the same day he offered to serve in the NZEF, Malone began to keep a detailed diary along with copies of his personal correspondence and some of his official or demi-official military correspondence. Like so many New Zealanders, Malone spent the first few days of August 1914 getting his personal affairs in order. He prepared a balance sheet of his assets and liabilities and on 11 August signed a new will.[74] All Malone's adult sons followed their father's example. Brian joined the force assembled to seize German Samoa and sailed from New Zealand on 15 August 1914. Terence and Edmond both enlisted in the Wellington Mounted Rifles on 15 August 1914 and Maurice volunteered in April 1915. Maurice added a year to his age so that he could enlist. His father, who would have been well aware of the age limits for service in the NZEF, seems to have turned a blind eye to Maurice's deception.[75]

The Wellington Infantry Battalion's organisation, like that of other units of

the expeditionary force, rested on the Territorial Force.
Each infantry regiment in the Wellington Military
District was responsible for recruiting a double
company of the new unit, which was named
after it and wore its badge. Such characteristics
fostered a strong sense of competition
between the different companies of the
battalion. The new battalion had four
companies the: 7th Wellington West
Coast Company [often referred to by
Malone as the West Coast Company],
the 11th Taranaki Company, the 9th
Hawkes Bay Company and the 17th
Ruahine Company. Each company was
227 strong and the whole battalion had
a strength of just over 1000. Malone
was fortunate in that he had a number
of exceptionally capable officers serving
in his unit; three of the battalion's five
majors, Herbert Hart, Robert Young and
William Cunningham, later rose to become
generals. The Wellington Infantry Battalion
adopted the distinctive lemon squeezer hat of
Malone's Territorial regiment. In 1916 the lemon
squeezer hat was adopted for use throughout the
New Zealand Expeditionary Force and still forms a
key part of the ceremonial uniform of the New Zealand
Army.[76]

When he was formally attested [enlisted] into the NZEF on 31 August
1914, Malone was described as having a fresh complexion, hazel eyes and
brown hair; being 5 feet 11 inches [1 metre 80 centimetres] tall and weighing
160 pounds [72.5 kilograms].[77] Malone did not welcome the Great War, but
he faced it confident that his years of preparation would stand him in good
stead and with a degree of excitement about what the conflict would mean
for him.[78]

Malone in about
1910, in full
dress uniform,
probably taken on
his promotion to
lieutenant-colonel.

Malone Family Collection
Wellington (now in ATL)

1
Saying goodbye and preparing for war

New Zealand to Egypt, August–December 1914

[MSX 2541]

August 6th 1914

War declared by Britain against Germany. I offered my services to NZ Defence Department for work in N[ew] Zealand or abroad.

August 8th 1914

My offer accepted and I [sic] appointed to command Wellington Infantry Regiment – being raised.

August 9th 1914

Saw Mayor of New Plymouth and tried to persuade him to get mayors of towns in the Wellington Military District to raise Regimental Funds for Wellington Regiment. I saw also Editors of *Taranaki Herald* and *Taranaki Daily News*. The Mayor and Herald Editor received my request somewhat coldly – "a prophet is not without honour except in his own country"! Returned with Mater and children to the Farlands, Stratford to prepare for my departure with my Regiment. Handed command of XI Regt (Taranaki Rifles) over to Major Bellringer,[1] my 2nd in command.

Above

'The Farlands', Stratford, the family home from which Malone went to war.

Malone Family Collection Wellington (now in ATL)

Right

The programme for a musical comedy put on in Masterton to raise funds to assist the men of the expeditionary force then assembling in Palmerston North. The show raised more than £100.

Wairarapa Archive

Malone attached great importance to the establishment of a regimental fund which could be used to purchase food to supplement government rations, comforts for wounded soldiers and a variety of other purposes. Malone thought such a fund would be especially useful in places 'where gold talks'. He was opposed to the establishment of small company funds and stressed that the regimental fund should have clear rules and keep proper accounts. Malone worked assiduously and effectively to convince community leaders to support the fund. Although less money was subscribed than he had hoped, the regimental fund proved a great boon to the men of the Wellington Infantry Battalion. It appears that the Wellington Battalion was the first NZEF unit to establish a welfare fund. This initiative is a good example of Malone's practical and thoughtful approach to his duties. ['Memorandum Re-Regimental Fund', nd but Sep 1914, Malone to Bellringer, 30 Aug 1914, MSX-2548, ATL; *Wanganui Chronicle*, 5 Sep 1914, pp. 4, 8, 12 Oct 1915, p. 6; *Hawera and Normanby Star*, 19 Sep 1914, p. 6.]

August 13th 1914

Proceeded to Palmerston N[orth] and to Camp at Awapuni. Appointing staff. Not satisfied with Adjutant appointed by G.O.C. to my Regt [acting Maj William Robinson].[2] Very pleased to find Major Hart my 2nd in command.[3] Only about 150 men came in.

August 17th 1914

Returned to Awapuni Camp. Matters bar Adjutant going all right. Major Hart reports adjutant as no good. Saw O/C I. [Infantry] Brigade as to shifting him.[4] He didn't like the idea.

August 18th 1914

Organising Regt. Testing adjutant. Quite satisfied he must go. Saw O/C Brigade again and said sending in written report and request for Adjutant's removal.

August 19th 1914

Still organising and equipping Regt. Written report to O/C Brigade requesting removal of adjutant and informing could not carry on with him.[5] Adjutant removed and my Adjutant of XI Regt (T Rifles) appointed[6] – to my pleasure.

August 20th to September 23rd 1914

Completing equipment and organisation of Regiment. Training same. Men improving as the O/C Brigade said astoundingly. They are of all classes. Sons of wealthy run holders, farmers, schoolmasters, scholars, M.A., B.A.s, musicians, tradesmen, mechanics, lawyers and all sorts. They will make good soldiers and the Regt I trust will lead the other Regts in the Brigade. I will do my best to make it. The weather has been glorious – no rain. We bivouacked three nights at Highden and one night at Feilding. We have established a Brass Band and it does well.

Malone was in many ways an austere man who drove those under his command hard in his efforts to make his battalion an outstanding unit. Nonetheless, he had a good sense of humour, as two incidents relating to Malone's insistence at Awapuni camp that the officers and men of the Wellington Infantry Battalion have their hair cut very short demonstrate. After ordering that all ranks receive a 'close crop', Malone held a full battalion parade. As he inspected the men he remarked with satisfaction: 'no flies on this Regiment – and, by God, no fleas.' He then noticed Private

Leonard McCracken 'had left a nice long lock in front to brush over. The old man's eye shone wrath and in a bellowing voice he asked Mac who was running the regiment. To the surprise of everyone McCracken replied, "Well, you're getting paid for it, Sir." For once the old man was bluffed and his eye twinkled as he moved on'. [*Primus in Armis: Journal of the Taranaki Regiment*, vol. 1, Jul 1936, p. 93.] At much the same time the question of hair length was raised at the camp officers' mess. Malone pointed out with pride the almost shaven head of one of his young officers. Lieutenant-Colonel William Meldrum, the commander of the Wellington Mounted Rifles, with which Malone's battalion had a friendly rivalry, responded by getting one of his officers who was bald to stand up and remarking: 'Gentlemen, this is how we do it in the Mounteds'. This exchange prompted hearty laughter from officers present with 'no one appreciating the joke more than Colonel Malone'. [A.H. Wilkie, *Official War History of the Wellington Mounted Rifles Regiment: 1914-1919* (Auckland, 1924), p. 4.]

[MSX 2548]

Awapuni
21 August 1914

My dear Harry and Charlie [Penn][7]

I enclose notes, etc, to help you in my affairs. I have been going 6 am to 10 pm here since I came down and until now . . . have had no time to write you further.

23 August 1914
I had no time to write further. I now have Harry's letter of 21st Inst. . . .

I am much obliged to you Harry for the £400. I am sorry that I didn't keep a closer hold on ready money, but I didn't anticipate the need.

Things here are going well. I have had a lot of trouble getting my staff together. The G.O.C. gave me an adjutant, no good and I had to put up with him for a week, then got him shifted and now have McDonnell who is right. My QM came in last night, Shepherd,[8] also Dr Home[9] so the show will soon be "going". The XI Taranaki Rifles, is well represented. My other officers are good and fair. I am not sure that I haven't made a mistake in giving Furby a show after all we will see.[10] The rank and file after a lot of weeding out will be all right. I am busy getting their hair cut!! Weather A1. We hope to be allowed to <u>march</u> to Wellington instead of entraining. I hope

Opposite

The Wellington Infantry Battalion, and the Wellington Mounted Rifles, drawn up in review order for inspection by Major-General Sir Alexander Godley on 24 August 1914, at Palmerston North's Awapuni racecourse. [*Auckland Weekly News*, 3 September 1914.]

Alexander Turnbull Library

Malone and the other officers of the Wellington Battalion at Awapuni Camp. Sitting, from left to right: Rev. Bush-King (Chaplain), Maj Brunt, Maj Saunders, Maj Hart (second in command), Lt-Col Malone (officer commanding), Capt McDonnell (adjutant), Maj Young, Maj Cunningham, Capt Home. Middle row: Lts Wilson, Bryan, Turnbull, Watson, McKinnon, Wells, Cowan, Morison, Furby, Jardine, Capt Short, Quartermaster Capt Shepherd. Back row: Lts Cross, Urquhart, Hugo, McColl, Narbey, Lee, Harston, McLernon. [*Auckland Weekly News*, 3 September 1914.]

that Stratford people will do something to give us a Regimental Fund. I could spend money now in "refreshment" of the men. A few cases of apples a day after a march would do them good and be much appreciated.

With love to you both and your respective wives.

Yours gratefully and affectionately,
Wm.G. Malone

———

Camp, Sunday
[23 August 1914]
My dear wife

I have a little time to spare so seize to write you a note. I have been expecting one from you but so far none. No doubt you are like me very busy. Things are going well now.

I have my staff complete. Capt McDonnell, Capt Home, Capt Shepherd (QM) came in last night and are right into the collar. Good men and true. The men are shaking down and when weeded over will do NZ credit. We keep on tramping them in and out. Yesterday I gave them a little variety, by giving them an imaginary enemy to scrap against as they marched along. They made lots of mistakes but on the whole did wonderfully well for men among whom were several, many who have only just now had a rifle put in their hands. They enjoyed it and it relieved the monotony of the march. I am getting very fit. Hart and I have started a mile run round the course every morning. The GOC inspects tomorrow. . . .

How are the boys and Mollie? Do they miss me? I am afraid not. Tell them to be good so as to please Daddy. The boys to be little straight men and Mollie her sweet self.

With all my love.
Your loving husband.

———

Awapuni
26 August 1914

Dear Mrs Wickham

. . . The men are in good health and spirits and will I am sure do credit to their country. I feel myself as if at last I could do something for my country. I used to have a feeling that I had done nothing. My dear wife is very brave.

She in no way tried to prevent me doing my duty, and would not stop me if she could. I am in the hands of the Almighty and if He so wills it, shall be back to home and my adopted country in due course.

With my kindest regards to you and you daughter.

Yours very sincerely,
Wm.G. Malone

Awapuni
26 August 1914

Dear Laurenson

. . . I am glad that I had so prepared, that I was able to offer services which are of use.

I leave a lucrative practice, a good and very happy home, a brave wife and children, without any hesitation. I feel that I am just beginning to live. Stodging[11] away money making, was no man's game. The old country, and its dependencies have almost their existence at stake and it is no time for those qualified to act to stand by. . . .

With kind regards.

Yours sincerely,
Wm.G. Malone

Awapuni Camp
26 August 1914

Dear Mrs Lepper[12]

. . . I shall be only too pleased to do what I can for your boy as well as all his comrades. Their mothers needn't worry about them. I have taken the responsibility of their care and will do my duty. . . .

Yours sincerely
Wm.G. Malone

Awapuni
4 September 1914

My dear Harry [Penn]

. . . Re house. You are quite right and will not be surprised if you cannot let it suitably.

Re <u>boots</u>. The Headquarters people should not have asked for boots (in specie). We wanted the money, so as to get a uniform suitable soldier's boot. The Government boot is a poor one. I made out a specification and on it Harris has supplied 250 pairs of splendid boots at 15/- [shillings] per pair. However, the bulk of the boots sent down will come in and are better than nothing. Too many good people acting. Thanks re Regimental Fund Wairarapa in one act gave us <u>£1,000</u> and will without hesitation make up the other £700 which we want for both MR [Mounted Rifles] and Infantry. Don't listen to any paltry ideas of putting us off with 10/- per man and then handing the rest of the money to <u>Government</u>! Already we could spend money to advantage. People talk about our going to garrison but there is not the least doubt in my mind from what I get from the "cognocente"

The Wairarapa Patriotic Committee organised local ladies to pack comfort parcels for the troops at the front. Woman played a vital and increasingly important role in New Zealand's war effort during the First World War.

Wairarapa Archive

[sic, cognoscenti] that we are going, after probably a month's training in England or France, to the front. There seems some doubt as to the ability of the Higher Commanders in the French Army, their trouble in the 1870-1 war. The men I believe to be A1 but rotten brutes like Clemenceau[13] and co (who prided themselves on having driven God out of the schools and said they would drive Him out of the country, and who blackmarked every true Catholic officer in the army) were obviously vicious and corrupt and approachable by vicious command seekers. I hope I am wrong, but it does seem that there is something wrong with the French Army. I am afraid that if little Belgium and England had not been to the fore, things would have been bad for France. . . .

W.G. Malone
The Regiment is breaking in well.

———

Awapuni
Sunday, 20 September 1914

My dear wife

I duly received your letter card and was sorry that you could not come up last night. I have been hanging about all day and have so wished that you were here.[14] It is a lovely day and all is well. I got Norah's postcard, but I could not get down. We get away very soon now and there are lots of things to see to and time is short. I have got my new boots and though they look

Wellington infantrymen march through the square in Palmerston North on 12 September, alongside loaded general service wagons. [*Auckland Weekly News*, 24 September 1914]

Alexander Turnbull Library

like glorified sandles [sic, sandals] or leather puddings, they fit me and my feet are comfortable. . . .

Don't forget my warm singlets and my 'washing'. I believe, however, we will go home via Australia, Colombo, Suez and the Mediterranean.

I hope that you are quite well. . . . I shall be so glad to see you on Wednesday. All my love to you.

Your husband.
Love to Norah.

———

Awapuni
22 September 1914

My dear wife

I have just got word from Norah of Denis's illness. I do hope that neither measles or fever will affect him. I am so sorry that the poor little chap should be laid up, and hope that in any case he will soon be all right. Give him a good kiss from me and tell him how disappointed I shall be at not seeing him on the wharf. I suppose that I shall not be able to see you either. It seems ages since I saw you and I was so looking forward to having the last hours of time in NZ with you. However, I might have been away weeks ago so I mustn't growl.

I was expecting a letter from you yesterday or today but I understand now how Denis's illness has upset you.

I enclose "Embarkation Orders".[15] I thought you might like to keep it and show it to the kiddies in later years as my name is on it. It is private at present until we go.

We are very busy packing up and fitting up. A beautiful day, our luck has been very good. With all my love.

Your loving husband.

———

Awapuni
22 September 1914

My dear Norah

Your letter to hand. I am so sorry to hear about Denis. I have written to Mater. Please send the letter on to her.

A photograph of senior NZEF officers published in the *Auckland Weekly News* of 24 September 1914.
Front row, from left: Maj J.G. Hughes, DSO; Lt-Col C.M. Hogg; Lt-Col C.E. Thomas; Lt-Col G.J. Reakes; Col W.J. Will, VD; Col A.H. Russell; Col E.W.C. Chaytor, TD; Maj-Gen Sir Alexander J. Godley, KCMG, CB; Lt-Col W.G. Braithwaite, DSO; Col F.E. Johnston; Lt-Col A. Bauchop, CMG; Lt-Col J.J. Esson; Lt-Col W.G. Malone; Lt-Col A. Plugge; Lt-Col J. Findlay.
Middle row, from left: Maj F. Chapman; Lt-Col T.W. McDonald; Lt-Col C.F.R. Mackesy; Capt H.G. Reid; Capt L.M. Shera; Lt-Col W. Meldrum; Capt J.R. Henderson; 2nd-Lt Tahu Rhodes, ADC; Maj A.C. Temperley; Capt N.W.B.E. Thoms; Capt C.L. Hawkins; Capt G.A. King; Capt J.H. Primmer; Capt F.G. Hume; Capt D.B. Blair.
Top row, from left: Capt A.C.B. Critchley-Salmonson; Capt C. Shawe; Maj J.H. Whyte; Lt-Col D.McB. Stewart; Capt H.C. Glendining; Capt F. Hudson; Capt H.M. Edwards; Capt A. Moore, DSO; Capt C.G. Powles; Capt M. McDonnell.

Alexander Turnbull Library

I shall be in Wellington tomorrow, arriving about 1.15 pm. From what the Hon Allen[16] said our time in NZ is now short. We will be pleased in a way to get off. Still we have had glorious weather and have put in plenty of good work. The men are A1 and will do NZ credit I really believe.

The war will be, I believe, of considerable length. Kitchener[17] says three years and he ought to know. I think a good bit less myself. We shall see. As the Spaniards say: *Veremos lo que veremos.*[18] You must my dear girl be a help to Mater while I am away. You will not I am sure think of running your own gait.[19] Mater has been better to all you children than any other one than your own mother could have been.[20] Be careful whose acquaintance you make and be not carried away by first impressions. You can always look to Mater for good advice and every consideration. I want you to be a good housekeeper and to remember that the Pagan Japanese deem domestic work <u>honourable</u>. All real work is. I have I think always worked hard myself and should like my children to follow in my steps.

Do what you have in hand with all your intelligence, will and might. We cannot be too thorough. Work first, fee second as Ruskin puts it.

I hope that you will write me as often and as fully as you can. Keep up your music. Be always true. Have nothing to do with deceit, no matter how petty. Help make the small ones good lads and nice[?] and Molly true and sweet.

With much love from your loving father.

[MSX 2541]

September 23rd 1914

We entrain for Wellington and embark. The embarkation staff is no good. Absolutely chaos on the ships. I wish I had gone down ahead of the troops. Very glad to see Mater and Norah again. Dined with Captain N.C. Hamilton, ASC.[21] He is a good chap and spoke well of Brian[22] and said [he] had recommended him for a commission. He said if he had known, that the 1st lot were going to Samoa he would have kept Brian for this force, for Europe.

September 24th 1914

Straightening up the transport No. 10., *Arawa*.[23] She is filthy. I do not understand the other men who embarked before us. All troops marched to Newtown Park for farewell ceremony. Too much speechifying and praying. Before show over rain fell. March back by the longest way to ship. Raining all the way, crowds of people lined the way. The transports moved out and anchored in the stream. My cabin A, which I have to myself, is very comfortable. Men settling down.

September 25th 1914

Blowing hard. Busy inspecting men's quarters and straightening things out. Men keen I think to be clean – but the Govt absolutely parsimonious in such small things as deck scrapers, sand soap and tea towels!! They do not understand "housekeeping". I am, if we get the chance, going to buy same out of R/fund [Regimental fund]. I fear greatly much sickness if we don't clean up and keep clean. Captain Clayden,[24] master of the ship, inspected. He is a clean man and all will be right I think. Lt Col Johnston, RA,[25] has his wife and one child Hilda on board. He is a real good fellow. His wife seems nice and sensible. I was pleased to hear her voice Mater's feelings

Opposite above

Wellington Infantry Battalion prepares to embark on the Shaw Savill & Albion liner, SS *Arawa*, renamed HMNZT No.10 for its NZEF charter, at the Railway Wharf, Wellington.

Fitchett Album, Alexander Turnbull Library

Opposite below

Wellington infantrymen formed up at Newtown Park to be farewelled by the Governor and the people of Wellington. Malone was more concerned with the state of his troopship, and felt there was 'too much speechifying and praying'.

Alexander Turnbull Library

as to "society" women golfing and "bridging". She too, like Mater, prefers to be at home to receive her husband and look after him and her family. Hilda is a good and nice child. I shall not I think have to "break her in" as I volunteered to do if required. We have been expecting to sail every hour. Now at 9 pm. I know that I shall be able to go and see Mater and Denis tomorrow. I am so glad. Things were so hurried that I did [not ?] seem able to say goodbye properly to Mater and Norah yesterday. Mater was looking very sweet and pretty and young. She is brave, all right. I feel very proud of her. Molly is a loving child and looks very well. Edmond and Terry are on the *Arawa*, in A Squadron, 2nd M.R. [Wellington Mounted Rifles]. I am glad that three of my boys volunteered without hesitation to serve and fight for their country. Maurice too will come next May when he is 20 – (youngest age for service) – if the war is not then over. I don't think it will be.

I feel very well. This life suits me, mind and body. It is a man's life. I wonder if I shall come back or leave my bones in Europe but I am content. I am in God's hands and no death can be better. But I do not feel anxious – I look forward to coming back to my dear wife and children. We have just heard that we do not sail for a time yet. We are all very disappointed. Still I wanted to see Denis – who Mater says is not well. We can too spend the time profitably in training. Plenty of marching – say to Trentham and target practice there. We tie up at the wharf again on Monday. The FA [Field Artillery] and MR disembark and camp at Hutt and Trentham respectively. We (WIR) [Wellington Infantry Regiment] remain on board but go ashore every day for training. Our equipment was not quite complete. I welcome the chance to buy more soap!, disinfectants!, scrapers and what not. Besides for myself I want some music.[26]

On 25 September before he heard that the sailing of the convoy had been delayed, Malone wrote a brief letter to Ida, which is not in the collection at the Alexander Turnbull Library, but is held by the Malone family in London:

My dearest

We are off in a very short time. It has been all so hurried that somehow we didn't seem able to say goodbye properly. Still we know how we feel and love one another. My thoughts will, when I am not on duty, be with you and the children. You are a brave woman and will I know bear yourself as a brave woman. . . . You know that it is as duty calls that I am leaving you and home and that I am in God's good hands and will be as safe abroad as at home.

Teach the children the doctrine of <u>work</u> and <u>duty</u> – duty to themselves – their fellows and above all to their country!

With all my love to you and all.

Your husband.

26th–29th September

Malone visited his wife and young children who were staying in Lower Hutt and was busy supervising his battalion's training at Miramar.

September 30th 1914

Malone's photograph of Ida and Norah at the Wellington wharves after they had said goodbye, 25 September 1914.

Malone Family Collection
London

Regiment marched to Miramar and returned to ship by 4.30 pm. I and Capt Cox[27] rode back to ship for lunch and then rode out to Karori to select ground for Coy [Company] attack practice on Friday next . . . We found good ground for our work. It blew great guns on the ridge. Good sheep country about 1½ to the acre. . . . No weeds but some gorse. A most lovely view is obtained from a high knoll on the ridge of Wellington Harbour and Bays and coast, across to South Island. There can hardly be anything finer. Some day I hope to take Mater up and show her. She would enjoy it I know. Rode back to ship for dinner. Went out to Lower Hutt and stayed with Mater until next morning.

October 1st 1914

Regt trained to Trentham. Target practice etc all day. Returned to ship by 5.30 pm. After dinner everybody ashore so I played or tried to play the new Schumann music Norah got for me. Mater was to have come in and gone with me to the theatre to see a good company and stay at Hotel Cecil the night. But as Denis was bad again she could not come much to my disappointment.

October 2nd 1914

Regt to Karori for attack practice. The Brigadier, Col F.E. Johnston spent most of the day with us. The work by Coy Commanders was not too good. The ground was rough and circumstance novel to them. An interesting and enjoyable day. Col J is a fine fellow, a New Zealander-born, his father the Hon Mr Johnston. Returned to ship by 4.30 pm.

October 3rd 1914

Regt remained on ship washing clothes, airing bedding and blankets. I inspected Regt and did a good growl, all round. Think it will do good. Paraded all officers and went for them for not arranging facilities for men to wash their clothes and criticized work (attack) of yesterday. Sports at Newtown Park this afternoon. I stay on ship expecting Mater to come on board and see it. Now 3.20 pm and she hasn't turned up. Speaking to Col Johnston, R.A. O/C Troops and not the Col Johnston our Brigadier. He said he had dined with Hon Allen Minister for Defence last night and had reported the Wellington Inf. Regt as best of troops, in discipline, drill and generally, and had given me the credit for its progress and satisfactory position. Very kind of him.

October 4th 1914 – Sunday

Went out to Lower Hutt. Denis much better but Barney sickening. Mater, Norah and I went for a walk round in the afternoon. Many pretty gardens. Flowers grow well.

October 5th 1914

Back to ship. Regt to Trentham, target practice. NCOs put under Sgt Major Parks[28] for instruction. Men's shooting improving and they are getting keen on it and are looking forward to shooting Germans.

Opposite

Wellington Battalion men relaxing during training at Karori.

Malone Family Collection London

October 6th 1914

Regiment to Karori Hills, company in attack practice – not well done. Officers don't rise to the occasion. Must peg away at them until they do.

October 7th 1914

Field operations at Miramar. We marched via Newtown and met the Otago Battalion, who attacked us in German fashion across the golf links. We were firing into them at 400 yards, while they were in columns of 4s. Their supports got up in masses – within 50 yards of front line. They however displayed wonderful vitality (thanks to blank cartridges) and tried to rush us. Result the umpires sounded "stand fast", just as I was putting my reserve (1 Coy) in counter attack on Otago left flank. The show absurdly hurried. Duration ¾ of an hour.

October 10th 1914

All troops marched to Lower Hutt and back – a vile day. Hurricane blowing 60 miles an hour. Left at 10 am, got back at 6 pm. The men marched well and none fell out. Col Chaytor,[29] A.G. [Adjutant General] came and specially congratulated the Regt on its march discipline and said we were easily first as compared with the other Regts. I felt rewarded for all my growling and work. I am quite proud of the Regt. Col Chaytor said it would create a sensation at home. Dined at Govt House with Mater. She looked so nice. She didn't want to come but enjoyed herself after all. . . . I had a good yarn with Her Excellency who referred to Mater's gift of lilac[30] last September. Stayed with Mater at Hotel Cecil.

October 13th 1914

. . . Went with Regt to Miramar – attack practice. Not Good Enough. I sailed[31] for two of Coy [Company] Commanders. Determined to go back to most elementary work and take each company myself or get Hart and McDonnell to do so. I have given the Commanders a good show and they cannot train their Coys because they don't know their work. I have been too considerate. . . .

October 14th 1914

HMS *Minotaur*, armoured cruiser and the Jap armoured cruiser *Ibuku* [sic *Ibuki*] arrived to convoy us or help convoy. HMS *Psyche* and [HMS] *Torch* are also here. We go soon. Went ashore to buy a razor and pay a bill. Got some money. Saw three Jap officers in Whitcombe & Tombs. Maps! were their quest, always out for intelligence. I suppose we shall be at war with them within 10 years. I like the look of the officers and have always admired the Jap people. They appear to me to be patriotic – abstemious, industrious, brave and clean. They worship their ancestors and their children. They would make I believe A1 Christians. They are I believe honest except as to their traders who form the ignoble class. Domestic labour is noble. Mater came to lunch and met Hon Mr Allen, the Minister for Defence and his daughter, a Mrs Montgomerie. Allen was quite nice to me which I thought remarkable after all my growling about the rotten embarkation arrangements. Not his fault tho'!, those arrangements.[32] At 4 pm we went out and anchored in stream as did all the other transports. It won't be long now! Poor Mater – broke down but is a brave woman and will soon be all right. Mot [Maurice Malone] was bringing the car down from Stratford and should have been here yesterday, but broke down at Sandon.[33] We shall soon be sailing now. The weather since we went into camp at Awapuni has been wonderful, not a real wet day. May our good luck continue. My influenza is nearly right. I want no more of it. I took photos of the men of war and transports.

October 15th 1914, Thursday

Still at anchor in Wellington Harbour – 13 transports, two a/[armoured] cruisers. A cold windy day. We expect to sail tomorrow morning at 6 am. So may it be. We go I believe via Australia and Suez Canal. Everybody in a good humour and stowing away. Miss Lawrence came off to see Lowe[34] and had quite a stay on board. A.W. Reid of Stratford turned up too to see his son.[35] I discovered that a Captain Vet Surgeon Walker is as fond of classical music as I am. I lent him my music and he enjoyed himself trying some of it. He doesn't play badly, about my equal.

October 16th 1914, Friday

The day. We sailed at about 6 am this morning. Everything almost was affective. It was a quiet calm grey and misty morning. Nature was mysterious – as befitted the quiet unannounced departure of our Force. No noise, anchor got up quietly and each ship seemed to slip away and take up its place in the line. HMS *Minotaur* led the way then followed in order, the Jap armoured cruiser *Ibuki*, the *Maunganui* (General Godley's ship), *Star of India*, *Hawkes Bay*, *Limerick*, *Tahiti*, (this ship) *Arawa*, *Athenic*, *Orari*, *Waimana*, HMS *Philomel* and HMS *Psyche*.[36] A most impressive sight, grim but harmonious. All was grey bar men. We were cheery and pleased to be moving at last. After we had got some 40 miles to sea, a convoy fleet was made up. . . .

The day turned out warm and sunny, the sea smooth. Our speed is about 11 knots an hour.[37] Our course apparently straight for Hobart. In the morning I was greatly put out by McDonnell – at 6.30 am Brunt and Saunders came and asked that men be excused physical drill that "they might see the Heads". I promptly refused. Then [all] of a sudden the band struck up! Too cheap for anything. Most inharmonious. In enquiry I found that McDonnell had taken on himself to order the band to play. I stopped it at once. I went for McDonnell. He won't try and run my Regiment again. It was about time he was put into his place. After officers' P/drill [Physical drill] I called all mine together and told them that the spirit of the Regiment was to be a doing of its work grimly and quietly without any beating of its chest or banging of drums! That to any right thinking soldier the striking up of our band with tune, I think, "<u>everybody's doing it</u>" or some such blatant air was shocking. I am afraid that they didn't all agree with me but they will learn. I again had to go for McDonnell. I had told my officers to wear belts on duty. He calmly said "It was against ships orders" (he prepared them as Ship's adjutant). I denied this and went off to see Col [G.N.] Johnston, O/C troops. I overheard McDonnell saying he (meaning me) can't go against King's Regulations. I promptly looked up King's Regulations and found that there was nothing in them <u>against</u> wearing of belts. They say officers <u>will</u> wear belts on duty. I promptly went for McDonnell and straightened him up. He is not loyal. He is spoilt. Partly my fault too – you can't make a silk purse out of [a] sows ear, and you can't make an "officer" in the best sense out of [a] sergeant major. McDonnell is still a sergeant major in character and is I am afraid too old to learn otherwise. If he does not alter his ways, I will leave him at the base. He asked to be relieved of the Regt adjutancy while he is ship's adjutant and I agreed, this before he kicked over the traces.[38] I am glad I agreed. I appointed Cox Acting and he and I can run things better without McDonnell.

At night we started on course of lectures. Col Johnston presided and I read extracts from Ruskin's Lecture on War (*Crown of Wild Olive*[39]). It was all right and will help a lot of our young officers I hope. . . They can't quite make me out as young Richmond[40] (Lt in Artillery) said. They thought I was too much a man of blood and iron to read Ruskin! And yet Ruskin says "Better to slay a man than cheat him"! At night all lights nearly were put out or covered.

October 17th 1914

Wet, cold and rough. P[physical]/drill made difficulties and many sick. We kept work going and I kept well. Enjoyed my meals. The other ships are making prodigious bows and dipping into the sea. We seem to be the best of them. At last I got some wind sails rigged, a great improvement. They take the fresh air to the bottom of the holds. Tonight Home [medical officer] lectures on sanitation. I told him not to forget "the <u>corners</u>"! Lecture off as Home not up to it and very few officers fit to listen.

October 19th 1914

A grey day, the sea smoothing down wonderfully. Everybody shorter faced, none snap. My order for officers to wear belts etc on duty is having an excellent effect. I cannot understand any one trying to argue that it is contrary to King's Reg. Captain McDonnell has a very limited view. I understand the objection to promotion of NCOs to commissions. Lack of education is a great misfortune. Had a yarn with Captain Greene, SA [Salvation Army].[41] He said he was greatly impressed with the idea of reading Ruskin's *Lecture on War* to our officers. He had never read Ruskin. I am prompting him to do so. Quotations would be of great help to all preachers. Ruskin knew his Bible better than most of them. Col Johnston is properly very irate at finding many of his artillery officers reading novels instead of their drill books, etc. We are putting up an extract from Ruskin's Lecture on War – beginning "never waste a moment", etc. Have just arranged class of instruction for NCOs. 20 might come and will announce holding of an exam at the end.

To my horror Col Johnston tells me that McDonnell holds the opinion that as men get dirty on active service, the sooner they begin to so get the better. He probably is not altogether serious but following on Captain Home's lecture on sanitation, I don't like it. Neither does Johnston. . . .

October 20th 1914

A bright breezy day. I have obtained most readily Col Johnston's permission to put day by day short quotations suitable to circumstances and helping to mould characters of our officers. I have prepared one for each day up to November 15th. Tomorrow's refers to its being anniversary of Battle of Trafalgar and quotes Nelson's famous signal. I then quote Wellington on 'Loyalty'. I hope and think the series will do good. Prepared and got typed synopsis of my lecture for tonight, "appreciation of the situation". Run 263 miles.

We reach Hobart at about noon tomorrow. All troops land and go for two hour route march. Men washed clothes today as water supply extra. Aired bedding too. Took a cruise round to see what <u>scrapers</u>,[42] 12 men, do.

Nothing. I shall sack Sgt Southam[43] and get another man. 12 men @ 5/- per day to do nothing is wicked. I could do the work myself in eight hours easily. QM Sgt Dallinger[44] will have to go too I think. He stalks and swells[45] about, but he has left the caustic soda in Wellington after all. I feel wild. Find that we join the Australian Division. They have 28 transports. What a fleet it will be, 38 transports and all the men of war.

[MSX 2549]

HMNZ Transport No. 10
(S/S *ARAWA*)
At sea, 20 October 1914

My dear wife,

Here I am in the best of health with all things reasonably well with me. I wish you were here too but it is no use wishing. I look forward to meeting you in England. I do hope that all is going well with you too. I carry with me a lovely picture of you, or rather a series of lovely pictures, going to Government House, being there, returning and staying. You looked so bonny I was quite proud of you and so pleased when Colonel Johnston said he had had the two nice girls, one on each side of him at dinner. He is a fine chap and I like him very much.

I am very comfortable. Have had an extra clean of my cabin, on my own. I get up at 6 am and lumber into my bath, which is ready for me, dress, go out and supervise the men's physical drill 6.30 to 7 am then do such drill with the other officers 7 am to 7.30 am, shave, walk until breakfast at 8.30, attend non-commissioned officer and officer class at 9 am to 9.15 am then supervise work of men 9.15 am to 12 noon, walk, lunch at 1.15 pm, 2 pm to 4.45 prepare work or lecture etc, supervise men at work or go round quarters and growl at the dirt, walk and talk, issue orders for next day, see all and sundry, dinner 6.30 pm. Good digestion waits on good appetite. 8 pm lecture to 9 pm, walk, to bed at 9.30 pm, read until 10 pm.

I send you copy of my diary which I hope will interest you.

The only fly in my ointment is McDonnell. I think, however, he is chastened and sorry. I keep him aloof. He is too big for his boots and I helped to make him so.

I hope that Maurice and Norah got down all right and that they are playing the game. I hope that Maurice will get something to do and do it.

Molly I presume is quite herself again, the dear little soul. Denis and Barney I suppose are back at school making up for lost time.

We get some war news every day and don't like to hear of the naval losses.

Just heard that we have a case of measles on board, an Auckland man, one of 20 put on to us at the last day. I didn't like the notion at the time, of "strays" being dumped on to us. Let us hope that the case can be kept to itself and landed at Hobart tomorrow. I wonder whether you have written and the authorities have sent on your letter to meet me at Hobart or Albany or Freemantle [sic, Fremantle]. I shall look forward to your letters.

I think of you all, you especially, every night before I go to sleep and pray that all may be well with all of us.

This is a great change in our lives but it was to be and we are doing our duty. Edmond is looking well and getting hard, thank goodness. Terry is all right. He was hard. I have got rid of all fat too. Goodbye now, my dearest. Love to you and the children.

Yours

[MSX 2541]

October 21st 1914

Trafalgar Day. "England expects that every man will do his duty".

Calm morning. We sighted land about 4 am. At about 9 am as channel narrowed we formed single line. The Japanese cruiser *Ibuki* impresses me as the most businesslike of our escort. She growls if any straggling or lights too bright. This is in keeping with my idea of the Jap. I understand him, I think in such matters. I took a snap of HMS *Philomel* as she came up from rear to head of lines. My lecture last night went off all right. Started a class for privates who wish to sit for promotion. S/M [Sergeant-Major] Parks conducts it. Edmond and Terry both well, neither been sick so the family was consistent. We had an interesting run to Hobart with land on both sides. Arrived there about 12 noon, anchored in stream, while 6 of the transports went alongside. I took several photos of shore points. In afternoon boat race, cutters, artillery, mounted rifles, one boat each. Wellington Inf two boats (one of these the Machine Gun section), 16 men to pull each boat. I stroked our boat and suggested that Meldrum should stroke his and Johnston the artillery but they could not see it, so they coxed instead. A hard race. We pulled down to the *Waimana* about two miles. Started there and finished at *Arawa* – wind and some tide against us, artillery 1st, MR 2nd, Wellington Inf 3rd but not a ½ boat's length between us. Our cox, young Harston,[46] steered on an erratic course and we should have beaten the MR but the artillery were too good for us. Our crew was very scratch, and about three of them didn't pull near their weight. Hard work but good fun. . . .

October 22nd 1914

Reveille 5 am. Route march, starting 8 am to Newton and back round over the hill and through town. Most enjoyable tramp but hot and close. Got back at 11 am. The Hobart people I believe put us a long way before their own troops, bigger and steadier and better every way. My Regt led coming home. We had no horses so I walked all the way – about 10 miles. Had a good bath on return and enjoyed my lunch! Hobart is a nice town. Houses built of stone and brick mostly. Beautiful flowers, roses especially. At one halt I was just opposite a house covered with roses. An old lady came out and told me to help myself. I did. She said her name was Brent (Miss) and asked me whence I came. She wound up by saying "Give it to those Germans"!! We had no leave so I did not see the shops. A small boy on the wharf sold us 5 picture post cards, all he had. I just managed to address them to the children and then went over to where the crowd of spectators were and asked a girl to post them. The crowd gave us an enthusiastic send off at about 12.30 pm. . . . At about 4 pm we sailed for Albany. Lecture by Col Johnston on military etiquette, all right. During night the transport had to sound sirens owing to fog.

October 25th 1914, Sunday

A beautiful day after a calm night. Our good luck sticks to us. Our physical drill is doing us heaps of good. Greene the SA [Salvation Army] Chap [Chaplain] is reducing or being reduced visibly! There are others who can stand reduction including myself. Church parade. Made my men parade in proper uniform with side arms. The others in their denims suffered badly by the comparison. I make my officers wear boots now when on duty and thus be completely properly dressed. I am satisfied that deck shoes, no belts, etc, leads to slackness and demoralisation. I am making the NCOs shave at least every other day and will thus get down to the men. I wonder what Mater and the family are doing. I hope that they are all well and happy.

A Lance Corporal[47] on *Ruapehu* died today and was buried. All transports stopped steaming and all hands were paraded and stood to attention for a ¼ hour during the burial. The *Ruapehu* steamed into centre between the two divisions of transports. We started classification of the men into classes (1) preliminarily qualified, (2) unqualified and can thus work up the latter at their own expense. We have started competitions between sections, platoons and companies of the Regt, complete units, not the <u>pick</u> of the men. It is the <u>worst</u> we want improved. We (Infantry Regt) have challenged the other Regts in this brigade to competition at 1st landing. Subjects: 1. Physical drill. 2. Squad drill. 3. Rifle exercises. 4. Firing exercises. 5. Semaphore signalling. My officers are not seeing with me too readily. They each want their own way and have some of them a supercilious air when I am telling them what I want and mean to have done. I call a conference and lay any new proposals before them and consult them so as to interest them and give them a say. But I am beginning to think the only way is to have a council of <u>one</u>, myself and simply issue orders. I have always been convinced that "Councils of War" are mistakes and am now almost convinced that councils of training, etc, when junior officers of ones own unit are present, are all mistakes too. You ask their opinion and 9 times out of 10 can't accept it. It is a big job the breaking in of a new Regiment. Over 1100 men to handle.

I am not at all pleased with Brunt[48] and Saunders[49], the only two Company Commanders on this transport. Cook[50] the 2nd in command of Hawkes Bay Coy is with us but has only ½ the Coy. He is all right. I am convinced that an officer must be a <u>gentlemen</u> bred. The lack of real education is a great

Major Brunt (right) with subalterns Jardine, Harston and McLernon. Brunt spent 10 years in colonial forces in South Africa. He had family connections in South Africa and emigrated there in 1920.

misfortune. Brunt I think is a Boer with Negro blood. Saunders is too small in the head. Neither of them are gentlemen. Cook is. Cunningham[51] and Young[52] are all right, tho' the latter is too "easy osy and plump["]. Cook his 2nd is the better man. I am cultivating the younger officers and shall not hesitate to supersede incompetents. I hope I shan't be too much disliked but I cannot pretend to like people if I don't. I find myself keeping aloof from most of my officers. I am glad I am with Col [G.N.] Johnston. I like him and I think he likes me so I spend what little spare time I have with him. At 5.30 pm he turns on the gramophone for my benefit. He is quite an education to me. His wife is very nice, shrewd, full of tact and common sense. The child is a good little soul – not at all spoilt and she and I are becoming quite friends. I would that Mater and Molly not to mention the others were here. Lecture by Col Johnston "Effect [of] artillery fire on Infantry". All right.

October 27th 1914

A wet day, grey, warm and misty. I had to go for QM Sgt Dallinger, ship's QM Sgt. I was very tired of the casual way in which decks were swept, food everywhere. . . so at 6.30 am I sent for Dallinger and dressed him down. He told me that the decks had been swept. I promptly and most emphatically told him not to lie. I was justly angry. Later he saw Col Johnston and wanted to resign. I had told him that if he didn't do his work I would get him sacked. Johnston saw me and I gave him the facts and he will back me in my efforts to clean up and keep clean. He gives me a free hand, and is pleased. General Godley[53] told him when he was at Wellington that he heard that the *Arawa* was the cleanest of the transports. . . . Bar the dirt, everything going well. My officers are knuckling down. Perhaps I have been thinking too hardly of them. I set a high standard I believe but no other is of any use. Worked all day appreciating situation, in tactical problems. . . .

October 28th 1914

Grey morning, ship rolling heavily but sea smooth and little wind. Land not in sight – now 7 am. We get up now at 5.45 am. Land in sight. . . .

We anchored in King George Sound, Albany at about 10.30 am this day – we found some if not all (28) of Australian transports anchored. They look a piebald lot. The Australian Government hasn't troubled to paint them man of war grey – as the New Zealand Government did the New Zealand transports. They (the Australians) therefore are all sorts of colours and do not look as businesslike as we do. Then they are lettered thus "A" with a number say A.3. We put up "H.M.N.Z.T." with a number. I understand however that the

Australians have plenty of room for men and horses, even sand rolls for the horses. We are dotted all over the sound. The men of war are anchored at entrance and the others in the inner harbour. . . .

Malone quickly made an impression on those under his command. One soldier on the *Arawa* wittily described him as: 'a parallelogram, that is an oblong, angular figure which cannot be described, but is <u>equal to anything</u>'. [28 Oct 1914, Memorial book compiled from the letters and diaries of L/Cpl Claude Comyns, Peter Liddle Collection, Brotherton Library, University of Leeds.]

29-31st October 1914
Anchored

November 1st 1914
Combined convoy sails (26 Australian and 10 New Zealand troopships) HMAS *Sydney* and HMAS *Melbourne* replace HMS *Philomel* and HMS *Psyche* as escorts.

The *Arawa* in its place at sea in the convoy with some of the Australian troopships ahead.

Malone Family Collection London

[MSX 2549]

28 October 1914
At Sea
Approaching Albany

My dear wife,

. . . . It is 7 am and I have a quarter of an hour to myself. I send you my diary which will give you such news as I have. The days pass better now but I do miss you so much. I often picture to myself the voyage if you were with me. It would be lovely. Some day ere[54] long we will journey together and I will be able to look back on this voyage with equanimity. I think of you every night and morning and hope that all is well with you and that you are having a good time. I am so hoping that there will be a letter from you for me at Albany. . . .

I am very fit and am looked upon as a wonder when I say I am 55. I certainly feel very active and light-footed. All the better for there will be endurance wanted later on in Europe. I am working hard, learning all I can of my job.

. . . We saw some whales one day spouting away. Wouldn't Denis have been delighted. One night we passed a shoal of phosphorescent jellyfish, great blobs of light.

It is warm. We got quite hot during our physical drill this morning.

I sent you a copy of the *Arrower*, our newspaper.[55] Home is Chief Editor. The reference to my hands is consequent upon the boat race. They were <u>not</u> blistered but I rubbed a bit of skin off another part of my anatomy. The thwart on which I sat was very rough! I have kept this fact to myself or it might have been "Arrowered". Do you have plenty of visitors? You must tell me all your doings. Why not keep a small diary as I am doing and send me a copy. These carbon books are good for the purpose. . . .

Do you get any news of us? I suppose not but remember the Honourable Mr Allen said "no news was good news". Did Mot get a job and how goes the car? . . .

I hope that Gordon sends you the rents promptly, and that you will be able to manage on the total amount. I have spent 18/- on one dozen films and 1/- on Lifebuoy soap so I shall save money. My washing is all right. Young Okey,[56] my batman does it. I gave him a lesson. He is a son of the Fred Okey[57] that was on the *Papamoa* with you.

Breakfast bugle has just gone. I am quite ready for the meal.

Goodbye my dear one. Don't forget all about me and write as often and as much as you can, but don't spend too much time over writing. I hope you are well. You will be able to get fat now. . . . My love to Norah who I hope is helpful to you and obedient. Tell Denis and Barney that I expect letters from them. I hope they got the postcard from Hobart. Give them all my love, and an extra lot to Molly. My greatest love to you who are dearest to me of all.

Your husband

[MSX 2541]

November 2nd 1914

The concert last night given by men of Hotel Cecil and was very good. Carbines[58] of Taranaki Coy (my Regt) at the piano was *facile princeps*.[59] His accompaniments improvised are really wonderful. There was a tenor (one Harrison), baritone respectively AI. There was a comical side to their singing too. Harrison a small podgy, no figure man in dirty deck shoes, Chinaman's denim trousers and a no cut denim tunic singing "Come into the garden Maud" like an angel and was as to dress too absurd for anything. Smith the baritone had a grand voice and almost a perfect enunciation. . . . Fine day but we are not steaming as fast as before we joined the Australians. Only 228 miles in this 24 hours. Heard today that we go via the Cape and not Colombo. Everybody very disappointed. Still it is all in the days march. We may it is surmized call at the Cape or somewhere [?] there and then at Durban or Port Ely [Port Elizabeth] both for water, etc.[60] . . . Though we little thought it would be under such circumstances. About 18 days voyage, weather warmer but plenty of bracing wind.

I had trouble with McDonnell again. Young Lepper[61] complained to me that McDonnell had called him a b_____ ass in front of the men and refused to apologise. I spoke to McDonnell and said he was to apologise. He tried to excuse himself on plea that [on the] occasion [he] was not "on duty". I ruled the plea out. Today I found that he had done nothing so I saw him again and expressed my astonishment at his attitude and asked him if he was going to apologise or not. He said no. I at once reported the matter to Col Johnston as O/C Troops and said the matter must be settled. He quite agreed with me and told McDonnell to apologise or we would report him to the General. McDonnell caved in. He is a fool. He thinks I am hard on him and doesn't seem to understand that I command my Regt and not he! If I have any more nonsense from him, I shall get rid of him. He is an ungrateful beast anyway. Lack of education is his misfortune. The Australians were a blaze of light last night. They don't seem to understand. The New Zealand ships were in absolute darkness to the outside world except for side lights (red and green) which cannot be seen many miles away. We carry no mast head lights at most times. On certain occasion (weather) the *Maunganui* carries head and stern lights (white). Sea somewhat rough.

November 4th 1914

Calmer. Last night we rolled famously. Kept most people including myself awake until about 2 am. The skipper seems inclined to think that we go Colombo after all. He says we are not steaming a course to fit in with crossing to the Cape. Wrestling match this afternoon between J. Robertson[62] of 2 MR and Hine[63] of Wellington Inf Regt, 10 stone 10 and 11.5 respectively. Robertson is a light weight champion of Scotland and elsewhere a tall lithe piece of steel. Hine the typical wrestler, short broad and round. Urquhart was referee. Prize £10, 25% going to Regtl Fund. 1st bout, 18 minutes, a splendid go. Robertson won it. 2nd bout, 6 minutes. Robertson ruled too much for Hine and won. He is a sport. He at once divided the purse with Hine. Col Johnston not well, stomach trouble. I don't care about telling him but he goes through the menu too freely. I told him to diet. Suggested no meat or soup and such things. He and his wife are most interesting people. . . .

November 5th 1914

A calm, warm morning. It is now 6.45 am so I write up remainder of yesterday's events and await physical drill at 7.15 am. I think Colombo is our next port of call right enough. I had to give a man field punishment yesterday for insubordination. He was up before me two days ago for same offence – after repeated appearances before his Coy Commander. I had given him 24 hours detention – which he, it was reported, said he enjoyed. I did my best to get him to promise to mend his ways and would then have not given him field punishment. He said "I promise nothing". So I had to inflict it. 24 hours in handcuffs, two of which to be passed attached to a fixed object. Before I turned in I sent Cox to tell the Sergeant of the Guard to give the man bedding and free him of handcuffs until daylight if he behaved.

Corporal 'Jock'
Robertson of the
Wellington Mounted
Rifles, the victor in
a wrestling match
on the *Arawa*,
4 November 1914.

Malone Family Collection
London

November 6th 1914

A grey calm warm morning. . . . The Commander of whole fleet (HMS
Minotaur) complimented the New Zealand transports on their obedience
to convoy orders and especially to their darkening all lights. He gave the
Australians a good dressing down. Time too – nearly every ship is full of
lights. They are endangering the fleet or rather some part or parts of it.
Why will not people take their job seriously? Even on this transport I go
round every evening and find a carelessness and want of thought. Ports
and doorways unscreened! A concert last night on boat deck in the dark
and consequently not a perfect success. A glee party appeared and sang
beautifully "Farewell". . . . I spent a couple of hours developing. I have only

one film now to do. I hope the printing will be a success. I started to read *Strategy* by . . . [sic]. Spent two hours and propose to set that time apart every day 4 pm to 6 pm for it. No lecture last night being an off night. Awnings put up, a great boon to the men drilling all day. A most lovely sunset last evening. A wonderful study in greys and pink. . . . I look forward to them but how I wish that Mater was here to enjoy them too. Nelson was the last place where we saw them together.

November 8th 1914

. . . It was very hot last night in bunk. Even a sheet was too much covering. Our trouble is that the salt water bath water is quite hot. It has something to do with the condenser. I must try and get some water drawn from the sea. Its temperature is possibly about 70° [21° C] but the bath water is over 100° [38° C]. I am in splendid condition though. I gave my officers a strong hint yesterday as to their diet. They were wanting my permission to go about in shirt sleeves and Lord[?] knows what. The MR and artillery officers are allowed to do so. But I have been insisting on my officers being properly uniformed and until the doctor tells me that health demands less clothing which I shall not readily believe they will have to be. I told them to eat less! That three full meat meals a day in the tropics was absurd. It is appalling the way most of them eat. They know no better I suppose. The inspection by Col Johnston went off all right. Some of the Company Commanders came asking as it was so hot would I put off the parade! No!! We have just received word of the naval disaster at Valparaiso.[64] Very bad management. We understand that we have 70 ships in the Pacific, the Germans only five and yet we cannot concentrate in superior numbers. The first principle of war neglected. I remember the Germans in their official account of the S.A. War were saying the British Generals dearly love dispersal and detachment of their forces. The navy has come badly out of the war so far. Everybody was saying the navy is the one up-to-date show of the British Forces, yet it is the army that leads. It is splendid, more power to it. The knowledge that the German ships are at Valparaiso make our minds easier here. The *Minotaur* left us this morning. I finished my developing on Friday. On the whole the photography is a success. I am going to do a print of each and send them to Mater from Colombo. Our run yesterday 249 miles. Today ought[?] to be a lot better. Col Johnston gave us a most interesting lecture last night. Comparison of British, German and French artillery. He is a good lecturer and knows his job. He was very complimentary about the Regt yesterday. But I told my officers that we would have to begin again, not thorough enough. They had to agree but they have been thinking that we were going too slow. The competitions opened their eyes. Still the men are keen and all will be well. I am writing this under most comfortable circumstances on the ship's deck in my deck chair – a lovely breeze is blowing. The temperature however is 93° [34° C] in the shade. How Mater would revel in it. Would that she were here. . . .

November 9th 1914, Monday

. . . It is now cool on the weather side of our shade deck but as soon as we walk about and go into meals we perspire! I am reviewing the training and am going to begin again! More work for the NCOs and officers and less for the men until the officers and NCOs are better able to teach, *Festina lente*.[65] Concert last night. I didn't go. I don't think the average soldiers comic song should be encouraged on Sunday. It is generally a bit *risqué*. Sunday with its three or four divine services to wind up in the evening with double entendre canticles is wrong. I don't mean that those songs are right at any time but the world has them and the authorities cannot very well interdict them on weekdays but it could on Sundays. Every day I know should be holy but Sunday is the Lord's day and there is a special command regarding it. I proposed to the O/C Troops to censor the programme but he didn't think it feasible. I will have a go at the concert directors. . . .

November 10th 1914

Fine hot. Sea smooth, rolly morning. Yesterday was an interesting day. The *Emden* (German a/cruiser, which has done deeds in this ocean for months passed) was smashed at Cocos Island by HMS [sic, HMAS] *Sydney*, one of our escort. The circumstances are somewhat extraordinary. At about 6.30 am the acting wireless operator (one Private Falconer of my regt) was on duty and got the call SOS (distress signal) from Cocos Island which we were then passing at a distance of about 50 miles. The call was repeated about 50 times – some other operator (the *Emden*) breaking in and trying to jumble the signal. Then the words "a strange man of war entering the harbour" were made out. Our operator was the only man who got the signal message, the reason being that one of the assistants to the wireless officer on the transport had brought with him a privately constructed detector of a very sensitive nature and had attached it to the ship's instruments. It was owing to this that the signal message was got and made out.[66] This assistant is a signaller in the army Signal Coy with us. We tried to get our flag ship by wireless. She is only a mile away but . . .

[MSX 2542]

Nov 10th 1914 [cont]

but as she was busy signalling on these matters – we didn't succeed. We tried to get HMS [sic, HMAS] *Melbourne* – but same result.

> At 6.50 am we got by semaphore the signal to *Maunganui* (HMNZT No. 3) our flagship.
>
> At 7.4 am – The *Maunganui* got HMAS *Melbourne*.
>
> At 7.10 am – HMAS *Sydney* left for Cocos Island.
>
> 9.32 am – *Sydney* sending code messages. *Emden* trying to block by sending at same time.
>
> 9.47 am – Everybody ordered to stop signalling.
>
> 11.7 am – HMAS *Sydney* to HMAS *Melbourne*. "Enemy beached to save herself from sinking".
>
> 11.27 am – HMAS *Sydney* "Pursuing merchant collier".[67]
>
> 11.29 am – HMS *Minotaur*, (which left us on 8th Inst on some other service) first spoke asking for movements of enemy.
>
> 11.41 am – HMAS *Sydney* to all stations. "*Emden* beached and done for."
>
> Noon – British casualties – 2 killed, and 13 wounded.

At 6.15 am today we got word per *Ibuki* that the *Emden* had her foremast and 3 funnels down and surrendered. *Sydney* intact – she is remaining to take off guns of *Emden* and the wounded and prisoners. She will rejoin us after 24 hours bringing the prisoners. Smart and good work. The *Emden* on night of 8th Inst must have been within 10 or 12 miles of us. But apparently didn't know of us. She is well out of the way. It was an extraordinary bit of bad luck for her our passing so close to Cocos Island and to our picking up the message from that island. . . .

It was amusing to see the Australian Transports last night. Hitherto they were a blaze of light. Last night hardly a light showing anywhere – the NZ Transport[s] have always been in dark – muchly to our discomfort. Still we were playing the game. How the *Emden* would have enjoyed a fling amongst us. I had been hoping that she would strike us. We are waiting to get full details of the "scrap".

Yesterday was very hot 90° [32° C] in the shade in our cabins – the worst is that we cannot get a cool bath in the morning or at any time. We mean to make the captain do something. Our physical drill takes the sweat out of us and then we have to cool down the best way we can. . . . I wonder how our horses will get on. They are just shedding the last of their NZ coats! Things are going smoothly – our beginning again will bear good fruit. I got all the NCOs together yesterday and bucked them up to redoubled efforts. More thoroughness. The effect was good I feel sure. Things have to be tightened up – not slacked – even if the weather is hot.

We served out our hammocks today but that wooden headed chump Dallinger, could only produce 130 instead of the 200 which I bought and the Wairarapa people paid for – and which Dallinger had to see on board. That is the last straw – when he takes up his Regimental duties again I sack him from QM Sgtcy. He is now Ship's QM Sgt and should be sacked from that job. Another of McDonnell's bad picks. The latter, by the way, is very sweet to me now but I don't mean to trust him very far all the same. I can very easily run the Reg't without him and really would prefer to do so. Capt Cox makes a very gentlemanly Adjutant and is attentive to his job and keeps his place.

Capt Hume lectured[68] last night 'Ammunition Supply' – It was a good lecture. I lecture tonight on The Attack so have been busy preparing and drawing on the blackboard – diagrams etc, etc.

Another lovely sunset last night. Greys and golds and yellow pinks. If only I could paint.

November 11th 1914

. . . My lecture tonight went off all right but it is a great strain for the listeners to sit in the saloon at temps 88° [31C] and pay attention for ¾ of an hour. Instead of formal following of textbook I gave them the Battle of Driefontein[69] – with maps – on the Blackboard and from it made all the points relating to the attack, from a Division down to a section of Infantry. Plenty of diagrams I hope made the matter clear. The Australians were alight again last night. They seem a slack lot. Perhaps it is my prejudice against Australians. I have it I know but cannot say why. I must be juster – and only judge on 1st hand evidence. Yet there is evidence of slackness on their part and a comparison unfavourable to them can be made every day. Our run yesterday was 250 miles. Good!

November 12th 1914

. . . We pass the Equator tomorrow and Neptune is coming aboard in state.[70]

Heard yesterday that all correspondence is to be censored. We can write nothing about the Convoy or Expedition. That means that I cannot send Mater the duplicate of these notes or any papers that I have been saving up for her. It is a dashed nuisance but still I suppose it is necessary. Mater will be content, so long as she knows that we are all right. When we get to England I presume we will be able (allowed) to send the news of this voyage. . . .

My Regt competitions (finals) are held today. It is now 6.15 and I can hear the various competing sections drilling all over the ship – practising. I am glad the men are so keen. And there are no prizes, except certificates. We will go on holding competitions. Every week. We will divide the sections into 3 classes and have competitions in each – so as to give all hands a chance to do something.

I am sorry to find that the Sports people have put on an event called a "Bun and Treacle" race. One of those more or less degrading things that the world still thinks good fun. I hate "scrambles" etc. They sort of teach the competitors to act like brute animals. I shall try and get my men not to enter for the race . . .

Electric fans are being erected in the men's holds. The good Wairarapa people put a dozen of such fans on board. I shall never forget them and Morrison their chairman.[71]

November 13th 1914

. . . Our competitions yesterday were a success. Some 100 men completed in sections and were quite good. We got the machine gun men to compete between themselves. They gave a good exhibition. In the Rifle Exercise a Ruahine Section was first, Taranaki filled 2nd, 3rd and 4th. The winners had decidedly more snap and vigour and so won. [Major John W.] Brunt the Taranaki Commander is a somewhat heavy thick slow man and conceived this notion that a stately action was the proper thing. I gave him the tip after the show was over to wake his men up then they could win. The Ruahine commander [Major Edward H. Saunders] is a somewhat puny man with little go, but he let his Sgt-Major run his men and they coming from a drier, harder country beat the mud plodders from moist, soft Taranaki. Australia can play cricket and New Zealand cannot for the same reasons.

This afternoon Neptune's advance party of Bath assistants – the proper ceremony owing to the rain being postponed to tomorrow, took charge and ducked all in sundry. They were a merry good-natured crowd – and all hands except Col Johnston and myself and one or two Majors took part. Personally I don't think any officer above rank of Subaltern should allow the men to collar and pitch them into the bath – a big canvas sail – still it is difficult I suppose to draw the line. A most unfortunate accident happened. Lt Surgeon [Ernest] Webb[72] lost his head and of his own accord took a header dive from the top of the horse boxes into the bath about 3ft deep and "broke his neck". He is not expected to live for more than 2 or 3 days. He is paralysed from the shoulders down. A really good able fellow. I like him and we often took a walk together. We are all very sad. The *Maunganui* sent 2 of their doctors over, but nothing could be done. Webb was unmarried, had no-one dependent on him. He is a Dunedin man. Had he been shot in action it would have been so different. Still is, was to be. We have another chap[73] in a dangerous condition. He had appendicitis and was operated on last night, a complicated case Home says.

> In his diary entry for 13 November, Corporal George Bollinger of the Wellington Battalion comments that the 'show got out of control and all ranks from Colonel downwards were dunked'. [George Bollinger diary, 13 Nov 1914, MS Papers 2350/1 ATL.]

November 14th 1914

The rain is over. We have a calm sea and grey morning. We left the main fleet yesterday, and are going ahead as fast as we (the New Zealanders) can. This to save time and we are more in want of water etc than the Australians owing to our longer journey. We are pleased and we expect to arrive at Colombo tomorrow morning. It has been announced that correspondence to New Zealand can be <u>closed</u> but closed letters will be delayed. They may be opened and censored but it is unlikely. I will therefore write Mater a formal open letter with practically no news and send another closed. . . . I am very fit – have reduced my waist by 2½ inches. A ½ hour physical drill in a temperature of 84° to 88° [29°–31°C] gets rid of fat. A large number of the officers have dropped out. They however are not proud of themselves. Yet they seem to somewhat resent the action of those who are sticking it out!! I am 10 years older than the oldest of them [except Brunt, who was 52] and am glad of the chance of getting really fit. The campaign in front of me is bound to be one of hardship. The fit man is going to do the best work. Our run yesterday 259 miles we crossed the Equator – about 11 am.

November 15th–16th 1914

The *Arawa* arrived in Colombo on 15 November and the following day Malone visited the city whose cosmopolitan population interested him. He toured a local gaol and the government radio station and was impressed by how clean and orderly everything was. He visited the home of a local official and his Anglo-Indian wife. Malone thought them 'very gentle civil people' and commented that 'he was committing an awful sin according to white Ceylon Ethics . . . in associating with them – but I don't feel guilty'.

After giving money to a young beggar he was surrounded by children who touched him 'gently and held out their hands – not a word – I soon got rid of my small coins. Quite awful I suppose but I couldn't help it. How glad I am that I wasn't born a native of ... any not white country'.

[MSX 2549]

Colombo Harbour
15 November 1914

My dear wife,

This is a formal letter, which can only contain matters not concerning our business. It is to be censored. We are allowed to write what is called a closed letter, which will be delayed here, so that any information deemed prejudicial will be practically out of date. I am writing you also a closed letter and sending you sundry papers, our newspaper and you will thus understand the brevity of this.

I am hoping that a letter from you may have got to Colombo and will be received by me. Needless to say it would be a great joy. We are all well. I am as fit as the proverbial fiddle. My waistline is 2½ inches less, and it was nothing very huge before. We have had a good passage, smooth seas, beautiful sunsets, a distant electrical display behind masses of clouds with a wonderful effect, one day's rain, which was helpful to the washing. Tell the youngsters that there are lots of flying fish. They fly 100 yards or more. We are working as hard as is possible with a temperature up to 88° Fahrenheit [31°C]. Practically no sickness, thank God, but a dreadful accident. Webb, one of our medicos at the Crossing the Line ceremony of Friday last, dived into the bath and so injured his spine that he cannot recover. He may linger on for a time. A grand young fellow, one of my right hand men in all sanitary matters. I liked him before most of the others. He said to me the other day, "When I first joined you, I thought there was rather much rousting[74] but I am convinced that it is now not so, to break in raw men and above all officers is a difficult job and one must roust and roust until they are broken in." It is very sad to see him lying paralysed from the shoulders down. But it

was to be and God's will is to be done. The next world after all to the good living man is the best after all.

And how are you all getting on? I think of you every day and hope that all is well with you and that all the children and not excepting Norah and Mot are all that they should be. Don't forget to get that photo of your sweet self taken and sent to me. With all my love to you all.

Your husband

November 17th 1914

We sailed from Colombo about 10 am. Some 28 of us. We go to Aden reach there in about 7 days. We will be Home in about 4 weeks. We have 30 German stokers on board, prisoners from the *Emden* – 2 Warrant Officers and a Lieutenant Engineer "Hass". We are not pleased. We had a crowded ship before and now we will have to keep a guard over these prisoners night and day. Poor devils they have had an awful experience. The *Sydney* smashed the *Emden* killing 130 and wounding seriously some 50 out of about 230. The killing too was horrible. The ship was a shambles men literally blown to pieces. . . . I haven't had a talk with Hass yet. We put him on parole and he lives and messes with us. He seems a very decent fellow. The men look a clean harmless lot. They are herded up in part of our boat deck under our awning with 3 armed sentries over them. Their presence brings home the reality of the war. Several of them are slightly wounded and Home is quite busy dressing the wounds. . . . I took a photo with their permission of the Germans on board here and of Lt Hass. He asked me not to put him in the newspapers. I told him I had no thought of doing so.

November 20th 1914

Another day fine and smooth sea. Warm, but a nice breeze from the N.E. I am all right as to inoculation result except for some tenderness in the flank. Some 20 privates of the Ruahine Coy are objecting to being inoculated. Also S/S/Ms Dallinger and Foster.[75] I had the two taken up before Col Johnston. I had the men

The *Emden*'s Lieutenant Hass (right) on the *Arawa* with Major Brunt.

Malone Family Collection London

up and did my best to get them to agree. Inoculation is not compulsory and the authorities forgot to make it a condition of enrolment. Only one man in Taranaki Company objected. He is a grandson of EM Smith[76] of NP and a son of Tom Smith.[77] I believe – a queer sort of a man. Major Brunt anyway thinks he can get the lad to submit. Any men who persist will be made the scavengers of the Regt and will not be taken to the front. I am inclined to take their rifles from them and treat them as non-combatants. I gave them until 4 pm tonight to make up their mind.

Have just heard that this transport, the *Maunganui*, *Star of India* and *Tahiti* with 10 of the Australians are going ahead of the rest, to Aden, to coal. We are glad the extra speed of 2½ knots per hour, seems to push us along, and we will thus see Aden – sun baked hole as it is called. . . . Our German prisoners now peel potatoes etc, and so save our own men.

I tried staying in bunk this morning. All parades have been cancelled for 3 days on account of the innoculations. I read a French book *La Piste Millicinanto*[78] a sort of Doctor detective story. I hope that by reading French I will soon be able to speak it again. I try and think of it during the day, from time to time.

Amongst Malone's papers were the following rhymes, which appear to have been circulating on the *Arawa*:

Sick nursing rhymes

For the Inoculated.

Sing a song of soreness, a little needle prick,
500,000,000 microbes in our flank shot quick,
When the swelling rises, the pain begins to grow,
WHY THE DEVIL SHOULD THE DOCTORS HURT OUR FEELINGS SO.

For the Uninoculated.

Sing a song of sickness, sunk cheeks and hollow eyes,
Forty typhoid cases, Lots of busy flies,
When the fever rises, they mutter every one –
"WHY THE DEVIL DIDN'T I HAVE THE INJECTION DONE."

[MFCL]

[MSX 2549]

HMNZ Transport No. 10
(*ARAWA*)
Arabian Sea
About 300 miles due east of Aden
[24 November 1914]

My dear wife,

. . . It is 6.15 am and I am sitting on deck dressed or rather undressed for physical drill at 7.15 am. It is a lovely grey morning, cool (81° Fahrenheit, in shade!!) [27°C], the sea quite smooth, a lovely sunrise. Greys, oranges, yellows and sepias, all shades like a sunset in reverse. We left Colombo on Tuesday last, a week ago today. Our voyage has been uneventful, smooth, fine, breezy and not oppressively hot, down to 80° Fahrenheit some mornings. We have all been inoculated for Typhoid. An hypodermic syringe is used on the left side of the abdomen. There is tenderness and malaise for some two to three days after injection of the serum or whatever the stuff is properly called. Some of the men (rotters) objected and our stupid medical authorities in New Zealand although providing for vaccination when a man enlisted, either didn't know of or forgot to provide for inoculation. I am not sure but that they thought that "vaccination" covered everything. One learned officer tried to argue that <u>vaccination</u> covered <u>inoculation</u> against typhoid (my spelling is getting weak!). He doesn't understand the value of words.

I am very much put out to think that any of my men are so exotic. There is only one man in the Taranaki Company and two in the Hawkes Bay Company, but 21 in the Ruahine Company. As to the Wellington West Coast Company on the *Maunganui* I cannot at present speak. We have tried them every way. As a last effort I had the objectors up before me and Home and asked them to state their objections. Childish! I got Home to explain the matter and then made them understand that if they persisted, I should have to treat them as a class by themselves, make "shoeshines" of them, not soldiers and would try and get them sent back to New Zealand at once, as useless. I must say some of them were men who never ought to have been accepted. The bulk of them, 66%, are not New Zealanders and have not long been in New Zealand. I am afraid that our immigration agents at home do not do their duty. Government ought to insist on only picked men and women be allowed to come to New Zealand. I had of course noticed odd men, unfit on our New Zealand standard and when we gathered them together, they were a queer sorry lot, undersized, weak jawed, ill formed, yet the fathers of future New Zealanders! I wonder whether our sometimes called statesmen ever think of their duty in nation building. I know that the immigrants are supposed to be selected, but it has been obvious for years past as you and I have ere now seen that the selectors don't do their duty. Dereliction of duty is I am afraid a common sin – lack of discipline everywhere. Statesmen, so called, afraid of "voters" and taking the line of ease and least resistance. The education of our part of the world is all wrong. I am afraid this is not interesting, but I write as I think. I cannot write about our business specially. I wonder when I shall get a letter from you. On arrival at our destination I hope.

Poor Webb died last Tuesday. The GOC at Colombo sent us a wireless message. The officers on this ship left £16 with the military authorities at Colombo to fix up Webb's grave and put up a cross over it. . . .

We are a healthy ship I am glad to say. We seem to be beating the measles too. We are starting to increase the work. My Lieutenants have two hours a day Tactical Classes now under Hart. I propose to hold an examination when we get to England. This will make them work, even supposing that their sense of responsibility is not sufficient to make them do so.

I wonder whether you have been having warm weather. I think every day how you would revel in what we call heat. I hope that you are keeping well and are not being worried in any way. I hope also that you are making nice friends and enjoying life. You are not to worry about me. I am in the best of hard and rude health and will keep so I have no fear. No hump on my back, now straight up and down always and feeling 10 years younger if not more. You I suppose are getting fat, and so satisfying your ambition. I hope that you will write me a good long letter every week and give me all your news.

Some day we will come this route together. Don't forget that you are to come to England when the war is over. Remember me to everybody who asks after me. I am sending some cards to the children. Have the boys gone back to Seatoun?

Edmond and Terry are well, the latter is acting Deck Sergeant still and is a good chap. Edmond hasn't any particular responsibilities. . . . Goodbye my dearest with all my love to you and the children. . . .

Your husband

[MSX 2542]

November 25th 1914

Arrived at Aden at about 6 am. . . . We heard today that 100,000 troops had already passed thro Aden. Tomorrow 40 Transports are due from Bombay with more troops. Lloyd George[79] seems to have made a fine speech in asking for authority to have another [£]225 millions. The resources of the British Empire are wonderful and all men have risen to the proper sense of their responsibilities to the Empire. As Lloyd George said we must finish things now and not leave our children to the German menace. Those who cannot give their lives can give their possessions. This war is the redemption of England and will leave the Empire better and greater in every sense. . . .

November 27th 1914

In the Red Sea a hot muggy morning. . . .

We had a lovely strong following wind last night. It was quite cool on deck. The wind has died away and we perspire. Still we all feel vigorous. At the moment they are doing their physical drill and there is plenty of

Regimental barracks Steamer Point

Gulf of aden

26.11.14

Carte postale

Britania Hôtel
The Anglo Jtalian Grocery Store
Samuel Benghiat, Behind the Hotel de l'Europe, Aden

This space may be used for correspondence ——— This space is for address only

My dear Norah.

we were anchored
just opposite the Port
of Aden. about 1½
miles away. The
buildings are artillery
Barracks. I believe.
from where we were
the country look
much higher. at
the back. All. were
Love from Father.

Mr ....

46 632 D

vigour and snap in the vollies [sic] of commands by the NCOs and the men respond with vim. We the officers do our p. [physical] drill in 20 minutes. The men's washing bothers me. They have not been allowed to wash clothes for 14 days and altho we were to get water for them y'day the Ship Captain said we would have to wait another week. Fancy with the limited outfit of under clothing of the men and all the hot weather and hard work they have had, not being able to wash for 3 weeks. I complained to Col Johnston and if we don't get water at once I shall complain to the General. There is plenty of water but it costs money to replenish – they say! as tho' cleanliness and consequent health is to be measured by money cost. I made a calculation that even at Aden price of water 7/- per ton, we could wash for £4.15.0 and allow every man 3 gallons of fresh water. Truly the European race is a dirty one, with little exception. I look at the *Ibuki* and week after week see well regulated lines of washed clothes drying literally covering the ship. And their own arrangements are so bad that our men, white men, some of whom call the Jap a brown monkey, cannot wash clothes for 3 weeks! The authorities cannot be expected to think about and provide for such paltry things! Reason, we are a dirty people. If we individually had to do our own work the white world would be like the white man, pigsty. I have some 24 officers on this boat and I doubt if more than 4 of them are really naturally clean. They don't understand what it means. If it were not for the stewards and their batmen, their quarters would be disgraceful. But enough!

November 28th 1914

6.10 am, temp. inside 86°F [30° C]. Last night on going to bunk it was 88°F [31° C]. . . . I spent my day today, apart from routine work, in solving tactical problems. Lt Hass our German officer prisoner, had to sign a written parole, and McDonnell drew up one, making him sign not to take up arms against Gt. Britain and her allies until the end of the war. But said nothing about not escaping. Col Johnston made him alter this limiting period to end of voyage. Fresh one prepared and signed. I happened to be about after its signature. I asked to see it and then had to point out that it missed the whole object of parole – which from an honourable foe-officer, is simply that he will not try to escape or escape – as to bearing arms, etc that is nonsense. If a prisoner is not on parole he is under guard and may escape if he can. An officer on parole is free of guard, on condition of his giving his word that he will not take advantage of his freedom and try to or escape. Obviously what is wanted is his word accordingly. So McDonnell who tried to argue as usual when he is wrong, that the document meant what it didn't say. That was the meaning of his argument. Col Johnston however made him go and rectify the error. McDonnell has a big lot of limitations. He is still a 1st Class Sgt Major, but is not and never will make a commissioned officer altho' he holds the rank. I am very disappointed in him. But am not trembling. I have got his measure. . . . There are now in the Red Sea, steaming N., our 38 Transports and 40 more from Bombay: 78 big ships full of soldiers, guns and horses. We estimate 75,000 men! and 100,000 horses we are told already gone N. Germany with all her thoroughness and wisdom, never calculated on such movement. Thank God, the few troops we had were able to hold up, with the French, the German host, and is still holding them, if not more. Time is all against the Germans and there can now be no doubt as to the result of the war. They have done their best and worst, and have not really succeeded. Our weight is coming. The wonder of it all, the gathering of men in all parts of the Empire, their equipment and training and then the flood of them towards and to the Front. The command of the World's seas! Well done those British Statesmen who have, in spite of active opposition of little Englanders, and the doubts of many of their friends, persisted in maintaining British supremacy at sea. The enormous cost is more than justified. It was but an insurance premium. If the same Statesmen could but have established universal military training in the British Isles there would have been no war. Lord Roberts was right and lived to see the proof.[80]

It is one of my regrets, that I cannot now see him. I had been looking forward to doing so. I had a message from old Captain Baillie[81] in Wellington to him. Captain Baillie's wife is some relation or connection of Lord Roberts.

Full marching order parade of my men today. They are busy cleaning up for it.

After appealing to the General we have got water to wash clothes with today. I am glad. But fancy having to fight to wash! I must now go to physical drill and get rid of what little adipose[82] tissue remains to me. It would be awful to be fat, in this heat. I feel really energetic and alert, mentally and physically, but one perspires sitting down in the open shade writing. . . .

Sick report y'day

Taranaki Coy	2 men
Hawkes Bay 1/2 Coy	1 man
Ruahine Coy	3 men

I am delighted – 3 out of the six were "sick" from bruises (accidental). What I call "soldier's sickness".

November 29th Sunday

. . . We got important news yesterday afternoon. We shall probably land at Suez to fight the Turks. It is a surprise to us. We had quite made up our minds that we should disembark in England. However it is all in our job, and Suez will be a much better place to winter in. Especially for our horses. If it is decided to disembark there we shall begin to land next Tuesday. The General on the *Maunganui* has gone ahead. We are making all arrangements to land and are not really sorry to be about to get off the ship. We have no doubt that in due time we will go to France and then on thro' Germany. We want to see and be in the big fighting.

My marching order parade yesterday morning was a success. It was an act of fortitude. 88°F [31°C] in the shade. The men have improved! Their steadiness, general turn out and arms etc were up to a good standard. They stood like rocks the perspiration running down their faces in streams. It took me an hour and a quarter and wasn't I wet when I finished. I am proud of my men. Full marching order, in the hottest part of the Red Sea, Home, as medico, was inclined to doubt the wisdom of it. I persisted however and no one was really the worse physically and all were the better morally. . . .

Church parade this morning, some 6 of the German prisoners off the *Emden* are Catholics and paraded with us. The 2nd inoculation starts today. I got my identity disc today, a piece of white thin metal round and about the size of a halfcrown, stamped.

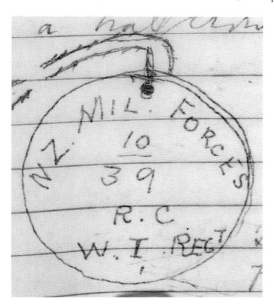

Malone's drawing of his identity disc.

Alexander Turnbull Library

10/39[83] is my number. R.C. means Roman Catholic. W.I. Regt Wellington Infantry Regiment. There is a small hole at the top, thro which is threaded a string by which the disc is suspended round ones neck. It is to be worn at all times, for, in case of need, identification purposes. I wonder whether Mater has got the former parts of the diary and whether it interests her much. It is not very exciting, but that cannot be helped. Let us hope there will be things more interesting and exciting to record. Later on I [will] find it somewhat of a resource, but it is getting I am afraid somewhat long winded. The short days are at hand. It is dark when we get up now. The men are just singing "God save the King" I stand up and think.

One of Malone's men was rather more direct about the need for identity disks, writing in his diary that they were required in cases 'where the effects of a shell leave the body otherwise unrecognisable.' [Oswald Meenken diary, 27 Nov 1914, Menken family.]

[MSX 2549]

In the Red Sea
About 500 miles south of Suez
Sunday 29 November 1914

My dearest one,

I wrote you at Aden a "censored" letter which is naturally a cool sort of public production. I had hoped to have been able to send you a little love letter, but it could not be. I must write you one now.

I miss you so much every day. While I am at work it is right enough but when I have finished and there is the long evening to go and it is too hot and too dark to work, I sit and think of you and all our best past, of the time when you met me at Lyttelton, our journey to Christchurch, my stay at Burkes at Papanui,[84] the day of our marriage, and ever since then the returning home to your bonny sweet self and later to the dear children, our little holidays together, our walks, our journeys and the delight when you put your arm in mine and leant on me as your true support in life. When I was away, the receipt of your longed for letters, the joy of arriving home and the disappointment if you were not about immediately on my arrival or if you appeared to casually receive me. You sometimes didn't like my apparent retirement to myself, but I loved you always. A man is often filled with business troubles and difficulties and must be affected, [?] some times he is tired and his nerves all of a jangle. I was often so I am sorry to think, but I was never content until I got home to you, and if I then remained in a cover of seeming selfishness, it was only a cover. You should know my dearest that you have been my only love. I have always loved you more than you did me. I loved you before and above everything and everybody, including the dear children. Whereas you know since the coming of our children that your love is divided and I think the children have the bigger half, that I believe on reflection to be only right and natural. I have I know at times seemed to resent it, but I know in my heart of hearts that the fact is one which endears you to me all the more. The maternal woman is the only true woman. God so made her. My resentment such as it was, was jealousy, an evil thing, a very evil thing out of it arose what little storms there have been in our wedded life. It was a great joy to me when you in time overcame it. You had no cause you know. On my part there never was any question, but as regarded our children, I am afraid that this appears somewhat like "the woman's always in the wrong". If so, forgive me. I am not acquitting myself of error. I might have been much nicer and better to you often and often and in many ways but I am as God made me, hard and unforgiving or rather resentful. Believe me when I was hardest I really loved the most and was miserable at heart. I won't write any more of this or think of it, only all the many many joys of our married life.

I had to leave off writing here. This is the longest parting of our lives, hard to both of us but especially so for you. Yet you have the children with you and I hope the novelty and pleasure of plenty of new friends in a new scene. Still I think when you have put the children to bed, you will sit and think about your husband, so far away on his new mission. When I wake in the morning I think of how it is evening with you and I try to picture you to myself, hearing Molly and the boys pray for their Daddy and his safe return. I pray too that God may keep you strong, well and happy and safe to welcome me on my return or to join me at this end of the world when the war is over. I look forward so much to that joyful day. We are probably going to land in Egypt and be there for some months. I think of your desire to see Egypt and do so wish that you could come and be near me. But I should not be able to see much of you and we expect to be fighting the Turks.[85] We are on the whole pleased at the idea of wintering in a good climate. It seems quite luxurious, but yet no doubt and I hope that there will be hardship.

. . . I hope that you have got my letters from Hobart, Albany and Colombo and that you are getting that photo of your dear self taken. I like the one I have very much, but I had had to paste a slip of paper over myself so as to have you by yourself. When I can get a moment I am going to cut you out and so fix up. I am sending you my diary leaves up to date which will give you my news and what not. . . . I wonder sometimes whether you feel tempted to take ship and come to me. How I envy Colonel Johnston having his wife with him. Not envy him his wife for she is nothing like my own dear girl. But it would be so lovely to sit on deck together, after dinner, in the dusk and cool and to have you about through the day. He doesn't seem to appreciate the position. They are very prosaic and matter of fact. She might be his sister. I was going to say mother, for she is very old in her ways. We all like her for she minds absolutely her own business and is in no way in the way. Holly is not a dear loving little soul like Molly and is allowed to eat ham and omelettes by the plateful. She sits opposite to me at breakfast and gets a bit on my nerves over her food. Dear Molly. If only we could swap Mrs Johnston and Holly for you and Molly it would be lovely. Give her a good hug and kissing for me and let her give you the same for me. I am afraid I should crush you up. I feel so strong with my physical drill and no business all day sittings. I only hope that you feel as well as I do. I am one of the fittest men on the ship. No fat now. My separation from you is my only trouble. I do so hope that you are managing all right without me. I feel that you are, but a woman by herself is without the support she needs. Still I know you love me and will on that account get along with independence and honour to yourself. Keep yourself well and strong for my sake and look forward always as I do night and morning to our reunion, never more let us hope in this world to part. The dear children too I have notwithstanding all my love for you, their father's love for them. Don't spoil them dear. I know you won't let them forget me. I hope they got or will get the elephants I sent them from Colombo. . . . With all my love and the memory of the kiss that was the sweetest to you of all those I have given you.

Your loving husband

Give each of the children a good kiss from me. Give my love to Norah and Mot. . . .

[MSX 2542]

November 30th 1914

. . . We are all feeling very much refreshed. No work today. Everybody tender after the 2nd inoculation. Some of the men who refused inoculation are now asking to be done. I am not inclined to allow them to be done. They are obviously either "wicked" or mentally deficient in some way and would probably almost certainly be a trouble by and by. Better I think get rid of them now, if I can. We went to a great deal of trouble to get them to consent, but they refused. Their surrender now is I think too late. They look in the main a bad erratic lot and we would be well quit of them. I spent of couple of hours last night playing Schumann. The salon was nice and cool. I quite enjoyed myself. His "Arabesque" which Granny used to play so often, from memory, was particularly attractive to me and awakened many memories of long, long ago. Granny used to play it perfectly. I am wondering about our letters from NZ. I do so want to hear from Mater. . . . The sooner the better. 45 days since we left Wellington.

. . . We hear now that we are to hand over our German prisoners to HMS *Hampshire* and that we are to go thro' the Canal and not disembark at Suez. Still obviously we are not going to England at present or we would not transfer our Germans. We shall know in a few days now.

We are. I did up my mail home, this afternoon, hoping to get it away by the censor Capt Shawe[86] without delay.

December 2nd 1914

. . . We transferred our German prisoners to HMS *Hampshire*. They were an inoffensive lot. Still we are not sorry to get rid of them. . . .

2

'In the cause of the age'

On active service, Egypt, December 1914 to April 1915

[MSX 2542]

December 3rd 1914

Arrived at Alexandria at day break [sic]. Steamed into the harbour under a shore pilot, a big ruffian in awfully baggy breeches, a long fine cloth overcoat and a fez. I went up on the bridge and took several photos of the harbour. It was full of sea-craft, big steamers, little one[s], ships, barques, brigs, schooners. Every imaginable sort of sailer. A great number of the big steamers are German prizes of war. Some 22 or so in number. We went alongside a quay, the Mah momdieh and tied up. Nobody seemed to know when we were to disembark, and nobody seemed to have troubled. None of us were allowed ashore. We completed getting ready. . . . The weather is surly and raining.

In his diary entry for 3 December, Private Oswald Meenken reports that large groups of men from the Wellington Battalion, who 'considered they were entitled to leave' rushed the picket on guard at the gangplank of the *Arawa*. This incident is noted by other members of the battalion and it is odd WGM makes no reference to it in his diary or letters. Perhaps he was too embarrassed to refer to this indiscipline in a diary he was sending to his wife.

[Oswald Meenken diary, 3 Dec 1914; George Bollinger diary, 3-4 Dec 1914; MS-Papers – 2350, ATL.]

December 4th 1914

One of Malone's companies left for Zeitoun on the outskirts of Cairo. Malone and Captain Cox went later for a walk through Alexandria. Malone wrote in his diary that:

It was most interesting but ugh! the filth and smells of the Arab streets and the dirt of the Arabs. There is a French-European part of the town, but the Arab town lies between it and the docks. Everything is like the pictures but one doesn't see the dirt and get the Malodorousness in the pictures. The Arab town is full of drinking places, seemingly every other shop or buildings is a place where the natives sit drinking, smoking, playing dominoes. Very few women about. Mostly veiled. Some apparently loose ones – unveiled a pity for they are the reverse of attractive or beautiful, and make the streets additionally objectionable.

[MSX 2549]

Alexandria
4 December 1914

My dear wife,

We arrived here yesterday morning and are busy disembarking and entraining for Zeitoun, four miles from Cairo. Some of the men go this afternoon and the rest will follow tomorrow or the next day. The *Maunganui* is going back to New Zealand and I have the chance to send this. You will wonder when you get it with New Zealand postmark. This is a big place, 320,000 population mostly natives, very dirty and smelly. I got a letter from Charlie Westerton[1] at Port Said. It was addressed to me, GPO London. He had heard that I was coming and seeing that some New Zealanders were in London, he thought I had arrived. The letter was sent on by our New Zealand Record Office. I am glad to find this because now I know that your letters will be sent here without delay. The landing arrangements here are not good, apparently no proper organisation. Everybody set up [?] on their own. We'll muddle through somehow though. This morning we route marched the men who had no work to do on board the Transport through the town to let them see the sights. No leave was given, this is a dangerous place to turn a lot of men loose as the drink is poisonous, and after total abstinence for seven weeks would have bowled them over at sight. I and Captain Cox, my acting adjutant, took a walk round, and were interested in the street life. How I wish you were here, going up to Cairo, which you have always longed to see. It is quite cool and there was rain last night and this morning. There is talk of England annexing Egypt. The Khedive has cleared out to Constantinople. 22 German ships['] captives, are lying here. The harbour is full of all sorts of shipping, lots of small barques, schooners, brigs, etc. It is a long time since I have seen so many sailing craft.

I send some more of my diary with all my love to you and the children.

Your loving husband.

[MSX 2542]

December 6th 1914

We go to Zeitoun today, all except a small party who have to stop and look after our waggons. Our horses got away yesterday. Just fancy, my Battalion and its transport, were spread over 4 ships! We could easily all have gone on the *Arawa* . . .

[MSX 2543]

. . . The journey was very interesting thro' level land, irrigated by the Nile, covered with green crops, Arab mud villages, more pretentious towns a mixture of European and Arabian. Water canals and channels, water wheels, turned by donkeys or bullocks, paths and tracks along side the canals. No fences. Lots of natives working in the fields and travelling camels, donkeys, bullocks. Goats and hairy sheep. Date palm groves, the great bunches of fruit covered with bags to I suppose keep the birds away. Flocks of kites as big as fowls. The scavengers of the country. We . . . got to Cairo at about 5:30 pm after a long wait we were . . . finally dumped out at a place called Esbet-El-Zeitoun. Piles of forage, stores, material, etc and lots of soldiers everywhere. The railway transport officer said he would send waggons along to cart our baggage – so away we went in the dark to our camping ground in the desert – a good road for a mile [1.6 kilometres] – we found our West

Coast and Ruahine Coys camp with tents pitched for themselves but our tents were at the Siding. We got a mug of cocoa and a small loaf of bread with a piece of Dutch cheese for our tea. We had a haversack ration on the train. For the night we bivouacked in the desert. It was hard but our fellows slept all right. We went back to the Siding and got our baggage . . .

December 7th 1914

Day light showed us a dreary waste on the edge of Zeitoun township . . . We found a very cold mist enveloping everything rain and damp most uncheerful – we got breakfast and then to work. By 10 am the sun came out bright and hot. We soon pitched camp. We took in more desert than allotted to us. I saw the Brigadier and also Genl Godley and they gave us carte blanche. So I laid off a spacious Camp next to the Otago Regiment. It is A1.

The men have put a small one stone high wall all round on the boundaries of roads and round each tent or else a sand wall.

The Govt is putting up the Dining Huts and cookhouses, which is more than we expected. The Imperial Chief of Engineers here Col Wright, whom I saw, insists that such huts, etc, are necessities and must be put up and he is boss. More power to him say me. We do not ourselves however consider that they are necessities. A bit of a cook shelter for each Coy is all that we thought of.

December 8th 1914

A cold night past very cold raw wet morning. We begin work and are settled down, much to the astonishment of the English Major in charge of the Egyptian Sappers along side of us. He thinks we are a wonderful people to so soon go to work. He is used to Egypt where "Tomorrow", for work comes very slowly. The stores, etc, of the force are being carted from the railway store to our depot by long strings of native carts – drawn by small horses or mules. Camels too carry loads. An everlasting long drawn out "Gee–e–e–ar" resounds night and day. It is the Arab drivers "Get up".

December 9th 1914

Foggy cold morning – busy squaring up camp and at work, hot day, cold night. We went some 4 or 5 miles [6.4 or 8 kilometres] across or rather into the desert for our days work. The sand is taking all the spring out of marching still in places the ground is fairly hard and covered with small stones and pebbles.

Some of Malone's men did not appreciate the extra work involved in 'squaring up' the camp. Arthur Swayne wrote in his diary: 'Granny Malone's order to beautify camp by placing stones around each tent . . . made it look like a lot of children's playhouses his ears must have been tingling with pride there was some smart speeches made about him'. Swayne's reference to 'Granny Malone' is unusual. He was most commonly referred to by his men as 'the Colonel', or 'our Colonel', but he was also affectionately referred to by others as the 'Old Man', 'our Molly' or 'Mollie Malone'. [A.J. Swayne diary, 9 Dec 1914, 1992-50, KMARL; Harston to IKM, 13 Aug 1913, MFCL; 'A Soldiers Book of Life' by Aubrey Tronson, pp. 1-2, MS-Papers – 2393, ATL; *Evening Post*, 13 Nov 1915, p. 13.]

[MSX 2549]

Esbet-el, Zeitoun
near Cairo
10 December 1914

My dearest,

Here I am in my tent on the Zeitoun desert sand and stones, not a weed, shrub or tree of any sort. It is 7 pm and I squatting on the ground on a bag and using the leather trunk as a table. The whole New Zealand Force is camped here. My Regiment is on the outside desert flank. I sent you a letter per *Maunganui* from Alexandria on 4th Inst. We stayed there until Sunday the 7th Inst midday or rather most of my men did. The disembarkation arrangements were no better than the embarkation ones so instead of the whole Regiment getting away in two trains, it was split up into four lots (main) and we still have to get our wagons. Still I won't bore you with our blunders. We saw the country between Alexandria and this place which we reached at 6 pm just dark. That country is flat and seems very fertile, covered with green crops, here and there Arab villages, date palm groves, mixed towns with good buildings, modern and mud houses and shrines. We crossed the Nile twice, also the Mahmoudieh [Mahmûdîyeh] fresh water canal, no fences, irrigation channels everywhere, water wheels, earth roads or paths, plenty of people in the fields and along the roads all natives riding on donkeys and camels or cows or bullocks. They sit right back on the donkeys' hips and ride without bridle or stirrups. Zeitoun was a small oasis about five miles from Cairo. Now there is a railway station and a small town with a good road and many suburban residences. It is close to Heliopolis, the

Opposite above

Malone's sketch map of the New Zealand Infantry Brigade camp at Zeitoun (left) and a more detailed map of his battalion's section of the camp (right).

Alexander Turnbull Library

Opposite below

This big horse, probably Don, towers over his master. Malone told his eight-year-old son Denis that his horse 'generally wants to run away with me when I am riding in the desert'. Herbert Hart, who succeeded Malone in command of the Wellington Battalion, took over Don and used him as his personal charger until the end of the First World War.

Malone Family Collection Wellington (now in ATL)

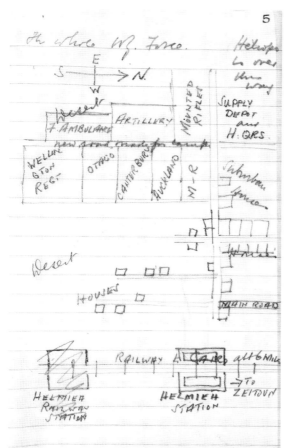

The whole NZ Force.

5

S ← E → N
W

Desert

7 Ambulance | Artillery | Mounted Rifles | Supply Depot and H.Qrs.

new road made for camp.

Wellington Regt | Otago | Canterbury | Auckland | M-R

Suburban fence

Desert

Houses

Water

Main Road

Railway | Cairo | abt 6 Miles → To Zeitoun

Helmieh Railway Station | Helmieh Station

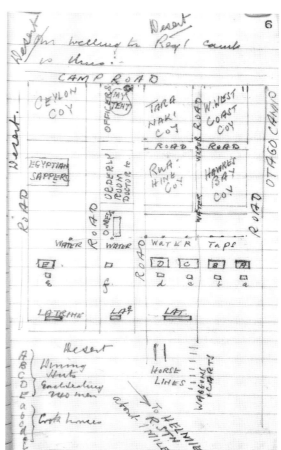

Desert — Our walk to Regl camp is this:—

6

Camp Road

Ceylon Coy | Officers [My Tent] | Tara Naki Coy | W. West Coast Coy

Desert Road | Road

Egyptian Sappers | Orderly Room Doctor to | R.W.A. Hine Coy | Hawkes Bay Coy

Road | Road

Water | Water | Water | Taps

E e | f | D d | C c | B b | A a

Latrine | Lat. | Lat.

Desert

A B C D E } Dining Huts — Each holding 240 men
a b c d e f } Cook houses

Horse Lines | Waggons & Carts

To Helmieh R. Stn about 1 Mile

Otago Camp

fashionable suburb of Cairo. Houses and streets and gardens are spreading out into the desert. The houses are built of stone in good moorish style, squares with flat roofs, porticos. I will send you a photo of a sample by next mail. We have been and are very busy fixing our camp. We find that by watering the sand floor of our tents, that it sets solidly, there being a lot of lime in the sand. Tramping makes it quite hard. I have bought for 4/- two large squares of native matting each about 12 feet by 8 feet and covered my floor with them. Tomorrow I get a few boxes, etc, and will then be comfortable. I am so glad I brought my stretcher. It is very cold here at night and we have had quite a lot of rain. The days, when the sun is out, are quite hot. It is winter. Don and Billy[2] are in splendid condition and stood the voyage well. I have not ridden them yet as no doubt their legs are tender, for seven weeks they were on their feet. The Regiment is together again and I am pleased with it. The Company and the ½ Company that were away are not as good as the rest but will soon come right. We have had the compliment paid us by the General of having joined to us a 5th Company, 231 strong, the Ceylon Planters Rifles. They, I am told, are all gentlemen of means. They equipped themselves, transported themselves and do without pay so they are the most exceptional lot of all His Majesty's Forces. They have been here three weeks and are at present in barracks. They come to us as soon as tents arrive from England in a day or two.[3] I have now 1,350 men under my command. May they do good work. Our Brigadier told me yesterday that he expects that we will be in action against the Turks in less than a month. We are all pleased and hope to do well. We may go across into Palestine and cut the railway to Mecca. There has been fighting already near Mt Sinai. It will do us a world of good to have been in action.

Captain McDonnell is all right now but he will have to keep in his place. I have got rid of my Quartermaster, Sergeant Dallinger. He is incompetent. He was insolent to me last night. I put him under arrest and am sending him up for court martial. He will, I believe, get dismissed [from] the Force. These Staff Corps and soldier men are a nuisance. If I had my way, I would have none of them bar my Regiment Sergeant Major, Mr Parks. He is a good man. I haven't seen much of Cairo. I went in with my assistant Adjutant [Captain John Rose] on Monday afternoon to get some materials and gear that we needed. We went by tram, first class single fare two piastres say 5d. The town at Cairo (Pont Limoun) Railway Station is very repulsive to my mind. A wide open space, the crossing of many roads and tram lines, all covered with litter and dirt, swarms of dirty natives squatting, standing or walking about. They are dressed in various coloured long robes or gowns reaching to the ground, mostly black or dirty white, their heads muffled up in dirty wraps, black or white. The women are mostly veiled. You can just see their eyes and a bit of forehead. Between and above the eyebrows they carry a brass roll about one inch in diameter, so from this hangs the yashmak or veil. Over their heads they wear a shawl. Everything is black. You see some leg without stockings, the ankles encircled with silver bangles, the feet in slippers without heels. Their skin is sallow, dirty yellow to brown. There is however a better part of the town, nearer to the Nile, Place de L'opera and Esbekiah [Ezbekiyeh] Gardens, some fine streets with fine buildings and shops, French and Italian. Wherever you have Arabs and Egyptians, you have squalor and dirt. The European parts of all these towns are decent and in many parts fine. I have had no time to see any sights. My assistant Adjutant and I did our business and then had afternoon tea at "Shepheards", the tourist Hotel, $^1\!/_3$d each! Not as good as Ellingfords. I took in my films for development and printing and will try and get them tomorrow and sent to you.

When at Alexandria . . . I went to mass at a church near the docks, an Italian church I was interested in and was of interest to the congregation. I called on the priest and had a yarn with an assistant in French. I shall with practise soon speak fluently.

All these towns seem full of drinking places where all the men nearby sit at little tables and play cards or dominos, smoke and drink very often coffee, etc. The streets in native parts are filthy and most malodorous. Some of the buildings are evidently hundreds of years old but out of repair and tumble down. I send you a lot of postcards which give you the general effect of everything except the dirt and malodorous. It is so good to get out in the desert where the air is sweet and the ground clean. There are lots of natives round and about the camp. They are carting night and day in one horse little carts our supplies, forage, food, baggage and ammunition. You here "Gee-e-e-ah" all times. It means "Gee up". Our own transport is not fit, the horses too tender yet.

So far no letter from you. I do so hope to hear from you soon. I trust that all is well with you and that you are not forgetting all about me. I am very well but feel the cold in the early morning. We turn out at 5.30 am in the dark and only candle light. A cold bath in the open desert in the dark sounds romantic but it is not very interesting or luxurious. I have, however, bought a spirit lamp and some Bovril and have a good pannikin full after my bath and that is a luxury.

I haven't seen Edmond or Terence since we left Alexandria – been too busy. But they are not far away, ½ a mile or so. There are 40,000 troops round here, Indians, Britishers, New Zealanders and Australians, not to mention my Ceylonese. The Turks have 100,000 but we are deemed to be good enough to tackle them.

My candles (2) are burnt down to the sockets and I am at the end of my news.

I do so miss you. It is right enough through the busy day but evenings and mornings I spend thinking about you and the family. I hope all is well with you all. Just heard that the *Scharnhorst*, *Gneisenau* and *Leipzig* have been sunk. Good news![4]

With all my love,
Your husband

[MSX 2543]

December 11th 1914

Dull drizzly cold morning – day fine and hot. We didn't exactly like turning out at 5:30 am, still we ought to be thankful that we are not on Salisbury Plain where we hear the mud, slush and cold is awful. The wet we are getting doesn't amount to much, and is exceptional. I believe the annual rainfall here is less than 2 inches! Everybody cheerful but Home and I are rather worried at our sick – over 130 reported this morning – nasal catarrh, cough. One man is very bad with pneumonia in hospital and will probably die. We expected the change to send our numbers of sick up but it ought to have eased off by now. I think it must be at its worst and will now mend. Let us hope so. The rest of us are all right. *Deo Gratias*.[5] We are hard at work. I am very displeased with the West Coast Coy (Cunningham) the Coy that was on the *Maunganui*. They are far behind the men – we brought in the *Arawa* – From nearly the best Coy – they are now absolutely the worst. They seem indifferent and quite slack – the officers' fault. I have now the job of straightening them up. The ½ Coy of Hawkes Bay that went on the *Limerick* are not so bad – not as good as the *Arawa* men but right enough.

December 12th 1914

Foggy morning but no rain – fine day – washing day. Everybody staying at home. England is deposing the Khedive and declaring his uncle one Hassain [sic, Hussein] an independent Sultan under the protection of England.[6] Egypt will be a Protectorate of England. It will manage all its own internal affairs but cannot meddle with international matters and England will see

Malone sets out what he wants done during training in the Egyptian desert.

Morison Album, Alexander Turnbull Library

that it is not meddled with. Turkey's suzerainty is ended and everybody said a good job too. There is to be a ceremony of installation of the new Sultan tomorrow week with a procession through Cairo. We are to help line the streets and keep order if needs be. Every man will carry 20 rounds of ball ammunition.

The proclamation of deposal of the Khedive and the constitution of the Sultanate or rather Protectorate has been issued.

December 13th 1914

Sunday – quite a fine morning. We (Catholics) went to Mass at Heliopolis. We marched with a Band at our head. The Church is like a tomb outside, sort of all domes built of buff coloured stone. So fresh, sweet and clean inside. Just as we got there, the people who had been to their own mass came out. Such a strange looking people all colours of brown, Egyptian Maltese, Italians, French, Levantines and a general mixture – not a real white man or woman among them. They stared at us some 600 stalwart men and we at them – our priest Father McMenamin[7] said mass and preached. In the afternoon I and our Brigadier, Col F.E. Johnston who is a Catholic, went to Mataria [El-Matariyeh] – 10 minutes walk from here to take part in the annual pilgrimage . . . . Quite a number of our men were present and we and the English soldiers (Catholics) had a place in the procession. In our turn we sang hymns in English. There was a sermon in French, which I understood easily. The good priests gave our officers coffee and wine. It was a most interesting event and ceremony. People came from all parts of Egypt. Many interesting types . . . . The faith of the people is great but I don't think they are very thorough.

December 14th 1914

Fine morning – cold – fine day. I went over with Col F.E. Johnston to watch an English Territorial Brigade of Infantry at work. The men seem all like boys so short, small and fair. It is astonishing. They are mostly very young. The officers seem a sort of their own – slow well done and not somehow or another altogether soldier like. I couldn't help thinking of the *Punch* Volunteer officer. They reminded me in many cases of him. I suppose it is that they are "fish out of water" – our Colonial officers in most cases are practical men and more or less readily take to soldiering. The English chaps don't appear to do so. I may be wrong and I ought not to express any opinion, but I have it all the same. They are good fellows I believe and anyway are doing their duty in volunteering to go to the front, and are I believe in earnest and doing their best. I had to meet Col Johnston at the Polygon Barracks, Abbasiah, and went across part of the desert. I met a General officer and I stuck him up to make sure of my way. He asked me to go along with him, as he was bound to the same place. He turned out to be General Prendergast of the Regular Army. He was very nice and is I diagnose a lover of practice[?]. We found the Territorial Brigade and I was asked to umpire one of the Battalions. The Brigade was attacking a position held by a real Force – another Brigade was cooperating in the attack starting from Mataria. I went along with my Battalion the 10th Manchesters and was quite pleased with the men or boys in the ranks. They trudged along, hardy and quietly and cheerfully with an air of its not being for them to ask the reason why. Their officers to my mind shied right off their objective and extended far too prematurely and generally acted somewhat unintelligently. Result the Battalion did a lot of tramping and running and laying down and getting up, all for nothing and were knocked off to go home just as the real show began to develop. The men never grumbled. I had a yarn with several of them as they trudged along. They nearly all came from Oldham Lancashire and had worked in the cotton mills there. With more age, they will make good soldiers. But the shortness of them is most striking. Our men seem like giants alongside of them.

December 16th 1914

. . . I don't think I have noted that a Company of Ceylon Planters Rifles have [on 8 December] been attached to my Regiment. They are organised on the British lines and are at full strength. They are all gentlemen Tea Planters, professional men, etc. We felt complimented at Genl Godley giving them to us. I had them over and inspected them and found them well-trained and really good hefty men. They put all their will into their work and every man uses his brains to do his bit thoroughly. They are alert and physically very fit. Their officers are really good. I wouldn't mind swapping some of mine. Their Commander is Major Hall-Brown a Tea Planter, a good chap but he feels a little bit I think his having to give up his general independence. He took orders from nobody except his Government. Now he takes them from me. We get on quite all right and I handle him gently. My Regiment is now 1350 strong in round figures. The Ceylon chaps know nothing about camp order, etc, but they will learn all right.

December 25th 1914

Xmas day. Mass at 6:30 am in Camp – Then I raked and swept and did up my tent and its surroundings until everything was tidy. My tent is quite homely now – my table with the NZ flag for a cover is a great comfort. I can sit and write with ease. I have been writing this up since the 8th, Spent most of the afternoon and all the evening up to now 9 pm. I want to send it to Mater by mail leaving next Monday. I hope I shall get another letter from her soon.

I am going to the Pyramids tomorrow, by tram, we have general holiday. We had quite a good dinner roast turkey, green (bottle) peas, plum pudding. I wonder where I shall be next Xmas. Capt Lampen[8] and the New Zealanders from England arrived today. We gave them 3 cheers, and then some of them in wheeling around, walked over my garden plots. I gave them gip[9] – while sitting here I heard one of the men describing the incident to his mates. Thus: "the NZ lot from London came in this morning and the Colonel called for 3 cheers for 'em, and they began to walk over his garden and then he gave them bally hell." He didn't know I could hear him. He thought it quite all right – Time I turned in.

[MSX2549]

Ezbet-El, Zeitoun
Egypt
28 December 1914

My dear Norah,

I was very glad to get your letter of 30th October last on Saturday week last. The mail goes out today. I too was very sorry to have missed you and Maurice on my leaving New Zealand. I am glad to hear that the car is running well. You are quite right to go on with your German, etc, but my dear daughter what about your music. You must go on with that too. It will always be a resource and I think it has always a refining and comforting effect. One sits and plays good music and one becomes possessed by the spirit of that music. Besides it may give pleasure to others. I am so glad to hear that Mater is well. You must always be a help and a comfort to her. I am sorry for Brian. I got a postcard from him. He didn't growl. I am sorry to hear that our reinforcements are so indifferent. We will straighten them up when we get them. We are very well but are disappointed that the Turks do not seem inclined to go on with their invasion of Egypt. We are certain to go

The 'cultivation of domestic virtues' required accommodation to be clean and in order. This is Malone's tent at Zeitoun Camp, Egypt.

to France by March next. Our camp is getting well settled down. My tent is quite comfortable. I have got a little table, for cover the New Zealand flag. I fold the Union Jack part in so that the part that shows is the blue with four red stars. I have Mater's and your photo on it and the little picture of the departure of King Charles or Monmouth from England leaning up against my book case. I am sending some photos, two of which give the interior of my tent but they were taken before I got my table. My work case, etc, is at bottom, a tea box with a shelf and at top a corned mutton box also with a shelf. The table is to the left of them, right close up. I have the brown pot that Mater gave me and in which I kept the lilac from New Zealand to Hobart. I have actually some mignonette and some roses in it, most lovely and sweet. The bees keep visiting them. . . .

I am very fit and well. We started again this morning an officers' physical drill class. It is not popular among the young officers because they have to get up earlier <u>but</u> it will do them and me a lot of good.

With love to you all.

Your loving father,
Wm.G. Malone

Ida, torn from the husband-and-wife photograph by McAllister. Malone would 'introduce' visitors to this portrait of his wife. On the back of the photograph Malone recorded his movements after he left New Zealand. The last entry is 'Happy Valley 6.8.15'.

Malone Family Collection London

The inside of Malone's tent in Egypt. The photograph of Ida that he always took with him is prominently displayed. Amongst the books visible are two by the leading British military writer Colonel G.F.R. Henderson: *The Science of War: A collection of essays and lectures 1891–1903* and *Stonewall Jackson and the American Civil War*.

Malone Family Collection London

Zeitoun
Egypt
28 December 1914

My dear Denis,[10]

For you yourself this letter. I send you some picture postcards to keep and to ask me questions about when I come home. I am sure that you are working hard at school and doing your best to be always tidy and clean and good. Give mummy a good love for me.

Your loving father

A lot of big guns are going by my tent, three Batteries, four guns in each. They look great.

x_____x

A letter Malone received from his youngest son, Barney, who was nearly seven years old.

Malone Family Collection London

Zeitoun
Egypt
28 December 1914

My dear Barney,[11]

A bee is flying about me as I write to you in my tent in the desert here. I have some nice flowers on my table and the bees are visiting them. I expect they are hungry as in the desert there are no flowers, grass, trees or shrubs, sand and stones as far as you can see N + E on the W + S. I can see date palms and houses and gardens and farms, green and flourishing.

Goodbye. Give your mummy a good love for me.

Your loving father
I send you some R.P.[12] cards.

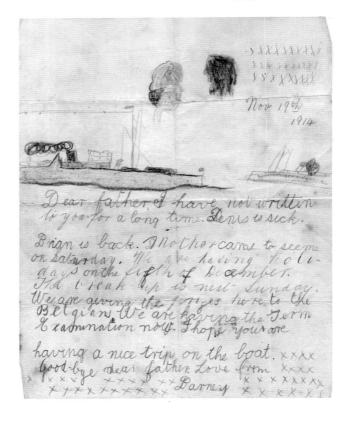

[MSX 2543]

December 29th 1914

Fine day. Physical drill. Did some work about camp pacing site of Regiment Canteen (wet) we will have a . . . garden in front and a shielded place or square where men can sit in front of canteen as they do in Cairo and other towns. . . . I have also allotted room for 2 big huts for the men to the S [Salvation] Army. Their 2nd in Command a Col Hunsworth just arrived from London, had lunch with us today, a good stamp of man and used to personal interviews with Royalty and big guns generally. He says that the King is very fond of the Australians and our New Zealand troops and thinks the world of them. May we do him honour. I took the opportunity of pointing out to Col Hunsworth who is a great friend, he says, of General Maxwell[13] as the Commander in Chief in Egypt – the unsuitability of our present working hours. Rise at 5:30 ½ an hour before daylight get out of camp by 8 am and yet get back with work finished for the day at 2 pm so that from 2 pm to 10 pm Tattoo[14] the men having nothing to do and general leave being the order of every day. Many of them naturally go off to Cairo and get into sore temptation. If I had my way I would get up at day light say 6 am, have physical drill ½ an hour, breakfast clean up properly and go out of camp say at 9 am returning at 4 or 4:30 pm. The men would be tired and by the time they had tea they would be content to go to bed. Then to my horror the GOC (ours) has approved certain measures for preventing certain frightful consequences of vice and so as to enable them to indulge in the vice with no fear of disease. At present we appeal to the men's better nature and to his morality at the same time letting him know the awful punishment of certain vice in this country. To do what is proposed is to destroy all moral restraint and lead to worse things. I was astonished when I heard what the GOC had approved. Col Hunsworth who used to be in this country, on my conferring with him said I was absolutely right, and that he would see General Maxwell and try and put things right. Right and not expediency is the only sound rule in life. I too would not give general leave, only leave to 25% of the men, day by day and to the good characters. People who prefer I think the easy way, keep saying "In this country you can't work after 2 pm," and men must have a break before doing any thing. Rot. I admit that between noon and say 2 o'clock it is wise to ease up, but the late afternoon is the best time of the day. Unfortunately we are here all together and if I do work at different hours and more work than the other Regiments my men naturally are discontented. They have been used to working the hours. I have stated I would have gone on with them as a matter of course were it not for the soft notion of the authorities.

December 30th 1914

Fine day. Heard that Col Hunsworth had seen General Maxwell, and that things are to be changed, in the way desired by me.[15] Companies busy with Coy training. I went into Cairo today, to get my photo films order and some cupboard boxes for the men's food, etc, one for each tent. I designed them. . . .

. . . Tomorrow, we the NZ Division will be inspected by General Birdwood[16] who is to command the Australian and New Zealand troops as an Army Corps. We were all introduced to him the other evening.

December 31st 1914

Inspection – up at 5 am. Parade at 7:30 am in the desert quite close to camp.
. . .

. . . At 10 am the Genl [Birdwood] and our Genl Godley and staff came riding along, taking the General salute from each Brigade – as he approached, when they got to my Regiment Genl Godley, spoke out "Colonel Malone – the Wellington Infantry Regiment". I was on Don right in front of the Regiment looking straight to my front – as much like a graven image as I could.

Then the whole division moved to the right – wheeled in successive Regiments to the left turned to the right and then marched past General Birdwood, Hon Thomas Mackenzie, New Zealand's High Commissioner, General Godley and other notabilities, standing by the New Zealand flag, which by the way our General borrowed from me. I have the only New Zealand flag in Egypt.[17] The show was a remarkable one. It went off well. The wonder of it a complete force of horse, artillery and foot and all details, brought from the Antipodes, in Egypt's desert close to the place where Napoleon's army defeated an immensely superior army of Turks. Where since 5000 years B.C. other eventful historical events have taken place. The might and cohesion of the British Empire was made evident 15 miles away close to the pyramids of Ghizeh – there were 25,000 Australian soldiers, horse, artillery foot too!

It was an inspiring sight and I felt proud to be an actor in the action. . . .

It was a brilliant day, not too hot but dust was raised by the tramp of so many feet. Our New Zealand flag floated out proudly, may the division always do it honour, in camp on the march, and in battle, etc. I believe the

Genl (Birdwood) was very pleased and said he'd never seen a finer body of men which I believe to be true enough. The show was over by 11:30 am and we went back to camp to dinner.

January 2nd 1915

Saturday. In camp after lunch Hart and I went to Cairo . . . Hart went shopping for the Mess and I waited about. We were to meet the Hon Thomas Mackenzie at 6:15 pm by special appointment. We had afternoon tea at the Continental, in a beautiful big sitting and reading room. At 6:15, we saw the Hon Mackenzie. He was very genial and told me that I was looking well and "not an oz [ounce] of spare flesh on you". I felt complimented. He gave us the news that we go to Marseilles and then to the Front about March-Feby always provided that we are not busy here with the Turks, who it is said may be here by the 10th Inst 80000 of them. We do so hope that they will come and that we have the benefit of fighting them – as part of our training. It would be the best training and do us a world of good. Colonel Johnston, our Artillery Brigadier, ... dined with General Birdwood a couple of nights ago. He told me today that Birdwood expects the Turks. Mackenzie says also, we are to get the new Rifle,[18] that our hats, the slouch ones, have to go.[19] They would advertise too much to the Germans, the arrival of new troops and then we should get an awful baptism of fire. . . . General Godley was announced so Hart and I took our departure. The Hon Thomas[?] is coming to see us on his return from Luxor where he was going last night. I asked Hart to dinner at Shepheards Hotel – where by the way our High Commissioner is staying in grandeur. . . . The dinner was good 5/- each which pleased me for I thought it would be 10/- which is what the Continental charged me a while ago. After dinner, we met Major Hall Brown, the O/C of the Ceylon Coy, attached to my Regiment and 3 or 4 more of the officer[s] and he asked us to stay and go to the Theatre "Kursaal" – variety show. I wasn't keen as I ½ expected the arrival of a New Zealand mail. However we stayed. The performance began at 9:30 pm (Dinner at 8 pm) and finished at 12:30 am!! It was to my fancy not good but it was very interesting watching the people. Hart and Hall Brown tried very hard to get me to have a whisky and soda but they failed. On getting back to Camp, I found 2 letters from Mater . . . and one from each Norah and Maurice. I could have kicked myself for stopping in town – I sat down and read my dear letters. Something strange however about their passage, for I got a letter dated NZ 19th Nov, on the 30th Ulto. It was good of Mater to write so often. I hope she will keep it up. While waiting at Shepheards last evening I wrote a letter to Mater. I met also

General Birdwood who gave first of all a most genial bow. I didn't recognise him. Later however he spoke to me, I felt honoured. He is only 46 and is spoken of very highly as a clever soldier.

[MSX 2549]

Zeitoun Camp
3 January 1915

My dearest,

Just a few words to thank you for your letters of 4th and 10th November last respectively. I wonder where they have been. Your letter of 19th November arrived on 30th Ulto. It was delightful to come in and find your two letters and one each from Norah and Maurice. I sat up until I had read and reread them. I got quite cold. Still I didn't mind.

I will briefly run through your letters and answer anything that seems to want answering. I wrote you on the 30th Ulto and again last night so this is the third letter you should get by this mail. That ought to tell you how much I love you. I hardly knew how much until I became separated from you for so long. I send you also some 23 pages of my diary up to date, also some photos. I hope everything will reach you safely. Many thanks for the calendar. It was so lovely to open it and find you looking at me but the photo is not so good as the one I have in a frame. I wanted a calendar too. You are a darling to think of sending so nice a one. I took my *Imitation of Christ*[20] to church with me this morning and was delighted too to find two little photos of you when you were in England in it. I am afraid I was distr [distracted?] for a time. . . .

Yes you should have no doubt as to my great love for you. You need never have had. . . . Your anxiety about the German mines and the *Emden* are now ended.

Yes I like my new life but the separation from you and the children is hard to bear. Thanks for the Zac [sic, Zak] photos. You must not write <u>short</u> letters as you say. They cannot be too long for me. I read and reread them. The joy and pleasure is great.

I am so glad that Norah is what she ought to be and that she is of use and is a comfort to you. She is a rare good sort I believe. Give her my love and tell her I will write by next mail, if not before.

I hope you found the Farlands in good order and are enjoying your stay but don't put in the winter there. How I wish you could fly to me here and spend the time while I am in Egypt near me. It would be heavenly but I am afraid very distracting. When the war is over, we will come here.

With all my love,

x_____x

Your loving husband

[MSX 2543]

January 4th 1915

We start Battalion training today. The Brigadier is in a hurry to rush us along at schemes and the top of the work. I am determined to begin at the bottom. He has been used to troops, who before they go to their regiments after enlisting have had 6 solid months recruits training a very different thing to ours where the men have only been 4 months together and 2 of them at sea on a transport with no room to work. We went away to our training area and after 2 hours marching in different formations. I put the men on to "musketry" under Section Comders as a change and rest. Just then our Corps Commander General Birdwood came up with Genl Godley and our Brigadier. Genl Birdwood sent for me and asked me what we had been doing and were doing. He quite agreed with our work and specially approved the hours musketry. Later Genl Godley had a yarn with me and he also approved the musketry.[21] I asked them both straight out because I thought that my non [sic] Commander Colonel Johnston didn't like it – after ½ an hour musketry, I formed the Bn up in mass and we went on with Bn movements. Genls Birdwood and Godley looking on. They left after a bit and then Colonel Johnston came up, and wanted to know why I had done what he called squad drill. He was some what put out. I stood to my guns and told him that the parade was mine – that I was responsible for the efficiency of my Bn, that I know better than he did what weak places there were, and that I was actually putting in more work, by 2 hours a day than any other Bn in his Brigade, and that if I gave him 6 hours of work according to his programme, I could do what I pleased in my other 2 hours. That it was all very well training nice tactical schemes and manoeuvres but that if the fire control was bad, not to mention the actual shooting, it was no good. That I wanted my Regiment to do something more than manoeuvre. He said he wouldn't allow the musketry or as he called it squad drill. I told him that he did not appreciate the situation that he had been used to a Regular Regiment where the men were thoroughly trained before the Regimental Commander got them. Where the NCOs had had many years of experience after being specially selected and where the officers also had had, as professionals, years of training. That he overlooked the fact that my Regiment was a newly taught one, with inexperienced NCOs and officers, etc, etc. He said "any way I was to do as he said and not as I wanted" and that, that was the end of it. I promptly asked him for permission to see the General, that is refer the matter to him. He refused, and rode away. I made up my mind to at once put in a letter through him to the General which he would have to send on. Later however he came along and said he misunderstood me and that I could do, as I wanted! so long as I did some definite Battalion work! I thanked him, and then told him that as a matter of fact, both General Birdwood and General Godley had absolutely agreed with my action and proposed action. I hope he won't bear me any ill will.

We got back to camp at 3 pm, after a useful and interesting day in the opinion of all hands.

Major Robert Young (left) and Lieutenant Leonard Jardine enjoy a drink during a hard day of training in the desert.

Morison Album, Alexander Turnbull Library

January 5th 1915

Battalion in camp until 2 pm. When we went out to stay out until 10 pm so as to practice night outposts and night marching. As I had noticed, very poor protection work by the different units sent out by Coy Commanders. I sent out the Ceylon Coy an hour before the Battalion and told them to lay up, for the Battalion, on its march out to its training area so as to test the Advanced Guard [A.G.]. I told no one else of my plans, as I wanted to see what would happen. I saw all right. The Advanced Guard, scouts, failed to do their work and the A.G. walked right by the Ceylon Coy who were stowed away behind, a disused railway embankment, at a distance of about 950 yards. The Flank Guard [F.G.] didn't protect itself even and walked right into the hands of part of the Ceylon Coy and were taken prisoner. The Main Body was caught in columns of route. I had ridden forward to the A.G. and on returning to the Main Body found things in a proper mess. I at once sent the artillery who were with us to open fire, and also a company to attack the Ceylon Coy, and put the other Coys under cover[?]. It was a great object lesson. If it had been the Turks instead of the Ceylon Coy we would have had a damnable mauling. I bet we will never be surprised again. If the A.G. and F.G. Commanders had sent only 1 man each to walk along the railway, the surprise could not have been effected. I was naturally or perhaps unnaturally delighted with the result of my plan. It was a most effective one and will save us in future. Everybody, men and all could see the A.G. and F.G. failures. Of course if the Turks were about no doubt they would have been more careful, and then as I had not told them that the Ceylon Coy were acting as a hostile force, they may have, in regards the scouts, not taken the . . . position, but the work was very faulty all the same. It was perhaps a cold blooded thing to do – to trip up my own Regiment, but it has learnt a lesson that every man in it will remember.

We finally mopped up the Ceylon Coy and then went on to our Bivouac, had tea and then put out all Coy's except one in out post [sic]. The One Coy (Ruahine) I ostensibly sent back to Camp but secretly told the Commander to turn off when out of sight go right round then cross over to the front of our outpost line, and tackle it in the dark. I gave him 2 hours to get round. In due time, he came up to the sentry line and then charged right into the outposts, in the German fashion, in 4 close lines one behind the other. No surprise this time and he didn't 'get right thro'. We marched home across the desert, in the dark, steering by star, in five columns (Coy in each) at 100 yards intervals, with a line of scouts out in front. We hit the camp exactly and the interval between had been kept practically exact.

January 6th 1915

The Battalion out on the attack – a scheme laid out by me was on the whole well carried out. We had a section of F.A. with us 2-18 pdrs, and I was connected up with them, by field telephone and able to get shrapnel fire on any part of the enemy's position as I desired it. It was a new experience for me, and very interesting cooperation between artillery and infantry is <u>the</u> thing in successful attack. It was very dusty marching home. A cold wind from the S[outh] had sprung up and naturally the air was full of sand and dust my tent was figuratively speaking full of it. It reminded me of the Mountain Wind (South Eastern) in New Plymouth in the summer time. It will probably last 3 days. I dusted out my tent, etc, twice before dinner (6 pm). But is no good.

January 8th 1915

Yesterday afternoon became beastly, wind, dust and sand but at about 6 pm to my great delight and refreshment came Mater's letters of Nov 23rd and 27th in one envelope. In the latter she gives 3-page description of her garden at the Farlands, where it was wet. It was so refreshing to read it surrounded as I am by arid desert, and in the midst of a dust and sand storm. It did me a lot of good. Strange to say, I am discontented with things here. One has to take things as they are and compared with the discomforts of those[?] at the Front – ours are nothing. Mater's letters must have come by a later mail.

This morning – the wind has gone down somewhat and we marched out to a point about 7 miles away on the Suez Road the whole Battalion, every man able to move and every horse and vehicle complete to go straight into the field. We were inspected by our Brigadier, Col F.E. Johnston. It is perhaps of interest to note what the soldier-private carries:

(1) A rifle and bayonet.

(2) An entrenching tool, in two parts, a handle and steel tool, the handle is carried in part attached to the bayonet scabbard. The tool part is in a web cover and is carried on the right hip.

(3) A pack, made of webbing carried high up on the back – the top in line with the shoulders and the bottom near the waist. In it are the great coat, pair of socks, towel, spare singlet and under pants, spare shirt, razor, strop, shaving brush, soap. Boot laces, a piece of string.

(4) Haversack – in it knife, fork and spoon. Pipe tobacco, etc, (if a smoker) 1 days ration of food.

(5) Water bottle, filled.

(6) 120 rounds of ball ammunition in 6 pouches, 2 packets (of 10 rounds each) to each pouch.

The total weight is 65lbs [29.5kg]. The Brigadier is very pleased and complimented us highly. I naturally felt proud and I must say the Bn looked well – fit and serviceable. Real soldiers!

We had quite a nice march out and back. We went through Heliopolis, on the hard roads and so escaped the sand and dust. We enjoyed it, marching on a good road and on the desert are two very very different things.

January 9th 1915

The New Zealand Force was fallen in without arms, on 3 sides of a square, round a platform from where Hon T. Mackenzie addressed us. There were with him Genls Maxwell and Birdwood. Our General Godley of course was at our head. There was only present Sir George Reid, High Commissioner for Australia, just like the picture of him in the *Bulletin*. It rained last night to our intense relief and delight and so there was an end of the dust and flying sand. The air was beautiful. My New Zealand flag came in [out?] again and floated over the platform and our distinguished visitors. The address by Hon T. Mackenzie was not too good. He had evidently prepared it – but had forgotten some of it. It was not spontaneous. I heard him at Te Wera to much greater advantage. Still it was over the average speech and good. Genl Godley called for 3 cheers for the King and 8000 lusty New Zealanders took off their hats and gave the cheers. My eyes got quite moist with emotion. God Bless the King!

We then went into camp and marched past Genl Maxwell in column of route. He took up a post on the central road of our Wellington Infantry Battalion camp. As soon as I, at the head got to the end of our lines I turned off and the Regiment marching past me (this is not regulation but I was letting my Companies break off as they turned in) and could see the columns as they went by General Maxwell. They looked splendid, solid, strong and steady. I think without conceit we can take 1st place expert onlookers said so anyhow. In the afternoon I motored, in Brigade motor to Abbassiah Hospital and visited my sick men, 49 of them. They were pleased. They are all I am glad to say getting on well. We have had 2 deaths (from pneumonia) so far. . . .

[MSX 2544]

January 13th 1915
Rode out across the desert to the Ranges. Met Genl Godley who complimented me on my Regiment saying "It is a good one". I was naturally very pleased, for the Genl very seldom gives special praise. I told him I was setting a high standard and hoped to reach it. . . .

January 14th 1915
Went to Cairo early, to see about necessary utensils and gear for company kitchens. Mr Crewe[22] who had a holiday, went with me and interpreted. We went thro' the Monsky[23] (Bazaars), and I bought some brass and silver work, and also a cashmere shawl for Mater and Norah and family. The shawl is about 80 years old and genuine. I saw some old Persian Rugs and am to see some more on Saturday and may buy. . . . We then went into a silk and Indian textiles shop, and saw some lovely things. I bought some to send home. Back to camp, after a busy but enjoyable day. I spent my month's allowance. Col Johnston (our Brigadier) and Major Temperley[24] came to dinner tonight, and were very affable and seemed pleased.

January 15th 1915
Motorcycled to range, and fired the course – shot erratically. Some practices very good, and others bad. I had to just take any rifle that was at hand, and

A busy street in central Cairo, early 1915.

couldn't gauge the elevation. Capt Rose[25] our musketry officer says I am a natural good shot, and with practice would do very well. The men enjoyed both my bad shooting and the good.

January 18th 1915

Battalion training. March. Protection on the move, 'Attack'. I had the AG [Advance Guard] stuck up and then put 3 Coys into attack. The work fairly done, but Coy Cmdrs do not cooperate, and the Flank Coy, as usual sprayed out too wide. In the afternoon I had a marked position laid out and put the whole Battlion (as part of Brigade Attack) into action pinning the Coy Comds down to an exact frontage, so that they may get the full picture of a properly built up firing and assaulting line. Their splaying out does away with weight in the assault. I like at least 3 men deep at the finish. Our Brigadier, who unknown to us had been watching the show, came and complimented me saying: the work was "exceedingly well done". He was easier pleased than I. There is lots of room for improvement. Back to camp by 4 pm, 8 hours work. Col Chaytor came to dinner.

January 23rd 1915

An off day, grey and cold – or it seems to me so, perhaps my vaccination make me shivery.

The General (Godley) held a meeting of all the NZ officers and gave us in the course of 1½ hours address, a lot of good advice on many things. He thinks the NZ Division will be the best division in the British Army! We go to Flanders when we are quite fit and properly trained, but may go elsewhere, first. The elsewhere is reckoned to be Syria. It is expected that we shall have a big fight with the Turkish Army – now said to be on its way to invade Egypt – near the Suez Canal, and then ourselves invade Syria and cut into Turkey's possession and communications, so as to make any further invasion of Egypt out of the question. It will be, if it comes off, an interesting and instructive finish to our training in these parts. Our men are itching to get moving and fighting. We got the Brigade Musketry state, on the practices that were completed last week. The Wellington Infantry Battalion – easily holds 1st place all round. I am naturally very pleased. We knew that we led in other things, but could not know as to musketry without trial. . . .

Work tells. Among our own 4 Coys – the W. West Coast Coy – which was on the *Maunganui* and away from us the whole voyage, is the worst of our Coys. Its average of marks for score was 89.2 as against 102.0 of the best Coy (Hawkes Bay), on the *Arawa*. We worked the men hard in theoretical

A Wellington Battalion machine gunner training in Egypt.

musketry and in musketry drill. We now have the reward of our labour. Last night Hart and I dined with the Crewes. A good dinner. Too good for me because afterwards sitting in a comfortable chair, in a closed room with a fire, I went to sleep while Hart and Crewe were talking!

January 24th 1915

My birthday, aged 56! Bar vaccination effect, I am very fit, hard and well. By the way I am afraid I somewhat too often record that fact. . . .

Capt Lampen came to see me today. He stayed to lunch. Poor fellow. His glory has gone. In England it was great. He and his British Section of New Zealanders were big – in the eyes of the public. Here they have been broken up and are sort of odd men out!

> Malone was inclined to scoff at the idea that the effects of vaccination against smallpox required men to have a few days on light duties. The medical officers responded by ensuring that Malone 'received that application of vaccine to which his rank entitled him. Thereafter the Commanding Officer had no hesitation in taking his two days' light duty'. [Cunningham et al., *Wellington Regiment*, p. 17.]

January 26th 1915

Last night our Brigadier informed me that the Wellington Bn (mine) and the Otago Bn were to be detached from the Brigade and be sent to El Kubri, about 5 miles N. of Suez, and that I was to command the Detachment. I was and am naturally very pleased. He said some nice things and wished me luck. We entrained, by 4 trains at intervals this morning. Captain Coningham[26] of 10th Gurka [sic, Gurkha] Rifles, is my staff officer. He and I came on to El Kubri by 9.26 am train, with half the Otago Bn. Reached El Kubri at 3.40 pm. It is about 5 miles N. of Suez. No town, or even village, just a railway siding in the desert about 1 mile from the Canal on the West side of it. It is close to where a caravan route comes in from the interior of Asia Minor. A Turkish Force is within 10 miles. My detachment is sent here to stiffen up the Indian troops who are holding the canal in a line of trenches and a series [of] redoubts. It is a dreary desolate spot. By 9 pm both the Bns had arrived, with all equipment horses and vehicles. We have with us a Section of the field amb. [ambulance] and a supply unit, 7 days rations and fodder, 600,000 rounds of SA ammunition, 8 machine guns, <u>no</u> tents etc. The force at present is to Bivouac. After settling things down I and Coningham, who unless I am very much mistaken I shall like very much, rode in to Suez to report to the GOC Genl Melliss[27] VC. His staff officer a Capt McKinnon piloted us in, and introduced us to the General, and his wife who is staying in Suez. Mrs Melliss said she was so glad that we had come. All the rest of the troops are Indians. She said it was a great relief to the white women that 2 British, as she called us, Regts had arrived. She seemed pleased. . . .

At about 3.40 am, we were awakened by heavy rifle fire from the other side of the canal. It turned out that about 500 Turks attacked the Beluchistan redoubt (just opposite our bivouac) on the East side of the canal. They were repulsed, and by daylight had all retired out of sight, taking their casualties with them. Some bullets came whizzing over us, but no harm was done. Our fellows were very anxious to get into the scrap but we were not needed.

January 27th to 29th 1915
Malone directs improvements to the defences occupied by his forces and visits General Melliss and other British (Indian Army) units in the area.

January 30th 1915
As yesterday, but tents have arrived, so I shall be able tonight to get out of Coningham's way. I like him very much. He is industrious and capable and in no way exceeds his duty. Nothing of the McDonnell about him. He makes it quite clear to everybody that I am the O/C of the NZ Detachment, which now numbers some 2300 men. I saw the General and made some suggestions, which he was pleased to welcome, and approve and adopt as "sound". I like him very much. He has earned the VC on 3 occasions, but on two of them, as he was CO he could not recommend himself. He doesn't at all like this passive defence. We often talk about it. I am trying to get him to lash out a bit and never mind what the authorities say. It is deadly to my mind to allow the Turks to concentrate day by day, and bit by bit a big force. We ought to go out and smash up the bits as they come along, debouching from the high country. It is difficult no doubt to go out to meet them, and it would not do to go more than say 10 miles owing to transport difficulties want of water etc, but they are now about 10 miles away only, and no doubt will attack us at night again soon. I have sent back to Cairo for a share of Brigade Reserve of tools so that we can improve our defences. Still very hot and dusty.

February 3rd 1915
About 12.15 pm last night, the Turks attacked Kubri Post, some few hundred of them. They attacked from 2 directions. Rifle fire only. . . . The Turks didn't

come closer than some 600 yards, and after 2.15 pm, retired. In the morning we found that they had dug a line of entrenchments, from which they had been firing, so probably, they suffered no casualties either. The next time they try the game on we hope we shall be allowed to go out on the flank and try and scupper them with the bayonet. We certainly are going to object to being turned out at night for nothing. It is probably part of their plan to keep our chaps from resting and to catch us on the hop, after numerous feints. . . . Today there was fighting out near Ismailia North of us – 2 New Zealanders and 30 Indians were wounded by shrapnel from big guns which out ranged our guns. Some 60 of the Turks were taken prisoner. . . .

I have shifted our HQ including my tent to the other side of the Railway, so as to be nearer to the trenches and to the telephones, the one to the GOC and the other to the O/C of Otago Bn who are in the trenches. I can thus better handle our men. Capt Coningham to my regret has been recalled to Cairo. I am very sorry for we have conceived a great liking for each other. He too is very sad about it. To have to go back to Cairo just when things have begun [to get] very interesting. I am appointing Capt Cook of Hawkes Bay Coy of the Wellington Bn, my staff officer in lieu of Coningham and we will manage all right. Genl Godley and Col F.E. Johnston visited the trenches today. They spent about an hour with us. The General was nice and seemed inclined to let me have the Engineers that I have been asking for and need, but Col Johnston threw cold water on it. He doesn't quite like the

Wellington Battalion men in the Suez Canal defences. After he got solidly to work in preparation for Gallipoli, defending the canal against the Turks was 'mere play' to Malone.

detachment, naturally so. His Brigade is cut in 2. My show is as big, as his and I am on my own, under Gen Melliss of course. Coningham says that he is jealous of us. We have been fixing up our orderly room etc. . . . My tent is fitted out as usual with shelves [?] and what not. I have got a table. I do love order and tidiness and can see no reason why they should not be observed, even if as Cook thinks, a shell may come and upset things. He doesn't like the change of quarters altogether. We were behind the Railway Embankment before, now we are in front of it, and no doubt as he says [will] make a good mark for the Turkish guns when they come. Still as I tell him, the risk is not very great and we are in God's hands. It is 10.10 pm and I must turn in, after a long day. . . .

February 7th – Sunday 1915

Mass and communion at 6.50 am and then I took the padre over to Kubri ferry on horse back. He said 2nd mass there. . . . [Major O'Neill, New Zealand Field Ambulance, Kubri Detachment] told me that one of the New Zealanders wounded on Thursday had died. A Nelson man named Ham.[28] New Zealand's 1st on the Roll of Honour, in <u>the</u> Cause of the Age.

In the afternoon I went into Suez. . . . I bought ½ a doz P/Post cards for Molly and Denis and Barney and then went to the Hotel Bel-air. Had dinner with the General and his wife. He was not very well. After dinner he proposed that I should take Mrs Melliss to the cinema, which proposal I managed to gracefully put aside. He showed me copies of all the orders and what not that had been found on dead and wounded Turks after the fighting of Thursday last. It was very interesting and enlightening. At 10 pm I went back to Kubri, or Campimento, as our camp is called, by a special railway engine, which the General insisted on providing for me. I felt quite a big gun. I wanted to go to Arbam – which is about 3 miles from our camp by ordinary train and then walk, but he wouldn't hear of it, said it was too risky. I was too valuable to get shot! He is too good to me. A cold night.

February 9th 1915

A dull day. Some rain. A quiet night. Drat the flies! They swarm. I have just finished a swatting turn, killed all in my tent, but they are coming in again. I have got 2 Egyptians (fellaheen [sic, fellahaheen[29]], farmer men who have some land close to the Sweet Water Canal) to come and take away all our horse manure. I hope thus to keep down the increase of flies. One of the men Mahmoud Arab, is a very good looking fellow, beautiful teeth and good features, and eyes. He has 6 acres of land, his own. He has a wife and

CANAL DE SUEZ. Drague.

Molly. 7/2/15

I often see this Canal. There are soldiers all along it now – forts + trenches – all sorts of soldiers. Big steamers still go thro' – but they have sand bags on the bridge so that the Turk won't shoot the Captain. – Love Daddy.

Carte postale Universelle.

CAIRO POSTCARD TRUST NO. 104

Above

On the back of this postcard he sent to Molly on 7 February 1915, Malone wrote: 'I often see this Canal. There are soldiers all along it now – forts and trenches – all sorts of soldiers. Big steamer ships go thro', but they have sand bags on the bridge so that the Turks won't shoot the Captain. Love Daddy'.

Malone Family Collection London

Left

The message on Malone's postcard to Molly of 7 February 1915.

Malone Family Collection London

2 children, 2 boys aged 5 and 2 years. He has a few date palms, grows bersem [sic, berseem].[30] Pays rates = about 14/- per anm. Lives in a mud house. Has no ambition, a patient peace and ease loving soul. Fairly industrious.

Word has just come in that the Turks are retiring. Pursuit is out of the question, so sit tight will be the order of the day.

February 14th 1915

. . . I have got an attack of dysentery myself. Home says it is caused by swallowing fine sand. . . . I am not going on sick list. Have put myself on bread and milk and less work. Most of us think the Turks have had enough and won't come again.

[MSX 2545]

February 15th 1915

All quiet. Foggy early morning. Later hot and sunny. The flies a d---d nuisance. I swat them in my spare moments. Still on bread and milk and less work. Home gave me a dose of castor oil and approves my own treatment.

February 16th 1915

I am quite all right again. Home last night gave me to take 2 sorts of tablets. I took neither!

We got news yesterday that some 40,000 Turks are supposed to be concentrating right east of our Section of the Canal Defence, and that they have abandoned the idea of further attacks north and will try and cross the Canal here, El Kubri – Suez. We are very pleased to hear it. Things were beginning to get monotonous. The G.O.C. of the whole Canal Defences, Genl Wilson, had a meeting at Suez yesterday. Probably more troops will be sent here. We look forward cheerfully to the Turk's attack. They are about 40 miles away, so it will be 3 or 4 days before they come, that is if they do come!

This afternoon I visited El Kubri Redoubt and had a pow-wow with Col Taylor O/C outposts re change of garrison etc. I had a look round the fortifications, which are much improved. Taylor spoke highly of the Taranaki Coy who are in the El Kubri Redoubt where Taylor has his HQ. I saw Brunt. He is working his men hard I am glad to say. As they change back to the West Bank trenches tomorrow, they are giving a farewell concert to the Gurkhas, their comrades in the Redoubt.

I and Ackland [sic, Acland[31]], our A.S.C. officer, went over to the Concert. We walked crossing the new bridge over the Sweet Water Canal. We crossed the Canal in a small boat to the Redoubt. There in a good big hollow level central place a wrestling mat had been pegged out, at one side a camp or bon fire, had been built and was burning gaily. Sand bag traverse, parapets and natural mounds of clay etc, rendered the spot fairly safe against rifle fire, if such came along. In a big circle, were the Taranaki Coy of New Zealanders, a company of 7th Gurkhas, some Lancashire Territorial Artillery men, some men of wars' men off the *Ocean*, all mixed up in friendly conclave. . . .

Indian camelry at a supply depot, El Kubri. Men of the Wellington Battalion can be seen in the background.

Malone Family Collection London

A photograph by Malone of his horses, Billy and Don in the Egyptian countryside. The officer in the photograph is Captain Charles Cook with whom Malone went riding. Cook replaced Coningham as Malone's staff officer at El Kubri.

February 20th 1915

The distant reconnaissance towards NEKHL[32] has gone out so in a few days we ought to know whether the Turks have really cleared from these parts.

Beer. I am troubled with the question of supply of beer to the men. The G.O.C. thinks as the men get no leave to go into Suez, that they ought to be able to get beer in camp. So far as I know none of us had wanted it but if the Turks have cleared out, the men will get sick of the position and seek to get into Suez. So maybe it will be better to arrange for them to get good beer, under strict control, in limited quantity. I am having a conference of Unit Commanders to settle the control question. . . .

Cook and I explored the West bank of the Sweet Water Canal to the north. Don and Billy objected to 2 young camels that were tethered on the Canal path. Billy snorted away and finally got into a ditch close to the path and Cook had to roll off. Billy cleared off back to camp in great style, the sight of an odd camel here and there kept him going as though Old Nick were after him, instead of me. I fetched Billy back and as Cook wouldn't let me try and ride him past the camels, got off Don, led him and also Billy (Cook kicking it on) past the camels. It wasn't as easy as it reads. Don is a philosopher. He was bad enough at first but has now just about made up his mind that "frightfulness" of camels, donkeys, mules, Lancers, Indians, Arabs and Egyptians is unnecessary.

February 21st 1915

Sunday. Mass at 6.30 am. Very cold. . . .

. . . Cook and I rode into Suez as I wanted to visit our sick in the hospital and also see a dentist as one of my teeth is giving me notice of trouble. We have 33 sick New Zealanders in the hospital, measles, dysentery, pneumonia, pleurisy, typhoid fever etc. Mrs Home[33] was hard at work. . . .

All our men are very much afraid that they will be put into the Reinforcements and left at the Base, when they leave hospital. They want to rejoin their Battalions in the trenches. We did our best to reassure them. Mrs Home asked us to lunch at the Hotel Bel–Air (close to the hospital) where she stops. We were quite a party Mrs Home, Dr Home, Major Hart, Cook and I. The change was much appreciated. The <u>butter</u> was A1. At camp we have tinned butter and it is very <u>so so</u>. . . .

February 22nd 1915

A hot day. Flies as usual. 2 aeroplanes went roaring overhead this morning. How I would like a flight in one. It must be lovely. We expect a NZ mail today. Our two objects in life at present are to get a smack at the Turks and to get our home letters.

February 23rd 1915

The NZ mail went through here today. Our Postal Clerk was prevented by order from Ismailia from getting our share of it and we shall now have to wait 60 hours (2½ days). It is too bad. I have written a strong letter of complaint to our AQMG and to our Chief Postal Officer and mean to follow the matter up. A fortnight ago we got our mail without delay and there can be no reason why we should not have repeated the performance. Some d---d red tape I suppose. It is very exasperating to know that your letters are being carried right past you unnecessarily and will be delayed for 2½ days.

The sun gets more power every day and the flies consequently swarm *En Suite*.[34] I wage war rigorously. General Melliss got me to meet him at Gare 152, with a spare horse. He arrived by motorboat from Suez at 3.30 pm. I had an awfully hot ride to meet him. I rode right alongside the Suez Canal. Lots of the men were enjoying a swim. I envied them. The General came to take, as he said, a last ride along our defences. We are all off back to Zeitoun on Friday. The Turks have retired a long way off and Genl Godley is anxious to get us back so that he can carry on Divisional training. Genl Melliss told me that he was very sorry that we were going and that he had intended to make me O/C of the Out Posts, that is the 5 Redoubts on the East Bank of the Canal and to put all the New Zealanders here (2 Battalions) and some of the Indian troops to occupy them. The change to take place next week. I felt greatly honoured and told him so. He said some nice things. It would have been a grand change, though of course a greater responsibility. And then if only the Turks came on again: we should have had a great time. In any case the change would have been enjoyable for me especially. Ships pass every day and sea bathing at one's tent door almost. If the Turks do come on again Genl Melliss will ask for us specially as reinforcements.

After our ride of inspection, he came to camp and had some tea and I then rode with him into Suez to the dentist. This about 6 pm. The Genl asked me to stay to dinner, which I did. As I had to see the Dentist, again I stayed at the Hotel Bel Air the night. I couldn't sleep for the strangeness of a bedroom and the closeness of it. I quite wished I had gone out and back. . . .

February 25th 1915

A visit to the dentist in the morning and then I rode out from Suez with the Genl [Melliss] to his Brgde HQ and then on to El Kubri. I got him to tell me of his war service and of a most exciting lion hunt, when he got badly mauled by a lion. He had a marvellous escape. . . . I am sorry we are leaving his command. He very kindly published in last night's orders a most complimentary reference to me and all my officers, NCOs and men and our work under him. His S.O. [Staff Officer] told me that he wrote it himself. We go to Zeitoun tomorrow by 4 trains. Very hot in the sun today.

Our mail arrived and there were three letters from Mater, one from Harry Penn and some from Denis and Barney. I was delighted and Mater says she is bringing Norah and the three little ones to England. I think she is quite right. It will give Norah and the little ones a better chance in this world to be broader minded etc etc. It will be strange if Mater and they go through the Canal, which we have been guarding and may yet guard again. But perhaps she will think the Canal not safe and go direct. I am very anxious to know whether she has sailed. If she comes via the Canal soon I shall most likely be able to see her at Suez or Port Said. What joy that would be. It is rumoured that we may go to attack Constantinople – that 68 transports are now waiting in Alexandria.

February 26th 1915

We entrained stock, lock and barrel or rather men, horses, vehicles, tents, ammunition etc, etc. Everything complete, in 4 trains, getting off. One train per hour punctually. We loaded up the last train in 25 minutes. . . . We got

to Helmieh at 5.20 pm, and by 7 pm we were all settled down again in our old lines. I heard that we are off again, probably to Constantinople way, within 10 days.

February 27th 1915

Busy re-squaring up our lines again. I had the reinforcements for my Regiment out for inspection. I gave them a good look over, then saw them drill a bit, and wound up by making them "attack" as a Company over about a mile of the desert. It was very hot and very dusty and they got a good gruelling. I was pleased with them and told them so. They were out some 5 hours, and got a surprise. Their officers said they thought they were only to be inspected. I asked them what they expected. Inspection to my mind meant finding out what they could do and how they did it. Their idea was that I would just walk up and down, look at them and then dismiss them! Not by long chalks! They are much better than I expected.

In the afternoon squared up camp and gave general leave. . . .

Wellington infantrymen watch a vessel steam through the Suez Canal. Malone wished his wife would travel through the canal on her way to England so he could see her after nearly six months apart.

Morison Album, Alexander Turnbull Library

[MSX 2550]

Zeitoun
27.2.15

My dear Harry [Penn],

. . . I am back here, after a month away helping defend the canal. Rules of censorship prevent me giving any details. The Turks seem to have retired for good, so we have come back to our Brigade and Division. You will probably have got some news of what has been going on from the newspapers. I don't understand the censor's rules here – so far as they relate to things which are public property, per the Press or otherwise. Still we are to give no information of a military nature and may be we are not able to distinguish between what is permissible and what not. I am very fit and well.

I cabled you last night. "Thoroughly approve England. Cable steamer and date leaving" which means that I quite agree with Mater's proposal and your approval. I don't know when we go to France, and we have not finished with the Turks yet. Before you get this you will I think have heard of our movements etc.

Mater said you would cable me when she was nearing the voyage end. Well I hope she hasn't gone through the canal yet, and that I may have the chance to see her at Suez or Port Said. The canal is safe for ships, or at least the passengers and the danger to any one very remote, because the authorities at each end know what is going on, and time the passage to suit. Yes, we are getting a most interesting experience, and I do like the work. One is of some use, even though small to the country. As to the seriousness of the position, you are quite right and it is astounding to think that people do not grasp it. . . .

Egypt is a wonderful country. It only wants wood and water. The land of marvellous fertility, 3 crops a year. Price £250 per acre. Talk about Waimate Plains land at £80 – after that if you can. The fellahaheen are patient, industrious (in a slow old-fashioned way) and generally (now) contented people, well made and good looking, that is the men and children; you can't see the women – for shawls and veils, mostly black.

The Arabs too are a fine race physically, that is the country people, except those from the deserts. They, the latter, are on the verge of starvation and are lean, smaller people. Cairo is a vicious place – a sink of iniquity.

Our New Zealanders gain good opinions everywhere and from all sorts. The Australians don't! We have had joined to us an Australian Brigade of

Infantry and one of Light Horse and form with a Division of all Australian troops, a New Zealand and Australian Army Corps. General Birdwood, Commander, one of Kitchener's men. General Godley is our Divisional Commander.[35] I think our New Zealand Infantry Brigade is the pick of the lot! The whole is a very fine body of men – but soldiers – Haldane[36] to the contrary notwithstanding – are not made under our circumstances in six months.

I inspected today the reinforcements to my Regiment that arrived about four weeks ago. They have only just joined us on our return. I am pleased to find that they are really good – some of them a bit old and stiff – for privates. A good chap as regards drill has been working them and that makes all the difference.

I am glad that Taranaki has a good season. I hope that you and Charlie are not too much bothered with my affairs. It is awfully good of you and him to look after them.

With love to you all and kind remembrance to all friends.

Yours sincerely,
Wm.G. Malone

[MSX 2545]

February 28th 1915

Sunday. Very hot in the sun and dusty, dreadfully so. Mass in the SA hut. Lunch with Genl and Lady Godley at Heliopolis House Hotel. They are both looking very well. There were 4 Australian Lt Colonels also at the lunch, from the Australian Infantry Brigade, that now forms part of the NZ Division. I was not taken by them. The Genl was very pleasant and asked me all about my Detachment at Kubri.

Afternoon tea at NZ Div HQ, by invitation with Capt Coningham who was my 1st SO at Kubri. He showed me two photos of his wife in England. She looks very nice. In the evening I called on Mr and Mrs Williams who live quite close to camp. They are both converts to the Catholic church. I met the new Catholic chaplain there, Fr Richards who came with the last reinforcements. Fathers McMenamin and Dore[37] were there also. I don't altogether care about the cut of Fr Richards jib.[38] Looks more like a coml [commercial] traveller or actor than a priest and is a bit fat looking which I suppose prejudices me. I had great trouble this morning over the

Protestant church service. For the first time the arrangements orders were left to Battalion Commanders. I promptly ordered separate service for each denomination. Hitherto Divisional HQ have ordered Bde "combined" service to which willy-nilly all Protestants had to go.

I strongly hold the view that every man has a right to go to a service of his particular denomination and cannot be compelled to go to any other. But the Protestant church authorities in New Zealand for some time have been joining in combined or united services (and by the way reflecting adversely on the Catholics for refusing to "combine") so that now when the different Protestant ministers asked the Genl to order separate services, he refused saying that what they did in New Zealand, they can, should and must the more easily do here and that the Catholics are the only ones who can have a separate service. It was case of being "hoist with ones own petard"! Still the Genl seems to have overlooked the fact that the individual soldier has his rights and that whatever the parsons did or do does not bind the individual, especially as I pointed out to the Wesleyan parson (Luxford)[39] who is in my Regiment, the Protestant religions are based on the right of "private judgement" in religious matter.

Some men and officers object strongly to being compelled to go to the "combined" service and to there being no provision for denominational church service.

On my order for such service Maj Luxford (Wesleyan minister) who claims to be Senior Chaplain of the Forces, saw me and objected to the order, and claimed the right to hold the combined service, and said I was squashing Gen Godley's arrangements. Could he see the Genl? I promptly repudiated the squashing and told Luxford he was not to go near the Genl with any complaint behind my back. He could lodge a complaint <u>through</u> me, against me to my Brigadier and if he had any complaint against the Brigadier he could then go to the Genl through the Brigadier. Result he caved in, and the separate services were held, much I think to everybody's pleasure except Major Luxford's. He is quite unsuited for his job. I am going to keep him up to his regimental work. He runs about too much to Cairo and everywhere, except our own lines.

Luxford described this day as the 'most unhappy Sunday I have had since leaving home'. He complained to Malone there were not enough tents available for each denomination to hold a service indoors, and by the time it came for Luxford to hold his church parade it 'was blowing an awful gale'. Luxford stated that he could not hold a church parade outside in such conditions; in response Malone dismissed his concerns, but later McDonnell came to see him and arranged for Luxford to use one of the mess tents. On 1 March Luxford went to see Malone, who complained bitterly about the persecution of Roman Catholics and told Luxford that he would not reconsider his decision. Luxford then privately complained to Colonel Chaytor who told him to write to Malone formally saying he wished to discuss the matter with Chaytor. [John A. Luxford diary, 28 Feb and 1 Mar 1915, MS-Papers – 4454-2, ATL.]

March 2nd 1915

Same as yesterday [Regimental training]. Edmond and Terry came over to see me. They had been over 3 times before but couldn't catch me. They are both well. We hear that we go for certain soon. The Australians are and have been for some time embarking. Genl Godley yesterday told me this but he either didn't know or wouldn't say what our destination is.

[MSX 2550]

Zeitoun, near Cairo,
Egypt
2.3.15

My dear Aunt Agnes [Vasey],

I am just back here from the Suez Canal defence operations, and expect to be off again on some further operations very soon. . . . The Turks as the world knows got a backhander and cleared off back, far back into the desert and don't seem to intend to come over again. . . .

I have news for you. My wife and Norah and the 3 small children, are coming to England, and will I think be landing there, at about the time, we were due to go to Flanders, say in 2 or 3 weeks time. I am expecting a cable giving the steamer's name and date of expected arrival in England. I of course will be unable to look after or make any arrangements for them, or even visit them, until probably the war is over. I am wondering whether any of the relatives would help them to settle down, or meet them and give them a little welcome. I had better perhaps say that they want no pecuniary assistance. My wife has an annual income of about £750,[40] and any special expenditure, for travelling, house furnishing etc, will be provided for by my attorneys in New Zealand. Her idea is to take a small house in say Reading near which town she has some relatives, and live there quietly, so that in the possible event of any casualty to me or the boys (Edmond, Terence, Brian and Maurice), all of whom will probably be in action before long, she would be near and could look after us in England, instead of fretting her soul out in New Zealand. She is a brave, grand woman and will be no real trouble to anyone. But I and she would appreciate very highly any kind action on the part of our respective relatives. Will you see about it and do what you can. . . .

I am very well, fit and hard and have the best Regiment in our Army Corps which is now being trained here. . . .

4.3.15

There is something else in which you may be able to help. The wife of Genl Melliss, under whom (General M) I have been serving, a while ago, took charge of 2 Belgian refugee girls (ladies) and they are still in a way in her charge. She is now in Egypt, and the girls are in England. I gather that the Melliss's are not in a position to stand the charge altogether, so their friends have been having the Belgian girls to stay for times, about a week or so here and there, Mrs Melliss paying their fare etc. It occurred to me that some of the relations or their friends might be able to help in the same way. . . .

I am afraid I am giving you a lot of trouble, but I know that you won't mind. . . .

With much love.

Your affect[ionate] nephew,
Wm.G. Malone

[MSX 2545]

March 4th 1915

A light morning for work. Conference of officers (mine), criticism of yesterday's work. Getting a new denture made as a standby in case of accident to the one I have, in a place where no dentist. A wise precaution suggested by one of my officers.

March 6th 1915

Last night we all that is the NZ and A Division left camp at 7.30 pm. Marched through Heliopolis to a point on the Suez Road about 8½ miles distant, then

Port Said Vu au Village arabe.

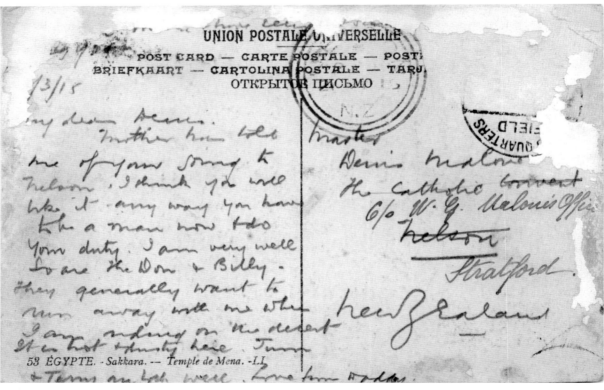

UNION POSTALE UNIVERSELLE
POST CARD — CARTE POSTALE — POST
BRIEFKAART — CARTOLINA POSTALE — TARJ
ОТКРЫТОЕ ПИСЬМО

13/15

My dear Deane,

Mother has told me of your going to Nelson. I think you will like it - any way you have to be a man now too. Your duty. I am very well so are the Don & Billy. They generally want to run away with me when I am riding on the desert. It is hot & dusty here. Jim & Terri are both well. Love from Teddy.

Master

Denis Malone

The Catholic Convent

C/o W. G. Malone's Office

Nelson

Stratford

New Zealand

N.Z.

HEADQUARTERS FIELD

53 ÉGYPTE. - Sakkara. -- Temple de Mena. - LL

took up a defensive position, entrenching it. We got out at about 11.30 pm. Disposed our men – 600 yards to each Bn. They dug themselves in manfully but the digging was frightfully hard, the ground like concrete. It took 5 Hours to make the trenches. At dawn an attack was made by a skeleton force. At 6.15 cease fire. Genl Godley and his staff rode along the position and then held a conference of mounted officers for criticism. The show was not a bad one, and the Genl was pleased. Then home, which we reached at about 9.30 am. Breakfast and the day off for everybody. My Bn marched in the whole distance without a halt and marched the Canterbury Bn to a standstill.

Last night's work gave me a lot more insight to the characters of my officers. They are a bit too glum to my fancy and appeared as though they thought they were being a bit badly done by. Still they did their work and the spirit of the men in keeping on digging was splendid, evidence I am pleased to think of good discipline. The better the discipline the better the digging and later on the better for us in less loss of men (casualties)!

Capt Cook, my SO at Kubri, arranged a dinner at Shepheards for the Kubri Detachment staff, I, Cook, Acland and Tracey [sic].[41] We enjoyed the dinner and after it went round to the Kursaal – where we saw some very vigorous Russian peasant dancing by a man and 4 women, no Nijinsky or Paplova [sic, Pavlova] about them. It was furious, but very noisy. Some Japanese conjuring was good. Finis 12 midnight! No tram until 12.45 am, so Acland who is our man about town and a jolly good chap too, took us into the Palmariam, a dancing hall where people sit and drink and smoke and get up as the spirit moves them to dance with ladies of doubtful character who are in regular attendance. The dancing is quite *en regle*[42] and there is nothing shocking to any one. Still there is an undercurrent of impropriety about the whole thing. The place was full of officers and men, mostly curious onlookers whom we joined. I soon left leaving the rest of our party to their refreshments. The show had absolutely no attraction for me.

March 7th 1915

Sunday. Mass at 10 am. Another hot dusty day. Invitation to dine with Genl Birdwood, our Corps Commander, tonight. I shall get fat if this goes on! Young Rapinet[43] turned up and brought me an invitation to afternoon tea from his mother. I went as did also Short,[44] and enjoyed it. There is a dear little girl of Molly's age, Andié [Andrée?], very fair and fluffy and shy. I made love to her and she soon surrounded me with her toys and when I left would accompany me with her brother Rene to the station to see me off. She speaks

Opposite

A postcard sent to Denis by Malone on 3[?] March 1915. The message on the reverse is: My dear Denis, Mother tells me you are going to Nelson. I think you will like it, anyway you have to be a man now and do your duty. I am very well. So are The Don and Billy. They generally want to run away with me when I am riding in the desert. It is hot and dusty here. Edmond and Terry are both well. Love from Daddy.

Malone Family Collection Wellington (now in ATL)

French so sweetly and is a very modest sweet little soul. I asked for *un grande baiser*[45] which she demurely gave me and waved her little hand to me as the train went off. How I wished I had Mater and Molly especially, here even for the couple of hours I had. Joy to come. . . .

I enjoyed my dinner with Genl Birdwood. He is a very genial and affable. Absolutely no side.[46] He is on the small side. I believe him to be a good man. He must be as he is one of Kitchener's men. He lives at Shepheards as does all his staff. After dinner he sat and talked to me until 10 pm. I made a move to get away at 9.30 pm but he wouldn't let me. He thinks the New Zealanders have improved "enormously". I couldn't agree with him and on being asked my opinion, gave it. . . .

I was glad to get to bunk, after such a week's dissipation. Genl Godley told us yesterday that we will embark for parts not named between 15th and 22nd Inst. He told us to take warm under-clothing. Rumour has it that we all go to Cyprus and then join other troops in readiness to land in Turkey or Greece, take Constantinople, settle the Turks then go up to Austria through Servia [Serbia], Vienna and then on to Germany! The armies would consist of British, French, Grecian, Servian, Romanians and probably Bulgarian troops. What a movement and mixture! *Veremos lo que veremos* as the Spaniards say.

March 8th 1915

A beastly day, blowing hard and a dust storm in consequence. It might be worse but I do <u>not</u> like dust. My tent and everything in it is being smothered. . . . This afternoon we will take a spell and at 5 pm march out to practice in Brigade "Night advance". The mail does not arrive until tomorrow. I must bear my soul in patience.

Just received a cable from Norah dated 3rd Inst that "Mater ill, departure postponed," which is worrying. I wonder what is wrong, nothing serious I hope. If Mater had been very ill Norah would have said so or perhaps not for fear of making me over anxious. I hope that Mater will soon be all right again and must cable for further news in a day or two. I was hoping to have seen her before we left Egypt but now there is no chance as we leave within 14 days.

March 10th 1915

Inter Infantry Brigade manoeuvres today. My Bn was Advance Guard, and later in Reserve, finally pulling the Brigade out of a mess, in the attack of the Australian Bde (Inf). The 2 attacking Bns Auckland and Canterbury, lost direction and had my Bn not appreciated the situation and gone forward without orders there would have been no Brigade attack! The Brigadier was very pleased with us and said it was a splendid bit of work. My men are splendid – 20 miles tramping across the hot and dusty desert and attack. A very hot day. Yet they marched into camp as though they had done nothing. I am very proud of them. They are a long, long way ahead of the other Battalions. The hot Khamsin[47] wind, with sand and dust, still keeping going.

March 11th 1915

Bn training. We marched out of the dust, to Avenue de Koubbeh, in the land of Goschen, a metalled road across the Railway lined with orange hedges and an avenue of acacia trees, green fields on both sides. We stayed close to the Ex Khedive's Palace and orchard, and were practically out of all the horrible dust. It was so restful. Billy, whom I rode, was almost unmanageable. He hates camels, and they were constantly passing along the road. He snorted and cavorted and bolted and played up all ways. The men were worked in musketry. I gave them a 2-hour spell in the middle of the day. I cruised round and inspected a small farm. . . . The owner of the small farm I inspected, is named Suleiman Jusef. He had his whole family with him at work on and

The industrious family of Suleiman Jusef whom Malone met in March 1915.

about the farm and well. His wife with a baby in arms, 3 small boys, and one small girl. His father and sister swelled the family. I got the children to wash their hands and faces by giving them "bacsheesh" [sic, baksheesh][48] ½ a piastre each. They soon learned what I wanted. They had no English and I had no Arabic, but sign language is universal. The well was huge and deep, cut in sandstone, the water very bright and clear and good. . . . Suleiman Jusef owned the land, and the crops. Busem [berseem?] beans and barley, were flourishing. He and his family got their whole living from his farm! Fancy 8 people living off 3 acres and looking fat, well and happy, and not too dirty, or ragged. In the sun all day. I took some photos of them, the farm and the well.

March 13th 1915

Saturday. Camp cleaning, washing day etc. I sent a cable to Mater, hoping that she was quite well, and saying that I was leaving Egypt in about a fortnight, so that she would know what to do with letters. It is still uncertain when and where we go, but the Navy is forcing the Dardanelles, and the French are getting ready an expedition of troops, to land in Turkey, to cooperate with the British and French naval forces so no doubt we shall join in soon. The change in weather is lovely.

March 14th 1915

Sunday. Went to a Greek (Orthodox) mass at the Basilica at Heliopolis, as did most of our soldier Catholics. A queer ceremony, 5 priests officiated. One was a Bishop. He wore his hair long, down to his waist, unbound. A choir sang in Arabic, queer music. We could not make head or tail of anything. It was not at all devotional and I would not have gone if I had known what it was like. Father Richards got me to go. I rode Don. After church I met a gentleman, a Syrian Catholic named Atala and took quite a liking to him. He asked me to afternoon tea at his sister's house next Thursday. She lives in Heliopolis. In the afternoon Terry and Edmond came to see me. They are fit and well.

March 15th 1915

Bn training but I had to go umpiring with the 2nd Light Horse (Australian) on an inter mounted Brigade Exercise. Up at 5 am and away across the desert at 6 am, a distance of 8 miles to ZAHR BAADEN. A most interesting morning. The NZ MR Bgde attacked the Australian L.H. Bgde. It was a poor show and neither Brigadiers in my opinion, seem to have a sound knowledge of their work. The NZder [Col Andrew Russell][49] was better than [the] Australian. The latter is really an English regular officer. I was not astonished, because I have long since found that very few officers (including all ranks) have a real knowledge of military principles – without such a knowledge it is impossible to be expert in any science. The science of war is no easier than any other. The show knocked off at about noon and I was home by 1.30 pm.

March 18th 1915

Last night's work a success, but strenuous. At 2 am my Bn and Otago Bn attacked an enemy in position. Swept right over them, and then dug fresh trenches to enable the position taken to be held. Very solid digging. My men dug 400 yards run of trenches, in frightfully hard, stony ground. The Genl was very pleased. No doubt the men are splendid; one hard thing too, is that they have always to fill in the trenches dug before we leave. We got home at 8 am and had the day off. We mostly had a sleep, after breakfast. In the afternoon I motor cycled to Heliopolis, and took 6 snap shots of its houses etc, then called on Me [Madame] Thomas, Mr Atala's sister and had afternoon tea. A very nice house-flat. Very nice tea and very nice people. She a widow of 10 years with five children, 21 to 10. Such nice children, educated at a convent of the Sacred Heart, the same order as the nuns at Island Bay. I practised my French[50] and received a pressing invitation to call again which I will.

March 20th 1915

Lecture by Genl Cunliffe-Owen on cooperation of artillery, infantry. He has lately come from the Front and there commanded both arms respectively. He was interesting though somewhat anecdotal. A hot day. Gen Godley said this morning, that within a fortnight, we would be in line with some of the flower of the British Army, who had been in Flanders, so our destination at present must be Turkey. We shall be glad to get to grips. The Canal work was only an "appetif" or rather "aperitif". . . .

March 21st 1915

Sunday. Camp inspection. Everything excellent. I growled hard last Sunday – Result, success. . . .

[MSX 2550]

Zeitoun
near Cairo,
Egypt
24.3.15

My dear cousin,[51]

Your welcome letter of 6th Inst to hand today.

I am so sorry to hear of Aunt Agnes' illness, and do hope that she will get well again. I do so want to see her – and for the matter of that all of the relations – but it is very uncertain, whether and when we shall be in England. We were to have gone there in the first instance, but got switched off here, through the arrangement to put this country under the Protection of England, and the possibility of Turkish invasion. We were very lucky to be landed here, as the English winter would have been very much against training. It is always fine and sunny here. We took part in the scraps on the Suez Canal, Early last month, when the Turks got set back. I had command of a detachment of our New Zealand Force, some 2460 men, right away from the Division. I was under General Melliss, V.C., with the 30th Infantry Brigade. He has very kindly recommended me for Brigade command.

We leave here very soon now and think our destination will be Turkey. Afterwards we expect to go to France and Germany.

My sons names are: Edmond, Terence, Brian and Maurice, in order of ages Edmond being the oldest. Since we left New Zealand Maurice reached the age at which he could enlist, or rather he reaches it next May, so he enlisted last month, and will come with a batch of our reinforcements in due course. Edmond and Terry are here in a Mounted Rifles Regiment – privates – Brian went to Samoa with our New Zealand Force, and is in the ASC (Army Service Corps), a sergeant. Maurice has joined a Mounted Rifles Regiment, as a private. . . .

My brother Austin has been killed by an accident, in New Zealand since we left.[52] He leaves a widow and 3 children. I got a cable a while since with the sad news.

My practice is in the hands of my clerks. I have treated it as no longer existing. I was very sick of churning away in it. If I get through the war all right, I doubt if I shall go back to my law profession. I am better suited where I now am.

We are all very fit and well and hard.

Give my love to any of the relations that you are in touch with.

Your affect[ionate] cousin,
Wm.G. Malone

[MSX 2545]

March 27th 1915

Saturday. Our 3rd reinforcements arrived last night.[53] 293 men and 7 officers for the Wellington Inf Bn. I had a short inspection of them this morning. They look all right, but are not fully equipped. Presumably they will take over the equipment of men, whom and when they replace. Bad staff arrangements. We had no definite notice of their coming. Result, we didn't meet them at R/ Station, and they wandered in to camp, the best way they could. I wonder why the Genl keeps incompetent men, in responsible positions. He is a bad picker of men. The Robinson-Henderson type is obviously a bad one, yet when I sacked Robinson from the adjutancy of my Bn, he was made an Embarkation Officer and promoted "Major"!!! Henderson[54] was sent back to New Zealand, not for his inability as an Embarkation Officer, but for some mess up of his in his former job in New Zealand. Today great fixing up of camp. Many laugh and say "now we will be off". So may it be, but if I knew we were going to pull stakes tomorrow I would still have order and cleanliness. I have some 1,500 men, being paid 5/- for the day, and if they cannot fix up, then I don't know who can. In the afternoon Miss Thomas, one of her sisters and her brother, . . . called to see the camp. I introduced them to Mater and they insisted that she could not be over 30 at most. I was very pleased. They also said *Qu'elle est jolie et intellectuelle*.[55] I gave them afternoon tea and showed them round. They seemed pleased.

At night 8.20 pm I went to Cairo, and sent Mater a cable hoping she was quite recovered and sending my love.

March 28th 1915

A horrible Khamsin wind day, the dust awful, so also the heat, 3 days of it I suppose. Went to mass at Heliopolis, and stayed at House Hotel there for lunch and to get out of the horrible dust at camp. Wrote to Mater, one letter to London another to New Zealand. Genl and Lady Godley came in while I at lunch. The Genl very genial, unusually so, and asked me to sit with them, but I was under way so stayed where I was. After lunch the Genl gave me particulars of the expedition on which we shortly go to help force the Dardanelles. An army of allies.

British	20,000
British Naval Troops	18,000
French	15,000
Russian	40,000 [56]
NZ's and A's	35,000
	128,000

Gen Sir Ian Hamilton [57] to command. He inspects us tomorrow.

The Genl told me to go and see Luxor. I said I would want 3 or 4 days leave. He said all right. I had worked very hard and had had no leave yet. I think I'll go. . . .

March 29th 1915

Review of NZ and A Division by Genl Sir Ian Hamilton, 12 noon to 4.30 pm, very hot and dusty. A good show. Put in for 4 days' leave and got it promptly. Entrained at 8 pm for Luxor. . . .

30th March to 1st April 1915

During his first period of leave since joining the NZEF Malone visited the important archaeological sites in the Luxor area; generally with Major Temperley and Captain Arthur Critchley-Salmonson,[58] adjutant of the Canterbury Infantry Battalion.

April 2nd 1915

Crossed the Nile, then per donkey to the Temple of Queen Hetetu, [?] a beautiful piece of work. Then to the Tomb of Queen Nefertari, 2nd wife of Ramese II or III,[59] visited also a private tomb or rather the tomb, of some court official. Then to the Temple of Medmet Habi [Medinet Habu]. To my mind this is the best of the temples. . . . Back to hotel by 1 pm. Lunch. Wrote to Mater, to London, because on Monday I got a cable from Harry Penn that she and family leaving on 8th inst, by *Rotorua*. I was so glad to get the cable and thus know that Mater is all right again, and something definite as to action. I have asked her to spend a honeymoon, on a dahabeh [sic, dahabeeyah][60] on the Nile, after the war is over.

Left Luxor by 6.10 pm train by which as it happened Genl Birdwood was travelling. He asked me to dine with him on the train, and as there was for the night no Restaurant car on, I was lucky. I got a jolly good dinner, and the most interesting of company. . . .

April 3rd 1915

Reported back at camp at 8 am. We are to embark next week for Turkey! Everybody getting ready. I am to be O/C Troops on HM Transport *Itonus*. We will sail about Thursday next which coincides, strangely, with Mater's sailing from New Zealand. Riot in Cairo last night. Some of the Australians and New Zealanders wrecked some brothels, where they had been badly treated. If they had burnt the quarter down, it would have been a good thing.

April 5th 1915

Inspection of troops by Transports. An awful day Khamsin wind, and accompanying sand and dust storm. It is like being in a hot dry fog, full of grit. The heat is sweltering, the wind is as coming from a furnace. Still we are cheerful knowing that we will soon be away, and that we might have been and be much worse off. All the same it is most unpleasant, to put it mildly, in the tents and outside —! One thing I expect a letter from Mater tomorrow and that will refresh me. Still the Khamsin generally lasts 3 days! The temperature is 100° Fahr! [38° C] The Maoris are off to Malta. I forget if I have recorded their arrival 500 strong, mostly big hulking gone-in-the-knees walking men. I think the War Lords don't quite know what to do with them. They look soft, and I fancy were not killed with work on the Transports. Captain McDonnell didn't get the command of them. A Major Herbert,[61] a Mounted Rifle officer has been appointed. McDonnell would have been a much better man. Our own destination is not at present known to us. England, I hear, expected Greece to come in and give us a base for the troops attacking the Dardanelles, and when she didn't come in, bought Lemnos Island, for a million or so of pounds.[62] Transports French and English were directed to Lemnos, but the troops didn't land, there is no water on it i.e. for troops in numbers!!! The French troops have landed at Alexandria and the English too. Now it is stated that we shall force a landing on Turkey and establish a base there. In the meanwhile Alexandria will be our base. We shall therefore apparently soon be up against the Turks. Heavy fighting is expected, but D.V.[63] we shall come out of it all right. Then, for a big flank attack on the Austrians and Germans, via Servia. Perhaps the Greeks, Italians, Bulgarians and Romanians will join in. If they [do] what a polyglot lot we shall be! . . .

April 6th 1915

Another hot dusty day. At last we have got definite orders for embarkation. My Bn entrains tomorrow night in 2 trains, leaving Helmieh at 11.20 pm and 1.20 am respectively. We go straight on board 2 ships *Achaia* and *Itonus*. I on the *Itonus*, taking also two companies of Canterbury Bn. Our destination is unknown to us at present, but we have a notion that we have to land in face of the enemy (Turks). Everybody busy fixing up and completing equipment. The Divn will take 3 days to embark. I got a letter from Norah last night and was very disappointed that there was nothing from Mater, poor girl, she was too ill to write. I am so glad to think that she is now all right, and hope the voyage home will set her up altogether. I wonder where and when I shall get her next letter.

[MSX 2550]

Zeitoun
Egypt
6.4.15

My dear Denis and Barney,

Many thanks for the letters etc you sent me. I am sending you some photos I took, also some P.P.cards [picture postcards]. I saw all the places depicted. I went to Luxor for 4 days on leave. Mummy has told me all about your staying at Nelson. I hope you will always be good boys, working hard at everything. I am very well. I hope to be able to see mummy, Norah and Molly, before very long, but I am afraid it will be a good long time yet. We are leaving Egypt this week and go to Turkey I think to take Constantinople. It is very hot and dusty here. It was 100° Fahrenheit inside my tent yesterday! but it is so dry one does not get knocked up. Don and Billy are very fit, and frisky. Billy bucks and kicks up. . . .

With much love,
Your Daddy

[MSX 2545]

April 7th 1915

Our departure is postponed for 24 hours. The Bn went out, as at war, every man fully equipped and formed, every horse, vehicle. We tramped in all

14 miles. It was very hot, and a feat of endurance for all hands. The march discipline was excellent. I was very pleased and am so proud of the Regiment. The others, though perhaps I shouldn't say so, are not in the same line.

A soldier in Malone's battalion, Private William Hampton, had a rather different view of the day. He wrote in his diary: 'Fall in 8 am. Had a dammed heavy march with full pack . . . about 18 miles. Very hot. All [the] men call Colonel Malone a rotter.' [W.A. Hampton diary, 7 Apr 1915, KMARL.]

April 9th 1915

We definitely depart tonight. Entraining at 2.20 and 5.20 am. I motor cycled in the afternoon and took photos of the graves of the 3 men of the Bn who have died, Campbell, Cooper and Simpson.[64] I thought their people would like the photos.

This morning busy packing up kit. Got it all into 1 roll. Left at base the leather trunk (E.L.M.), one Gladstone bag and contents, one green canvas bag and contents, one box of books etc. Sending these by Mrs Home, to Mater to whom I wrote today.

The grave of Private John Campbell. Malone wrote in his diary that 'Campbell was a Catholic, a good soldier.'

3

'The world never saw better men or braver'

Gallipoli: The landing and the struggle for Walker's Ridge
April–May 1915

[MSX 2546]

April 10th 1915

Left Zeitoun last night, 10.20 pm, by troop train carrying ½ Auckland Bn in advance of my Bn so that I might see that things in order on HMT *Itonus*. Arrived at Alexandria at 4.15 am. The *Itonus* was out in the stream, but I only found this out after I had tramped round the biggest part of the Docks. She came alongside at 8 am. . . . She is properly fitted up as a troopship, but only for 800 men. We will be over 1100, still we will be all right. The hammocks however are not available unless we care to take the risk of measles. The last troops she brought from Australia had measles, and the authorities had refused to have the hammocks fumigated. We decided to take no risks and the men will sleep on the bare decks, which are wooden. On the *Achaia* however, which carried ½ my Bn, the decks are <u>iron</u> and hard sleeping that – no mattresses, no straw.

We soon embarked, and hauled out at about 3.30 pm, and sailed for Lemnos, where we get further orders. The troop ships are sailing independently and without escort. We are going to land on the Galipoli

[sic] peninsula. The landing may be in face of the Turks, and will be within 3 weeks. The voyage to Lemnos takes normally about 50 hours, but we are towing a steam-tug and 2 big barges, and cannot [sic] only steam at 2/3rd speed for fear of swamping them. I was very much impressed by the naval transport officers at Alexandria. We wanted certain things, life-belts cleaning materials, and a cooking range, for the 'Achaia'. I and Hart went to see the NTO and met a Mr Peacock I think. He was admirable. He listened to our requests, asked a plain question or two and at once acceded to our requests. No argument no petty objections, no evading responsibility, no callousness to needs of our men, a careful consideration and prompt decision. So different to our experience with our own staff. They either promise and don't perform or else bluff or cheese pare[1] or refuse and say buy what you want and pay for it yourselves out of your regimental fund. The injustice of it all.

I have a roomy 3 berth cabin to myself, and the captain and officers of the ship are most obliging and pleasant. Our voyage is they say to be a smooth one. I turned in early.

April 11th 1915 – Sunday

Sea smooth weather fine but with a decided cold twang about it. Busy all day getting a good hold of everybody and everything. It is really interesting having ½ the Canterbury Bn to handle. We could soon bring them up to our standard. They have been loosely handled. Mass at 10 am. Fr. McMenamin is now our Chaplain in lieu of old Luxford, who is transferred to Otago Bn.[2] Everybody is glad. He (Luxford) ought to have been left at the base. He is a useless specimen of an army chaplain, but has curried favour with the Genl and others. Young active amicable and amiable parsons left behind and he the reverse of those things taken to the Front. We are on the lookout for submarines, one is supposed to have torpedoed a transport off Smyrna[3] last week.

This boat carries a Lascar[4] crew, miserable specimens of humanity. The 1st officer amused me today. We have not enough lifebelts, by some 100 and not enough boat room for some 500 of us, in addition to these Lascars some 120 in number. In arranging about boats in case of collision or torpedoing etc. he said that we were to have all the boats and the Lascars could swim or drown. We were far too valuable beings and they too worthless! He meant it too and I think he is right, but I told him it could not be so, the ship's company gets 1st serve and we take what is left of the boats. We are sorting out all those who are good swimmers and telling them off to any gratings, seats, benches etc available. If anything happens to us we expect our wireless would bring help within a few hours – so the position is not very bad. Still it is not pleasant to think that some of us may drown like rats. One thing everybody accepts the position most philosophically. The men are splendid. They have settled down without any bother and there are no complaints.

April 12th 1915

. . . Up early and about, seeing if all other officers properly supervising. I took special notice of the Canterbury men [Canterbury Infantry Battalion]. They are good stuff, but want shaking up. Not their fault – their COs. The officers are I think quite a good lot, and are responding keenly to our demands. . . .

April 13th 1915

A wet rough morning. The tug and 2 barges that we were towing broke away from us last night. We stood by and picked them up this morning, and started towing them to lee of an island 3 Lascars and the 1st and 2nd mates got into them. It came on to blow harder and harder and the sea was running high. Before we got under the lee of the island the tow line parted and then we had a big job, getting round and picking the men and mates up. The tug was sunk. The barges are all right but we had to let them go. . . .

Port Mudros on Lemnos crowded with ships as the Mediterranean Expeditionary Force prepares for the Gallipoli landings, April 1915.

Malone Family Collection London

Our soldier men acted well. Two boat crews, from my Bn were told off, and got into the boats ready for lowering one of the boats swung in and out and began to smash things, obviously with considerable danger to the men in her. Yet they sat cooly still and took their danger as a matter of course. It was only when I told them to come out that they moved and then without flurry they came aboard. It was a good job we didn't have to lower the boat. I doubt if she could have lived in the big sea that was running. It was a good thing to see also how the 1st and 2nd mates got the 3 miserable Lascars aboard, before they moved themselves. . . .

Arrived at Lemnos, Port Mudros at 6 am. A good harbour. It is almost full of men-of-war (British, French and 1 Russian) and Transports: A great sight. The shore is hills up to 1,000ft here and there, but mostly undulating land. Several small towns. . . . No trees to be seen anywhere. Hardly a shrub. Farmhouses here and there. Generally the country looks like sheep country, one can see sheep and cattle. . . . The port is protected by a line of netting bouyed [sic] from shore to shore, with guns mounted at each end. We anchored out in the Bay until about 4 pm and then the Assistant Kings Harbour-Master [AKH] came off and took us thro' the boom to the harbour, where we again anchored. The A.K.H. Master was on the *Ocean*, which was

sunk in the Dardanelles. She was torpedoed from the shore.[5] He says there are 150,000 Turks and 16,000 Germans on the Gallipoli Peninsula, and that we will get a warm reception. Apparently they cannot force the Dardanelles without a land force – to demolish or complete the demolition of the Turkish forts. That will be our job after we have driven back the Turkish army. The job is going to be a big one. There will be difficulty about water. There is none on Lemnos (for an army) and we will have to depend on ships for all our water and supplies. We have to darken the ship tonight. 2 Turkish or German aeroplanes were over the harbour yesterday and dropped bombs. . . . The crew, [of the *Itonus*] Lascars, are a queer lot – very small and weedy, yet good workers and attentive. . . .

[The lecture outlined below gives a good insight into Malone's thinking. There is, however, no indication in the diary that he delivered this lecture.]

[MSX 2551]

Lecture HM T[ransport] ITONUS
Lemnos 14 April 1915

Subject: Officers' Efficiency and how to obtain it. . .

Preparation: Habits
Cleanliness, order and method, industry, early rising, abstemiousness, thoughtfulness. Special study of books. Which?

Ingrainment of principles
Application question constant [sic] if such and such happened. What will I do. Concentration, modesty, always room, and power to learn, consult experts. No jumping to conclusions. Appreciation of situation – all thro. General Birdwoods four Cs: concealment, cover, communication, control.

Practice: Physical fitness. Know job, do it to exactitude. Punctuality, care, complete, no "near eno". Habit of thoro'ness.
Good form always. Clear command. Insistence [on] performance. Supervision. Non interference.

Position: Word of command. Determination.

Relations with superiors, equals, inferiors

Superiors:	Absolute loyalty.
	Non criticism.
	Obedience to orders.
	Orders: "Nil nisi bonum"[6]
Equals:	Courtesy – loyalty too.
	Cooperation.
	Competition not opposition in job.
	Good form always.
Inferiors:	Dignity.
	Manners [?].
	Civility.
	Camaraderie, not friendship.
	Care, health, comfort.
	Knowledge without intimacy.
	Example to.
	Lead, not drive.
Conclusion	Self Criticism and Examination of Conscience.
	Highest standard. Every man has limitations. Modesty non conceit. Have I done my duty? Why not. Sorrow[?], intention, amendment. Renewal of original good intention.
	Amendment.

[MSX 2546]

April 15th 1915

Went off to HMS *Arcadian* naval HQ ship, to see whether our Divl or Bde HQ ships were in. Later went off to *Lutzow*, Divl HQ ship. She was one of the Nord Deutche boats – captured and now a transport! A fine boat, luxurious. . . . I saw Genl Godley. He was genial! I asked him to sanction disembarking all the troops on my ship, as practice. He most readily agreed and at once issued an order for all troops to do the same. Got permission to buy flour and fresh meat for the men. They have been on bully beef and biscuit since Friday last. After lunch went ashore with Capt Carey, Master

of *Itonus* and explored Mudros Town. . . . The people seem friendly and are all Greeks. Population 2000. It is quite refreshing to see Europeans, men women and children. The women are rather good looking but mostly old. I think the young ones keep in, with so many soldier men, filling the town. The children seem strong and healthy, and are good looking. The men are not tall but strong. All seem fairly clean and tidy. . . . Soldiers and sailors, English French, Australian and New Zealand are everywhere – well behaved and quiet. We quite enjoyed our walk round. In the harbour there are now some 100 ships. Say 25 men of war 75 transports. The *Queen Elizabeth* is here, tho' most of the other men of war seem somewhat old fashioned. It is a great sight and a stirring one.[7] Weather fresh, breezy but fine.

April 16th 1915

Sent all troops ashore today and so practised disembarkation. We used 5 of the ships boats. It took us about 4 hours to get the men ashore. We are over 2 miles from the landing. They went for route marches, and all got back to the ship by 6 pm. I mean to do the work quicker next time. Too much waiting about. I and Carey went ashore by last boat after lunch and went for a walk to top of a high ridge, west of the town. The land is on the hills very rocky, but every little bit of land that can be ploughed is ploughed. Crops mostly wheat, a few peas. . . Back on the ship by 6 pm.

Malone was very fond of children. Here he has photographed a group of Greek children at Mudros.

Genl Birdwood has issued a circular memo to the troops telling us that we have a big job in front of us, and a rough and hard time, but that he is confident that we shall succeed. So may it be. I saw and had a good look at lots of French and English Regular troops today. Our NZ men stand out as something far superior. Grand stalwart soldiers.

April 17th 1915 – Saturday

Washing and airing blankets. Conference all the morning with officers. A talk to the NCOs, emphasising Genl Birdwood's circular. Went thro' the topography of Gallipoli peninsula, with all officers then exercised them in their duties on disembarkation in boats etc. Boats crew (our men) exercised too.

Called to *Minnewaska* army HQ boat, instructions as to landing. We all to have 2 steamers and 4 lighters – according to Col Skeen, the landing officer. We are to have hot fighting. He said we would move in a short time now where we are to land is still to us a secret. We got definite news of the attack by a Turkish torpedo boat on one of our transports [HMT *Manitau*], just south of this island. The transport had all artillery on board. The Turks gave them 3 minutes to get out and then fired 3 torpedoes. 2 missed and the other failed to explode. A couple of British men of war came up so the Turks ran for one of the islands and beached their boat. Some 50 of the artillery were drowned in boat confusion and accident. On our voyage over I had told off and exercised our men to line the ships side and give any submarine plenty of rifle fire. Some of the officers laughed at the idea, but I thought it better to be prepared for anything and not get put out without a fight. We today got Divisional orders for all Transports to make similar preparations. I am sure that if the Turkish torpedo boat had tackled us that we could have kept her off. Divsl HQ anyhow say it can be done.

April 18th 1915 – Sunday

Mass and Communion at 6.30 am. Wrote to Mater and also Norah. I wonder when I shall get a letter from Mater. One I hope is following us up and will be delivered before we start for and land on Gallipoli.

Called on Col Monash[8] – Brigadier 4th Australian Inf Bde. He is on the *See - angchora* [sic, *Seangchun*] linked to us. – (A large number of transports are linked together in pairs, side to side touching to save room in the harbour.) Col Monash asked me to lunch. He is a big stout man, as is his Brigade Major. He showed me the map of Gallipoli peninsula, marked up with the latest aerial reconnaissance information: The Turks seem to have covered it with trenches, redoubts and gun emplacements and batteries, but our naval artillery is going to give them a hot time, a hotter one than they will give us.

Practiced boat drill and loading, this afternoon. Every man, in full marching order, got off the ship into a boat, and then after the boat shoved off and returned, climbed on board again. The men go down and climb up – a Jacobs ladder – a rotten trumpery[9] one too.

After dinner went ashore for a walk – did about 3 miles and then back by moonlight. Saw a steamer with a captive balloon on board, also saw the balloon go up. More and more ships keep coming. There must be some 125 all told now, exclusive of small craft, a great and stirring sight.

[MSX 2551]

At a place not to be stated
18 April 1915

My dear wife,

I wrote you last Friday week from _____ [Alexandria 9 April] where I was then, and told you that we were off that night for our destination unknown. Well we got here on Wednesday morning last, after a somewhat exciting passage – all safe and well. We are off for another destination very soon now. By the time you get this, the newspapers will have given the news of our movements. Everything is going well and confidence prevails – also good spirits. You are at sea and 10 days of your journey are over. I think of you every day – the first and last things and pray that you and the children are well and in good heart and that our separation will not be unduly prolonged. I know your feelings and the great conflict that goes on in your thoughts. I am proud to know that my wife is so brave and so full of the sense of duty to country, that her own personal desires and interests are readily set aside. Perhaps not readily, yet certainly, we have all along been agreed on what my duty was. To me that is a great comfort. Yours is the harder part, as is that of the women who *per force* must stay at home, while their men go forth to war. Still my dear one, we have had great happiness together, and please God will be reunited when the war is over never in this life to separate again. I have a great feeling of confidence that all will go well with me, and so do not grieve. In any case we have done our duty.

I will write something every week if it is possible, so that by the time you get to London, you should have quite a pile of letters. I have been hoping

The Wellington
Battalion practising
embarking and
disembarking at
Port Mudros in
preparation for the
Gallipoli operation.

that a letter would come from you. A mail is due, but of course it is difficult
to catch us up. The last letter I got was from Norah, telling me of your
illness, and that you were unable to write. I know of course that you got all
right again. I was so glad. You must be careful for the future. I am carrying
your dear photograph with me always. It is now hanging up in my cabin and
when I disembark goes with my map case. I am looking forward so keenly
to seeing the original again and telling her of the travels of the likeness. I do
so hope that you will be comfortable in England. I am very glad that you are
going there and I am sure that everybody will welcome you.

We are without full war news, as are you no doubt also, but everything
seems to be going well. We have heard that the Turks have had another go
at the canal. If so no doubt Edmond and Terry had a look in. They would be
glad. They and their mates were getting sick of inaction.

It is spring weather here, and thank goodness, no dust and no flies, and
no great heat.

We are in luck. We have a priest with us, Father McMenamin (a close
friend I believe of Father Maples). We had mass this morning and nearly
all the Catholic men had squared their "yards"[10] and filled their Easter duty.

It is not easy to write a newsy letter, when it has to be censored or rather has to comply with the military rules relating to correspondence. If you don't get letters from me regularly, don't worry, you can easily understand that it will be difficult to carry out postal work. No news will be good news!

I am very fit and well, but, I am afraid, putting on a bit of fat. I don't worry because it will do to come and go on in case of shortness of tucker. I sent you by Mrs Home, a lot of photos and the parts of my diary that I had been unable to send before. I have my camera with me and some ½ dozen films, so you may later on get more photos.

With all my love,
Your loving husband

My love to Molly. I am writing a little note to Norah.

18/4/15
My dear Norah,

I duly got your letter of I think Feby 21st telling me of Mater's illness. Thank you very much for writing. I hope there will be another letter from you, if not one from Mater herself. You are 10 days at sea now. I hope all is and will be well with you. I too am on shipboard. She is a good boat, sweet, dry and clean, miles ahead of the *Arawa*. I am O/C Ship. Everything goes well and everybody is cheerful.

You will have a lot of news to read up when you get home. We too are out of war news except our own. I hope that you will like England. I feel sure that you will. I am glad that you view the war position as you do, and I am proud of you and Mater. If all the girls and women were like you and her, there would not be much wrong with the world.

With much love,
Yr loving father

[MSX 2546]

April 19th 1915

Nothing fresh. The troops exercise in landing, starting at 7 am. All went ashore, did a route march, in full kit, and then came aboard again. We only had 5 boats. The first boat got away from the ship, with 32 men, in 3½ minutes. There were 27 boat loads – average time of filling them and shoving off from ship 5 minutes. The men have to go over and down the side by a slender jacobs ladder. A 2 mile pull ashore and 2 miles back mean that it takes 4 good hours to land the Bn. The men are getting quite handy, and we have the business now well organised. It was quite hot today. I went ashore at noon and had a walk round. . . . Saw the biggest part of the Battalion of Lancashire Fusiliers, Regulars, long servers about 8 years. I had a real good look at them and didn't like their looks. Their faces are not good, they look very young, boys many of them. They are small men. Nothing smart about them. Good stuff no doubt but if they are as they have been called, the flower of the British army then I understand Genl Godley's statement that the NZ Divn should be the best in the army. Of course I have not seen them work – but in a critical first look I would want 1½ or 2 Bns of them for 1 NZ Bn. When we get into action I shall be better able to judge. One thing our men on the whole look like gentlemen and the Tommies don't. As for the French they look very slack and soft.

After dinner, on board, went per boat round the *Queen Elizabeth*. She is mighty, almost all mighty 8-15" guns, besides numbers of others. She is power all over, grand lines, very sharp in the bows. I will try and go on board tomorrow.

April 20th 1915

Northerly gale, very fresh, orders for NZ Inf Bde to practise disembarking tomorrow. I am to command the Bde, apparently our Brigadier has not yet arrived from Alexandria. No word of our sailing yet but it cannot be long before we do. . . .

April 21st 1915

. . . In the evening I got secret operation orders for our disembarkation at Gallipoli peninsula, with full details of the whole movement. I will not set them down now, lest the secrecy be endangered. I was told to deliver copies of the secret orders to O/C units on my ship, but as I did not and do not think it wise to do so until we have sailed I shall keep the orders to myself. I am sorry to say it but I believe that if I issued the orders as instructed they would be all over the ship in a very short time. The place of landing is much as I expected it to be. I know where the British 29th Divn and our own A & NZ Army Corps are to land, but there is no word as to the French and Russians. It won't be long now before we are hard at it with the Turks.

April 22nd 1915

I heard last night that a NZ mail had arrived on HMT *Goslar,* so at 5.30 am today I sent a boat to fetch our share. It was blowing "some" so it took the crew 4 hours to go and return. To my delight there was a little letter from Mater. . . . It was a very great pleasure to hear from her. I immediately wrote to acknowledge it as we may be away very soon now. . . . Genl Sir Ian Hamilton has issued the following special order.

———

General Headquarters
21.4.15

Soldier of France and of the King

Before us lies an adventure unprecedented in modern war. Together with our comrades of the Fleet we are about to force a landing upon an open beach in face of positions which have been vaunted by our enemies as impregnable.

The landing will be made good, by the help of God and the Navy, the positions will be stormed, and the war brought one step nearer to a glorious close. "Remember" said Lord Kitchener when bidding adieu to your Commander, "Remember once you set foot upon the Gallipoli Peninsula you must fight the thing through to a finish".

The whole world will be watching our progress. Let us prove ourselves worthy of the great feat of arms entrusted to us.

———

The combination of the Army and Navy is going to be complete. We are going to see and hear a tremendous artillery attack from the sea on positions on the land. That attack is to be stopped by the leading infantry lines, when the time for their assault of the positions has arrived, by the waving of red and yellow flags which the Infantry are to carry. This flag business is new in European armies tho', I believe the Japs used it in their war against the Russians, to stop their own artillery fire. When the assault was ready to be launched, or rather to launch itself, we don't want the *Queen Elizabeth* to pitch her all but one ton shells among ourselves! It is going to be a great fight and we must succeed. The preparation seems very thoro'. Our Genl Birdwood is one of K's [Kitchener's] men and K's motto is "Thorough". From what I have seen of Birdwood he takes after his chief.

[MSX 2551]

On board a ship
22/4/15

My dear wife,

I have <u>just</u> got your little letter of 7.3.15. About 2 hours ago I got one from Mrs Cook, telling me of your illness, and I was afraid there was no other letter. I did so long for one from you. Still I knew that you would have written if you could. You can imagine my delight to see your dear handwriting again and to learn that you were up and on the high road to complete recovery. I learnt last evening that a mail had followed us and was so wild that the HQ people had seemingly made no arrangement to get it delivered. At 5.30 am today I sent a boat away to fetch it. It was blowing hard and the crew had a job to get back. It took them some four hours. I wrote you on 18th. We are still at the same place.

I am so glad that you are taking Denis and Barney after all. The leaving them was the one thing I didn't quite like, tho' I knew that you would do what was best. . . . I suppose Denis and Barney were overjoyed when they rejoined you again, and will be pleased with their life on shipboard and in the old country. I sent them some postcards, to Nelson.

I have just got a letter from Aunt Agnes, which I enclose. I have no place to keep letters now and will shortly have to carry all my belongings on my back! I am looking forward specially to seeing Aunt Agnes, of all the relations. Give her my love when you see her. I may not have time to answer her letter, but will do my best to do so. Thanks for the lavender; it smelt so sweet. I pictured you on the verandah, putting it in your letter to me. I have put one piece in the locket I always carry with my identity disc round my neck and the other piece I put in that little housewife[11] you made for me. I send you some flowers I picked ashore near where I am writing. I picked them for you, thinking how lovely it would be if only you were with me. Some day we will pick flowers together again – please God.

As to address, you had better address me, with full name and rank, Regiment, and Force as before, but at Record Office, London, putting in front of "Record Office" the name of our country. They will forward.

It is quite cold here at times 50° Fht in [10° C] the shade. A while ago I was in 105° Fahrenheit [41° C]! I have put on a little warmer clothing, and am as usual quite well.

I am counting the days to when you will reach Home. I know you do not like the sea and shipboard, but time passes, all the same. Pray for me always that I may do right.

With all my love,

Your loving husband

Their father's love to Norah, Denis, Barney and Mollie.

[MSX 2546]

April 23rd 1915

A quiet day. All hands making final preparations for landing movement of transports and men of war to the outer harbour. The French Division has arrived. There is a quiet but businesslike quickening, everywhere. At last after the preparation of months, we are to get solidly to work. The canal business was mere play.

We sent some bread over to the *Achaia* – some 200 loaves we had in hand. It would be a great treat. I promised to give them all tomorrows bread and our fellows can do a day on biscuit again. I am arranging also to give every man a pound of raisins to take ashore. They are sustaining and will help to keep the men's mouths shut and so prevent parching. With the raisins and 3 days rations, I think we can put in 5 days without further supplies. In 5 days surely we shall be masters of enough of the Peninsula to give us plenty of water and enable landing regularly of full supplies etc.

The men are going to carry a big load. 200 rounds of ammunition each, weigh 12lbs. In all they will carry close on 75lbs [34kg]. The regulation weight is 61lbs and I think a quarter oz. Each man is carrying extra to Regulations. An oil sheet, some firewood, 1 extra iron ration and an extra ½ days food, 50 rounds SA Ammunition, 1lb of raisins.

The weather bids fair. I heard today when we sail.

April 24th 1915

A fine day with wind from the East. If it continues, it will be good for our landing. I went to a conference of officers with Gen Godley on the *Lutzow* this morning and did not get away until 2 pm. We had to row to the outer harbour and back. I relieved the stroke and quite enjoyed an hours rowing. A head wind made it hard work, but it did me good. Plenty of movement all day. Transports and men of war from battleships down to torpedo boats and submarines, supply ships and hospital ships. A great sight. Britannia rules the waves – right Enough! We sail at 6 am tomorrow morning and expect to land between noon and 5 pm.

I have just arranged with Home to issue to every Platoon Commander, a phial of morphia tabloids[12] so that any wounded men can be at once given by the nearest man, a tabloid or two to put under his tongue and thus get relief from pain. The tabloid will take from 10 to 15 minutes to dissolve and to work, but it will be a great blessing to the wounded men and a great help to the nerves of their mates who will be saved quickly the hearing of the wounded men's cries.

We gave the men rice and dried apricots stewed, for their tea tonight as an extra. It was an unexpected treat, and very welcome. Tomorrow we give them for their last meal on board rice and stewed prunes. After that bully beef and biscuit will be the order of the day for a long time.

April 25th 1915

A lovely calm spring morning. We left Port Mudros at 6 am. An auspicious departure. I wonder what our landing will be like. I fancy that it will [be] easy. The weather conditions seem perfect and I can but think that our enormous artillery power will blast most of the Turkish resistance off the face of the peninsula. The British Divn lands at Cape Helles and Seddil Bahr [sic, Sedd el Bahr][13] at South of Peninsula. Our army corps land on beach just north of Gaba Tepe on West coast, the place is about due west of where the Narrows take a NE turn into the sea of Marmara.[14] The idea is to cut off the Turks who are south of such point. The landing was to begin at 3.30 am this morning. The Australian Division being the 1st to land at 4 am. Some of our fellows heard the big guns going. So no doubt as I write, fighting is going on. We are – as I write just leaving the eastern most part of Lemnos.

[MS Papers 4130]

[WGM wrote two entries in different diaries for 25 April 1915 – both are included, but a small section where he uses exactly the same words has been deleted.]

25th [–26th] April 1915

Left Port Mudros Lemnos at 6.10 am for Gaba Tepe, Pen[insula] of Gallipoli, with other transports, having been preceded by Advance Landing Troops of the Australian Division. We towed 2 barges in which to land troops and horses. A lovely calm and in nature a peaceful day. But the huge 15" guns of the *Queen Elizabeth* could be heard at 60 miles distance bombarding forts etc. at Cape Helles and SEDD-EL-BAHR, where the 29th British Division was landing. As we got in we could see the action. Quite a number of Men of War, British, French and Russian blazing away. Transports steaming in close to the shore and landing troops in boats and barges. The Naval shells were bursting all along the Turkish position which seemed strongly held. We did not steam nearer than about six miles but with glasses could see what a great and furious fight was going on. The French Division was making a feint on the coast of Asia Minor so as to keep Turks there. We sailed on Northwards and as we got near Gaba Tepe which is about 10 miles North of Cape Helles found that our Army was landing at a bay some 2 miles NE of Gaba Tepe. It had commenced landing at 3.30 am and had been most gallantly, nay recklessly carried out. The men of war *Majestic*, *Triumph*, *Queen*, *Inflexible* and ors [others] were firing furiously. Transports were landing troops etc. The action was a [at] Cape Helles. The Australians had carried the heights surrounding the bay but instead of being content with that and then digging in hard and fast had scally wagged for miles, into the interior some 3 to 4 miles got scattered and so became a prey to the Turks, who had been surprised in the 1st place and had (it is said) only some 500 defending troops at our landing place.[15] Their troops encamped at Bijuk Anafarta and Kojader [sic, Koja Dere][16] were brought against the scattered Australians and slaughtered them.

As the New Zealanders landed, they were rushed up to the heights, mixed up higgledy piggledy among themselves and with the Australians, with resulting in the case of my men anyhow (in my opinion) in serious avoidable loss. At 4.30 pm my first troops went ashore. Taken off by HMS *Bulldog*, torpedo boat. I sent 2 Coys of Canterbury Bn and ½ Taranaki Coy, the latter in the man barge we had towed. I went with this consignment. When we got within about 1 mile of the shore we got into our ships boats and rowed ashore. The Turks welcomed us with shrapnel and sprayed up the sea all about us, but very few of us got hit. The beach was crowded with all sorts of beings, men, mules, donkeys, horses, ammunition, supplies, naval beach parties. In getting out of the boats many men got a salt-water bath all over. They had full packs, 200 Rds of ammn, 3 days food etc., so easily slipped and fell. There didn't seem much organisation on the shore, in fact it was disorganisation. We evidently haven't got a Kitchener about. On paper it was all right, but in practice no good. Still Britishers always muddle thro somehow or another. The Heads like General Birdwood and Godley <u>plan</u> all right, but the executive officers in the main are no good. Have no idea of order, method etc. They as I put it "hang up everything on the ground." The whole army does. After I got Canterbury Coys ashore I got the ½ Taranaki Coy, and used them in extended order as guide posts along the beach. Soon however Col Braithwaite our GSO [General Staff Officer][17] told me to attach them to one Col Pope's (Australian) Bn and they were marched up some heights. Major Brunt was with them. They got messed up by the Australians and lost in a short time some 15 killed and 19 wounded. After they had gone I struck our Genls B & G [Birdwood and Godley] and they were very disappointed when they found my Bn (bar ½ Coy) was still on the sea. The naval people for some unknown reason knocked off disembarkation. I got the General to wireless to the ship to carry on and about midnight the remaining 1½ Coy of mine on *Itonus* got ashore, and were sent to hold a ridge just above the beach. They had no tools, as our Bn['s tools] were in the *Achaia* with the other half Bn! I had asked to get ½ of them at Port Mudros, so that when we landed, we would be independent but it was not allowed, by our Brigadier. However, I got some of my HQ details to go along the beach and collect all the tools they could, and they got quite a number and then I sent them up to the ridge to enable the men to dig in. I had rather an amusing incident. I was going along the beach close to the cliffs, where there were crowds of men sleeping, finding out who they were so as to help reorganisation of units. Quoth I to one group "who are you fellows?" Low and 'bold' they were Generals Birdwood, Godley and Bridges and their staff 'low and bold'[18] there were quite a number of picks and shovels in their quarters – the open beach. I soon got all these tools and sent them up to my men. By daylight Hart and the 2 Coy off *Achaia* landed. We were ordered into Reserve alongside Army Head Quarters as an army reserve. We placed ourselves up a gully narrow and steep, full of scrub and remained there until about 4 pm of the next day **[April 26th]** when we were ordered to go up this gully onto the Plateau and report to General Walker[19] who was our acting Brigadier, Col F.E. Johnston being ill with gastric influenza. We had an awful climb, and found General Walker and reported but he didn't know what to do with us, but in the end put us in reserve. All this time, the 24 hours round the big ship guns were booming away, also quick firing Howitzers, mountain guns and rifles. Endless fighting. Shrapnel bursting on and close to the beach. Boats and barges going to and fro the ships and beach, landing all sorts of men and things. In the night of Sunday I know there were some question among the Generals of our having to re-embark, personally I could see nothing to require it. As General Walker's plateau was congested with men without my Battalion I asked and obtained leave to take them below the crest. We got settled down into dug-outs, and then got an army order to go back into our original reserve (Army) position. This from Genl Birdwood himself. We had been up the hill and now down again. Still we are all philosophers now.

[Tuesday 27th April 1915]

Next morning, Tuesday 27th we were sent up another gully in which 2 Howitzers were placed, and then to a place in the beach N of Divisional Headquarters and then told to draw 2 days' rations and march N. along the beach to where a big ridge came down from the high country surrounding the bay. Duly away we went. Arrived at foot of the ridge – found General Walker, and heard a roar for reinforcements coming down the hill, irresponsible men, Australian privates passing the word for "Reinforcements at the double!!" General Walker told me to at once send a company up – packs to the left at the bottom. I enquired "what they were to do?, where to go and what the position was?" I was told they would be met at the top and put right. So away they went. No sooner gone than more yells of the same sort from the Australians. Another Coy of mine ordered to follow the 1st one. The Coys were (1st) Wellington West Coast, (2nd) Hawkes Bay, some 450 of the best soldier men in the world: They were being sent to chaos, and slaughter nay murder. I then brought up the remaining 1½ Coys to about ½ way, which the A[Acting]/Brigadier [Walker] told me to hold in Reserve. On doing this more yells for reinforcements.

I took [it] on myself to stop the yells and say no more reinforcements should go up in that irresponsible way. I went up myself to find out the position – A long climb along and up a ridge. I struck a sort of natural fort along it. Entrenched and occupied by about 40 Australians and 2 M [machine] guns, one Major a fat chap. I asked him what he was doing there, sending down yell for reinforcements. He said he was passing the yells on. I asked him why he didn't go himself and take his men with him. He said he had orders to stay. I went on passing scores of Australian unwounded lying all along the track. Finally I got to a Col Braund[20] who said he was in command of the show. Asked for some explanation of the position and why he had left his men when down the ridge and called for reinforcements from the New Zealanders. He didn't know and knew nothing. Had no defensive position, no plan, nothing but a murderous notion, that the nice thing to do was to plunge troops out of the neck of the ridge into the jungle beyond.

There Turks of whom very few were seen by any of my officers, were lying down shooting down all the bits of track that led from the ridge outwards, having range marks fixed, and dropping our men wholesale. Major Young and Cunningham grasped the situation soon and told who they could to dig in, this was begun but Col Braund came along and ordered the Platoon Commander to go on and plunge into the jungle further and further. On their protesting, he claimed as Senior Officer their obedience to his order and so on and on they went, and got slaughtered. Lt Wilson[21] and his machine guns (2) were treated in the same way. I made Col Braund send back and take all his Australians forward and to shift his HQ – forward. I then went back to Brigade Headquarters to report and was told to bring up my remaining 1½ Coys to the fort. After getting them up I started to go forward again, up the track to get a grip of things but was met by a lot of Australians tearing down the track yelling "fix bayonets, the Turks are coming". I whipped back on [?] to the fort, put 2 M [machine] guns on front slope with a line of the best shots of the Ruahine [Coy] and sorted the other men up in readiness to hold back the Turks. I really believed we were in for a solid thing and told the men we would have to stick it out at all costs. I then went forward and

The Wellington Battalion digging in on Walker's Ridge.

Malone Family Collection London

found that the panic, for such it was had been stopped, thanks mainly to Major Hart who had been sent on by me ahead of the Reserves to get a hang of things and report to me when I came back. He like the good chap he is steadied the men and was helped by Captain Cox. I sent forward a platoon of Ruahine Coy to help stiffen things up, and on order being restored and no Turks appearing went forward to a spot close to the top of the ridge and established my Headquarters. By now wounded men by the score were being brought back and laid along the track, all sorts of wounds. The stretcher bearers couldn't cope with the number and soon there were no stretchers. I got an immediate demand from Col Braund for more reinforcements but sent him a firm refusal. He then said as I would send him no more reinforcements he would have to retire to his first position. I told him he never ought to have left it.

I sent to Young and Cunningham and told them to dig in and link up if possible secure their flanks and hang on. Got replies they were doing so. Col Braund then came to see me and on my asking why he had been doing as he had, said the truth was, he feared that if he didn't go on his men would run away. I said that was no reason to sacrifice aimlessly my men. I went and reported to General Walker and asked that the whole of the Australians be withdrawn as soon as possible. He came back with me to the position. We struck lots of Australians who hadn't moved. I ordered them up and drove them ahead pelting the leading one on the track where they stopped with stones and putting my toe into the rear ones.

By this time wounded men were being brought back in scores (My Bn's casualties out of 2¼ coys say 450 men were about 45 killed and 150 wounded, in about 1st hours of action), and left on track no stretchers being available. They were all very brave. No cries or even groans, one man kept saying "oh Daddy oh Daddy" in a low voice. Many greeted me cheerfully. ["] Well Colonel I've got it." Many smiled. My men are wonderful. The world never saw better men or braver, I am sure. After the frightful murdering slaughter bungled by Col B. of the Australians they hung on, fired at from all quarters and yet unable in the jungle to see many of their enemy, dug themselves in. I went up with Hart and we divided up the ground held. Sent up picks and shovels and all night was passed by all hands, dig dig digging. Turks firing from a distance all the night with shrapnel, machine guns and rifles. Hart poor chap directing operations got shot thro the leg, flesh wound only I am glad to say. He will be back in about a fortnight. He was shot by a Turk within a few yards. The Turks threw hand grenades at us thro' the night.

Captain Jesse Wallingford, an experienced New Zealand Staff Corps officer, was dispatched to the ridge by Brigadier-General Walker on 26 April in response to reports that the defending forces were badly disorganised. Like Malone, Wallingford was highly critical of the chaotic state of affairs on Walker's Ridge. He later noted in his diary that 'Malone does well and glad he is here he will keep the old woman Col B [Braund] of the Australians from evacuating.' He found the 'Australians jumpy and their Col – dam [sic] his soul – is dreadfully so . . . Col B is brave but oh such an old woman. He talks such utter rot that makes all his men jumpy.' [Jesse Wallingford diary, 26 Apr 1915 (this diary entry appears to cover events both on 26 and 27 Apr), Wallingford family collection Wellington.]

Although it is headed Kaba (sic Gaba) Tepe, this sketch map by Lt Harston shows the Walker's Ridge area.

28th April 1915

We are well dug in. The Turks keep trying to blast us away and thro the day killed 3 or 4 and wounded 8 or 9. Our position is something like this.

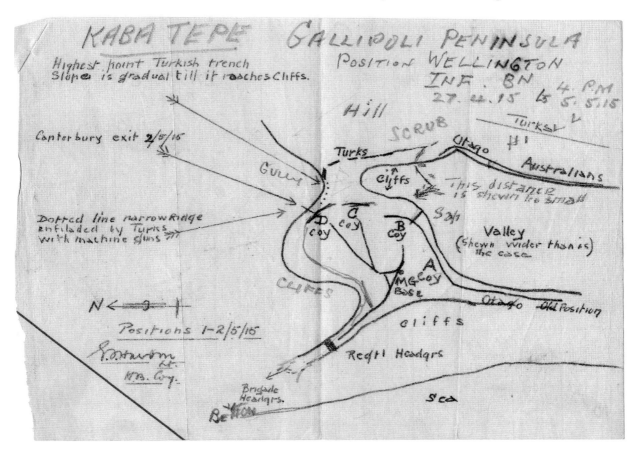

The ground is covered with scrub. We go on digging and are shelled and rifle fired at night and day, but thanks to our excellent digging our casualties get less. I insisted on the Australians being all withdrawn. General Walker asked if I could hold on without them. I told him they were a source of weakness. All last night they kept up a blaze of rifle fire, into the dark at the Turks who they could not see and thus drew fire. The Turks knowing where we were. I tried to stop them but it was useless. About 1 am Col Braund came to me for more ammunition. I refused to give it to him telling him he was wasting enough and only informing the Turks that he was scared. He insisted and I said responsibility on me. I sat tight and told him to go see General Walker as without his order I absolutely refused to give him any more ammunition. At 6 am the Australians left. It was an enormous relief to see the last of them. I believe they are spasmodically brave and probably the best of them had been killed or wounded. They have been I venture to think badly handled and trained, officers in most cases no good. I am thinking of asking for a Court Martial on Col Braund. It makes me mad when I think of my grand men being sacrificed by his incapacity and folly. He is I believe a brave chap because he did not keep out of the racket. If he had it would have been better for us. I would not have minded losing the men, if only in a fair go, but to have them thrown away, is heartbreaking.

Poor Lt Wilson and all his NCOs except one Corporal knocked out. He killed. They did great work but ought not to have been plunged into the jungle. It was skirmishing with M. guns. Quite wrong my officers knew better but Col B [Braund] took the attitude I am your senior officer and the senior officer here and I order you to do what I tell you! They did it, to our frightful cost. We are unable to bury many of our killed. The whole of the scrubby slope opposite to us is full of snipers, dead shots. They pick off even our periscopes and to go out is sure death. Still at night men . . . go out and we have buried all those lying in the least exposed places.

My officers are alright. We as well as our men have no blankets or kit, Army Headquarters have apparently decided not to land Echelon B which is Horses, Vehicles, Baggage etc. We have had no sleep since Saturday night yet are cheerful, fortunately the weather is fine and fairly warm.

Brigadier-General Walker would later praise Malone's role in the defence of what became known as Walker's Ridge. In a letter to James Allen he wrote that Malone 'pushed forward vigorously, supported the Australians at a critical moment, reorganised the firing line, and by his initiative made good the position. . . He worked strenuously at his trenches, organised his defences, saw to the feeding of his regiment, and generally showed himself to be a man of resource as well as a good leader.' [*Wanganui Chronicle*, 16 Jul 1915, p. 5.]

29th April 1915

Today as yesterday in morning dig dig and dig, getting safer every hour. Last night I had a close call. I was reconnoitring with General Walker and the snipers were trying to get us. At last a bullet just cut my hair on the back of my neck, and goodness knows it is short enough. Still it wanted cutting! So this morning I got one of my orderlies to finish the job. I am glad to say my nerve is quite allright [sic] and my experience at the Canal was compared with now absolutely nil. I have had and have no inclination to duck which I thought everyone had. Any amount of good men about do so at every near burst. I thank my regular life. I was inclined to think that I was too high strung to stand the racket of real hard war. It is not so. Dreadful things are all round – yet no dread. It seems the same with all of us. Enemy only sniping vigorously all morning. In afternoon, they opened a terrific M [machine] gun and rifle and some shrapnel fire on our position: We kept low and let them blaze away. They are about 300 to 400 yds away. We cannot see them and for the matter of that only look for them with periscopes. I got our Howitzer O/C [Major Norris Falla][22] to let me have 2 guns to work. I had after a lot of trouble got a phone put in my forward trenches and connected with my HQ which was connected with the Howitzer Battery through the Brigade HQ by phone. I also was also in touch with some of the Naval guns. I had the great pleasure of directing the fire of the Howitzers and Naval guns. The Howitzer made excellent practice, and in a short time we paralysed the Turks fire.[23] Then we began to find their trenches and when they ran our men got up and let them have it. We gave them fits and got some of our own back. Our men were delighted. It was a good stimulant for them.

Genl Godley had been offering us rum, but I refused it. I told him I should be sorry to think that my men wanted "Dutch courage". The trouble is the army is short of Howitzer ammunition, and when we have fired 20 or 30 rounds Headquarters sing out about <u>waste</u> as they call it. I asked if killing Turks and getting back at them was waste and they didn't know what to say except we are very short and somebody says you are wasting ammn.

We had a quiet night, comparatively, as a result. Only 2 killed and 2 wounded and the S.M. Bonar[24] was one. Poor McGlade[25] was killed the first day. We have had 2 officers killed and 6 wounded – Hart, Wilson and Hugo.[26] Jardine,[27] Furby, McColl,[28] Turnbull[29] and Bryan.[30] Jardine got hit by shrapnel from our own naval guns. He is a good chap. He was shot through the back, yet walked out, and came and sat with me and drew me a plan of the position where he had come from. They are all splendid. I cannot sufficiently express my intense admiration of them all. None better in the world.

30th April 1915

A fairly quiet night. Still the Turks shelled us here and there now and again and lots of riflemen kept up fire. We don't answer except occasionally with short M. Gun bursts. No-one hit. Digging as usual. All water and food has to be carried up (500 feet) from the beach, nearly a mile up a steep track, and the carriers are under sniper fire all day. Now and again one gets shot. Still they go on climbing sweating grunting falling but no grousing or complaining. We have some mules helping now. If only we could get plenty and save the men I would be glad. I am arranging every day to send some men to the beach for a swim and a few hours spell from the trenches. Whenever one sits down, one goes to sleep, without effort! We are getting back on the snipers and think we bag about 50 a day. The boys think it good sport and recompense for all their hardships. It rained last night. We were all cold and wet but <u>not</u> miserable. I am rigging out a home – part dug out, part sand bag . . . no roof. A lovely look-out to beach and sea. I am perched on a ridge say 400ft above sea level. Shrub round about a steep cliff to my left and the track leading down the ridge on my right. Men dig-in all round, everywhere. It is a delightful spot in very sharp contrast to the fighting going on. There is not a second that some weapon is not being fired from 15in guns to the rifle. Shells bursting now and again. Huge shells arriving from probably the Sea of Marmara and plunging into the sea amidst our shipping. M. guns rattle-rattle. Crack and smack [of] the rifles. Boom and blast [of] the big guns. Men are killed and wounded. Very few now among my men, I am proud to say thanks to their splendid discipline and consequent good digging, and so the world goes on.

1st May 1915

Our friends treated us to some four hours violent rifle shooting last night. Sheets of lead passed over us. We didn't fire a shot back. Casualties nil, but we can't sleep. A fine warm day digging still. A quiet morning but in the afternoon, the Turks opened a terrific fire on our position. I got the Howitzers working again and after a time settled them and our men got a turn. At one time about 1000 of them moved towards the Australians and so got across

The Indian mountain battery nestled into crevices on Walker's Ridge.

our front. Our fellows let them have it, and as the Australians afterwards said "slaughtered them". It was most stimulating, just what our men wanted. An Indian Mountain Gun Battery arrived, on the Ridge and dug emplacements. 26th Battery, Captain Whitting in command, Major Bruce, I think Brigadier. We don't quite like their coming, they are bound to specially draw the Turks artillery fire and can't do much good. Their field of fire is limited to a flank from which the Turk do not attack. Genl Godley came and had a look round. He was very complimentary to us and I think meant it. He didn't stay long. [Sentence deleted by WGM.] He is very tall and had to stoop and bend to get out of the sight of the snipers.

2nd May 1915

Fine, fairly quiet day. The big shells from Sea of Marmara all but got one of the Transports. The shell to us seemed to hit her fair on the stern, one huge blaze of fire and then thick smoke. But the shell had just passed over and exploded alongside. Later I found that the shell had gone into an open hatch full of coal. [this sentence inserted later] 1 man killed, 2 or 3 wounded. All ships up anchored and started steaming from danger spot as quickly as they could. Today an observation post of Turks was found on Anafarta Point.[31] It had been shelled, and a couple of batteries blown up some few days ago. A platoon of Canterbury Bn were sent by sea – landed and surprised some 2 officers and 15 men in a deep pit. They showed fight and got 2 or 3 killed and wounded. We got no more shell fire on the beach for a time. We are still digging – still being shot at night and day. Last night the Otago Bn was to

A Wellington
machine gunner in
action on Walker's
Ridge.

Hampton Album, Alexander
Turnbull Library

have gone out and taken an advanced line, but at the last moment the order
was cancelled. At about 5 pm the Turks opened up again a tremendous rifle
fire, m/guns also our artillery replied and after about 3 hours the thing died
out. We had 2 men wounded only. Many many thanks to our digging power.
It was a great pity we thought that the order for Otago to go was cancelled.
The Turks had a good basting.

Tonight at 7 pm the naval guns and our Howitzers and 18 Pdr QFs
[Quick Firing] bombarded the Turks position for fifteen minutes but the
practice was no good, the naval shells fell a thousand yards or so too far.
The Otago Bn were to advance at 7.15 from Australians position but got
delayed somehow and didn't start until after 8 pm. It was dark. They soon
got against the Turks and after 3 charges, were driven back. We cheered
them on from the start and the Turks I expect wondered what was up. They
poured lead onto our position from 3,000 rifles, Col F.E. Johnston estimated.
I was with him observing near one of our machine guns. The racket went on
until about 2 am. The Canterbury Bn was to have gone in thro' our left and
joined up with Otago, but Otago didn't get thro' [so the] Canterbury people
couldn't go on. A lion in the path to wit a machine gun barred the only track.
Some of the Otago people hung on and dug in, but the bulk of them retired
and were sent down to the beach, to rest. They lost some 100 men, and
several officers. In my opinion the plan was no good and doomed from start.
They tried to go in where the Turks had been attacked for days. They should
have gone in from our left, ie almost other end of Turks. My remaining Corpl
of machine guns Copeland[32] was killed. I was within 9ft of him. I had just
recommended him for a Comn [commission] and he deserved it. Poor lad
shot thro' the heart. Not a sound. Another gunner was wounded.

3rd May 1915

We hear we are to be relieved today. We haven't asked for it but won't refuse a spell, out of the actual fire. Later we are not to be relieved. So on we go with our digging. Sang froid, is our motto, also "cheeriness". Everybody jokes, smiles, and laughs. Good men pass out and we don't wince. Our turn next perhaps but we are doing our job and it's all in the days "march".

My dug out is quite homely now, a bunk of sand bags, tree feathers as I call twigs and leaves for a bed, an old scrim tiffin sack for a blanket. My great coat on, a dead Australian soldier's (great coat) for a coverlet, a pack full of leaves for a pillow and I get some sleep – al fresco [sic] at present. I wash in a pint [0.57 litre] of water at night, save it and wash all over with a sponge in the morning, or rather ½ of me one day and the other ½ the next, in the same water, and then perhaps the water left does to wash a pair of socks! Great economy. I have a box or two for odds and ends, 4 bayonets picked up, stuck in my sand bag wall do to hang up all my gear on. I am getting a table. 2 oil sheets overhead now keep off the sun.

Turks still snipe away and we snipe back. We are beating them at their own game and our boys enjoy the sport. We get 20 to 100 a day, and lose

Malone called this photograph, taken of him by one of his subalterns at Walker's Ridge, 'the famous one'. It is sometimes incorrectly captioned as being at Quinn's Post.

hardly any. Every night the Turks give us a furious rifle shoot for about 2 hrs. We reply not. We think they have the jim jams,[33] and think we are attacking them in the dark. The trouble is that night is turned into day, and made hideous.

Been trying all day to arrange our artillery bombardment of Turks position, but Divn HQ say as a few scouts are out, we musn't shoot. The Turks are digging like mad or perhaps like us and the game is stalemate. As we couldn't get the artillery going I went out for a little scout on our left flank [deleted in original, but legible.]

4th May 1915

Fine day. Again trying to get an artillery bombardment. Major Bruce, 26 Indian Mountain Battery, very keen too and helping. I hope at least to get his guns at work only 10 Pdrs but still something. Div HQ again step in and stop us. I am getting sick of it. The war is a "JOKE WAR". Ever since Aug last we have been getting "Notes" from, the front,[34] all emphasising that modern war is a question of 1) artillery 2) digging, 3) telephones, 4) periscopes. We are constantly told to read and digest. We do so but when we want artillery to help us, phones and periscopes to enable us to work quickly and safely, we get almost[35] nil results.

Our howitzers are short of ammunition, our 18 pounders don't seem to be able to get into action, and the naval guns can't talk soldier gunnery. As to phones – after losing life after life I got two small field phones, cost near enough 25/- each. They were old and worth about 5/0. Very soon one was taken away. As to periscopes – 4 per Company were issued. Every man or two ought to have had one. If it were not so serious – the penalty – one could roar with laughter at the preach and no practice. As to digging – if we had to depend on others we should go short, but that we can do, but even then it is hard to get hold of tools.

The Briton is a muddler all right. Still he gets there. That is how we feel. If only some of the German thoro'ness could be put into us. What a people we would make.

Feeling a bit sick of trying to help big things a bit, I went in on a little scout by myself on our left. I took a rifle and slithered into the scrub, found several dead Turks about, poor devils, been there since 25 April. Not pleasant to look at. Some women are wondering about them and will weep. I will try and get them buried tonight. Unfortunately we cannot bury lots of our own poor chaps. We can see them here and there but it is almost certain death to go out to them. There are two I would specially like to bury Lt Wilson and a bugler lad Bissett[36] from Hawera. He lies with his bugle on his back face downwards, shot in his tracks. I hear day by day of innumerable acts of special bravery on the part of our men. One could fill a book – one Roberts[37] carried 3 wounded men out of the inferno and came back for another man and was then killed himself. It is a wonder that many of our 1st 2 Coys came through. Menteath[38] of West Coast Coy was telling me that he was with a lot of Australians who gathered round him and wanted to retire. He wouldn't let them so they stayed and were killed one after an other. He was surrounded with dead men. How he escaped he cannot tell. (Menteath was killed later at Krithia Battle 8/5/15 [inserted by WGM later]) To go back to my scout, I wanted to see if HMS *Canopus* could fire direct on to some new Turk trenches without hitting us. I got a good way out and found that she could and was then picked up by Corpl Sievers.[39] He had heard that I had gone out and came after me to warn me against <u>our own</u> snipers. I was in Turk country and could most likely be taken for a Turk. I went back quick and lively. I brought a Turks pack with a camel hair blanket – brown with 3 red stripes and a great rent in it. The blanket will do for a cover for my table. The Turks name is [Arabic script] such was written on his pack.

On getting back I saw our Brigadier and asked him to arrange for the *Canopus* to fire on the Turks new trenches. He told me we re-embark tomorrow for destination unknown. Some flank movement I suppose. We are to be replaced by the Naval Division troops. We are sorry to go in spite of everything. I wanted to get at the Turks on our left and I think it could be done. Still we must do as we are ordered.

5th May 1915

Last night Turk fusillade grew but it was mostly against the Australians across the gully and except for the noise and the necessity of being on the alert we had a quiet night. Only 3 of our men wounded yesterday. We are to re-embark back tonight it is thought for Cape Helles to help the 29th Divn. The Naval Divn people have arrived such boys they look, still they must be sturdy. There are no troops like ours to look at and now I know as regards my Bn for work no regiment in the world could have done better. Into action on 27th 40% loss [corrected by WGM previously "45% loss almost"] of troops engaged fight and dig night and day for 8 days. No blankets. All food and water to be carried up hill a long way. Living in trenches. Yet cheery and unshaken. I was busy with Major Bruce of 26 Indian Mtn Battery, trying to get the new Turk trenches on our left shelled. It seems strange that there is such difficulty about it. My Brigadier won't let me go to Divl HQ about

it and is busy himself with other things I suppose. I find, and am glad to say, Major Bruce very keen to help and I think as he can get away on his own the Turks will get blown out of the trenches. He has promised me to go off to the warship on our flank which is in line with the trenches. The *Canopus* has gone, the *Majestic* taking her place. The "Nelson" Bn of Naval Brigade took over our position today. The Colonel Eversley [sic, Evelegh][40] is a mild mannered elderly man. He is lucky to get my dugout. It was very comfortable, just finished. At about 2 pm the Brigade Major (Naval Bde) came along, and I went with him to put up a flag at extreme left of our position so that the *Majestic* could fire without mistake. The flag not being much and dark blue, I put a helio[41] at the point to flash to the *Majestic*. At about 4 the *Majestic* opened fire with 12" guns (I think) and got the Turk trenches 1st pop. She fired about 5 shells and blew the trenches and a lot of Turks to pieces. They went up, in bits. Then we got our Howitzer to fire on the Turks who were running for their lives. A lot of Taranaki Coy men too got busy with their rifles. Unfortunately unknown to me our machine guns had been dismounted, and the naval guns not put up or we would have slaughtered the Turks. As it was we bagged a lot of them. We are all very pleased at a good finish as it were to our occupation of the position. But I should have liked to have followed up with another bombardment to night and then attacked with my Bn. I believe we could have swept and taken the whole front line of the Turks trenches.

At 8.15 we marched to embarking piers and went off to Destroyers. A long cold job because after getting into all sorts of cutters and pinnaces we had to wait some 4 hours without moving. Finally, we got on board. I went on HMS *Mosquito*. Her officers made us at home. I enjoyed a cup of cocoa, biscuits, 2 oranges, chocolate and chocolate creams!! Quite a feast, at 1 am. We reached Tekke Burnu [Sedd el Bahr – crossed out][42] about 3 am and soon landed waiting for remainder of Bn. I turned in on the beach and got a couple of hours sleep until daylight.

Opposite above

Ships off Anzac Cove, as seen from Walker's Ridge.

Malone Family Collection London

Opposite below

The beach at Anzac Cove during late April or early May 1915.

Malone Family Collection London

4

'It was hell'

The Second Battle of Krithia, May 1915

[MS 4130]

6th May 1915

We then marched from beach past Sedd el Bahr Fort to a Bivouac about 2 miles inland. The fort is all smashed to pieces. We saw as we passed 2 huge guns lying crumbled, as it were. An easterly wind was blowing, very cold and dusty. It is a great sight the Head from Tekke Burnu to Sedd el Bahr.

The sea covered with ships of all sorts. The beach with men, horses, mules, guns, wagons, stores, soldiers, sailors, landsmen,[1] donkeys. A huge camp or series of camps, French and British. We soon settled down at our Bivouac, in green fields, with elms and walnuts on the boundaries, a running stream of clayey water or two – wildflowers, dog roses, poppies and others strange to me. Yet big guns and rifles were firing away in our front, odd bullets coming into us. We are within easy shrapnel range of the Turks, but we soon dug in. My bivouac is in a sort of bank and stone wall just above the creek. We are to be in reserve today and well our men deserve it. We came from our position in the Gaba Tepe heights and were all night embarking and disembarking, no sleep worth talking about. We may have to move today, a big battle is going on just in front. We have the British 29th Div on left, the French on right and 2 Bns Naval Bde in centre. Some 40,000 men attacking, the Turks who are in position.

Guns of all sorts naval 12", French 75s, British 18 pdr QF and Howitzers are blazing and blaze all day long, send some 30 shells every minute agst [against] the Turks. The batteries are close to us, so sleep was almost out of the question. I had a good wash and shave and then climbed a small hill nearby, and spent most of the day watching the battle. It is ideal fighting country, open undulating country. I could see our troops and the French advancing but not one of the Turks yet an incessant roll of rifle fire goes all day. Next to us is an Australian Bde, then there are Indian troops. We all take things as a matter of course, after our experience at Gaba Teppe [sic] this is a sham fight. Yet now and again we get shrapnel fired at us and an odd man gets hit.

By dark we had gained quite a lot of ground. Our artillery is immensely superior to that of the Turks. We turned in at 7 pm, but the firing went on all night, at times furiously. It was a very cold night. We couldn't sleep for it. The men got up and walked about to keep warm. I do wish we could get them some blankets – or rather get our blankets. The officers are in the same boat. I am not so badly off. I got a small blanket off a dead Turk, the other day, for a table cover, it is better than nothing.

Sketch map by Malone showing position at Krithia, 6 May 1915.

Alexander Turnbull Library

Key
A. British 29th
   Division attack
B. French attack
C. Naval Brigade
   attack
D. ⎤
F. ⎬ Turkish
E. ⎦ positions

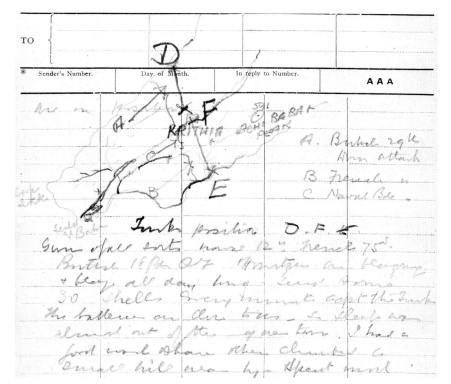

7th May 1915

The battle still raging. We are busy fixing up our Bivouacs. I have made mine quite snug per a stone wall, two boxes for side board etc and can now sit on the side of my bunk in the bank. Dog roses blooming all round me. The Brigadier Col F.E. Johnston called. I made him clean his boots! lending him my gear. We move I think this evening to N.W. to about the A in my sketch. We will then be behind the 29th Divn. The battle is going well, only about 250 casualties yesterday, which out of 40,000 is trivial.[2] It is a relief to get in where war is being waged scientifically and where we are clear of the Australians. They seem to swarm about our lines like flies. I keep getting them sent out. They are like masterless men, going their own ways. I found one just now crawling like a big brown fly over my Bivouac. I straightened him up, not a bad lad either I believe, but a 10ft road was not good enough for him, he wanted to walk or climb on a 6" ledge – strange!! I sent off a note to Mater, by a man going to Alexandria, to give to Lt Col Charters[3] to send when proper.

At about 4 am we moved to sea cliff, westerly and then along cliff N.E. to a gully leading inland, in rear of the 29th Divn fighting line to reinforce that Divn. We were exposed to shrapnel, but fortunately suffered no loss. We were to remain at foot of gully for the night, and had made ourselves comfortable in bivouacs, when at about 9 pm we were ordered to move

Malone and his bivouac at the reserve camp, Cape Helles, May 1915.

up the gully to occupy trenches. We plodded along and by about 1 am got settled down. A very cold night, and we feel the want of a blanket. Nobody growls, but we are getting well tried right enough. My HQ are alongside a white low stone hut which is frequently shelled by the Turks.

8th May 1915

Up early to see about rations. I found and took over a lot that had been sent up for a Lancashire Fusilier Bde that had been retired. I revelled in straightening up the cases of stores and taking stock. Bacon C/Beef [corned beef] (tinned), biscuits, iron rations, tea, sugar, salt, jam, some dried vegetables. It was a veritable godsend. If we had had to draw from the Base it would have been midday before we could have got supplied. We have no transport. Still in the *Achaia*. At 10.30 am we were ordered to attack. We advanced under heavy shell and rifle fire, on a front of about 600 yards, Auckland and Canterbury Bns on our right. By about 4 pm we had got forward about 1200 yds [yards] and within 200 to 400 yds of the Turk trenches. Owing to enfilade machine gun and rifle fire, we were unable to get further. We passed [thro deleted] over trenches held by 1st Inniskillings[4] (2) Hants[5] (3) Royal Fusiliers (4) Essex,[6] Bns. We dug in. On our left were a detachment from Inniskillings and across the gully on our left, the S.W. [South Wales] Borderers. At 5.30 a general advance was ordered in a very airy fashion, by people behind who

Malone in a reflective moment at his bivouac in the reserve camp, Cape Helles.

spoke about going right through and doing all sorts of wonderful things. But an attack of a line at less than 1 Rifle per yd, with the next line 200 yds to the rear and the next 300 yds and the next 500 yds is not war. We were all ordered to start at 5.30 pm and did so. I pointed out to my Brigadier that until the Bns on my right, which were 300 yds in rear of the prolongation of our line came up, it was no good pushing my men forward. We had gone 300 yds in advance of any other troops and were hanging on to what we had gained. He said you must push on. Result, my right went forward about 150 yds more and then got badly cut up and stopped, a platoon of Essex, reached us, didn't like the fire and went back. No other troops reached us, except about 10 Otago men and a few Auckland. So I am proud to say my men went further than any others and hung on and continued to hang on. The Auckland Bn I hear retired after being badly cut up, so my right flank is in the air. During the night we got out our casualties, estimated at about 30 killed and 120 wounded. [Inserted by WGM later] They turned out to be 50 killed 150 wounded. We got up rations and water but the men had a rough night, digging. No great coats – very cold. It was a warm sunny day. I came thro safely but had some four very narrow shaves. A shrapnel shell burst in front of me and several bullets rapped some timber close to my head on the right. I am somehow or other immune. I took Colonel Moore, Otago along to show him best way for 2 of his Coys to advance. A bullet passed between our heads and went right through the lobe of his ear. I must be more careful though as the loss of officers is getting very serious. I can't do much good going ahead, but I do not like sitting at my Hd. Qrs with my telephone. Still I can control things better if I keep in my place. *Deo Gratias*.[7]

9th May 1915

We had a quiet night. A small Turk counter attack, which we easily settled. Their defence is very solid, trenches everywhere also machine guns. Evidently the Germans are organising things. Officers who were in Flanders say that bar the weather Flanders fighting is a picnic to this. The British and French losses have been very great and our progress is slow. Today is a lovely day. We are W.I.B. holding about 750 yds with about 500 men. I am asking for a full bn to be sent with 4 m/guns to fill up. It is dead against rules for 500 men to hold 750 yds, hastily made trenches. I don't generally believe in asking for reinforcements, but my line must be closed in – which would be the proper thing – to about 200 yds. We are expected to go on advancing and I must have in my opinion at least 3 Rifles per yd. The French I hear are doing well on our right. Poor Menteath was killed yesterday – a

Malone's panorama of the Krithia battlefield, with the objectives – the village of Krithia and heights of Achi Baba – indicated in the sketch map in his diary on 7 May 1915 (see p. 179).

Malone Family Collection Wellington (now in ATL)

splendid soldier. He lived through an inferno at Gaba Tepe Heights and I really thought he was immune. 200 reinforcements for my battalion arrived and these are our own from NZ. They will make up yesterdays casualties – 5 officers with them. Taylor [sic, Tayler] of Eltham and Hartnell of New Plymouth I know.[8]

10th May 1915

I got 4 machine guns out of Genl Marshall[9] yesterday pt [part ?] Motor Maxim Squadron. At dusk I took them up the gully on our left to the left of our line, some 1200 yds ahead. We passed a Bn of Gurkhas (6th) who were relieving the S.W. Borderers, Sikhs 24th were relieving Inniskillings on our left. We got as far as we could with the mules, and I went ahead to find Lt Preston[10] my m/gun O/C. The Turks opened up shrapnel and rifle fire, and things were very heavy for half an hour. As my orderly said it was a "lovely fusillade". I handed the guns over and got back to HQ at 11 pm. The Brigadier was wanting to know if I had relieved the Royal Fusiliers [RF]! I told him that unless I withdrew some of my men from the front I couldn't. That as we were 1200 yds in front the RFs didn't want any formal relief as they were only a moral support to my men.

I am not hitting it to well with our Brigadier. He seems to resent my asking for information and for not too readily allowing my men to be plunged ahead, without reconnaissance or information. I ask also for barbed wire, engineer detachments, the moving up of so called supporting troops, who are not in any touch whatever with me, and generally everything that can enable me and my men to do our job thoroughly. He says I am more bother to him than [all deleted] the three other C.O.s together. They say yes to everything, and seem to blunder along but I am not seeking popularity, only efficiency. [Deletion four lines of text – marked "deleted by me W.G.M."]

We and the other troops have suffered tremendous losses because our directors [written over the word leaders] failed to quickly appreciate that this is the day of digging and machine guns, and that prepared positions cannot be <u>rushed</u>. The naval opening, shelling the forts was a huge mistake, it gave notice of Britain's intentions, and the Turks had 6 weeks under thoro German officers to cover the Peninsula with trenches and to fix artillery and m/gun positions: with exact range to every approach. Had the operation begun by the landing of the army, then probably the rushing tactics now used would have succeeded, but now it is going to be sap, sap, dig, dig. The war of Flanders again. I expect every day to be told to in our Brigadier's words "fix bayonets and go right through – no shilly shallying about, everybody going in." If I do there is a 500 yard slope in front of me, over which my men must pass and it is absolutely commanded and enfiladed by a number of machine guns across a big gully.

11th May 1915

No advance by anybody. Men busy improving trenches. They are shelled intermittently but suffer very little loss. They keep down. I have been busy reconnoitring country to [the] right of my Bn lines, so as to fix certain Turkish trenches, which enfilade us more or less. I made an eye sketch of country right back to KRITHIA. On my travels I came across a lot of dead Turks – about 100 in two patches lying as they fell, mostly face downwards. They ought to be buried but it is not safe to send men to do so. Snipers are firing all day long at any body who goes out into the open. Strange to say, tho the Turks who have been killed some 14 days are really a horrible sight, I do not care to write the details. I and seemingly no one is horrified. I had a look for papers on several, so was as close as could be. I am going to try to get them buried. There is an odd New Zealander and Britisher among them men evidently sniped and killed crossing the ground. Our artillery support is not right. We get quite a number of our own shells in our trenches, and some times a naval big shell lands behind, but close to us or just in front. The Turks have got our range and shell us vigorously, but do really very little harm. We are getting home on the snipers but it is a difficult job. Our Brigadier has just ordered me to relieve the Essex [Bn]. I had to tell him that unless he wished me to withdraw men from the front trenches I could not do so. I asked why he didn't send the Otago men who have been in reserve, and I then found that really the Auckland and Otago Bns are all to pieces. They have suffered horribly but are not the disciplined men that mine are, and thro' this I believe their losses have been greatly increased. I always thought the Wellington Bn was easily the best in the Bde. I now know that it is. Both the Auckland and Otago Bns have gone back to put it in politely [sic] and their morale is all to pieces. Even Col M.[Moore][11] who commands the Otago Bn is quite shattered up, and not much good just now. An active service man of the Regular Army too. It will tone him down a bit. He had a cock sure, better than any Territorial CO who had not seen active service air about him that was somewhat annoying. The Wellington Inf Bn is the only one that is a working organized unit and we have lost 16 officer[s] and some 400 men. *Revenons aux nos moutons.*[12] I suddenly thought of the reinforcements for my Bn who had arrived and could not while the Coys were in the firing line be incorporated with their respective companies, so I said to the Brigadier I could send them. He was quite pleased. It is not possible without loss to move troops by daylight so at dusk I sent the reinforcements along, but they got lost, as to some 100 of them and had to come back. I gave their officer a good talking too [sic]. Still night work is most difficult, and they were new chums.

12th May 1915

I made the reinforcements clean up. Oh the mess and litter of rifles, ammunition, equipment of all sorts. The country is littered. Then the rubbish tins and odds and ends of food, not to say filth. Ugh! A battlefield is a much littered and untidy thing. We have been having a hard job getting out and evacuating our wounded. Had it not been for my reinforcements, we could have done but little. Captain Home our RMO is a real good worker. He has had some 48 hours without rest or sleep, and has no assistant doctor. I have forgiven him his untidy ways, for the sterling work he has done. Our stretcher bearers, bandsmen, have worked heroically, going out under fire, by day and night, carrying in the wounded. I hope I shall be able to tell the people of NZ what grand fellows their soldier men are: nothing better in the world! The Imperial (Regular) officers and men are full of admiration and speak of the splendid advance made. It opened their eyes, they say they never saw anything better or finer. And it was good. My Bn advanced 1200 yds under shell, machine gun, rifle fire, crossed several trenches which must have been most tempting to stop in, kept their intervals and never fired a shot until they were within 200 to 400 yds of the Turkish trenches. They lost heavily, but advanced as tho they were on a parade ground. It was splendid. I never saw them do anything like it during their peace training. I used to growl and growl, but there was no room for any complaint. They were in dead open ground. The Tommies have christened my men the

"White Ghurkas" [sic, Gurkhas].[13] We are very proud of the sobriquet and mean to live up to it.

We are to be relieved tonight by the Manchester Brigade of English Territorials. Our men can do with a spell, it is impossible to light fires in the trenches so cooked meals are minus.

At 2.45 pm I went to HQ across country, to the usual sniping accompaniment. There is a line of trenches leading to it, but I can't stand dodging along them. I did think the Brigadier could have given me full instructions on the phone. We are connected by it. Still it was all right. I met the Manchester Rgt officers and took a Col and 5 others back with me to prepare for the change over. At dusk it started. But it was 24 hours before finished. When we started to change, the Turks seemed to know what we were at and let us have shrapnel *ad* galore.[14] Then we had to go to a strange bivouac close to where we were, when we landed. It came on to rain and in the dark we couldn't find the turn in the so called road and got down to the beach. Pitch dark and raining cats and dogs, so we decided to stop and get what cover we could. We were among the stores, and transport. Stacks of ammn, boxes of stores etc etc gave some shelter. I found a little mimi [sic, maimai][15] of boards and sacks and felt and found only one man in, a beach worker I presumed, so started to crawl in as there seemed room for two. The inmate sat up. I asked "only one in here and room for me". He said "one" and no more. So I crawled right in and lay down alongside him. He said not a word and seemed astonished. Presently Major Young outside got up against someone else, who in a tongue which I thought was Turkish raised a big talk. My man then chipped in. Turk, I said to myself. Presently he lay down and like a good Christian pushed a blanket over me. So what with a great coat, very small that I had picked up and the blanket, I was fairly comfortable, dry anyhow, and out of the rain. I got some sleep. On getting up, I found my bed fellow – the bed by the way being "mother earth" and a board or two on it, covered up in another blanket. So I crawled out without waking him. Outside I found an officer and told him what a Christian I had stuck and gave him 2/- to give to mine host. Just then he came out and to my astonishment, he was an Indian as black as the ace of spades! By name "Naring Sam" (Naran Sammey) [corrected name added later by WGM] a cooper in the Indian Army. I gave him the 2/- and my best thanks. A strange bed fellow right enough!! Still a clean and sweet one. I noticed he at once folded things up and tidied up and I trudged off and finally found our bivouac proper a muddy filthy place it is. A most vicious wind. Rain it rained. My batman, young Okey and also Whitmore[16] a sort of body attendant of mine, and the other orderlies, were very glad to see me. They had gone on with my gear and had prepared a bivvy for me, and were somewhat alarmed at my non arrival. I soon had some tea and then got to work in the rain fixing up a proper bivvy. I found the one I had used before, but a road had been driven thro it across the creek. I soon bunged the road up, with stone walls dug and scraped shaped and after some hours work was quite alright. We got very wet, but then was nothing else to do and I like a "HOME". Col Richardson[17] (NZ S [Staff] Corps)[18] who is on General Paris's[19] staff, came to see me and asked me to dinner tonight.

13th May 1915

I enjoyed my dinner. Met General Paris and his son and several other officers who were all very nice to me. The dinner was a change too to our own rations. I was glad to turn in, and tho' everything was rather wet, slept well. Today is hot and sunny and the mud and all wet things are drying up fast. I have spent the day drying clothes etc. The fight with the Turks goes on, all the same, but we hardly notice the sound of the big guns and rifles. Shells keep passing over us and arouse sometimes a little curiosity as to what damage they will do or have done, if we only notice the explosion. Yesterday the Brigadier sent for me to advise as to my Major Young taking command of the Auckland Bn. I naturally don't want to lose my officers but the Wellington Inf Bn <u>can</u> run even if it does lose its officers. I recommended Young who has improved as a fighting soldier out of all knowledge. When Hart comes back he will get the Canterbury Bn, and so far as I can see, we will officer, in the higher commands, all the other Bns. We are proud of the fact, but still we begin to wonder how our own Bn will get on if our best are transferred. Young is to be made temporary Lt Col. Promotions are plentiful. I have just recommended 7 NCOs for comms [commissions] to fill vacancies in my Coys. A private now commands the machine gun section. Lieutenant Wilson and all NCOs have been killed or wounded. The section did splendid work. Young Preston is the new O/C, a 2nd Lt. He was astonished when I got him appointed. He is a good chap and only 23. He concentrates. We nearly got blown out of our quarters today by our own artillery. There is an English battery about 600 yards just behind us and they had 3 premature shell bursts, we got the pieces of shell and shrapnel bullets. I went down and told them they were very rude, and that if they shot us up any more we should have to shoot back! We expect Turkish shells to annoy us but expect our own to go <u>over</u> and not <u>into</u> us. Fortunately no one was hurt except an Indian. I ought to have said the Inniskillings, SW Borderers,

Hants and Essex and Royal Fusiliers who were close to us here relieved by an Indian Brigade, 6 Gurkhas, 89 Punjabis and 2 other Regts. O/C General Cox who I met and liked. He dislikes disorder etc as much as I do.

We have just got word that a NZ mail bag arrived. Hurrah! I shall enjoy a letter from Mater. My HOME is nice and dry and straight now and it will be a luxury. I am thinking of taking off my clothes tonight. Ever since we disembarked I have slept in my clothes – 18 days!

14th May 1915

I took off my clothes last night and slept in my shirt and a cardigan jacket I picked up on the battlefield (I have had it washed), but it was not a success. Too cold. Today is a lovely sunny one. The Bn was allowed to go down to the beach after breakfast and to return by 10 am. I went for a ride. Col. Richardson very kindly lent me his horse and Whitmore my <u>bodyguard</u>! got Colonel Ives [Ives's horse]. We went through the French line to Sedd El Bahr village and fort. A mass of ruins. Stone houses, narrow streets, full of horses, mules and French troops. The old fort is an [sic] Hospital. I went in and had a look round. It dates I believe from the crusades. Our big shells had smashed it in many parts too [sic] pieces. I went up on the rampart and took a photo of the *River Clyde* s-/s/ [steamship] and the beach. The *R. Clyde* had been used as a landing stage, ? a death trap. Run ashore and then some 8 sally ports discharged our 29th Divn troops, to be badly shot up. I had a yarn with *le Pere Bertin Liebaux des Augustins de L'Assomption*,[20] late of

A view from the old fort at Sedd el Bahr, with the *River Clyde* on the left, taken by Malone on 14 May 1915.

Malone Family Collection Wellington (now in ATL)

Strange bedfellows: Malone and Naran Sammey, 14 May 1915.

the College Francais Gallipoli now a French Army chaplain. He has been a long time in Turkey. He says that if the troops had landed at the same time as the naval bombardment, the Turks would have given up. The whole thing has been badly mismanaged. No sound appreciation of the situation, and now a plunging policy. I got and sent Mater a French army Postcard, as a curiosity. The mail was not a regular one and there were only a letter from old Major Sandford[21] at NP and Fred Westerton respectively. Nothing from Mater. I was very disappointed and am wild because I feel that the mail is somewhere about, probably at Gaba Tepe and negligently delayed. Our last mail was delivered at Port Mudros about 23rd Ulto. Still I feel absolutely sure that Mater has written. She and the family will soon be in England now and I hope they have had a good voyage and are well. I then rode on and had a photo taken of "Naran Sammey" and myself alongside his "Mimi". He is of the Supply and Transport Corps, 29th Indian Infantry Bde, a Madrassee Hindoo. He is "mine host" of the other night. I will send him a copy of the photo, if it comes out all right. I wonder when the film will be developed. I then went on to the Fld Hospital to see any of my men there. I only found one, sick dysentery. He had been blown out of the trench by a shell.

[MS PAPERS 4130 Second Book]

14th May 1915 (Contd) and got naturally a severe shock. I bucked him and several other sick men of diff [different] units (British) up. He was very grateful to me for calling in. All the wounded were on board transports, used as Hospital Ships, and which as they are filled go to Alexandria or Malta and discharge the men to shore hospitals. The casualty list is great. My Bn up to yesterday has lost – 80 killed, 306 wounded, 42 missing, total 428. The missing I am afraid are nearly all killed. A great price to pay. [13 lines deleted by WGM of which four were torn off the bottom of the diary page. The first words of the deletion 'for so little' are, however, legible.]

I find that things on Saturday last were worse than I knew. On the second advance at 5.30 pm, my W [Wellington] West Coast Coy, was actually stopped by <u>our</u> <u>own</u> shells. Bursting right in front of them instead of on the Turks trenches. The Artillery cooperation is often a cooperation with the Turks. No proper observation. No telephones for us.

I suppose everybody is well meaning but there seems no firm able hand anywhere. Actually we got messages to observe the artillery fire and send word by a messenger, who would have to go back say 1200 yds under heavy fire. Fancy waiting for such observation! It is too dreadful. I am going to try and get a 4 Coy outfit of tphones [telephones] from our Regt Fund. It will save many a life. I lost 3 orderlies out of 8 the other day carrying messages to the firing line – all for the want of the phone.

I got back to Bivouac at 12.10 pm in time for lunch at 12.30. I had to go with other O/C Bns to the Brigadier. [8-9 lines deleted.] A blundering plunging into action will gain nothing.

The Army HQ have now sent round a circular memo, practically saying that there is to be no more plunging. Semi siege warfare is the order of the day and the future: sap and sap, and mine and dig and night attack, and make good against c/ [counter] attack.

The Flanders war. That is a slow game. If I were G.O.C. I should make good a defensive line on the ground, we have gained, make it impregnable then garrison it with the weakest troops, except a few take all the best troops north by night to Gaba Tepe, or Anzac Bay as I believe is the right name of our landing place N of here. Then prepare a plan of attack on Hill 971[22] from NIBRUNESI PT [Point].[23] Get every available man of war to come up and at night take position at sea commanding [Hill] 971 and line thence to 224 D.5.[24] Which is the crest of the ridge, a frontage of about 2800 yards. Then all our FA Batteries and Howitzers to take up position about Nibrunesi Pt.

and about knolls Sq 250 R.N.J. and in advance of same. Ranges (1st) 7000 to 4500 [possibly 11,500] yards then march say 3 Divns, say 45000 men to take up position to attack. 1 Dvn: with its right on the Beach (Frontal) and L [Left?] on line parallel say 1500 yds N.E. and the other 2 Dvns left on line sq 250.F and R [Right?] in line 1st Dvn (Flank).

Everything and everybody in position by night and attack commenced at dawn, the forward line could be right wheeled along road W° [due West?] to BIYUK ANAFARTA[25] and thence right moved to foot hills and make some progress up them before dawn. At dawn the troops now at Anzac Bay to make a feint and so engage Turks now facing them. Aerial reconnaissance, would I believe show that the Turks have not really fortified the NW slopes of the position to be attacked. The crest gained, dig in, bring up guns etc and prepare for further advance either immediate or next day to MAL TEPE[26] and thence to KILIA TEPE.[27] This would cut the Turks communication. Position gained to be fortified, and held awaiting any T. [Turkish] attack from S. and N. until whole show reorganized etc. Put a line of trenches on right across ANZAC BAY [Anzac Cove] to sea at KILIA TEPE.

At present it is stalemate, and attacks direct on ACHI BABA[28] or 971, must be slow and costly, sap and sap. Manoeuvre is the antidote to entrenchment. I hope to be able to get G. HQ. to consider such a plan, if one is not already under weigh [sic]. I saw Colonel Richardson today of General Paris' staff, and he seemed impressed with the idea as a sound one.

[15th May 1915]

Today I had lunch with Col R. [Richardson] and Genl P. [Paris] and his staff. The men are, as to 500 of them, at work on the beaches and roads. Fine sunny day. I spent some time darning my only pair [of trousers], and strengthening the seat, which was almost thread bare. One of my Subs[29] wanted to photo me, sitting on edge of my bivvy with my only pair off and on my knees, and I darning and stitching!!!! But I didn't want any companion picture to the famous one. I went and called on Col Evelegh Comdg Nelson Coy [sic, Bn] R.N.D. he relieved us at Gaba Tepe heights,[30] and has just come back here, being relieved by the Auckland and Wellington M. R. so I suppose, Edmond and Terry are getting a look in at last. I hear we go back to the trenches tomorrow night, but we have to find 600 men for beach work tomorrow Sunday. I wrote a long letter to H. Penn re the doings of my men. Our aero planes [sic] very busy today also our guns. We were shelled pretty often thro the day, but we pay no attention.

I found some new, to me, wild flowers today, and some honeysuckle just about to bloom. The fields and track sides are lovely – dog roses, poppies big white daisies and many yellow purple lilac blues and white flowers also some tawny reds.

16th May 1915, Sunday

A lovely morning. Mass at 6.30 am, in the open bivouac an occasional shell bursting over head or close to. Distant rifle fire. The "shriiing" [sic] of our own shells passing over, all taken as a matter of course. There is to be a 2nd Mass at 10.30 am – 600 of men gone to beaches to work at unloading stores and material. We have no word yet of going back to the trenches. The Brigadier sent for me for my advice as to his appointing a C.O. to Auckland Bn vice Plugge[31] wounded. He fancies Major Young of my Hawkes Bay Coy. I at once recommended Young. He has come on wonderful[ly] in action, Enjoys it. I asked whether the Auckland officers would loyally back Young up, because if not it would be a difficult job to straighten the Bn up. Their peace training was slack and I attribute their losses to want of discipline and good leadership. They were a sacrifice to their own inefficiency. It is pitiable. Young is to get the Command with tpy [temporary] rank of Lt Col. When Hart gets back he is to get the Canterbury Bn – so very soon the Wellington Bn will officer the Brigade!

17th May 1915, Monday

Fine day. Things as usual. Went with Col Richardson, (NZ but on General Paris's staff) to beach to go off to *Franconia* for some things he wanted, a little holiday for me. We walked down but *Franconia* was taking the Australian Brigade back to ANZAC Cove (GABA TEPE). So we had a look round the supply and ordnance depot. I got a ball of string, 2 candles, 2 bamboo rods and some stationery. Met a Gen Elliott who was very nice an engineer, he is making a road round the beach. He was very nice and chatty but rather worried about his son, who is in front observing for the artillery. I discovered he had no periscope which is madness so I impressed on the Genl to get one or make one, and gave him a design. The beaches and land along side is literally covered with men, horses, carts, mules, stores and supplies. We have come to stay right enough. . . .

At night I presided over an Anglo-French concert, Taranaki Coy and French gunners under a huge walnut tree. We wound up with the Marseillaise and God Save the King.

[MSX 2552]

17 May 1915

Dear Major Sandford

Many thanks for your letter of 14.3.15 which came to my hand 2 days ago. Glad to hear your news. I cannot give you much back of importance owing to censor rules, tho probably you and the world at large pretty well know all that has been doing. I cannot say where I write this, but I think I can say that the Bn which I have the great honour to Command (and which you know) has been fighting from 27th April to 5th May inclusive at one place, and then went to another and was fighting from 7th May to 13th May, hard and continuously – night and day. We are now having a spell, but are still under shell fire and long distance rifle fire the latter not aimed at us, but at our troops in front. Still an odd man gets hit but we look upon the fire as quite harmless – as most shell fire is. I can give you a recent instance. About ½ an hour ago I was crossing a field, which by the way is a lovely blaze of scarlet poppies, white big daisies, and great quantities of wild flowers, strangers to me – but most beautiful, all colours and shades. Well a bit to my right a Lyddite[32] shell landed apparently right on to a mounted orderly. Up went a big column of smoke and dust, the mtd man was enveloped, and one could think blown to bits. No fear, presently he rode out somewhat shocked and very angry, but not hurt. His language was free!!

I had been down to the beach to Ordnance Stores, about periscopes and telephones for my companies, and was on my way back. Don't think I was an heroic figure, I wasn't. I had 4 fresh baked buns in a flour sack and 2 long bamboo rods on my shoulder. I had just left a General Elliott who had shown me a new road he was having made, in return for a design of a rough periscope I had given him. I had run across a Field Bakery and as I and my HQ mess (Capt McDonnell, Capt (Surgeon) Home, Capt Chaplain McMenamin, and Capt Cox (of Hawera) acting as my staff officer in lieu of Major Hart (wounded) had had no baked bread since 25 April last. I made love to the chief baker, and got 4 loaves. I asked for a loaf and then said it was a pity to separate one, and he gave me 2. I then got a flour sack and told the baker that the 2 were lonely by themselves, and it was a pity to separate such close companions. (They are baked in lots of 4 together), and would he make everybody happy. He did. I told him I might remember him in my will.

The bamboo rods are to help in fixing up my bivouac shelter. We landed with what we stood up [in] and what we could carry, officers and men alike in our packs and no blankets. So we are up to all sorts of patents to protect us from weather and cold. And it is cold at nights, tho' the days except 1 have been lovely. Our rations are all right, Biscuits (great jaw muscle developers) Bully beef, jam, cheese, bacon, tea and sugar. These with good appetite for sauce, go down cheerfully.[33] We are all very well and fit, never better in our lives. There was a great shortage of sleep up to 13th but we are making up the arrears fast. Except for the separation from my wife and family, I am enjoying life as I never enjoyed it before. The fighting part is full of horrors and dreadful things – but to us, there is no horror or dread. We don't altogether understand it. You know our casualties (I am not allowed to mention their number) and you can imagine what the fighting has been like, and what we must see. Yet very few even wince. I reason it out that there is "an absolute acceptance of fact" on our part. War is war. There is one thing we don't like, but it does not worry us, that is the impossibility in many cases to bury the dead. At my last HQ during the action out of which we came on the 13th, there were over 100 dead Turks, in the same paddock, within a stones throw and among them an odd New Zealander or Britisher. The Turks had been killed about 15 days before, they were all on a patch about 1 acre. The others had been killed within 6 days. I crossed the place 2 or 3 times while reconnoitring but to send out men to dig and bury meant heavy casualties. The field was slashed with shrapnel and rifle fire whenever any number of men went over it and at times, apparently on spec. I had the New Zealanders and Britishers – 4 in number [–] buried at night by a man going to each and digging lying down alongside. Thus we did the job without loss. The Turks were too big a proposition, tho' we did bury a good many of them, in the least exposed places. At the place where we were fighting before we came here, we dug in on the ground gained, and in time dug communication trenches, and in the end enclosed a good piece of ground. Well in our midst, numbers of Turks, Australians and our own mates lay dead, but it was impossible to bury them. If you put a finger up, you would very soon get it shot off. We had started to sap to the bodies to bury them, but came away before we had done so. All this I am afraid is rather Ghoulish and I don't know why I have written so much about it, except, that it is the one outstanding thing that I don't like. Kill your man but don't leave him unburied. [Added later by WGM] An armistice to bury dead, I suppose is the thing, but now-a-day it is out of the question. As to my men, they are splendid and Brave as they make 'em patient, enduring, clever, cheerful, nothing upsets them. Heroes all. I am so proud of them. Sandford I love them. Strings of wounded men go by me "Well Colonel, I've got it. I hope you are satisfied with us" always with a smile, often with a little laugh or an attempt at one. No cries or groans, not a whimper or complaint. The only cry I heard was from one poor chap who was shot up most ghastly, and his wasn't a cry, it was a repeated "Oh Daddy" "Oh Daddy". Intense suffering in his voice, which was soft and affectionate. He was I suppose somewhat delirious. New Zealand can be justly proud of her sons. They are gallant gentlemen.

My men have earned the sobriquet, from the British Regulars who saw them advance over 1200 yards of shell, machine gun and rifle fire swept open ground – of "The White Gurkhas". I never saw or read of anything finer. They got out of a rear line of trenches, 3 companies in one line, each sending its 4 Platoons one behind the other, interval about 5 paces, the rear Platoon carrying picks and shovels. They advanced as though on a show ground, steadily walking forward. No lying down, no firing. They went over 3 lines of trenches filled with British Regulars, who were except as to the front line, spectators. These trenches were havens of safety, but my men got into them and got out again or else jumped them. As they went shrapnel slashed them – then machine gun and rifle fire – men began to fall, but the rest bored steadily on and on, at last they reached the front line of British trenches some 500 to 700 yards [originally 480 to 600] in front of the 1st Turkish trenches – passed over them, went 200 to 300 yards further and were struck by enfilade machine gun and rifle fire from both flanks, as well as shrapnel. At last down they had to go only now did they begin to fire. Then dig and dig. It was impossible to go further. [WGM later inserted the following sentence in the margin: "These Britishers at first had orders not

In a note later added to this sketch map of the Second Battle of Krithia, Malone explained that in his original letter to Sandford containing the map the troops involved had not been identified as it was against censorship rules to do so.

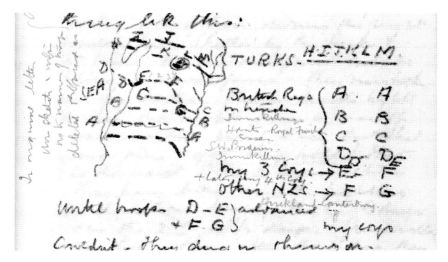

to advance, but later at 5.30 pm they got orders to do so."] The troops on our left had been ordered not to attack, so that when our left had got some distance past them, it was against all reason to go further. The troops on our right had had their advance stopped, and thus we were unsupported on our right. We had got within 200 to 300 yards [originally WGM wrote 400 yards, but then amended the figure] of the Turkish trenches and had gained some 200 to 300 yards of fresh ground. The position is something like this.

Until troops D-E and F to G advanced my coys couldn't. They dug in and hung on. At 5.30 pm (we started at 10.30 am) a general advance was ordered with the bayonet. I sent in my reserve coy and they advanced magnificently, and reinforced my right, which advanced until it was stopped by our own shell fire, not to say anything about the enemy's. My Bn was the only one to gain fresh ground and hang on to it. We dug in and were in the trenches for 4 whole days and a night. Then without request by us relieved, when the whole Brigade was relieved. The price was paid you know. But you can understand why I love my men. In the trenches, no fires, no blankets and in most cases no great coats. Food got in during the night under fire. Shelled by the Turks and at times by our own guns – field artillery and naval guns. They mistook us for Turks. Played search lights on us one night from a man of war. I am proud to say that what my men get they hold! That is the result of the 2 severe[?] actions they have been in. The fighting in the actions, being the 1st 9 days and in the 2nd 4½ days. Practically no sleep. Then after the 1st day, they begin to get their own back. They are very clever, out-sniping the clouds of snipers who lay for us. I vowed to have at least 2 Turks for every one of mine hit, and I am sure that we have got it already. The lads are great sportsmen, so keen and clever. I have lost less than any other Bn. This I attribute to better discipline and training. We were told long ago in notes from the front, that the best disciplined lost the least and dug the best. My men are great diggers. When we get back to NZ we are going in for earth work contracts. So I say to them as I go among them, we shall be *facile princeps*. 'Eat to live' is old – 'Dig to live' is the new tag. One night I calculated we had 2,700,000 (two million seven hundred thousand) rifle bullets shot at our trenches (at a distance of 300 to 500 yds) and presumably at us. Result, all the shrubs and small trees were cut off close to the ground. Our trench crests were levelled off but only 1 man killed and 1 wounded. We sat at the bottom of the trenches and never fired a shot. We couldn't. We fire in the daytime. We think the Turks get the jim jams and fire like mad to keep us from attacking them. One night we all sat up and kept up a tremendous cheer to puzzle 'em. Didn't they let fly! The more they fired the more we cheered. At last we could cheer no more. We were dry and every drip of water had to be carried, under fire of snipers, about 3/4 of a mile up a ridge some 500 feet to the top, as was also our food. Everybody has done well. Even our – in – peace-time, much-abused[34] bandsmen, as stretcher bearers have done great things working night and day, walking, climbing, carrying wounded, mostly under fire. They render 1st aid then carry to the Regimental Aid Station. Captain Home is a brick.[35] He had no doctor or surgeon to help him and worked long long hours. I suppose everybody did, but sometimes this must be a rotten job. Far from free from danger too. Many of us carry charmed lives or seem to. We know that we are in the hands of the Almighty and don't worry.

Tell all the Taranaki people who have sons or relatives here who have been casualtied [sic] that I would like to write to each one and tell them of their lads, but that is not possible. Some day I hope to see them and tell them personally what I think of their lads, and how great is my regard and affection for them. Perhaps you would tell them something of what I have written here. The whole Bn has done excellently, and I am not prepared to distinguish between any of the Coys. I don't think I could. My sympathy and that of the whole Bn goes to those who have lost son or relative and we are heartily sorry for them. But for the men themselves we feel that they have met a glorious death *Dulce est pro patria mori*.[36]

There are lots of officers and men here who have been in France and Flanders and they say the work there is a picnic to ours here. But I always say we have not had the ice and snow and rain and mud. We did have 2 nights and 1 days rain. And I must say the mud was delicious, Rich and thick and so sticky. Water here is within (in most places where we bivouac) 1½ feet of the surface. Our bivvys mostly holes dug in the ground were during the rain filled with water. We have very little sickness tho'.

Remember me to Col Bellringer and the 11th [Taranaki Regiment] and all other friends in your parts. Perhaps you would kindly show this to Bellringer and tell him I would like to hear from him. Letters are very scarce, but much appreciated.

With kind regards to Mrs Sandford and yourself.

Yrs sincerely
W.G. Malone

Extracts from this letter were published in the *Hawera and Normanby Star* in mid-July 1915. Several of Malone's letters were, like hundreds of others from soldiers serving at Gallipoli, published in New Zealand newspapers. The military censorship system was not as effective during the first year of the war as it became later and these published letters, as well as the private circulation of soldiers' letters, helped ensure that the New Zealand public had a fairly good understanding of conditions during the Gallipoli campaign. [*Hawera and Normanby Star,* 17 Jul 1915, p. 5; Glyn Harper (ed.), *Letters from Gallipoli: New Zealand Soldiers Write Home* (Auckland, 2011), pp. x–xi, 163–65.]

[MS 4130]

18th May 1915, Tuesday

Fine day. Shells very lively about the camp last night, just missing us. One man lying in this bivvy got hit by a rifle bullet, thro the sole of his foot. Wrote a long letter yesterday to Major Sandford the only man in New Zealand who has troubled to send me any news. I got interested and gave him quite a long a/c [account] of the Wellington Bn doings, as a return for his goodness in writing. I do wish I could get my NZ mail it must be about somewhere. It is too bad the neglect of our authorities. We shall be glad to get back to the firing line. A spell is very nice, but we have had it, and are getting tired of doing nothing. I heard today that the NZ Inf Bde are Army Corps troops, that the Composite Divn to which we were attached is dissolved and that the RN Divn which formed the major portion of it remains as RN Divn.[37] [Deletion of 11 lines, of which five have been torn off the bottom of the page.]

If it wasn't for my good men and officers I would try and get a job elsewhere. Today we are being shelled, bad luck 2 Otago men killed and 3 [5?] wounded by one shrapnel burst coming back from the beach. Our dear padre Father McMenamin had a shell pass just over his head and explode in the ground beyond him – Major Moir (Otago) was with him. Mater arrives in England in 2 days I hope all is well with her and the family.

May 19th 1915

The Turks shelled our bivouac a good deal last evening, but we all went to cover and so escaped. This morning they resumed the shelling from the N [North] and have opened on us as our R [Right] flank from across the Dardanelles from 2 different places. It is unpleasant. Bang. bang, bang, bang, the shells go in 4s at once, then single ones and so on. Odd horses and men get hit. We have not built our bivouac shelters to cover us from our flanks. I suppose we should do so but everybody is very indifferent about it. It seems hardly worth while.

No mail yet. Drat it. There must be 2 somewhere about probably at Gaba Tepe. It is too bad, the neglect to forward. The men and everyone are very properly growling about it. It is extraordinary how subservient officers are. They shun every form of trying to make their superiors do their job. If only they would politely but firmly insist on their just needs being attended to, they would be. There is no reason why they shouldn't. They are keen eno in jumping on those below them, but butter won't melt in their mouth when dealing with those above. A reform is absolutely necessary, but as I know the path of the reformer is hard. I learn that Auckland and Otago Bns are shattered in morale. Poor devils, they are paying for their leaders faults. Their discipline and training was not too good and they didn't get a fair show. And now the CO of Otago Lt Col Moore jumped up from Capt and adjutant to command the Bn because he was an Imperial Officer and had seen active service, turns round on his own Bn which thro' his own fault is not good, and says "Colonials are no good". It is a d-d shame, no better material in the world, but [in] this Bn it is the CO.

We are to re-embark tonight for ANZAC COVE GABA TEPE and rejoin our division at 7.30 pm we moved off. I went with 1st Coy. Interviewed the N.T.O. [Naval Transport Officer] on *River Clyde* the steamer that was run ashore as one part of landing stage on Sunday 25th ulto on attack [sic]. She proved a death trap then, but is useful now, tho she does get shelled every day. Capt Lambert was the NTO. He asked me to dinner and tho it was a case of "And me full of turnips", I couldn't resist a proper sit down dinner, soup, roast meat, asparagus, canned pears and apricots, lime and soda, coffee and I don't think I am either a glutton or an epicure. We had some good talk to – there were about 7 Naval officers Middies or 'Snotties'[38] as they are endearingly called, lieutenants and captains. They told me about the landings. Heroic but deadly business. The Snotties in my opinion deserve the credit of credit. Boys, yet they steered the boats in and out and in and out. Loads of soldiers one after another, shelled and shot at. And they had to sit and steer and wait, often their boats full or half full of dead and wounded men. Then after landing effected they had the taking off of the thousands and thousands of wounded, also often under fire. Good Boys! At about 11 pm I and Capt Cox went off, with one of the Coys in a minesweeper late trawler No 318 to the *Eddystone* a big supply ship. On arrival on the *Eddystone* we found everybody staff and all turned in and apparently every inch of deck space occupied by sleeping men. An utter lack of organisation. The 1st men on had taken all the handy deck room and apparently there was no room for mine – but there were at least 2 holds the farthest away quite empty and instead of filling these first and leaving the vacant space nearest to the embarking ladders, the reverse was done. Only 1 ladder to climb on board with on each [east?] side. I fairly roared asking "Whose handling this embarkation?" I found Temperley, our Bde Major comfortably asleep on a couch. He replied the NTO. I sought him and found he had no military help so I promptly went to a ward room where I saw a lot of officers lying on the deck asleep, and soon emphatically ordered 3 Wellington and 3 Canterbury officers to get out and help things. Went myself. Then I found the only means of getting the men down to the lower holds was over the ship's single break neck iron perpendicular ladder!! And as every man carries about 70 lbs weight it was a slow not to say dangerous job. The men had to walk over the lying men. It was practically impossible to get these lying men up and stowed away at this stage. I and Cox and the officers I poked up, stick [stuck?] to it and after some hours work got every body stowed away.

I am glad to say I was able to treat the whole thing as joke, which was the best way to keep the men in good and patient humour. I then found a roost for myself and Major Turnbull who was helping me in a boat, on the floor of it. My cap made a good pillow and I got a couple of hours sleep. We were out of the wind, and yet had ventilation.

[MSX 2552]

19.5.15

Dear Morison

It occurs to me that you would like to know how your son[39] has shaped. He has made absolutely good – as for the matter of that, has the Battalion. His and their conduct has been most gallant and yet with all thoroughly sound and soldierly. I never had any doubt myself – after some study of him, that he would be all right, and told you so in Wellington, but the proof of the pudding is in the eating and your son is very good "eating"! The water has been hot and furiously boiling as you probably have gathered and not good for ordinary puddings but one can stand anything.

I have recommended him and our other 2nd Lt for promotion of 1st Lt. He is very fit and well. . . .

We are all apart from the separation from our people enjoying life as we have never enjoyed it before. There are of course lots of horrors and dreadful things but there is remarkable absence of horror and dread. I do not think that it is callousness. I put it down to an "absolute acceptance of fact". War is war. Nothing more is to be said or thought.

New Zealand can be very proud of her sons, especially her soldier sons. None better in the world. Brave as they make 'em cool determined enduring, clever patient, kindly and cheerful.

Our Battalion has been dubbed by the British Regulars, who saw them make one of the finest advances under very serious fire, been made "The White Gurkhas" which we think a great compliment. . . .

Your boy was in all this and I am glad to say got through scatheless. And sometimes mind you Morison it was "hell".

I am so proud of the Bn, I can tell you. I love them. The wounded are wonderful. No cries or groans or moans. Stoics and heroes all. . . . You must know I have been everlastingly growling at them, on the least provocation. So hoping to make good soldiers of them. My belief that the best disciplined Battalions loose [sic] the least has been justified. . . . Your son and his fellow officers are the same stuff, and you and their people all can be glad and proud that it is so good. . . .

W.G. Malone

> The letter above was addressed to Charles Morison, a Wellington King's Counsel who may have been known to Malone. Morison's son, Second Lieutenant [later Captain] Bruce Haultain Morison, had somewhat controversially received a commission in the Wellington Battalion even though he had no military experience apart from a period of service with his high school cadet company. What especially concerned some officers was that Morison was commissioned at a time when Territorial Force officers were so anxious to serve that they were enlisting in the ranks of the NZEF. [Officer Commanding Wellington District to Headquarters New Zealand Military Forces, 14 Sep 1914, AD1, 9/49, ANZ.]

[MS 4130]

20th May 1915, Thursday

I got up soon after day break and found we were off ANZAC COVE GABA TEPE, our original landing place. Then on to a destroyer, where the O/C made us welcome and gave us some tea. These Naval chaps are awfully good. Hospitality itself and they seem to think a real lot of us. Then to lighters and ashore. Then to a gully – in reserve. Going along the beach at one <u>point</u> snipers were laying for us and wounded 6 men in a few minutes. So we had to halt and try another track which as it happens is free from snipers. At the point I got a letter from Mater of 21.3.15. Major Hughes had given it to Temperley to give to us. I was so delighted. I took advantage of the halt to read nay devour it. It is so good to hear from ones loved ones. As I read bullet after bullet pitched into the sea within 20 ft of me but I was quite safe sitting in a bank on the beach. I think there is another letter for me. Our mail was sent to Sedd El Bahr, as we left. Mismanagement. I am going to get to the bottom of postal things – somebody wants sacking. I am sure. We finally stacked up in a gully just behind our position of 26 April to 5th May. My own bivvy is right in the water channel selected by Cox who is no good at it.[40] Still I must put up with it. We got our kits, from *Itonus* so I had a sailor's delight. I am changing into light clothes. It is very hot.

I sent in special mentions re action 26th ulto Majors Hart, Cunningham and Young, Lt Wilson, L Corp Bennett, Pte Hayden and Swan.[41] There were several others who did very spcl [special] work re wounded men, but the Brigadier (I think rightly) does not want names of such. It is quite clear

The view out to sea from Malone's bivouac on Wellington Terrace in Reserve Gully, Anzac, May 1915.

Malone Family Collection Wellington (now in ATL)

A dressing station at Anzac Cove.

that it is very dangerous both to wounded and rescuer to do anything and it is not a case of leaving wounded men to savages or at all. Both Lts Hugo and Meanteath I am afraid after being wounded was [sic, were] killed thro' attempts to rescue them.

Cpl Woodhead[42] did work which at one time would have been rewarded by VC with also 2 or 3 others, but it is wrong.

Very glad to get something to eat at 3 pm, cup of tea and a biscuits at 6 am, only other food. Turned in early on my <u>stretcher</u>! Sybarite! But some fleas have followed in [us?] from Sedd El Bahr! Orders to stand to arms at 3 am and be ready to reinforce Col Monashs Bde. Genl Godley came to see me – an honour.

May 21st 1915

Stood to arms at 3 am. Later Col Johnston complained about want of obedience to orders. Went and had it out with him. He withdrew his complaint and apologized. Had a good talk with him. His heart is all right but Temperley, I feel sure is a "poisonous" sneak. I asked Col Johnston to carpet me every time he got any complaint and so hear the other side. He said he would. He admitted that I and my Bn had worked hard and had turned out to be the most solid Bn in his Bde. The air is cleared. We apparently will be in Reserve for a few days. The Turks attacked twice 2 days ago *en masse* and got badly smashed and repulsed 2000 dead and 5000 wounded. There is an 8-acre patch of dead. Brave and determined but rash. A German Genl Liman von Sanders is directing their operations.[43] They had received 15000 to 20000 reinforcement from Constantinople. We are all pleased at our success.

I found in connection with our action of 26th Ulto that the Turks were in much greater force than I had thought and moreover that we inflicted great loss on them. Young Preston who was on one of the machine guns gave me details of slaughter of several hundreds by his guns alone under Capt Wallingford[44] after Lt Wilson killed. It is good news. Young Preston is solid. Poor Wilson seems to have been somewhat rash and stood up too much. Hard to blame him. I do it myself, but I am meaning to be more careful in future.

Terry is here I hear. They posted me in Egypt as killed, and then wounded. Terry is reported to have told Major Whyte[45] who told him I was all right. "I know that my father did [not] come out to get killed["]. I will try and see him tonight.

Went up the ridge, to our old trenches which are now held by the 2nd M.R. (Wellington) and Auckland M.R. Col Meldrum[46] was in my old bivouac. He and his officers were very pleased to see me. He sent for Terry, but I couldn't wait, so didn't see him. Meldrum will send him down to lunch with me tomorrow. I went round the trenches, and found that they had been improved a good deal. They now have some 18 Pdr Q.F. and some Mountain Guns up: a great help. I had heard that a 'plunge' attack by 100 men of the 2 M.R. had been ordered by HQ for a couple of days ago. A mad fatal thing. It was to be a dash across open ground, commanded by machine guns and rifles, to the Turkish trenches and then back. It meant destruction to the 100 men. Meldrum saw the folly of it and got it counter-commanded. I went up partly to shake his hand on his action, and did so. I found later that Terry was one of the 100, so feel we have to thank Meldrum for Terry's life. A forlorn hope, with no real object is ghastly.

May 22nd 1915

It rained last night, and this morning up to 1 pm. Oh! The mud in our gully. Still we are cheerful. I got my kit, which had been landed from the *Itonus* and had a sailor's delight – slept in pyjamas on my stretcher, with plenty of blankets. What a sybarite, I! Orders to go and view the Australian position, with other C.O.s. A heavy, muddy, climbing, trench squeezing job. Saw the Turks trenches which in some places are only 15 yards away. The countryside is one mass of trenches tier upon tier. I saw lots of dead Turks. It is clear to me that an attack should be made from the North. Progress to our present front must be snail-like. The Australians to me, do not seem anything so keen as our men. Only an odd one observing the Turks and no sort of plan to deal with them; every man on his own. We organise parties of our men to deal with every bit of the Turk's trenches and have got them so impressed with our vigilance and quick shooting, that they keep very quiet and low.

I was glad to get back to my bivouac after a very hard, hot and muddy, and unuseful [sic] trip. I found Terry awaiting me looking very fit and well. He had been out sniping and reckoned he had had good "killing". He brought in 2 Turk rifles and wanted me to try and keep them for him. He stayed to tea. While at tea Genl Birdwood came to see me. I felt greatly honored because it is a climb to get to me. He was very nice and said he was very glad to get me and my men back, and that he had heard that we had done splendidly at Sedd El Bahr. He had got a smack on the head from a bullet, I found. By the way Genl Bridges[47] died from wounds, the other day. He had been going round having a look and was caught by a stray bullet. We go out as inlying picket tonight at foot of Walkers Ridge, stand to arms at 3.30 am and come home at 5.30 am.

Saw Major Bruce today. He was very pleased, apparently to see me, and told me of his Mountain Gun Battery. They have been doing good work but have lost 69 men. Things are hot right enough.

I forgot to say that on my return from Australian lines I was welcomed by a letter and 3 lovely photos of Mater. They are very good and do her credit. She looks lovely and younger than ever. I have a great longing to see her in person, but must be content. Then I began to get letters, another from Mater, one from Norah one from Brian – March 11th date. It was delightful the longest looked for mail. It was 4 weeks since arrival of last one.

May 23rd 1915

Sunday – Back from picquett [sic]. Fixed up my bivvy some more – levelled and paved and squared and straightened up generally. Then to my delight another letter from Mater March 15th and then later on still another April 1st. It seemed to pour letters. The last was I am pretty sure the last from NZ. She was leaving in 3 or 4 days for Wellington and then for England. She will be in England now. I hope she got my letters and what not, on her arrival, and was welcomed by her and my relations. I have passed the day looking at her photos and reading and re-reading her letters. I must write to her at once. I heard today that I had been specially 'mentioned' in connection with our actions and recommended for DSO.[48] But there must be lots of others who did more. I only did my job. It seems that General Walker had specially mentioned me as well as my own Brigadier.

On picquet last night, very quiet, only strings of mules and carts going by taking rations and water to the positions. Indians run the service.

May 24th 1915

Wet morning. Wrote Mater, thanking her for the lovely photos and for 4 letters. Sent her a few flowers, from around my shelter. An armistice for 9 Hours from 7.30 am this morning has been granted to the Turks to enable them to bury their dead and remove wounded. It seems so strange the quiet consequent on the cease [sic, cessation] of firing. Ever since 25 April, night and day there has been continuous firing, varying of course in volume from the tremendous roar and roll of big naval gun Howitzers Q. Firers Mountain Gun and rifles, down to the smack – smack of the snipers shot. It is quite uncanny the silence. We have just heard that Italy will declare war. A vote of 407 to 74 having been carried for Extraordinary Powers Bill,[49] which of course means Military Powers.

Mud – sticky – very sticky mud is with us again. But I think the rain will soon be over. An enemy submarine is about and keeps our shipping moving. 3 German officers killed yesterday! The blighters.

At 10 am. I went up over the cliff, and into and past our original position so dearly gained on 27th April last. The armistice was in full swing: A delimitation line was agreed upon, practically ½ way between our lines and those of the Turks, along this line at intervals of about 20 paces, pairs of sentries without arms were posted, one British ie Austn, NZer and one Turk. Each had a little white flag. Then between such line and the respective trench lines parties of men with white bands on their arms with medical men and assistants and stretcher bearers, sought the wounded, and other parties acted as burial parties. It seemed strange such numbers of men and officers moving about on the ground between our positions and not a shot being fired. I had a special look round for our own dead and those of the Turks. I wanted I admit to get a count of the Turks, so as to know, whether we had given as good as we got. I found quantities of dead Turks, just on the position and in it where we had the fierce fight of 27th April. I counted over 100. There were only some 12 of ours lying there. We had got in and buried all we could at the time. Poor shattered humanity – exposed for 27 days, as dreadful a sight I suppose as could be seen. They lay as they fell. In one

The armistice at Anzac called on 24 May 1915 to bury the dead. In the distance the Turks are burying their dead.

track about 50 Turks in a sort of double line of about 50 yards. In another place there was a curious tangle – a Turk lying face down across, his legs and lying back down a Ruahine private (one of my Bn) and then across his legs another Turk. I tried to reconstruct the scene. [Small diagram here.] I think some how, they were fighting in close order, and then got killed by fire from other troops who were firing into the jungle without a visible human target. Our men had to carry the dead Turks to the ½ way line – a gruesome job. One poor devil of a Turk had had his leg blown off at the knee, below, only his foot there. I did not go over any other part of the position but from what I saw in front of us, and from what other officers who did go over all the ground [saw,] the Turks have suffered great losses. The ground seemed littered with them. It is a good thing to have the dead buried. The air about was poisoned. The trenches are very close, in front of us, only some 60 feet away.

I saw a German officer. I hated him at sight. His manner was most offensive. Our men were burying a line of Turks who were so decomposed that it was almost impossible to lift them, and of course a sort of line or trench had to be dug. This pig accused us of digging a sap. A rotten job to bury their men and then to be accused of sapping made me wild. I told some of our chaps if he said any thing more to squash a dead Turk on to him. He snarled, but got more civil.

We got Wilson's body and also that of the Bugler lad Bissett and buried them. I am glad. I am quite satisfied about our nerves. The most awful dreadful sights and yet no awe or dread. A great regret that, the killed cannot be buried at once. It is a desecration of the human body to leave it shot up, and unburied for long.

I had no lunch, but got some tea and biscuit and jam at B/Gen Russell's HQ thanks to a Captain Levin[50] whom I had met at Palmerston North some years ago.

At 4.23 the armistice ended, and the firing recommenced. I had a good look at the Turkish soldiers they look good, and well fed and clothed, and seemed cherry [sic] and friendly enough. At 7 p.m. Hawkes Bay Coy gave a concert, but the rifle firing became so furious and noisy that it was impossible to hear, so we sang God Save the King and went to bed, at about 7.30 p.m.

[MSX 2552]

24.5.15

My dearest,

It is Monday morning, raining some, and there is an armistice of 9 hours from 7.30 am, (It is now 8.15 am) to enable the Turks who asked for it to bury their dead and remove wounded. 4 days ago they attacked and were repulsed with loss to them of some 2000 killed and 5000 wounded. Those killed are close up to our trenches and we shall be glad to get the ground cleared. It is so strangely quiet – night and day since we landed – one heard firing of all sorts. That is all the war news I am going to bother you with. I meant to have only told you of the armistice, but then it was clear it was better to give you the reason – lest you might think we had been asking for it, and were in trouble. We are quite all right, but progress may be slow. It is the day of trenches and there are less and less of them in front of us. Finis, war.

I am sitting in my shelter quite dry, but it takes some skilful operation with sword and rifle to induce the rain not to come thro in driblets at places. The sword is a Turkish officers, that one of the boys took off a dead Turk and brought in for his Colonel, the rifles are 2 Turkish ones that Terry brought in from the front of his troop's position and wanted me to try and cart along for him. My shelter is up near the head of a gully. I get just a peep of the sea. The gully sides are covered with scrub and many beautiful flowers, and the shelters of our Brigade. We are in reserve, and so are having a sort of ½ holiday. We got back to the 1st place of disembarkation, rejoining our Divn last Thursday, (I think but dates and days get lost!). I think I have told you in a previous letter of our trip away to another part of the Peninsula.

I am apart from the separation from you very happy, and just now tho the longing to be with you again or at least to see you is greater than ever, yet is endurable, because I yesterday received those beautiful photographs of your dear, sweet and lovely self. You look younger than ever. I sit and lie and gaze and gaze and devour you. I am not sure after all that they do enable me to endure better, our separation. If I were a stranger I should fall in love with you at the sight of them, but you know I am already fully in love with the bravest, and sweetest and loveliest woman in my world. I think I like the one photo, in which you are sitting on a sofa with a far away look in your eyes and (to me) intense look and pose of listening, or probably thought of your far away husband. It seems to me as tho you were striving to be in communication with me. The coming to me of the photo completes the connection and almost renders it physical. Was this so? The head is very lovely, and wistful, but to me there is not that intense character and greatness that there is in the other. One is beauty, the other is lovely greatness.

Thank you so much for them. Everybody here to whom I show them promptly falls in love with you. My dearest what rapture it will be when we meet and meet again. I feel sure, we will. God is and will be good to us. Our lives will be full of bliss and love. All unworthiness, narrowness and pettiness driven out of us by this eventful experience. I think and trust that I am a better man in every respect, and that all my selfishness and badness have gone, for good. I pray God that I may never forget what you have endured for me and be able to recompense you in full. You my ideal woman and wife.

To add to my great pleasure there were 4 actually <u>four</u> letters from you March 11th, 15th, 26th and April 1st, one from Norah and one from Brian. It was the happiest private day I have had. But it shows how badly we are served by our P.O. I had been growling and growling, but had cold water thrown over me. It is the one thing above all that we want, our mail. I hope you got all my letters on your arrival, and that you were welcomed by your people and by mine. I have been trying to picture your arrival, and hoping that you did not find the voyage too trying and that you have got quite strong and well again. All right I'll fix up about your overdraft, don't try and pay it off yourself. Don't stint yourself. Get all the pleasure and enjoyment you can, and you will thus be pleasing me greatly, for you will be well and strong and more lovely than ever when I come back to you. I suppose H. Penn knows that you are to have the rent of The Farlands, as well as the other rents. Did you make a mistake when you said we expected to get £236 per ann [annum], but would take £200 pa. I did not expect to get anything like that, not that it is not worth it but there are so few people, who could pay it. I am so glad you took Denis and Barney.[51] Give them all my love and a good hug and kiss each. My dear little Mollie shall have her arms around her Daddy again. The dear loving little soul. So like her dear and lovely mother. You speak about the kisses I shall have to give you. Will you give me some?! Those paper ones are not satisfying – x_____x x_____x x_____x x_____x. There! Neither are those are they?

I suppose you know all about our doings here. We are well fed, and are thriving on our food. Biscuit (great jaw muscle developers), bully beef, bacon, jam, tea and sugar, and sometimes dried potatoes. Appetite is a good sauce right enough, but honestly I don't ask anything better. It agrees with us. We have very few sick. My Battalion has 6. In Egypt they commonly numbered 60. The men are splendid gallantly brave, yet cool and enduring, great and clever fighters, keen, patient, I love them. They are heroes and stoics, always cheery. The wounded don't cry, groan or moan. It seems incredible but it is true. Among them one has no horror thro' sound. In any case we have no horror or dread. Thanks be to God. I sometimes however get tears in my eyes. Whenever a wounded man who can speak, sees me, he says something like this "well Colonel I've got it", a little smile showing the courage and spirit within. Then with a touch of anxiety "I hope you are satisfied with us". (You must know, I have been from the beginning up to the very last minute growling and growling at my men, at the least provocation, in the belief that that makes for good soldiery! [)] I tell them what I think of them and thank and praise. Then "we've done our best" – a final little laugh. Wan enough God knows. It is very pathetic so you will understand the tears in my eyes. They are not there generally. I am really very callous and hard.

The mail man waits so I must close.

Love – all my love (husbands love) to you.

My further love to the children

Yours for aye
Your loving husband.

[MS 4130]

May 25th 1915

Rain in the night. Fair day. Conference with MO re sanitation. The gully is congested and it is difficult to provide proper latrines. The ground is very steep. We have decided on a plan which should work. At lunch today, we saw a lot of the men looking out to sea from vantage points. It was said that the Turks were shelling our ships at Imbros. Then we heard that one of our men of war HMS *Triumph* had been torpedoed by a submarine.[52] I met Lt Harston and he said it was so he saw the ship sink. She was quite close to our landing place. He said[?] a number of destroyers had dashed in and he thought had rescued the crew let us hope so. The submarine was here a couple of days ago, we heard. The position is awkward. We are dependent on the sea transport for everything including most of our water. I suppose some sort of torpedo safe harbour or area will be made into which our ships can come and unload. It rained hard for a couple of hours this afternoon, but it is now hot and sunny. My shelter is reasonably rain proofed.

[MSX 2552]

25.5.15

My dear Norah

. . . I hope you enjoyed your stay with Aunt Louie, and that you will thoroughly enjoy England.

I liked the Cherinavski[53] [sic] celloist the best. We get some music here all vocal. Last night one of my companies gave a concert. 'Mary of Argyle', 'Sweet and Low', and The Veterans Song (Long Live the King – don't you hear them shouting – is the one I mean) were very well sung, but after about 6 songs, we had to bunk off. The machine gun and rifle fire, with an odd shell burst, made such a row that we couldn't hear. Night and day we get it in varying volumes of sound. We had an armistice yesterday (at the Turks request to enable them to bury dead etc) for some 9 Hours, and the quiet was quite uncanny.

. . . The men are splendidly brave and cool. I wish you could see the gully. The sides run up in spurs to a plateau with 2 main ridges. At the bottom there is a dry water course which we have levelled, it is about 12 feet wide. That is the only continuous piece of fairly level land. The men some

3000 stowed away in all sorts of dugouts and shelters, on the spur sides. There is in places scrub, and any amount of beautiful flowers. It is something like the steep parts of Wellington but each house is a little "bivvy" as the men call their shelters, an oil sheet for roof or may be a blanket. In fine weather it is all right, but in rain, no good. We have just had rain, one night ½ a day and now 2 hours solid. My bivvy and I am one of the best builders in the Divn, is high up the water course bed near the cliff. I have built a stone wall on one side and the stone balk on the other. At a 3rd side I have cut into the bank, and from it stretched an oil sheet for roof. The other side is open. I have paved a little yard. I am very comfortable. I give you a plan.

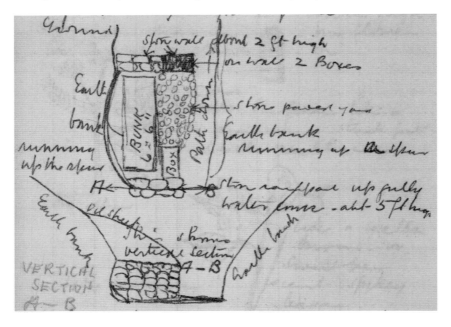

Malone's plan of his bivvy.

Alexander Turnbull Library

In front opening I have the NZ flag I brought with me. It keeps out the Westerly sun, which is very glaring and hot. I rig up cupboards with biscuit boxes. Two on the stone wall, for shaving and washing gear, brushes, and odds and ends. Two along side my bunk for a table, and books and papers. A candle stick inside is protected and hidden, and enables me to read a bit before I go to sleep. I have a blue signal flag, picked up a long way from here for a table cloth. I have actually some flowers. For vase a shell that didn't break up (shrapnel), about 8 inches high and 3½ inches diameter. My flowers are lovely yellow ones.

But I will enclose some. I am charmed with the lovely flowers here and find time in spite of the fighting to enjoy them. Pick them as I go along. Terry

Malone and his well-constructed bivouac, Anzac, May 1915. His New Zealand flag was one of a handful at Gallipoli.

is very well – at present in the front trenches. His troop were being sent on a sort of forlorn hope the other day – just a little local show – but Colonel Meldrum, good soldier that he is [,] saw that it was hopeless and meant certain death to the troops and their leader Hardham VC[54] and got the order withdrawn. It was a mad thing. I had heard of it without knowing that Terry was so directly interested, and so appreciated Meldrum's good judgement, that I made a special visit to see him and shake hands with him over it. It takes a lot of moral courage to point out to superiors mistakes of that sort, and I felt I must go and back Meldrum up. When I heard from Terry the next day that it was his troop that had been detailed for the job, and was actually waiting ready to dash out, I naturally felt glad. They would have gone, but none of them could have come back. It was what I call a "touch wood" business at best, and we can't afford to play games of that sort here.

How wonderful everything must seem to you in England. You must my dear first write and give me your impressions. We do so enjoy getting letters, and are always looking out for them. Look after mater well and help her all you can.

With much love
Yr loving father.

25.5.15

My very dear Denis

Many thanks for your letter and painting. You are getting on. Keep it up always. I hope to see you all soon. I miss mummy and all of you very much, but I generally have lots to do. Just now we are having a spell so I can write letters and read them and think about you all. The Turks make a great racket with their guns and rifles, but we hardly notice it now. I see aeroplanes every day sailing up so high, and lots of ships and boats. All sorts of soldiers, I was at a place not long ago where there were lots of French soldiers, and Indians. One night I was out in very heavy rain and had no place to go to to sleep. (We never have any tents only little shelters that we make for ourselves.) It was about 2 in the morning so I and the soldiers with me did the best we could. It

was near a landing beach, and there were lots of stacks of food and boxes etc about. I found a little shelter and crawled in and found somebody in it. It belonged to him, but there was room for two, so took it. It was very dark. The man sat up, but didn't say anything. I thought he was a Turk workman. I think he was frightened. By and bye he put a blanket over me, so I kept dry or rather didn't get any wetter. I was very wet, and it was fairly warm. I snuggled up against the other man for warmth. I got to sleep. The floor and bed was boards loose and earth. In the morning I got up. The other man was covered up in another blanket, so I didn't like to wake him up and thank him. I saw an officer outside and gave him 2/- to give to my host, but just then he got up. Wasn't I surprised. He was a black man, so very black with gold earrings!! And I had been snuggling up to him to get some warmth out of him! Fancy my surprise! Didn't I laugh. He was nice and clean tho and very tidy. His name

Naran Sammey a Madrassee Hindu of the Indian army. Wasn't that a joke? I went back some days after and got a photo taken of the shelter with me and Mr Naran Sammey alongside. I gave him the 2/- and he was very pleased.

Goodbye now with lots of love
Yr loving father.

Malone's young boys drew him pictures of the adventures they thought he was having. These drawings are by Denis, who was eight.

25.5.15

My dear Barney

You haven't sent me a letter, but I will write you a little one. How do you like England and what did you think of the ship and the voyage? You must write and tell me. I see lots of strange things here too. Big ships and little ones. Aeroplanes and all sorts of guns and things. Soldiers and sailors, mules and horses and donkeys. The other [day] a tortoise called on me. There were 2 or 3 of them living in a bank close to where I slept. I lived in the bank too. There were lots of frogs. I didn't see them, but they made such a funny croaking not like our frogs. Something like birds with a bad cold. I see such lots of beautiful flowers, and things. The sea and islands and a big salt lake and capes and bays and beaches. Fields red with poppies. Stone houses. Everyone has got a big bakers oven. I am very well, but it is very different to the Farlands – no cows! and therefore no milk or butter not to mention cream. No eggs, no puddings, but we do enjoy our meals and don't miss anything except mummy and our dear little boys and girls. Pray for your Daddy and perhaps [I will, words missing from carbon copy] see you, if only for a little while.

Lots of love
from your loving Daddy

25.5.15

My dear Mollie,

I got your lovely long letter a day or two ago. It was good of you to send it. I suppose you told me of the big kisses you are making and keeping for me. I hope it will not be long before you can give them to me. I think when we finish here, that we may come to England for a little rest before going to France, and then won't it be jolly. You must be such a big girl now, and you have seen such lots of new things. I am sure everybody loved you and the boys on the ship that is if you were very good. And I am sure you were. I don't see any little boys and girls now, and we are where there are no houses, or streets. I can see a Turkish village about 5 miles away, and there was a fisherman's hut near where we are. The fisherman has gone away, so we don't get any fish. The fields or some of them are red with poppies and there are such lots of other more lovely flowers. Some day I hope you and mummy and I will come and see them. Terry is very well. Edmond hurt his leg and is still in Egypt.

Goodbye my dear darling Molly.

Lots of love from your very loving Daddy

[MS 4130]

May 26th 1915

Fine day. Everything drying up beautifully. But lots of mud about. Took 3 Photos of the gully. Orders to go on picquet tonight on our left flank. Repaved my yard and put a small water drain in it. Went out and reconnoitered our left flank in readiness and in case of any action tonight. Found one line of trenches but parapet too high for most people to fire over. Suggested to O/C to fix same up and to fix wire right along under which all rifle barrels to be put and so kept down to sweep the ground in advance. I remember Sir Ian Hamilton writing at time of Japan Russia war recommending this.[55] I little thought I should be under his command! No support trenches either! We are very casual. Then there are two detached posts on some unconnected ridges a long way in advance. Instead of these having a regular garrison troops go out and come in every night. Too much movement and everybody strange to surroundings, ranges etc.

Went out with Bn at 7.30 pm and bivouced close to position. At 3.30 am stood to arms and remained under arms until 5 am when back to our quarters. A lot of firing in the night at other parts, none on ours.

May 27th 1915

Fine day. Hot. Mud all dried up. Had a sleep to make up for last night. Just heard the *Majestic* torpedoed by submarine last night. Sunk in ¾ hours. This at Cape Helles. Presume not much loss of life. Rather dreadful – such – rotten way of going under.[56] Wonder how the situation will be met or are we to do without naval support. It hardly seems just, but somehow or another we have got a notion that the navy, messes things up and are getting messed up. Grand fellows all the men we meet and "they do us proud" whenever we are near them, but they seem something not *comme il faut*.[57]

On our requisition for some sticks of timber to enable us to erect latrines that suit our peculiar and congested circumstance the Ordnance people reply "No timber available". Yet Home whom I sent to see whether there was not timber about found more than enough for our most urgent and necessary purposes used as lines to dry shirts etc on near Divl HQ! I put a letter into our Brigadier informing him. Let us hope he will shift things. If our sanitation is not fixed up, we are threatened with some serious epidemics of sickness. The lack of sanitation thro' out this Divn is dreadful. Things are beastly in most places. I can stand a month [of] dead and unburied corpses, but I cannot stand the filthy ways of living beings. McColl rejoined yesterday. He was shot on the 29th April thro the chest high up. The bullet missed every thing.

[MSX 2552]

27.5.15

My dear Hart

I was so glad to get your letter of 17th Inst and to hear that you are getting on well. Don't come back until you are quite all right.

I am as usual very fit, and apart from the separation from my wife and people very happy. Living as I never lived before sounds brutal, but somehow I don't think it is. . . .

We are back at our first landing place, and are having sort of ½ holiday. The Bn I am proud to say, has come out of the show the most solid of this Bde. A [Auckland] & O [Otago] went all to pieces. C [Canterbury] has not been so sorely tried. The Bn advance at 2nd place was magnificent. Quite a show performance and long steady advance, no lying down, no shooting for over 1200 yds, result minimum of loss, gaining 2/300 yds new ground and <u>hanging on</u> to it. Our officers and men are splendid. Trumps every one. An armistice here day before yesterday at request of Turks to bury dead. Their dead estimated at 3000, and I don't think it far out. I went and had a count in front of our position. When you got hit I had wanted 2 Turks for every 1 of our casualties and I think we have got it. Some of the poor devils had been killed for nearly a month, and weren't good to look at. We got poor Wilson's body and buried it.

The Turks trenches and ours are on some places only 15 yds apart. Funny business, modern warfare, but the Turks ought to be blasted off the slope of the hill in front of us and I don't understand why they arn't. I am wondering what the next move will be. We have ordered a 5 set telephone outfit for the

Bn, out of R/fund. Hope you will approve. It is an absolute necessity. We have lost too many already for the want of it.

Kindest regards
Yrs W.G. Malone

––––––––

27.5.15

My dearest

. . . Sorry your weather was so bad, let us hope that England will give you of its best. As I have already told you I heartily approve all you have done especially taking our little boys with you. I hope you are better than ever, you were on 11th March on the road to recovery. Your letter of 15th March. It was a good idea making the drawing room into your sick room. And so you had almost made up your mind to stay in N.Z. I should have been sorry if you had. N.Z. seems an awful long way off.

It was sad about Austin. I wonder often how Jesse [Austin's widow] is managing, and whether we can help her. I suppose there was some "compensation" under the Act.

Yes I remember sitting up high away at M^e [Madame] Barnards with you and how lovely it was, tho if I remember aright you were inclined to poke a little fun at me. We will be together again, surely. I am a lucky being and God will surely answer all the prayers for my safety.

Constantinople is a bit far away yet.

Miss Chapman sent me a little letter of thanks for the things I sent her. You never told me whether you really like the things I sent you and whether they suited you, the colours. I have an idea they didn't, still it gave me very great pleasure to send them to you. We have no need of money, no sellers and nothing to buy. I want nothing, as a matter of fact I have got too much stuff. All the lovely warm under things you bought for me, will have to wait until I spend next winter in England with you. We have no transport. That is horses and carts and we have to carry everything ourselves, so we are not looking for a load. Don and Billy were sent back to Alexandria, with all the horses and vehicles, none here.

I ought to have written to Mollie for her 5th birthday but somehow didn't. Your letter March 26th: I hope the 50 nurses on [the] *Rotorua*[58] were nice. They will be useful. I understand some of our wounded are being sent to England. If this is so, do like the good woman you are, go and see them, tell them who you are and give them my best regards. Thank them for me for their splendid conduct here and tell them I am very proud of them and hope that they will speedily recover and come back to us. Tell them I have not forgotten them, but that we have no means of knowing where they are and how they are getting on. Tell them that the Wellington Battalion, has maintained its reputation and in spite of everything retained its morale and came out of two intensely fierce actions spread over 9 days and 5 days respectively a solid fighting force fit for anything. It was the only Battalion out of 8 to gain and hold new ground. <u>It always holds what it takes</u>. This is not by way of boast, but I think it will help our wounded chaps along the road to recovery, and let them know that their services and sufferings was not futile. Don't fag[59] yourself in visiting them. If you pay them one visit, it will be as much I like to ask you to do. I almost wish now I had said nothing about this, and have half a mind not to send this part of my letter. I will let it stand tho', but your duty is to yourself, our children and to me, to keep strong and well and not to fag yourself and worry yourself over my wounded.

I had to break off at "see" on previous page. Terry called to clean up two Turkish rifles that he had brought in from in front. I had cleaned them, but we oiled them etc and then packed them up with a Turkish officer's sword that I have got in a bundle ready to send away and to store to take back to New Zealand as mementoes. Terry is very well like his father. He stayed to tea. It was quite late before we finished. . . .

In your letter of 26th March you say "I should so like to know what you think about it, whether you would rather we did not go. But surely you would cable if you felt like that." Well my dearie, I cabled about I think end of February – heartily approving.

I hope you were not very anxious about the German submarines the risk you took. I think you very properly took, and it shows me how much you love me, tho I didn't want any proof.

Yes we always thought 'Anglers Emulsion' good stuff.

Terry Malone in the uniform of the Wellington Mounted Rifles, 1915.

Malone Family Collection Wellington (now in ATL)

And so at last you managed to dream about me, and your dreams were happy ones. I am so glad. I go to sleep and wake up in the morning, that is when I wake and am not awoken, thinking of you, but some how I don't dream of you. I think I don't dream of anything. Generally sleep is precious. My nerves are like steel, so off I go, if it be only for an hour or two, and don't worry about anything no matter what racket has been or is going on.

I am sorry you were bothered about the letting of The Farlands. I am afraid some of my letters would miss you, but I wrote latterly in duplicate and sent one writing to London and the others to N.Z. Do tell me in detail what letters you got on arrival.

<u>Sergeant</u> McDonnell as you call him (you mean Captain) is quite broken in and is a faithful admirer and hench man of mine now, and all trouble is over and has been for a long time. I severely put him in his place and he now knows it, and is quite a good chap now, and loyal to me. Hard service shakes or drives everything and everybody into its or his place, and there is no mistake about it. One gets one [sic, one's] level, pretty quickly.

Don't worry, my dearest, about my having to endure anything. I endure nothing, it is one great pleasure of the best sort. The pleasure – or perhaps *"la joie"* of <u>living</u>, of doing a new job, of feeling physically and mentally absolutely fit to do it, of doing something for ones country, when it needs the service of its men. There are no real hardships, under the circumstances, or so it seems to me, but I am very strong and can make a joke I have discovered of any capsize. It helps everybody wonderfully if you laugh instead of grouse or grump. I often fume to myself over incompetences that I see and I sometimes let fly but that is the only hardship. The putting up with incompetence – ignorance – neglect or inability.

I feel intensely the separation from you and the children, and long to see you all, but some sacrifice must be made, and that is the one I make. It is to me a big one, but I know you bravely join in its being made. I have been just interrupted by Col F.E. Johnston our Brigadier. He congratulated me on being given a DSO. I am sure, I was going to say I <u>think</u>, you will be glad to know this. I can't say that I feel that I deserve it. I did my job and worked hard, as I hope I always do and will.

Mail man wants me to finish. He is waiting

With all my love to you
Your very loving husband
x_____x
Love to Norah and the children.

[MSX 2546]

May 29th 1915

Fine day. The Turks made a determined attack upon 'Quinns Post'. Exploded a mine, sapped up to our trenches, at the same time one of ours exploded in their trenches. They made a dash immediately after the explosion, and got into part of the fire trench. A counter attack recaptured the trench, 43 Turks being killed and 17 made prisoner. A large number of Turks were killed and wounded outside the trenches. Our casualties, about 190, only about 20 being killed. My Bn takes over Courtneys Post tomorrow and ensuing days – 1 Coy per day. On our left and right we took small trenches respectively.

[MSX 2552]

29.5.15

My dear Louie[60]

Many thanks for your letter of 8th Ulto, to hand yesterday. We are having a sort of ½ holiday so I seize the opportunity to write. By we I mean my Battalion. The somewhat quaint censor rules, prevent me saying where I am though I suppose the place in regards my Bde is concerned is published in every paper. Anyhow the Turks know we are here. I am always fit and well and enjoying life and never enjoyed it before, bar the separation from Mater and the children. The life suits me. We have had a pretty fierce time since the 25th April when we landed, and fighting goes on more or less and night and day. Some troops of course are always in reserve, as we are for the time, and so get a rest of a sort. My Battalion has been in two big things – one over 9 days and the other 4½ days, by days I mean 24 hours because often there is more firing at night than day. My men have acted splendidly. NZ can be proud of them. I class them as heroes and stoics. I suppose by the time you get this, you will have had newspaper a/cs [accounts] of things.

This is a lovely country and the weather on the whole delightful. Wild flowers the most beautiful abound and are a constant source of joy to me. . . .

We are well fed and thanks to weather conditions are able to make ourselves comfortable, in all sorts of holes, and in trenches. . . . Water has been and is our trouble, 2 quarts [2.27 litres] a day per man for everything – imported from Malta and carried by us up heights and for considerable distances very often under hostile fire. However we are a cheery lot of philosophers.

Yes I heard about Austin. He hadn't a very joyful life I am afraid. I wonder as one often does, when it is too late. Whether I could not have done something to have made his lot more pleasant. I am afraid I have been far too selfishly engaged in myself and my own affairs. I must try to do better in the future. This life widens ones outlook tremendously. If you had asked me at one time to have cut myself away from my personal affairs even for a month or two I should have said that it was <u>impossible</u> in big letters. If I come out all right (as I feel certain sometimes or another that I shall) of this war. I will do something if I can for Austin's boys not to say Jesse and Ellie. It is not easy to handle the matter now. I am writing my attorneys T.H. and C. Penn to try and get her to accept an allowance of the 10/- a week she wouldn't take from the Trimbles.[61] It is not much, but it should help, and I think I can easily manage it. . . .

I hope to revisit Lille but this show . . . is not going to be over in a day. The Navy has made, we think, a bad mess of things, and made our job a tough one – *Tr' importun* [?][62] . . .

I shall be glad if you will write me now and again. The receipt of and the replying to letters is about our only recreation. Country walks tho' most beautiful are not healthy! Too many snipers. We have a concert now and again, but big gun, machine gun [and] rifle fire makes such a racket, that often we cannot hear, and have to knock off. We never know when we can have comparative quiet.

Love to you and Walter

Your loving brother Willie

––––––

29.5.15

My dear Maurice

Many thanks for your letter of 10th Ulto. Glad to hear you have been accepted, and hope you will break [?] in at your drill and work, and become thoroughly fit and well trained. We shall look out for you, let us hope in France or rather Germany. We are – where no doubt – the newspapers have told you but we cannot. The censor rules are a bit quaint. I hope Brian too will be with us. Terry is here, where I am, but Edmond got his leg hurt and had to stay in Egypt, until it is well.

I am very fit and well and as hard as nails. We get well fed, but the army ration, doesn't make fat. Biscuits (very hard), bully beef, bacon, cheese, jam, dried potatoes, tea and sugar. We don't seem to miss the other things generally looked upon as necessities. We live in holes and trenches, and are very up to date in our shelters. The weather is lovely. Only 3 rains in a month. Thank goodness all the same. This is a lovely country, lots of wonderful wild flowers. The farming or what little we have seen of it, helps the weeds and hence the wild flowers. The newspapers will have told you mostly about our doings, and in any case I wrote you with Harry [Penn] a longish letter about them which no doubt he will let you see. I am hoping to soon hear from Mater from England, where she should have got on 20th Inst.

Glad you have been making yourself useful in the office, which I hear is doing well. I am enjoying my life very much, tho' of course I don't like the separation from Mater and the family. . . . Wool at 1/2 ½ [1 shilling 2½ pence] per lb is all right. Fat sheep too I suppose will have made big money. Don and Billy are at Alexandria, sent back from here as no use for them at present. Lots of fighting here night and day. The Wellington Inf Bn have done all right and I am proud of my men. They are heroes and stoics.

With love
Your loving father Wm G Malone

5

'Steady fighting work'

Courtney's and Quinn's Posts, June–July 1915

[MSX 2546]

May 30th, Sunday

Mass and communion at 6.30 am at the Bde Depot near beach. After breakfast went over to Courtneys Post and reconnoitred it. West Coast Coy goes in today, Taranaki tomorrow, and then 1 Coy per day. It is a slow process. On Bn picquet tonight.

Quite hot today. Young Parrington,[1] one of my observers who sleeps close to me, got a bullet wound on side of his head last night while asleep. A ricochet I think as we are not under direct fire. I woke up thinking such a bullet had got me in the calf of my leg, but it was only a bite from some particularly venomous insect, which I couldn't find. I didn't know of Parringtons accident at the time.

A general attack by the Turks is expected tonight, before the moon rises, and we are all to stand by. 5 weeks today since we landed! We haven't gone far, but we have had a good dose of fighting, and have consolidated our landing.

May 31st 1915

We had a comparatively quiet night. There were spasmodic outbreaks of heavy firing, but no determined attack. Still sleep was almost out of the question. At 3 am we stood to arms, knocking off at 5 am, having been knocked off during the night at 10 pm. We started relieving the Australian 4th Brigade (Inf) yesterday. I am to command what is known as "Courtneys Post", and will be under Col Chauvel.[2] Taranaki Coy went over today. I and remainder of Bn go tomorrow. Glad to be at steady fighting work again. It is getting very slow. Fine day.

June 1st 1915

Went over and took over Courtneys Post, a very higgle[dy] piggledy show. People all over the place. There are 4 different machine gun detachments, 3 Australian and 1 NZ. I put Major Cunningham in charge of my Bn and began to take hold as O/C. Post. Built a new HQ bivouac and propose to terrace the ground, and so make room for the men. I put all the machine gun men in one place. The Australians didn't like having to shift but I insisted. There is a lot of work to do remodelling, but we will get it done soon. The men are keen. We have got a Japanese mortar, which throws a bomb almost perpendicularly and can be seen coming down. It explodes with a tremendous force and must be terrifying to the Turks.[3] The latter have been having the upper hand in sniping, etc., but I expect our fellows will reverse the position. At dark the usual big firing began. The Turks have been turning night into day.

At 9 p.m. our people in next Post, known as Quinn's, went out to blow up a sand bag and timber erection that the Turks had put up[. A]t 10 p.m. A tremendous explosion announced success. We bombed away to help and turned on some machine guns as well.

June 2nd 1915

Interviewed Col Chauvel as to alteration in position – sand bags, periscopic rifles, flares, bombs, tools, etc. – and asked for extra supplies so as to have a store in hand. He was very nice, agreed to everything.[4]

We have told off a special sniping party to deal with some snipers who have ever since landing practically commanded, the valley, on the southern cliff of which our posts are, and have killed and wounded a large number of men, including Genl Bridges. Today we bagged two of the snipers and have quite altered the atmosphere. Yesterday morning 6 men Australians were wounded within 1 hour. Today no casualties, except the 2 Turks killed.

Moreover the Turks in trenches in front of us have are [sic] learning that there is a change. We got several of them, including an officer.[5] They are callous people. They sling the dead out of and over the trenches. We have started our terracing and made quite a change. My Bn will only be here for 8 days, but I shall be here at least 32 days, as O/C Post. The Otago Bn comes in, next Sunday, 1 Coy and so on, and my Bn goes into reserve for a spell. I would like to keep my Bn altogether and will have a try. It depends how they are. They have each Coy 48 hours in actual trenches practically without sleep, and then 48 hours off. Terry got wounded yesterday, so Major Whyte rang me up to say. Shrapnel, 1 ball in the arm and 2 in the leg. I couldn't go down and see him, but understand he will be all right, and was in good heart.

Very hot today and the flies are already a plague. A most unpleasant one, when one thinks of all the dead Turks about unburied. Finished my Bivvy and am very comfortable, but it is back to prevailing wind, and in the day, a sweltering place. It has a good outlook to sea and Imbros. I am writing this 9 pm, to accompaniment of continuous rifle fire – "Smack", "whine", "whiz", "sheet" go the bullets overhead – the valley echoes some of the sound and so adds to the clatter. Still we are used to it. Just been round the trenches to see all right. The men are in great heart. Capt Cox of Hawera has been promoted Major and commands Ruahine Coy, vice Saunders wounded. Capt Short is my staff officer, a good solid chap. Major Bruce 26th Mtn Battery was killed the other day. Sniped. I had taken a great fancy to him and he seemed to like me. A very keen officer and a real good sort I am sure RIP. I feel so sorry for his wife, of whom he spoke to me the other day.

June 3rd 1915

An uneventful night. I turned out at 3.30 am, when all hands stand to arms. Turned in again at 5 am. At 6 am sent in my daily report. I must try and get O/C Section (Col Chauvel) to fix 9 am for this report. It means, as it is now, that one gets practically no morning sleep. And as a rule from dark up to about midnight there is the Devil's own clatter and bang and boom, and smack and ratattat.

Rang up Col Johnston about getting away to see Terry. He was very good about it and said he would make all arrangements for a boat etc. Terry is of course on one of the Hospital ships. Soon I got word that all was arranged and away I went. Met Genl Godley on the road. He too was very good. Enquired about Terry and said he had instructed Col Lesslie [?] the RMO [Regimental Medical Officer], to see to a boat etc. He told me not to hurry back. He seemed genuinely affected. I feel very grateful to both him and Col Johnston. They couldn't have done more, if it had been a case of their own sons.

1st visit to the beach since 2nd landing. Quite a town has sprung up, and it seems well ordered. Huge piles of stores and food, for man and beast, right along and on the beach, 4 landing ramps, with all sorts of boats and barges alongside. A field hospital, wireless stations (2), ordnance and supply depots. Hundreds of dugouts and shelters of all sorts, backed into the hills and up the gullies. It is from, safety view, an almost ideal landing place. Shells do get the beach, but it is very fine shooting. I found that I might have to wait for 2 or 3 hours before a boat went off to the *Gascon* on which Terry was, so I tackled the P. [Port] Naval officer, a Commander Dix, he was awfully good, at once took me down to a piquet boat (motor) and told the middy [midshipman] in charge to take me off to Trawler No. 327 and to tell the

Quinn's Post at a fairly early stage, about May 1915. Note the extensive use of sandbags around the dugouts.

Australian War Memorial

Capt thereof to up anchor and take me out to the *Gascon* and then await my orders. We were soon away and alongside. I found to Father McMenamin, on board, On sick list, he took me to Terry – ward 7. However he was asleep, so I let him be. Later I saw him. He was quite cheerful tho' there was I was pleased to see a tear in his eye, when he saw me. Terry feels more than he shows I am sure. He had been hit by shrapnel. 1 bullet thro' the Right forearm, 3 thro' Right leg (2 above and 1 below the knee). He had also a graze on the upper R. arm and one on the abdomen. I think he will be quite all right, but the doctor wouldn't say. I got Terry some cigarettes, gave him Mater's address (c/- the NBNZLd [National Bank of NZ Ltd] London), and a letter to Col Charters at Alexandria, to advance him any money required. I hadn't a sou here. I hope they will send him to England. I understand they are sending a good number of our wounded there. I invited myself to lunch with the Ships Captain. She is a 'Castle' liner, a fine boat. The lunch was A1. Butter for almost the 1st time since 25 April, a great treat, not to say anything about cucumber and lettuce and oranges!

Genl Birdwood came on board, and chatted to me. A cruiser came up from Cape Helles guarded by some 5 destroyers and shelled village of Anafurta [sic, Anafarta] into which Birdwood told me the Turks were pouring troops, a new Division from Bulair,[6] 16,000 men. We couldn't see the village from the *Gascon* and didn't hear the result of the shelling. The General took me off to the *Sicilia* another Hospital ship. The *Gascon* sailing as soon as we left.

On the *Sicilia*, I bought for the mess 15 Tins fruit, and 3 Tins swiss milk. The Purser who was very nice threw in 3 Tins fruit. Cost £1 which I borrowed from my orderly, young Parrington.

Got back to Post at 6 pm. Dinner with Col Johnston, who was most solicitous about Terry.

Usual night racket. At 10 pm we made a special fire demonstration to draw all the fire we could. It was limited to 5 rounds per man. Every man, who was in fire trenches fired along all [the] front. It drew the Turks all right. In front of my post, we wrecked their fire trench, which was not very stoutly built.

June 4th 1915

Usual turn out at 3.30 am. Morning busy with engineer officer Lt Savage, a young Australian, a nice lad. Scheduled all work and workers – Genls Birdwood and Walker visited the post at about noon, discussed my supporting an attack to be made tonight by Quinn's Post, on trench in front of them at 11 pm tonight and also an attack on German Officers Trench,

A Turkish shell bursting on Courtney's Post.

Alexander Turnbull Library

on our right. Made all arrangements. Col Johnston visited the Post. Later, Col Smythe, O/C 2nd A. [Australian] Inf Bde came re support. He is on my Right. 6 men wounded in shelters this morning by snipers from distant ridges, also 2 men killed walking along track in Monash's Gully, a bad track. It was there Genl Bridges killed.

Arranging support for tonight's attack. At 11 pm the ball commenced. All hands and guns opened fire, a really terrific [changed from terrible] business. Pitch dark, flashes and reports of rifles and machine guns on all sides. Shells, red hot coming from our own guns, just over our heads, and from cross emplacements. The shells seemed to be coming straight at one – they are fired from a lower elevation. Crash, bang, then the return shells – bombs and star shells. Such a roar, crash, "hunch", bang rat tat tat, smack, swish, boing, pop and plop and an odd boom. A veritable inferno. I seemed to be in the centre of things . . . but I was really, bar very bad luck quite safe. The real danger was from premature bursts or short ranged shells from our own batteries.

It was a weird experience. Our guns made beautiful shooting just skimming the crest of the hill about 18 feet over my head. 18 feet doesn't seem much to come and go on. [In the old diary transcript, based on the now lost top copy of the diary, WGM apparently added: "Young Savage our Engineer says it is only 18 feet."] It is somewhat fascinating to see a flash, then a red point travelling up to you at a terrific speed and then over you, and the hill. Then flash, bang. One gets the sound of the cartridge explosion, just about as the red shell passes, depending on distance of the gun. It was my first experience of such a concentrated performance, and I wasn't sorry that the shells were not being aimed <u>at</u> me and my position. One of my orderlies tho' within 10 feet of me was wounded by a shrapnel bullet, premature burst from one of our guns.

The shooting raged all night, slacking off a bit towards daylight and then recommencing. Quinn's Post sortie had taken the Turk's trench and 28 prisoners, but were enfiladed and bombed and grenaded, and had to vacate at daylight, taking their prisoners. Great work, Canterbury Bn NZ Inf Bde. We think the Turks reserves in rear got cut up. Not heard yet our casualties. Only 4 in my post which shows one is safe in the midst of an apparent

Just how close the opposing forces were at Quinn's Post is illustrated by this photograph taken in 1919. The Turkish trench in the foreground is only separated from the ANZAC trench by a bomb-stop (a pile of earth).

Australian War Memorial

B = Bomb-stop, C = Courtney's Post, GOT = German Officers' Trench, P = 400 Plateau (Jolly and Pine), Q = Quinn's Post, S = Steele's Post, W = Wire Gully.

inferno if you are well entrenched, and your own people are good shooters and you have good ammunition.

The attack on German Officers Trench succeeded in getting the trench, and smashing things up, but it is not certain that a machine gun in a sort of fort (small) is out of action.

June 5th 1915

The firing still raging, on part of Turks, who are wasting ammunition at a great rate. We are pursuing the even tenor of our way, trying to get some sleep. Got a cable, dated 22.5.15 from Mater in London announcing safe arrival, all well. It had been to Alexandria and then posted on here. So glad to know she escaped the German submarines tho' I really didn't think there was great risk. I hope she got all my letters and that I shall soon get a letter from her. I sent her a note, while on the *Gascon*. A cold night, but very hot this afternoon. Just received copy of secret intelligence report "A recent arrival from Turkey states that the fame of the Australian and New Zealand troops has gone far and wide. Even the Germans admit their splendid fighting qualities and the Turks think them marvels. They talk of them as 'being more terrible than the Bulgars'!"

The flies are becoming an awful nuisance. The area is full of them – blow flies – and the small house fly. So many unburied bodies about. So many unsanitary latrines, and general dirtiness. This [is] not a clean army in its ways and even actual washing is very difficult. We are on ½ a gallon [2.27 litres] of water a day again. And corned beef and salt bacon makes one very thirsty, quite apart from the heat. Still no doubt the best is being done.

Col Braithwaite WG [William Garnett] visited the post. I gave him some tea and he gave me an ORANGE!

Major Cunningham who is running my Bn is doing very well. Keen, untiring and attentive to everything. I am glad he has had the chance to act. Hart has had to have his leg opened up again to get out some lead, and expects to be away another 14 days. I give him more. Jardine is nearly fit. McLernon[7] still bad. Furby sent to England for special operation. No news of Saunders or the others. Young Cargo[8] who had recently been promoted to Lt was killed in the trenches the night before last. A splendid young fellow – soldier-officer. Very sad really. Still no better death.

June 6th 1915

A quiet night, at 3 am all sections except ours made a demonstration fire. This morning, casualties on my Post 1 man killed, 2 wounded by snipers.

Saw Col Chauvel, as to requirements for post – sandbags, phones. Fine day. Bush King[9] holding Divine Service on terrace just alongside. Shrapnel bullet just came into <u>my shelter</u> – not into <u>me</u>.

Busy fixing terraces for men who are having a hard time, 48 hours in trenches, on end with practically no sleep. Certainly no comfort, no shade. I hope to get overhead cover for terraces which will thus be both safe and comfortable.

Hear we are not to go into Reserve – at end of 8 days – but into Quinns Post, which I gather ought to be abandoned. The Australians, who won't work and first got the position instead of sapping out and making forward trenches, just sat tight on the edge of the cliff and allowed the Turks to sap and trench right up to them, only some 10 feet away now. The Turks are sapping and no doubt intend to blow the Post up and into the gully. Nice place to have to take over! The Courtney's Post has taken a lot of straightening up, and it will be a bit tough if after we have got it fixed up, we go out and tackle a new messed up post. All the more honour, but it is very wearing and not altogether fair or reasonable.

June 7th 1915

Details taking over Quinns Post settled. We start on 9th. Some 250 reinforcements[10] have arrived for my Bn, and will thus make it up to full strength. A bit of a job in incorporating them at this juncture. Genl Godley called to see me and had a chat. Sent Cunningham up to see Quinn's Post. He reports it as in a filthy unsanitary condition. I went saw [Robert] Young the O/C and gave him notice that I will <u>not</u> take over unless it is thoroughly cleaned up. They are making a sortie tonight, and we help by fire. I think when we get settled down in the Post, we will be able to get the Turks under. At present they seem to boss the situation. Here in Courtneys Post my men have got an absolute fire superiority over the enemy, so that they hardly dare fire at all, in day time.

June 8th 1915

Mail arrived, but only a cable of congratulations to me and men from Stratford Patriotic Committee, dated 24th ulto – posted to me from Alexandria. I suppose some announcement has been made in NZ.

Last night's sortie from Quinn's by Canterbury Bn men, was a failure. 3 killed and 24 wounded. I think another "touch wood" bit of business, not worth the casualties. I suppose I shall be poked up and ordered to continue the game, but I shall take some forcing until I am satisfied of chances of success or necessity of operation. Isolated local attacks at the most salient point of our position are not in my opinion sound. There has been gross, I think, neglect in the early stages, when such movements would have succeeded and kept the Turks back. The Australians seemingly just sat down and waited and waited and did nothing. That seems to be their character, dash forward like mad things and then instead of working and making good, sit down and loaf, and then get "scary". That is not only my opinion but that of Australians themselves. We have succeeded what they call their worst, and a bad Brigade (Monash's). Bad luck for us. Still it is all in the days march, and please God, we will see it thro' and may be able to straighten things up a bit. I fear trouble however with my HQ, who I am inclined to think do not properly appreciate the situation.

Getting very hot, and the flies increase every hour, drat them! I am looking forward to Maters 1st letter from England. It is now 17 days since she landed and I am sure she would write very soon after landing. I do so hope, she has quite recovered and is not worrying.

Jackie Hughes[11] has been given the Canterbury Bn *vice* Brown[12] wounded.

View of Quinn's Post located in an indentation in the top of a spur accessible from Monash Valley that led from Anzac Cove to high ground beyond the beach. This photograph was taken before the construction of the terracing and other improvements carried out at Malone's direction.

[MSX 2552]

8.6.15

Dear Kirkwood,

I have just written a formal letter of thanks to the Chairman Stratford Patriotic Committee, for a cable of congratulations to me and men. I don't know who such Chairman is, but have ½ a notion that it is yourself. In any case I would like to add a few lines to the formal letter. I don't know whether the congratulations is special or general. My Bn has been in a couple of very special jobs, and done very well, and is now on another, in which it is making its mark. Any way the cable was welcome, and I am communicating it to the men and especially the Stratford men: than whom none have done better. We have had and are having a strenuous time, but it suits us.

We have had, as you can probably picture from our casualty list, a somewhat rocky time, but are very fit and well, that is the rest of us. Weather A.1. (but hot and too many flies!) Food, army ration, all right. Work, plenty, night and day.

Give my kind regards to all your people, and all other friends.

Yours sincerely
W.G. Malone

[MSX 2546]

June 9th 1915

Took over Quinn's Post at 9 am with 2 of my coys. Had a good look round. On the whole I like the change, but there is an awful lot of work to do. Such a dirty dilapidated, unorganised post. Still I like work and will revel in straightening things up. Quite a length of the trench unoccupiable, owing to bomb throwing superiority of Turks. No places for men to fall in. The local reserve is posted too far away and yet there is at present no ground prepared on which they could be comfortably put. I selected a new HQ shelter for myself, and gave orders that every rifle shot and bomb from the Turks was to be promptly returned at least twofold. We can and will beat them at their own game.

Lieutenant Terence McSharry, the Australian adjutant of Quinn's Post who

Opposite

An aerial view showing part of the maze of trenches that made up the ANZAC and Turkish front lines, June 1915.

Australian War Memorial

had played a leading part in its defence, initially stayed on to assist Malone. His first impression was not favourable. McSharry wrote in his diary that Malone was 'an old woman . . . I am fed up you don't expect too much red tape in the presence of <u>the</u> enemy. One good fight will perhaps tune [?] him up.' He did not appreciate Malone's tongue-in-cheek remarks about planting a garden at Quinn's, and on 14 June wrote: 'I hope the Turks don't attack while he is here.' [Terence McSharry diary, 9 and 14 Jun 1915, 3DRL 3250, Australian War Memorial, Canberra; Peter Stanley, *Quinn's Post, Anzac, Gallipoli* (Crows Nest, 2005), pp. 107-9.]

June 9th to 24th July 1915

Been very busy right thro', too busy to write this up. We soon got the upper hand of the Turk riflemen and bomb throwers, and have completely changed the position. The Auckland and Canterbury Bns which we relieved, went off as if they were leaving a death trap. They were cowed, and dreaded being in the position. We have terraced the ground so that the troops in reserve are together instead of being dotted about in all sorts of holes, like conies[13] and somewhere in the Bible it speaks about "the conies in the hills being feeble folk". We have made roads to the top of the hill at the back so that we can counter attack. Fire positions have been fixed for the supporting troops and in less than a minute we can sheet the hillcrest with lead from 200 rifles, the men being side by side in lines under their NCO's and officers. I got 2 machine guns mounted to sweep ½ of our front which before had to depend on some 50 rifles to stop the Turks who had only some 15 yards to cross to get from their trench to ours. Above all the men are inspired with the conviction that they have superiority over the Turks and are getting a fair run for their lives. We have so wrecked and racked the Turks trenches, that they now have the 'dread' and have almost abandoned their front trenches opposite us. Improvements made every day, overhead cover erected over terraces, making them sun and shrapnel and bomb proof. Blankets nailed along West fronts keep out the glare and heat of the Westerly sun and can be rolled up at night, out of the way. The Post has become absolutely the best in the Defence and the safest. A Turk deserter told our HQ "That the Turks had found the mining and fighting so hazardous opposite Quinn's Post (this one) that they had to call for volunteers to man the trenches opposite it, and that every such volunteer was promoted to corporal. That the shooting of the soldiers in Quinn's Post was so deadly that they (the Turks) had closed up all their loopholes and men were forbidden to use them. They had lost such a number of men shot thro the loophole in the head and killed."

Opposite above

Terraces and shelters on the hillside at Quinn's Post, July 1915. The extent of the improvements carried out under Malone's command can be clearly seen.

Australian War Memorial

Opposite below

July 1915. A view of the shelters at Quinn's Post, looking towards Pope's and Russell's Top.

Australian War Memorial

Good on the Wellington Bn, my gallant men. They outshot and outbombed their opponents and in 8 days had obtained such superiority, that they had got all over the Turks. We recovered, regained the 50 yards of abandoned trench, and now one can walk from one end to the other of the front fire trench. The place has been scraped and cleaned and repaired, and put in order. We have been congratulated by Generals Birdwood, Godley and Lotbiniere[14] and their anxiety is at an end. They were very nice to me. The life has been strenuous we have thrown on an average 200 bombs in the 24 hours, and rifle shooting goes on steadily thro' the day but mostly at distant targets, for the Turks hardly ever fire out of their trenches in the day time. They do a bit at night. Our casualties have been small, 4 or 5 killed, say 20 wounded, including 3 officers: Jardine (2nd time) Wells and Carrington.[15]

I got the skin knocked off my right cheek by the casing of a bullet, that came just passed my head having struck an iron loop hole and on another occasion I was straightening up some wire entanglement and a bullet or bomb struck it and splashed my hands and face with small bits of the casing. I can now say I have actually shed blood! A few drops. Nothing like that spent from a razor cut! I am a lucky one all the same. The garrison is 900

A photograph of Quinn's Post taken by C.E.W. Bean during his visit on 17 July 1915.

men, and stays in 8 days and then goes out for 8 days rest. I stop [stay?] on all the time. The Canterbury Bn alternate with the Wellington Bn and sometimes some Auckland or Otago men come in to make up numbers. After 5 continuous weeks work by me, the Brigadier said he would like me to take a rest. I said if I could go to Imbros all right, but that it would be no rest to go into a rest gully, and that I would sooner stop and work in the Post. He soon got Genl Birdwood's and Genl Godley's warm approval and away I went with Short my staff officer to Imbros. Went over by SS *El Kaheri* staying on board all night, landing at Pyrgos[16] near Cape Kephalos, at about 9 am next morning, a Tuesday [**6 July**].

By noon, Short and I went off for a walking tour round the Island. Our itinerary was Pyrgos to the Capital Panaghia, then to Kastro, back to Panaghia past Gliki, then to San Theodoros, back to Panaghia then to Skimude, to Pyrgos on South Coast. Then by South Coast to starting point which we reached at 5 pm on the Saturday. Met Genl Godley, with Admiral de Robeck[17] (who commands the Fleet here). Genl Godley was very genial and told me to take 2 or 3 days more and have a <u>rest</u>. I and Short had made up our mind to go back that night. We were glad to stop, as our trip had not been physically restful. Admiral de Robeck on my being introduced said "Oh, you are the man that turned the Turks down at Quinn's Post. You deserve a rest." Imbros, our Mulberry Island as I think of it, owing to that being the only fruit in season. Huge trees, by the wayside, smothered with luscious fruit-common property. It will not "carry", and is not picked except by the children and probably a few jam makers. The Island is very hilly, but there are considerable areas of flat valley land, well cultivated – Grapes, figs, walnuts, pears, plums etc. The people, blue eyed Greeks, lead the simple life, self contained, growing everything almost that they want. Old time cultivation tools and methods. We enjoyed the trip immensely. Back to Quinn's Post on Tuesday [**13 July**] morning. On the whole glad to be back. Found a welcome letter from Mater awaiting me. Visited by [**17 July**], Capt Bean, Australian war correspondent, Mr Nivenson,[18] [sic, Nevinson] English provincial do/do [ditto] Mr Ross, NZ do/do. I liked Nevinson, <u>especially</u> Bean, seemed Australian or ½ so. Ross, nondescript. On another day Ashmead Bartlett the, English W/Cpdent came with the others, and actually kinematographed part of the Post, at back, taking in the terraces, and the men at work etc. Then I took him into the fire trench and he took some more pictures. He seemed a bit swollen-headed, and full of his own importance. I gave him a couple of thrills, by taking him to places open to Turk fire at about 300 yds range, and then pointing out to him the Turks

A chute used to
remove spoil from
one of the many
mine shafts dug at
Quinn's Post.

trenches. I had asked him if he wanted to see them. But generally they are looked at thro' a periscope.

Mater seems [to be] settling down at home, but is evidently fretting over the war and our separation. She writes often, as do I. I get spare time every day. We the last 3 nights have been expecting a massed attack by the Turks. They have received 100,000 reinforcements, and are expected by their Govt to drive us into the sea. Yesterday was their Constitution Day,[19] and we all expected them to mark it by a big attack. But so far it has not come off. We do so wish they would come on. We do so wish that they would. It has been slow waiting waiting, shooting and bombing at small things.

I had a trip on the Destroyer *Colne* to have a look at the country N of our army position, with view to an attack on [Hill] 971 from that side. I like on the whole, the look of the country. It looks as tho' the plan I outlined weeks ago, will be – or something like carried out.

Today **[24 July]** at midday, the Turks discharged a mine opposite our No. 4 sub post, close to their own trenches. We think they got scared and let off prematurely. They have in 2 months fired 3 mines, we – 28! Brilliant weather all thro'. Hot, but except at about 3 to 7 pm, a nice northerly breeze. Many of the men go about with only shorts, boots and socks and hats – not forgetting identity disc.

Edmond was wounded 3 or 4 days ago [on 20 July]. A bomb exploded near him on Walkers Ridge position and drove a bullet thro' his leg above the knee. He will be all right.

I must try and keep the diary going now day by day.

Second Lieutenant Charles Saunders DCM, a capable and strong-willed New Zealand engineer officer, was responsible for much of the construction work undertaken at Quinn's Post when Malone was in command. Entries in his diary about the construction of bomb-proof shelters give a good insight into Malone's command style and conditions at the post:

June 27th 1915: I discussed with Colonel M [Malone] how I should do the job; he was [sic] an amateur Architect and had great ideas of a bottom plate let in the ground, uprights dovetailed in it and then a top plate . . . Now timber was scarce and I saw I could save the bottom plate by sharpening the uprights and driving them in with an mawl and just nail the top plate across the tops of the uprights. He wouldn't have it, so I said no more but decided I must do it that way as I hadn't enough timber for his way.

June 29th 1915: Got quite a lot done on
terraces. Making a good job of them; no need
for levelling; we just drive the uprights in a little
more where necessary; quite a quick job. Colonel M
looked it over then called me into his dugout. He
told me that this way was far better than his, in that
it was quicker and quite strong enough, although
his way was a stronger job; he wanted to know why
I had done it this way after our talk yesterday [sic]. I
told him I had measured up, found I hadn't enough
timber [for] his way and couldn't get any more. He
was quite satisfied.

No wonder flies are multiplying. Almost every
upright we drove in, went into a grave — the whole hillside at this spot
was one huge grave — Turk and Colonial together. It was awful. [C. W.
Saunders diary (copy), MS-Papers-73336-1, Alexander Turnbull Library.]

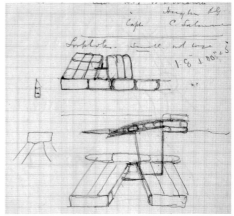

Malone's design
for a loophole at
Quinn's Post.

Alexander Turnbull Library

[MSX 2551]

10-6-15

My very dear wife,

I was very glad to get your cable of 22nd May, telling me of your safe arrival.
I only got it 2 or 3 days ago. I have been anxiously awaiting a letter from
you giving me all your news, but so far it has not arrived. No doubt you
have written but our mail is very much delayed. I am very busy indeed and
have been for some time. I was given charge of a Post – got it into order and
then was changed over to another Post which is the most important of all. It
entails a big lot of work, requiring as it did reorganising pretty well from top
to bottom. I am very well, but we turn out at 3 am, so don't get too much
sleep.

The change of home is a bit of a bother as I do like to be fixed up
decently. As I write I look out to sea. The flies as usual are our chief trouble.
Ken Munro[20] should be here soon. A lot of reinforcements arrived and he
was with them but stayed back, ….. [illegible] as he was not very well.

I do so hope that you are comfortably settled.

With all my love to you,
Yr loving husband

[MSX 2553]

[10-15 June?]

Quinn's Post Anzac. Pa [Peninsula] of Gallipoli[21]

List Work

The O/C No 3 Section
[Brig Gen F.E. Johnston]

Anzac Defence

I beg to ask you to reconsider your decision that working parties be furnished by the garrison of this post and not by the General Reserve. My reasons for asking this are:

1. That both the Divisional and Army Commanders have respectively emphatically impressed upon me, and especially upon Post Commander generally the absolute necessity of the garrison being constantly in the most alert and ready state possible.

2. That both the other commander of No 3 Section (Colonel Chauvel and Colonel Hughes) unhesitatingly decided that these parties were to be found by the General Reserve.

3. That the turn of active duty in the post is 24 hours, out of every 48 hours.

    That the [most convenient deleted by WGM] hour for changing relief is 9 am each day.

4. That the work done by these working parties is of a permanent or quasi permanent nature relating to the Post itself and its defence and not to the garrison itself except indirectly.

5. That if the garrison in addition to its tour of duty of 24 Hours has to work for 4 hours, the men employed will have done, out of 48 hours, 28 hours work, in addition of course to certain necessary fatigues particularly[?] of their own. And that their efficiency in the defence of the Post will suffer and the degree of alertness and readiness insisted upon by the Army and Divnsl Commanders not be maintained.

6. That the parties can easily be found by the General Reserve, and that if they are not so found, the work due by the respective units will be as follows:

a   the Garrison employed 28 hours out of 48 hours.

b   The General Reserve 8 to 12 hours out of 48 hours.

I trust that you will see your way to provide that the parties are found by the General Reserve. If you cannot see your way to do that I respectfully ask that the matter be referred to the Divisional Commander for a ruling.

[MSX 2551]

Flag Lieutenant H.S. Bowlby, RN   ANZAC
HMS *Triad*   16 June 1915

Dear Mr Bowlby,

Yours of 10 Inst to hand. I have made enquiries about your cousin, Lt Menteath and can now answer your questions:

1. In endeavour to make further advance with his Platoon, he tried to cross a machine gun swept zone, but was hit, in the wrist, then in the groin. Lance Corporal Haynes[22] went along and bandaged him up and then tried to carry him into a safer place, but unfortunately Menteath was then shot thro' the head. He gave Lance Corporal Haynes his will.

2. He was buried in a marked place about 20 feet behind the trenches which had been dug, by his company when further advance was impossible. A wooden cross was put over the grave which is near a growing pine tree, and can be located in the future.

3. I cannot find out anything about the message on the envelope.

I would like to say that it was at Menteath's special request, that Haynes tried to carry him out. Haynes first of all tried to drag him, then tried to carry him crawling, but ultimately had to stand up and pick him up.

One might think that Haynes should have left him where he was after bandaging, which experience now shows is generally the best thing to do, while firing is going on, but Menteath unfortunately thought otherwise. In any case the 2nd wound in the groin was I believe a fatal one but no one can say. His watch was smashed by the bullet that hit his wrist. His sword should be with his kit in the *Achaia*.

I would like to say that your cousin was essentially a soldier – very brave, determined and keen. He was truly a gallant gentleman. He had been thro' another inferno here on 27th April, when 17 men were killed right round him. I had a great personal liking and regard for him, as had all those who knew him. Please accept and convey to your and his people, my sympathy in the great loss sustained. . . .

Wm.G. Malone

16th June 1915

My Beloved,

I sent you a letter on 10th Inst and a scenic post card. Since the 10th I got your letter of 13th May (also dated 15th and 18th May) posted 20th May and your letter of 23rd May. It was and is such a great joy getting your letters and it was a relief to know that you were safely landed and established with Norah and the 3 small ones. I hope that everything will continue to go well with you. England should be beautiful now.

I am very very busy here – reorganising, re-arming and generally putting things in the best possible condition. I am to stay on as O/C of this Post. My Battalion which came in with me and have done splendid work, goes out tomorrow for a rest and another Bn comes in. The responsibility is great, but soon I hope to have things so fixed up that there will be no anxiety. This Post has been a source of anxiety to the whole Army, so I was honored [sic] by being taken away from another, the next most important, and put in charge of this. The only difficulty I have is in getting people above me to give me what I know are essentials (and which they ought to know). My path is consequently not rose strewn. Still I am getting gradually my way. Both Genls Birdwood (our Army Commander) and Godley (our Divisional Commander) called on me or rather saw me yesterday and said that they were "delighted" that I was in charge of the Post, which is a very high compliment. Genl Birdwood said also that he had written the Hon T. Mackenzie. NZs High Comr in London telling him the same thing. The job is strenuous, but I am revelling in it, and needless to say doing all I can. I get to bunk generally about 10 pm and then subject to alarms etc, don't turn out until 3 am.

I had a touch of dysentery yesterday but will be all right by tomorrow. Have put myself on milk (Swiss) and biscuits, which worked my cure at El Kubri, otherwise I am very fit and well as usual. The flies are my only annoyance, but I have a sort of hut, on the side of a hill, and by putting a bit of muslin (which I fortunately brought with me as a mosquito net) as a window and blocking up the door with a blanket, I can periodically chase the flies out and keep clear of them for a time. I am out and about most of the daytime so get along fairly well. The weather is gloriously fine and sunny, but hot in the daytime, the nights cool. Some dust, this a few days ago when there was a S wind. I look out and see the sea and Imbros in the distance. Our Section Commander is sick – pleurisy and Col Johnston, our Brigadier, also ? Enteric, so it is on the board that I get the Brigade and then the Section, which is generally commanded by a "General". It will comfort you I think to know, that the higher the command I get the further I get away, for most of the time, from the frontline, and from the "fire". I hope always that I shall be able to do my duty. I will do my best without "fear or favour" and God, thanks to so many prayers that are put up for me, will help me.

It must have been a great trial to you, the risk of being torpedoed and I am glad the nurses helped you. The "Huns" are too barbarous for words. They are "swine" as we class human swine. [23] . . .

I am glad the Vaseys and Fred Westerton met you and did all they could for you. You must have been glad you dear girl, to have got at your journey's end and settled down. Rest all you can and get fat! as you have always desired, though I must say you look quite plump in your last lovely photos. I have them before me as I write. It is a wet morning and so I am taking time to write.

I am glad you got your letters all right. You can be sure that it is the Post that is out, if you get no letter when you should. I write every week a little letter at least, and will always do so. I can tell you where, the letters of 18th and 22 April were written from, on board a ship. It was the *Itonus*, a Transport from Alexandria to Port Mudros in Lemnos, and the place not to be stated was Port Mudros. We sailed thence on Sunday 25th April and landed at ANZAC COVE about 2 miles North of GABA TEPE which you can find on a map of the Peninsula. It is very rugged country round Anzac Cove – great gullies and hills and razor back tracks. We stayed until 6th May and then went to Cape Helles, Sedd-el. Bahr, and were in the battle of 8th May. Then in trenches dug by ourselves, returning here on 19th May. And here we are near ANZAC COVE. My Battalion has made a name for itself and deserves it. I will tell you all about it when I see you, tho I suppose the newspapers have something to say. . . .

As to sending me vests etc, please don't do so. I have the 2 silk shirts and the 3 light vests, you got me. The winter ones I have never worn, and are away at the Base. What I have are quite good, and I cannot carry any more. I will let you know when I am in want of anything. I want you, as you know. If you could only fly over for a little visit, it would be a great joy, but that is not possible. There is a talk of Bulgaria coming in. If she does, this part of the war might be over in 10 days so Genl Birdwood told me. And then I think we would get a chance of going to England before going to Flanders; that is if we don't go to Germany via Servia and Austria.[24] As you say my dearest, it will not matter when we go, so long as we are together, but I bar the "<u>desert</u>" unless it is wintertime. Still I want you to see the places I have seen while away from you. Capt Home has at last been promoted Major as from 1/9/15. All sorts of Doctors were landings here with rank as Major, who had not done any military service before and it was not fair, so I backed Home up and have at last succeeded.

With all my love,
Yr loving husband

ANZAC – near Gaba Tepe
19.6.15

My very dear Aunt [Agnes Vasey],

Your letter of 2nd March but addressed to me in New Zealand has just come to hand.

By now, my wife and Norah will have been to see you. I have heard from my wife that she got to England on 19th May – all well. I was very glad and a bit relieved because there was some danger of the *Rotorua* being torpedoed.

I am very well, and have gone through the work here without a scratch. Thanks to our Lord. I am always very busy, and there is always a great lot to do. The weather is lovely, but very hot in the middle of the day and afternoon. We have a plague of flies – the brutes! Battlefields such as we have here, produce them woefully and then most soldiers, on active service especially are very untidy and not very clean in their ways. We have however practically no sickness.

With much love and looking forward to seeing you in a few months time.

Yr affect nephew,
Wm.G. Malone

[MSX 2552]

Quinn's Post
Anzac
19.6.15

Dear Richardson

Yours of yesterday to hand. Thanks for same and news. Things are a bit slow here too. The NZ.I. Bde has taken over the position held by the 4th Austn I. Bgde, and it is a bit of a clean up I can tell you. In this post we are right up against the Turks, 15 yards away at one place, mostly 50 yds. We bomb each other gaily, with superiority to us <u>now</u>.

It is a bit late for that winning movement, or rather it will be much more difficult. When a month ago the door was wide open, it is now shut more or less with ? a Divn [Division] of Turks and lines of entrenchment. In front of us here, tiers and tiers of trenches, which being on the forward slope, ought be untenable, but artillery or its ammunition is scarce.

One Major Sykes with a NZ 18 pdr Battery does some very fine shooting right over me. He cuts it down sometimes to 18 feet over <u>my</u> head. In the dark, those red balls seem to be coming straight at me. He shoots from a bit lower level. I am right in his line of fire. I am very busy and have a touch of diarrhoea [dys crossed out by WGM]. Very well and fit.

Col Johnston is sick so I am Acting Brigadier. The billet has been and is since we came here a sinecure and I <u>work</u> as O/C of this Post. The Bns are handed over to Os/C Posts, under a Defence Section Commander. Hence the sinecure. When the present job is finished, I think I shall have to try and get on[?] out of the Brigade. I don't seem to be able to get on with Col J., my last communication with him he dubbed "extremely insubordinate".[25] He had refused a request for a working party, and I asked him to refer the matter to Divl HQ for a ruling. Glad to hear you are all well, and hope good luck will always be with you and the RND [Royal Naval Division] staff, of whom I have such pleasant recollections.

Have you, any spare <u>sand bags</u>, or machine guns at Cape Helles? . . .

Yours sincerely
W.G. Malone

[MSX 2551]

ANZAC
Quinn's Post
20.6.15

My dear Hart,

I was so glad to hear from you, . . . and yet sorry to hear that your wound has turned out serious. I have missed you very much, as has everyone I am sure, and hope you will be absolutely all right not later than the doctor folk say. I know how you feel about missing the work here, but that cannot be helped, the fortune of war. We heard that you were to get a DSO and I have been waiting for official announcement, but so far it has not so far as we know been made. In case as we all hope that it is correct and accept my very hearty congratulations.[26]

Did you get any letters from me. I wrote twice, and Cox wrote sending you a blank cheque on R/Fund, to help our fellows in case of need, but I gather from your letter that you did not get his letter or the cheque. We are very glad that you and [Major Edward] Saunders took the bull by the horns, and I will get your action confirmed.[27]

We have been getting on all right. Stayed on the Ridge where you were wounded – now known as Walker's Ridge – for about 9 days, digging, digging, made it impregnable, then shipped to Cape Helles, 6th May. Took part in Battle of Krithia on 8th May. The Bn making one of the finest advances possible, some 1200 to 1400 yds steady unstopping advance, over shrapnel, machine gun and rifle fire swept ground . . .

The continually moving target beat the artillerymen and our losses were (what looked like miraculously) small, over 3 or 4 lines of trenches held by British Regulars, then 200 to 300 yards further when enfilade by gun and rifle fire and shrapnel and the stop of the troops on our flanks, sent our chaps down for practically the first time to shoot and dig and dig . . .

Start [of the advance] at 10.30 am! if you please. Positions sketched about 11 am up to 4 pm. Then Ruahine Coy sent in to back W.W. Coast Coy up, as a general advance of all troops ordered for 5.30 pm, but it went off to Right and prolonged our Bn line, somewhat. At 5.30, in spite of my pointing out that unless the troops on our flanks came up and went forward we couldn't, we were ordered to "fix bayonets, go right through, no shilly-shally", Colonel F.E. Johnston thus giving me the order! I pointed out that for troops at varying distance, from 0 to 1400 to 1500 yards to start an attack at same instant didn't give the 0 people (the Wellington Bn being the only Bn that had gained any fresh ground) a chance, in face of enfilade m. [machine] gun and rifle fire, not to mention direct artillery fire and all against an invisible foe, in scrub. I was sat on, and was practically told I was more bother than I was worth! Anyhow, A Coy and D Coy went forward some, until stopped by our own shrapnel fire, not to mention, the Turks cross enfilade m [machine]-gun and rifle fire etc. Auckland came up same and then went right back, and then they (A and D Coys) had to go back to the trenches they had dug – prolonging those of B and C Coys. The rear lines of troops never came right up. We hung on and at night improved and by morning after repulsing a weak Turk counter attack, were secure. We stayed in 4 days and nights. I got up 4 extra machine guns into the position after the 1st day. The net result of the NZ I Bde and Austln Bde attack, was the bit of ground say 250 yds gained by the Wellington Inf Bn. The cost I may not tell you, but we WIB, lost over 200. By a night advance I am quite satisfied we could have gained the same ground and if not more, with probably no loss at all!! Such is the sense of war as practised by people who are supposed to know better. *C'est magnifique, mais ce n'est pas la guerre*[28]. That is my criticism of this war in these parts so far. We were relieved. I am quite satisfied, that the NZ officers have absolutely nothing to learn from the imported man and that active service has taught the latter nothing. On 19th May we came back here, went into reserve, for about 10 days to enable Auckland and Otago who were more or less demoralised – that is between you and me – to recover, and then the Bde took over from an Austn Bde part of their defence position. I was O/C Courtenay's [sic, Courtney's] Post, with our Bn, then when the Bn expected to go into reserve after 8 days strenuous trench work was sent with our Bn into Quinn's Post, which everybody, in Major Youngs words considered "b____y hell" (Young temporarily commands the Auckland Bn – vice Plugge wounded). I am O/C and remain in I suppose while the NZ Bde is here. The garrison is changed every 8 days. Canterbury are in now. It has been and is a job reorganising, rearranging etc. The Turk trenches are only 15 yds to 50 yds away, and when we came in had superiority of fire and bombing. We altered that in 3 days. I ordered for every shot or bomb fired at least two should go back. The Post was too dilapidated for words. Now it is becoming one of the show places, and in another week, any anxiety on my part will I believe be at an end. I am already inclined to pray for the Turks to come on. Still one gets very little rest – always out at 3 am. One thing we are so close to the Turks that they cannot shell us, without hitting their own works, and vice versa, but all sorts of bombs are hurled to and fro at all hours, sometimes we get a Japanese bomb from one of our other posts, fired at the Turks, but misdirected. Yesterday one burst over and close to my shelter – wounded 6 of the garrison! I am asking for an enquiry. It was fired by Australians, at they said 4 or 5 Turks. Fancy using a mortar bomb for such a purpose!

Cunningham is running the Bn and doing all right. Cox has his majority as O/C Ruahine Coy. Harston is running HB Coy and doing well. In fact my dear Hart our officers, N.C.O.s and men have turned up thoro' trumps. I am full of regard and admiration for them.

Home has been and is a regular brick with our wounded. He has got his majority. One of my sons, has been wounded 3 shrapnel bullets thro' the leg and one thro' the forearm and 2 grazes, doing all right when I saw him. I have been and am very well, bar a 5-day course of dysentery – now just about finished – and have got off free of injury, though yesterday my 1st blood was drawn, a splash of nickel just cutting the skin on my cheek! I am quite proud of it!

Our weather is lovely tho' hot. The flies are awful. Col Johnston is on sick list. I had Bde for 2 days and then Col Braithwaite was appointed. I am thinking of asking what I have done! I am afraid the NZ Army is <u>not</u> for NZ officers (no matter how hard we work) in its higher commands. Genls Birdwood and Godley respectively tell me, they are delighted that I am O/C Quinn's Post, but they or rather Genl G. is not delighted enough to let me even temporarily command the NZ I Bde. The work at present in the Bde is an absolute sinecure. Goodbye, my dear Hart. With my affectionate regards.

Yr sincerely,
Wm.G. Malone

Anzac
Quinn's Post
22.6.15

My beloved

. . . All goes well here, and I am over my little complaint (after 6 days tho') without having had to go on the sick list. The Post is improving every day, but I shall be glad when my own Battalion comes back as garrison. It is by far the best in the Bde tho' I say so. The flies multiply, but if I have to be inside in the daytime, shut out the daylight from my shelter and light a candle after drawing out the flies.

If you would send me a muslin cage, say 6 ft square, without a bottom, I should be glad, just any cheap muslin would do. I could then get my meals in peace and be quite a luxurious soldier. But you know how I hate flies, and there are extra reasons here to dislike them.

Weather is lovely, but hot in the daytime. I suppose you have seen Aunt Agnes by now. . . . Give her my love and tell her I am looking forward to seeing her ere [before] the year is out. It is expected here that as Venizelos[29] has been returned with a big majority, that Greece will join the Allies in the war and that then Bulgaria must join too. Therefore Turkey will soon have to make peace. Progress is slow here. Trench warfare – all the same as Flanders.

I have been shortened! Gone into "shorts". They are so cool and free. They are very much in fashion. I still clean my boots everyday and shave and manage to get a body wash everyday, but water is scarce. Many go down to the sea and bathe, but I am like a Captain on the Bridge, and cannot get away. I am sitting at a biscuit box *escritoire*,[30] with your dear photo at my right hand. My shelter is like this:

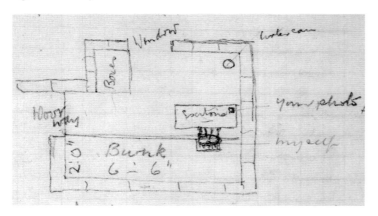

Above

Malone's drawing of his escritoire, which was made out of biscuit boxes.

Alexander Turnbull Library

Left

The layout of Malone's dugout.

Alexander Turnbull Library

Walls are part dugout and part sandbags. I sit on edge my bunk, where shown. I can look out down a huge gully to the sea, with Imbros in the distance, the sea about 1½ miles away. My shelter is on the side of the gully cliff near the tops. My escritoire (I think I shall patent it) is much admired and is very useful. One can't sit on it as made owing to its legs being somewhat fragile, 4 strips of the box lid 2" x ½". Not many flowers here, too many soldiers on a somewhat limited area, tho' away in the gullies there are plenty. The longest day is over and they are long here – 3.30 am to 9 pm. But we have started keeping naval signal time that is 24 hours in the day – midnight 0 – midday 12, 1 pm 13, 2 pm 14 and so on. It is now 8 pm i.e. 20.00 and now 21.35. I have just come back from a tour round the position seeing things in order for the night and making special provision at two points. It is a beautiful moonlight night. The evening and nights are delightful, except for the everlasting smack and crack, and clatter-clatter-clatter and boom and bang and "hunch" of rifle, machine gun, gun and bomb, which however we hardly notice nearly two months of such noises night and day makes them almost unnoticed. I think we shall have a quiet night and I shall be able to sleep until 3 am (I mean 3.00). I am feeling quite all right tonight and full of go. Thanks be to God.

. . . . I see England is shaping towards increased military training. She must adopt it. Had she done so in 1908 when Lord Roberts pleaded and argued so strongly for it, the war would never have started or if it had, it would have been over by now. I am not at all favourably impressed by the Territorial troops I have seen here. They are only ¼ as good as our NZ troops. We were attached at Cape Helles to the Royal Naval Division, Churchill's troops and we saw also Lancashire and Manchester Territorial Division troops. This was at the Battle of Krithia and I was disappointed. We fought thro' and over and with the 29th Division, Regulars, and they are good stuff, but not as good as ours. Still we must remember, that the introduction to "fire" was sudden and very hot. I have unwittingly let myself write about things that I didn't mean to but it is so astounding to me to think that England and Englishmen, Britishers have been so narrow-minded and foolish to go on as they have been and be found unready from [sic, for] war. [Two lines deleted.] I have deleted these lines as against censor rules. We too have suffered here from that unreadiness. Haldane ought to be crucified. Still, I will knock off. Why bother you with the subject. I know you have always been and are at one with me in the matter.

How do the children like England. I know that you and Norah are delighted, that is apart from the war. I am sure that everybody is pleased to see you and will do their best to make your life as pleasant as can be. I think of you always in my spare time, and long for our reunion. I am content tho' to see my work thro', especially now that I know I am really of use. Goodbye with all my love.

Yr loving husband,

x_____x

[MSX-2552]

[25 June 1915]
Quinn's Post
Anzac
Gallipoli Peninsula

Dear Miss Stuart-Menteath

Your letter of 27th Ulto has only recently reached me. On the 16th Inst, I wrote to your cousin Flag Lt H.S. Bowlby on the *Triad*, in reply to a letter from him, giving him as much information as I could as to your brave brother's death. I send you a copy of the letter, in case there is any delay in the original being communicated to you.

The action I refer to as of the 27th April was one in which my Battalion and especially your brother's Coy distinguished itself. It took place 2 days after the 1st landing was affected. We were sent up a long steep ridge opening out on to a flat, covered with high scrub, some 500 feet above the beach, to reinforce some Australian troops. The Turks were in great strength and had machine guns and rifles trained, from across a gully so as to sweep the flat. Tracks led from the ridge track and these were marked with range marks and commanded by rifle fire. The fighting was consequently wood fighting of the severest. My men could see nothing, but were mowed down, as they charged with the bayonet thro the scrub. Our casualties were over 40% all in about the 1st hour of the fighting. The 2 leading Coys (that of your brother was the 1st to go in), gained the edge of the gully and the crest of a neck which connected the flat with a plateau beyond, and then dug in under the very severe fire. By night we had dug right in, and made absolutely safe the left of the whole Division – nay army. We stayed in the trenches dug, for 9 days and nights, repulsing all attacks, with slight loss to ourselves. (We were then relieved and sent to Cape Helles, to help in the attack on KRITHIA.) Your brother particularly distinguished himself. At one time a number of the Australians who had lost their officers, were inclined to retire but your brother took them under his charge and stiffened them up, so that they went on fighting valiantly, until they were nearly all killed, round and about him. It seemed a miracle that anyone escaped without hurt, on that flat, but your brother didn't get even a scratch. I really thought and hoped after that, that he had a charmed life, and would go thro the war unhurt. I regret his death very much, and you all have my very sincere sympathy. His death however was one of the best a man can die. He had been with me since August of last year, and I had formed a great liking, respect and admiration for him.

If I can do anything for you at any time I am at your service.

Yours sincerely
W.G. Malone

––––––––

Quinn's Post
Anzac
Gallipoli Peninsula
25.6.15

My dear Charles [Westerton]

. . . I am extremely busy here, . . . I am O/C of this Post one which was causing our Generals great anxiety. . . . I was shifted with my Bn, from another post, and told that I was relied on to improve things. I have been here 16 days. . . . "The Turks [according to a deserter] think our troops here are wonderful shots and on account of the number of men shot in the head and face through the loopholes in the trenches, orders have been issued that men are to keep away from loopholes and when using them simply to put the rifle into position and fire."

It has been and is strenuous work, night and day, rifles and bombs. Our daily average of bombs thrown is 182. Our frontage is only 200 yards. Owing to the Turks bombing 50 yards of our fire trench had been abandoned, that is no one could go into it, as the Turks from their trench 15 yards away pitched bombs into it. Bombing cuts two ways so the 1st day I came in I ordered 2 bombs to be thrown for every one of the Turks. Result, we have resumed occupation of the abandoned trench and the Turks trench opposite is an awful wreck. The more my men get to do the more they distinguish themselves. I am naturally very proud of them. No better soldiers in the world. But enough of Turks. . . .

W.G. Malone

MSX 2551

Quinn's Post
Anzac
26.6.15

My dear Terry,

I am so glad to hear from you that you are on the right road to recovery. I have been wondering how you were getting on and where you were. I asked Home to try and get you sent to England, so as to give you the best chance. I heard that it was frightfully hot in Cairo. . . . I am well, but have had about 8 days of dysentery. Managed to keep off the sick list and am now I think and hope round the corner. . . .

It is hot here, and the flies are a great nuisance. Too many unburied dead Turks, close to our trenches.

Goodbye my dear boy – get quite well soon and take care of yourself.

Your loving father,
Wm.G. Malone

Quinn's Post
ANZAC
Gallipoli Peninsula
26.6.15

My beloved,

I am sending you some photos, which I have managed to get taken and printed. I hope you won't mind me sending you the one of the dead Turks. It is a memento of a remarkable day, and place and I want to keep it. If I don't send it to you, it may get lost here.

. . . . I showed Capt Coningham (10 Gurkha Rifles), who was my Staff Officer at El Kubri, your photos today. He said she is a "lovely girl" and so say I and all of us. Goodnight my beloved. With all my love.

Yours for aye,
Your husband

Quinn's Post
Anzac
29.6.15

Genl Sir Wm Birdwood

Dear General,

Allow me to congratulate you on the new honour [KCMG] bestowed upon
you by His G. Majesty. All my officers ask to be allowed to join me in the
congratulations. We all hope that you will have honour added to honour to
the full measure of life.

  This Post is now quite a haven of safety. One can put one's head and
shoulders over the parapet of the front trenches without even drawing fire.

Yours obediently,
Wm.G. Malone

Quinn's Post
Anzac
3.7.15

My best beloved,

At last letters from you, 4 all in a heap, dates 26th May, June 4th, 8th and
15th. It is over 3 weeks since the receipt of word from you. Imagine my
delight. . . . . I write, you can be sure, at least weekly.

  . . . . I hope that long ago you have got my letters. Of course your change
of address, may cause some delay. . . . I must tell you, how extra delightful
it was to get your letters today. I had been up since 3 am and had just at 12
(noon) come down from part of the post, on to which the Turks had brought
a new surprise gun and bombed one of our machine gun positions. I had
been for about 3 hours very busy with my machine gun officer and some
engineers, planning "deceit" and a new position just alongside the old one.
I think we have worked our point. It was a very interesting morning and I
was just coming in, thinking the mail will be in tomorrow, when lo as I got to
my shelter, I was handed 3 of your letters and 2 from Norah. Your 4th came
when I was reading the others. I waved my letters to Major Cunningham
who is commanding the Wellington Battalion while I am commanding
this Post, and some other officers. They all congratulated me and were so

pleased. They know how I love my wife and look forward to her letters. I plunged into my "home" telling my Staff Officer that I would see no one, for an hour, unless on "urgent" affairs and then spread myself to get all the joy and delight I could out of the dear letters. I drove out the flies, put the letters in due date order and then read and reread, for an hour. The dear little photo of you and the Pickerings at Montevideo is a delight too. You do look so young and slim and pretty and aristocratic. But how I wished that it was I and not Mr Pickering that was with you. At 1 o'clock or rather 13.00 I had lunch with my S.O. we 2 mess together, the garrison troops change every 8 days, but we stay on. We had, I think I must tell you lest you believe we are badly fed, for lunch, lentils and toast, tinned kippered herring, cheese and tea no milk however. Tonight however some tinned milk arrives, from Imbros Nestles 1/- per tin! Also some sardines and canned fruits are coming! Prices you may be interested to know: sardines 8d 2lb, tin fruit 2/-. Still we must have a little change of diet, and we have nothing else to spend money on!

I am all right again now, but have, I am not sorry to say, got rid of all superfluous fat, and so don't feel the heat much. I am like "all steel" now, bones, flesh, muscle and nerves. I can climb and spring like a goat, and a young one at that. We get plenty of climbing here! Last night we had some rain, so everything is fresh and cool today, but there is some sticky mud about. All goes well here, generally and with me and this post, specially. We have revolutionised it. When we came into it, it was looked upon and called "hell". The Army was anxious about being able to hold it. The Turk trenches were and are, in some places only 15 feet away, mostly 20 to 25 yards, the furthest 50 yards. Well my men (Wellington Bn) who came in with me, soon got all over the Turks and this is what a deserter who came in the other day reported to our Army HQ: "The mining and fighting opposite Quinn's Post is looked upon by the Turks as so hazardous, that they have to call for volunteers to go into the trenches and promote every volunteer to Corporal. The shooting by the soldiers in Quinn's Post is so deadly (not to mention the bomb throwing) that the Turks have had to close every loophole"! It is, as I told Genl Birdwood 2 days ago, the safest Post <u>now,</u> in the show. . . . We have in 3 weeks so wrecked and mined and blown up and bombed and shot up [sic] the trenches in front of us, that they are like a big railway accident and are practically abandoned by the Turks. 3 weeks ago you couldn't put your little finger up over our trenches, now you can put head and shoulders, in broad daylight and not run great risk. The trenches however are no good to us. They are enfiladed from both flanks by the Turks other trenches. You

Quinn's Post,
showing the layout
of the Allied and
Turkish trenches.

Alexander Turnbull Library

must know that Quinn's Post is a pronounced salient striking out all by itself into Turk ground, something like this. [see above]

We came from Courtney's Post into this one. I am glad and proud to say that our casualties have been what I call "slight". We have been congratulated all round on our success. The whole secret of it as I tell our Generals is "the cultivation of the domestic virtues", inspiring the men with confidence, cleaning ones boots, having a daily bath even in a pint of water, the keeping calm, no matter what racket or noise (explosions) goes on, getting and keeping everything as near normal as possible, no pigging it, no letting things slide, no "near enough", because it is war we are at (the fond excuse of incompetent people). At the same time the intense [?] preparation to meet every possible contingency to the best of one's ability. The insisting that every man and officer constantly asks himself "If such or such a thing happens, what will I do?" and answering and memorising the answers to the questions. The bombs were the terror of this Post, but we laid down the rule that for every bomb thrown by the Turks at us, we threw two, if not more, at them. They soon got the tenor but enough such talk. I had meant to not write war news to you but perhaps it is better to say something, or you would imagine me [?] all sorts of things. We are now allowed by the censor to give news such as I send, because it is no more than what the Turks well know. One thing that makes Quinn's Post so safe now, is that we are so close to the Turkish trenches – they do not shell us much, because they are as likely as not to hit their own people! They have had 2 goes yesterday and today but when they hit their own trenches, knocked off. Our casualties, nil. We can make good all the damage they did to us in a few hours.

Edmond came to see me yesterday. He came from Egypt two days ago. He looks well and glad to be here. Terry got wounded about end of May, in leg and arm. He is now out of Hospital at Cairo, convalescing at the home of Sir Alex Baird, at Matarieh near Zeitoun. He will have a good time, plenty of motor cars. I didn't say anything before. I wanted to say he was all right which he is. You must not worry about me, if you hear nothing it means good news. You are bound to get word at once if I get hit, so until you hear be content and confident. Worry is no good my dearest. I think it will not be very long now before we meet. We are, I think, sure to have a short visit to England before we go to Flanders or France. . . .

And so Jessie Brown (Childs that was) has been to see you. I was very fond of the Sam Childs as we called them. She is one of them. But I thought her husband was dead. Has she married again? You speak of her husband as tho' he were alive. I back you to be right in your opinion of Mrs G.V.[31] In any case she is a German and would be no good if not true to her race. Still she must now be honourably <u>neutral,</u> or else go back to Germany.

. . . Hampton Court must have been lovely. Next time, you and I will do the Pictures by ourselves tho' my beloved I am sure that I shall only want to look at and be with you. There is nothing so lovely in my eyes. I shall feast them soon I hope. As I write your dear photo, is within 8 inches of my hand and I look at you every time I lift my eyes from writing. It is always there on my *escritoire*! Part of my act of war, the cultivation of domestic virtues. But all the same this would be no place for you in *proprie persona*,[32] and I wouldn't have you here, if I could. That doesn't read nicely, but you know what I mean. My work here has to be done. Your photo, <u>calms</u> and <u>helps</u> me. Your person would <u>distract</u> me. I am only human, and if you were here, it would be <u>all you</u> . . . [illegible]. The lovely photos taken in Wgton told me that, but Norah's snap shows that it is absolutely so. I am so glad. But I hope you won't think I am too dreadfully old. I feel young thank God. The dry climate suits me, and I think I was never better in my life.

Major Hart is in England somewhere. He was wounded on 27th April, sent to Cairo, and on 9th Ulto to England as his wound wouldn't heal in the heat of Egypt. He was shot in the thigh. He is a good fellow, and chafes I know at not being back sooner. You might try and see him, probably the High Comn for NZ could give you his address. We hadn't heard until lately that he got a DSO. We get very little news here. I wrote to him c/o the High Comn on 20th Ulto, congratulating him, if it were true we had a rumour of it. I miss him very much, but my officers as well as my men have all turned up trumps. I am sorry to say I don't get on with my Brigadier (Col F.E. Johnston) and our Brigade Major (Temperley). They think I am a nuisance, because I have an opinion of my own and do not slavishly toady to them. All the worse for me. If I want telephones, machine guns, work done, water, things for my men, I will not take no for an answer and keep on until I get what I want. But that is not the way of what we call the "Imperial Army". There apparently the junior officer always takes no for an answer. Because I insisted on having the Brigadier's refusal to give me certain men for special work, referred to the General for <u>his</u> decision, I was called "extremely insubordinate". I insisted and had the matter out before the General, and told him straight that the Brigadier seemed to try and thwart me whenever he could, and didn't treat me fairly, and that I had got to the point of asking to be relieved of my command in the Brigade and to be given another job! The General was very nice, as he can be. Since then the Brigadier has become a different being altogether. Temperley is no good. But I do my job, without fear and don't look for favours. My Battalion is absolutely the best here, bar none, and has done on every occasion the best work. The revolution worked in this Post is an outstanding proof of its capacity and efficiency, yet not one word of encouragement, praise or thanks has the Brigadier or his staff ever given us. They seem to dislike our success. Some people say that that is, what is wrong with us. The Brigade as a Brigade has not distinguished itself. My Battalion as a Battalion has, on every occasion (3 very important ones).

(1.) The landing and making good and safe the Army's left flank, after 8 days and nights severe fighting.

(2.) The Battle of Krithia, 4 days and nights fighting.

(3.) Quinn's Post.

That has been my only trouble and apparently, things will be all right now. I hope so.

The Brigadier I believe at least is not a bad sort, but as I told the General, in his presence, his mind is poisoned against me. It is said that Temperley was and is looking to get the Brigade if anything goes wrong with Colonel Johnston. (He was too sick to take part in landing and has been more or less sick ever since. Had to go away sick the other day). And I am the next for promotion[33] and in Temperley's way. But as Col Johnston, a Major in the Imperial Army [was] jumped up to Col over me . . . and given the Brigade so <u>Major</u> Temperley of the <u>Imperial</u> Army, probably can see no reason why the act should not be repeated. If it is I and I hope the Govt and people of

NZ who find the men and pay the Piper, will have something to say. Rightly or wrongly, we NZ Army officers feel that, the <u>Imperial</u> Army officer has had and still gets all the pull.[34] Their so called "experience" has been and is not as of as much value as our "experience". They are not <u>practical</u> men, there are exceptions of course. When we get back to NZ I feel pretty sure that the NZ officers will run the show and the Imperial officer will have to go. It was so once before and History repeats itself.[35] Now why on earth I have lumbered you up with all this I don't know, but it has been in my mind for some time and had to be delivered. Forgive me, if I have bored you and don't think that I am worried. I have a feeling of injustice "but the way of the Reformer is hard," and I have the great satisfaction that I have done my job and that none of my men have suffered by any act or omission on my part.

All this is between you and me. I have though personally expressed congratulations and good opinion of my Army Corps and also of my Divl Commander so I can do without that of my Brigadier and his staff.

Now to your letters – again, after such a terrible divergence. You cannot feel too strongly about the need for the salvation of old England – you are absolutely right. It does me good to know and I am so proud to think, that you feel and write like you do. England must have at least that which we have in NZ.

. . . I am glad Denis is getting on more condition. What joy it will be to see him and Barney and Mollie, not leaving out <u>you</u> and Norah. But you know my beloved how I feel about you. You have <u>all</u> my <u>husband</u> love, and will not begrudge them their father's, <u>father</u> love.

Don't worry about the NZ casualties. I have a charmed life, or rather God, with so many prayers offered up for me, cares for me and keeps me safe.

. . . You are quite right your news and letters are most welcome, like the Tatter[36] man. We don't want <u>war</u> news. What I want is to hear that you are well, content, not mourning or being nervous and that you are enjoying England, that everybody is nice to you, that you are, as you deserve, to be made much of, but above all that you love me more than anything or anybody as I do you. Tell me all the people you meet and what they are like and how you like them. Your diary hasn't turned up. You said you were sending it.

I hope Bridport[37] for the boys will be all right, but can they be properly <u>fed</u> and looked after for 8/- a week each? School fare is never anything much, but good food is such a necessity. I did not think any school boarding could be got under £40 a year. Do my dearest make quite sure about this and see that the school is a good one, with a good class of scholar. Forgive me if this seems doubting your selection, but the fee seems to me to condemn the school. I know your flowers will grow and be lovely. 3/6 a day is a long way off our NZ 8/- isn't it? It is very late and my candle is all but burnt out. I must to bunk and finish this tomorrow. Goodnight sweetheart x_____x

<u>Sunday 4.7.15.</u> It was after midnight when I finished last night, and to my great delight I actually discovered that you were with me, in my left arm. I dreamt that and then awoke, to rifle fire report and bomb explosions. Just the ordinary night music, and day too, for the matter of that. Out at 3 am. Quite a quiet night. The Post has been for some time now and is comparatively very peaceful. It is now about 3 pm (1500) and I must finish this soon as our mail closes. A new Bn the Canterbury came in today. Little Major Hughes that was is O/C [sic], you will remember him, I think at Newtown Park he escorted you. I am to have I think a few days holiday. I have had 35 days right on end in Courtney's Post 8 days and 27 here. I have not asked for, it but will not refuse. If I can I and my SO will go over to Imbros, right away from the fighting area. It is only two or three hours steam to Imbros from here.

Col Chaytor got shot in the arm and will be all right. Yes apparently we are looked upon as all Australians. The NZers are out on their own as the best troops here. Better disciplined much more steadfast <u>workers</u>. I cannot take to the Australians as a Force at all. In fact I always clear them out if they come anywhere near me. On our landing I was sent to reinforce an Australian Bn and was mixed up with them for some hours in very fierce fighting (my No. 1 occasion). Well I soon told Genl Walker (our acting Brigadier, Col F.E. Johnston was on the ship, sick) that he <u>must</u> take all the Australians away. He said ["] But can you hold on without them?" I said they are only a source of weakness and must go! At daybreak, I got them all cleared out and wasn't I glad to see the last of them. We held on all right.

So far your cable hasn't come, but don't cable. It takes weeks to get here from Alexandria and you will only be worrying because there is no prompt reply.

I am so glad it is summer time and England at its best, so my dearest try and enjoy it. I know how you love it and I am so looking forward to seeing it too, with you. We will have another honeymoon together, sweetheart when the war is over. Good luck to you always.

With all my love,
Your loving husband

———

Quinn's Post
Anzac
4.7.15

My very dear daughter [Norah],

Your very welcome letters of 26.5.15 and 1.6.15 respectively with the snapshots to hand yesterday. I had quite a field day of letters, 4 from Mater, but I had had a weary wait. I have written Mater a long letter and she will give you my news. You mustn't be or let Mater be anxious about me on a/c [account] of lack of letters. The mails are unsatisfactory. Your snapshots are very good, especially the one of the children in a boat on the lake at Regents Park. It is almost perfect. I like too the one of Mater at Montevideo the group, but do take a snap now and again of Mater by herself or with the children and send to me. Get someone to snap you too. It brings one up to date. I sent Mater some photos, in 4 of which I appear. How great England must be to you, and I do so hope that you will enjoy every bit of it. Write me your impressions and tell me of the relations. Yes the Thames is a lovely river and the riverside houses and gardens, delightful. You must go to Sunbury[38] sometime. As a boy I often went there – some aunts lived there.

Terry is all right, but 3 bullets thro' 1 leg and another bullet thro' the arm, was enough shrapnel. Yes I too am looking forward to meeting you all in London. What a reunion it will be. I am very fit and hard, and enjoy my work. The more I have to do, the better I like it.

The mailman is waiting so good luck my dear daughter. With love to you and D [Denis] and B [Barney] and M [Mollie].

Yr loving father

[MSX 2553]

In early July Malone and his staff officer, Captain John Short, had four days' leave during which they went on a walking tour of the island of Imbros. The first part of this letter to Ida Malone is missing and this page begins with a description of a visit to a Greek peasant family.

Pyrgos [Imbros] 11-7-15

. . . Invited into the house and getting through a square hole, about 4 feet by 3 feet, we were seated on the only furniture a long wooden box, about 10

Opposite

Some of Malone's men in the trenches during a hot day.

Hampton Album, Alexander Turnbull Library

feet long. The room was clean and tidy, with many strange things, a stone fireplace, cupboards in the solid wall (which is about 2 feet thick), cushions were produced. Soon eggs were boiled, brown bread fresh from the oven (a big stone affair outside), a dish of beans like broad beans, dry, over which <u>for us</u> was poured a liberal quantity of olive oil. The family and our driver did not get the oil. I would gladly have dispensed with it – dried olives, onions raw. White curd cheese a goat hair rug was placed on the floor, on it the food. The men sat round and the wife and her daughter, a dear little girl of about 9, waited on all hands. We got the milk – the others drank water. We made quite a good meal – laughing away and making signs. I showed the woman the snaps of you and the 3 children at Montevideo and explained where you were. She was very bright and sympathetic. After dinner I took 3 photos of the family outside their house, which I hope will turn out all right. On leaving I offered payment but they wouldn't accept so I gave the girl a 2/6 [2 shillings and sixpence]. We shook hands all round, the little girl kissing mine. Her name is Kodina: she took off down the hill like a young goat and was back with some nearly ripe plums, before we got away. They seemed an ideal family, natural, unsophisticated, absolutely united. I wish you could meet them. . . . Skimude is as its name sounds, sort of skinny, a poor place, like the country. Houses old, and not in good order, streets ditto, people ditto. We made for the cafe, and in it was like the place – nothing pretty or comfortable about it. The usual terrace outside but instead of grapevines some stiffish[?] trees. We were well stared at by the customers. A Greek priest there, we salaamed to and asked to join us in cafe. Soon a chap turned up who could speak some French, then another. They took us round the town, sights nil except a cheese, butter and olive oil factory. Oh such a place! and oh such butter! like sperm oil, and such hard cheeses, such dirt and primitive plant! Almost inconceivable. We were glad to leave Skimude. . . . [Malone and his party visited the home of a Greek priest Father Antonios Larsodotis who showed them round his farm.] Then to the house, and at <u>9 pm</u>! a meal. Bread, boiled eggs, vegetables warmed in rice, covered with olive oil, a salad of lettuce, onions and green peppers, also covered with oil, milk, rice and spice milk pudding. I did very well, with all but the oil covered dishes. Red wine was also on the table. To bed – no sheets just one of the large quilts each. Too smothersome for me so I put it under me and used my plaid shawl. Plenty of air. Breakfast at 7 am. Toast, tea, eggs and jam, and ½ ripe pears. I took photos of the priest, his housekeeper and her mother and of the monastery. We left a £1 for the House, gave the housekeeper 2/6 and away at 9 am. . . .

. . . Thro' a rocky ravine with a running mountain stream meeting a man driving 6 goats tied together in an ingenuous fashion. We walked nearly all the way, as I did the day before. . . . We got no lunch. At 5 we reached our journey's end, Pyrgos at Kephalos our starting point – a most welcome meal – a wash over and to bed. I saw Genl Godley and he insisted that instead of going back to Anzac as we had intended, we should take what he called 2 or 3 days rest, here. I was in no way loath as there was nothing going on . . . at Anzac, and I was not due in Quinn's Post until Tuesday. The Genl was with Admiral de Robeck, our Fleet Admiral and introduced me to him. The latter said, to my astonishment, "I've heard of you, you are the man who turned the Turks down at Quinn's Post – you deserve a good rest." Naturally I felt very flattered. He is such a fine looking man the Admiral beau ideal.

Today I had breakfast with the Supply Officer, one Harley, and then with Short went to the beach and in for a swim. It was lovely. Lunch with 2 NZ officers and now I am in a QM's marquee the coolest and freest from flies place I could find, finishing my letter to my sweetheart. I am expecting there will be a letter for me from her on my arrival. I am tempted to go back sooner for the letter, but it is not sure that it is there and a loapher [sic, a loafer[39]?] will do me good and haven't I had a lovely holiday my beloved. All the time I was thinking of you and wishing to have you here and show you everything and enjoy all the beauty and interest of everything.

The General says the war is going on all right. I can hear the big guns rumbling as I write.

When I finish this I am going for another swim, and loaf on the beach. There are no flies near the water's edge, but there is no shade. The harbour is full of shipping. Tomorrow we are going round to the shops to see if we can buy some tinned milk, fruit, cocoa etc to take back to Quinn's Post. One thing I forgot to tell you. The mulberry trees here are plentiful and bear profusely – the most delicious fruit. It is common property. Big trees laden, with fruit in all stages. I did enjoy it so, especially if I could get milk with it. Can see too that figs and walnuts and all other fruits will be as plentiful. Good bye now my best beloved I know you will rejoice in the good time I have had and am having – with all my love. I am for aye your husband.

11.7.15

Quinn's Post
Anzac
15.7.15

Dear McDonnell

Glad to get yours of 4th Inst, but sorry to hear you have had and are having such a bad time. . . . Brunt has just gone off with pneumonia – 2 months job. Short is taking the Coy; I am still O/C Quinn's Post, and it is getting quite comfortable, and spick and span. Over head cover to the terraces, earth on top makes bomb and shrapnel proof and gives cool shade, blankets (Govt) nailed along western front, keeps out glare of afternoon sun. It has got to the armchair state and I am getting one made, out of a box. The Turks have periodically given us best. I had my head and shoulders up over the fire trench, at different places along our front, and don't really think I was running much risk. We have recovered the whole of the abandoned trench, and driven Johnny Turk out of the crater. A small gun got on to our left flank a while ago and plunked, at about 300 yards range, some 30 shells hit us. No casualties and very little damage. We had to shift our left, machine gun, about 6 feet, to a better place!

   When you come back, bring me some 2 lb Tins canned fruits and some milk, some pickles, dates figs semolina and sago. . . . I hope we won't be stuck here until all those go, but I can always dispose of them. Jardine got

This sketch of the view from the No 2 Sap of No 1 Trench at Quinn's Post was drawn on 8 July 1915. The approximate position of the annoyance of the moment, a Turkish gun firing on No 3 Trench (to the right of the cornfields behind the ridge), is marked with a cross.

Malone Family Collection Wellington (now in ATL)

Dugouts faced with blankets to keep the sun out, Quinn's Post.

wounded again, McLernon is back also Turnbull: Very fit and well myself. Kind regards from all to you and all others.

Yours sincerely
W.G. Malone

———

Quinn's Post
Near Gaba Tepe
Gallipoli Pen
15.7.15

My dear Mrs Wickham

Many many thanks for your kind letter of 19th May last. I am so glad to hear from you and to receive your good wishes I am, thanks be to God, very fit and well and except for a very tiny cut in my cheek from a bullet and a bruise on my chest from a bomb projectile have escaped scatheless, thro' all the fighting. I am one of the very lucky ones or rather as I believe am especially cared for by our Lord in answer to the prayers of my many good friends. . . .

I see that at last New Zealand realise what this war is and what it means to our Empire. I am afraid a good many people in New Zealand looked upon it as something that didn't concern them very much, and that the Germans were beaten long ago. That our NZ Exped. Force was a picnic or tourist party! I felt that the casualty lists would bring home to NZ people what war such as this does mean. The fighting has been and is very stern and hard here, but NZ's lads and men have proven themselves the equal of the best soldiers of the world. My officers and men are splendid. I admire – nay – dear Mrs Wickham I love them so. So gallant enduring and cheerful. They are wonderful. Their people cannot be too proud of them. The wounded are so patient, so quiet, so brave and uncomplaining. They bear all their pain like stoics – no other troops like them. I hope to tell, personally, their parents, relations and friends, what I think of them, and will if God spares me do so when the war is over.

I hope you and your daughter will continue to enjoy good health and contentment [?]. With kindest regards.

Yours sincerely
W.G. Malone

———

Quinn's Post
Anzac
Gallipoli Pa
17.7.15

My beloved

Saturday night 8 pm good day light, sitting outside my shelter, and with an hour or two to spare unless anything untoward to spare [sic]. Plenty of bomb explosions, rifle shots about, but custom makes us deaf and unconcerned. I wrote you last from Imbros and posted letter on last Sunday 11th Inst. On my return here I got your very welcome letter of 19th June, from Bridport. I had hoped for 2 or 3, still it was a great joy and comfort to get the one. I do so hope you soon got my letters that were overdue. You mustn't worry about the letters. Postal matters are very casual here, but so far apparently all letters have been delivered. On Monday Short and I went for a picnic on the sea beach and spent a quiet time, swimming and resting during the heat of the day. In the evening we got a sailboat and went off to HMS *Talbot*, to see if we could get some stores. We got cream, canned tomatoes and canned tongues, stayed to dinner and had quite a good time. It was nice to sit in an easy chair. The next morning we came back here per a trawler, and by noon were in full training again. Things are going all right. General Birdwood came to see me yesterday morning and gave me lot of news, and was very nice to me. The post [is] getting as I call it to the armchair stage, I am having one made out of a box, more cultivation of domestic virtue. You know my maxim: The art of the war is the cultivation of the domestic virtues.

It is very hot, but I can't give you the Fahrenheit measure of it, no thermometer about. Still we get a brief now and again. Today 3 newspaper war correspondents called on me to see the Post. . . . They saw the Post and I gave them afternoon tea to a "bomb" orchestra. They seemed to enjoy themselves.

And so the Bridport school is all right. Did you go to Weymouth or Dorchester? I used to know the former place very well. England no doubt is lovely now. About the letters from me, my dearest, it is not the fighting that causes any delay. I can nearly always manage to write some lines or another at least once a week and will always do so. As to the photos and there being no letters from me with them, well I sent the films to Cairo by a sick man, and told him to get the prints sent to you direct. I myself wrote at the time from Cape Helles, or Sedd el Bahr. The print of land[ing] would be of a practice landing at Mudros in Lemnos and not here. There was no time for photography then. The one of me outside, a dug out would I suppose be at Walkers Ridge, where we drove back the Turks and dug in (entrenched and made the left flank of our army safe[)]. I always try to get a photo of each of my "homes" and myself with it. I always rig one up and make it comfortable, cultivation of domestic virtue. I see by the papers that at last New Zealand has awoken to the meaning of the war. The loss of the *Lusitania* and our casualty lists brought it home to them, now that they are public there is no harm in me telling you what the NZ Infantry suffered – 2300 casualties out of 4000! an almost incredible number. My Bn owing, in my opinion to its better discipline and training lost less than the others still we lost over 200 at Walkers Ridge and over 200 at Krithia. Here at Quinn's Post, we lose on an average only 2 or 3 a day.

I see NZ is talking of sending 50000 men. If this is done it will mean at least 3 more Infantry Brigades. I wonder whether they are going to be officered by New Zealanders or NZ army officers, or by Imperial officers. I am half afraid, the outsiders will get the plums!

NZ is sending a hospital ship, the *Maheno*. Lots of Convalescent Homes are being given, in NZ. I must turn in now. I didn't have too good a night last night. It is 9.30 pm several men been in about one thing or another good night my sweetheart. I shall go to sleep thinking about you. Always the last and first things of my sleeping hours I think of you.

[Illegible note] Sunday 18/7/15

I have a little time, which I can take to finish this letter. Everything is in order and we had a fairly quiet night.

Major Cunningham is away sick also Major Brunt the latter has pneumonia. Capt McDonnell is in Egypt sick too. Also Captain Shepherd, sort of run down. Heat, flies, rations monotony and general strain.

Edmond came to see me a couple of days ago. He is very well, but dressed or rather undressed like a Red Indian absolutely nothing on but a pair of shorts like bathing pants, boots and socks, a hat, his identity disc and his water bottle. Lots of the men always go about like that – a majority naked above waist. They are sun burnt brown as brown as Maoris. They beat the lice better this way, and find it cooler. Terry is getting on all right. Your diary has not turned up. Mine is at a stand still. Been too busy to keep it going while in the Post. I meant to have written it up at Imbros but couldn't settle down to it and it was not convenient. Harry Penn wrote me that the Stratford Patriotic Comtee were asking if he would let the Farlands as a Convalescent Home to returned NZ troops. He seemed to think he might do worse. I hope he will soon let it, because it will mean more income to you. I hope you can manage on what you have.

General Godley has just called and I have been all round the Post with him.

I managed to send all my exposed films (of photos at Imbros etc) to Alexandria and hope soon to get the prints to send to you with all my love my darling.

Yours

x____x

Love to Norah and the children.

Quinn's Post
July 18th 1915
Gallipoli Peninsula
W.H.T. Winter Esqre

Dear Sir

Your letter of 30th June last just received.

Your son Adrian[40] was killed in action on 29th <u>April</u> last, at a place since called Walkers Ridge.

His Company (Wellington West Coast) had been sent up the Ridge to reinforce an Australian Bn. The fighting was very fierce, in high scrub. Another of my companies joined the 1st and ultimately the whole Bn was in. We dug in, held on and made good. The left flank of our Army, your son, as did all his comrades acted most gallantly. His platoon commander has since been killed – were it not for this I could probably have given you more details. Your son was a fine lad and a splendid soldier. You have my sympathy in the great loss you have sustained. If I can do anything more for you pray command me.

Yours truly
W.G. Malone

[MSX 2551]

Quinn's Post
Gallipoli Pa
19.7.15

My dear Harry,[41]

I wrote to you last, I think on 29th May last. On that day my Brigade took over certain Posts, Courtney and Quinns respectively, part of our Defences near Gaba Tepe, from an Australian Brigade. I was put in charge of Courtney's Post, and after 8 days (day always means <u>night</u> and day here because the Turks seem to prefer to turn night into day and keep up a more or less continuous fire at night) instead of going into "rest" for 8 days as was the practice, I and my Bn (Wellington Inf) were sent into this Post, I as O/C Post. It was in a parlous condition, and a source of anxiety to our Army and Divisional Commanders. The Turks had been allowed by the Australians to come down on top of them and on top of them, so close that in one place, there was only about 15 feet between the Turks and us. Then they had allowed the Turks to get such superiority of "fire and bombing", that it was impossible to put up even a periscope without getting it shot away at sight, then 50 yards of the front fire trench had been practically abandoned. (The frontage of the Post is about 200 yards.) The men in it looked upon the Post and called it "Hell". It adjoins ground named "The Bloody Angle", and "Dead Man's Ridge", for good cause. They expected to be undermined and blown off the edge of the cliff, on which the Post rests. Two of our NZ Bns went into it when my Bn went into Courtney's Post, and they also looked upon the Post as "Hell". Their O/C, when I took over from him, told me it was "b——y Hell". And so it was a dilapidated, demoralised and filthy Hell. But all it wanted was cleaning, reorganising, re-arming, repairing and the "cultivation of the domestic virtues". Within a week of our taking over, my men got all over the Turks, shot and bombed them. We scraped and cleaned and reorganised, repaired, put in machine-guns. I had been told there was no place for them, and so cultivated the domestic virtues that the whole character of the place was absolutely altered. We recovered the whole of the abandoned trench. The "terror" had passed to the Turks. They practically abandoned their front trench and gave us best[42]. . . .

It is now absolutely the safest Post in the whole defences, and the most comfortable. We are praying for the Turks to come (the more the better) and try to put us out of it. It is comparatively "Heaven" now. Both Generals Birdwood (Army) and Godley (Divn) are delighted and relieved. And all this Harry is, thanks to my men (the Wellington Infantry Bn). I can only take a bit of credit for the training and the inspiring of them, and for insisting on the practice of domestic virtue, that we keep calm, confident, clean and orderly, taking every precaution and making every precaution for all contingencies. In addition I laid down 1 simple rule, viz that for every shot or bomb fired or thrown by the Turk, we fired or threw two. I am so proud of my men, Harry. To come out of Courtney after 8 days' strenuous trench fighting and go into Quinns and within 8 days to settle the Turks, opposite to it and practically turn Hell into Heaven, is an achievement as great as that of any Bn that ever fought. Our casualties too were ridiculously small. Of this I am prouder than anything. I enjoyed the work, tho' it was strenuous enough. Terribly broken sleep. In 4 weeks, we fired 16 mines, under Turkish lines, threw say 5600 Bombs and got thrown at us say 2000 bombs. I leave out the rounds of Rifle ammunition. We never fired our machine guns (they are kept as surprise packets in case of a big attack) but got any amount of m/gun fire, front and flanks. This Post you must know is a pronounced salient and its front trenches are mostly only about 20 to 30 yards away from the Turks trenches. The greatest distance is 50 yards, the nearest 15 feet. It is something like this: [see opposite]

This is not against censor rules, because the Turks can see as much or more than I send.

23.7.15

. . . Yes our NZers are rather absorbed by the Australians, thro' Australasians. The facts are that there is an Australian and NZ Army Corps, consisting

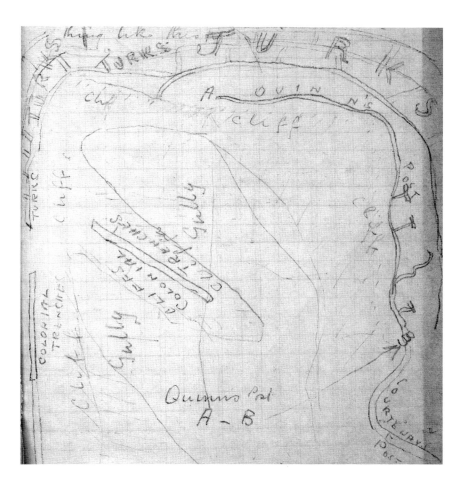

A sketch map of
Quinn's Post.

of 2 Divisions, the 1st an Australian one pure and simple and the other a
NZ and Australian one, about ½ of each, so that there [is] something like
3 Australians to one NZ. Outsiders soon lose idea of distinction between
Australians and Australasians and N Zealand is sad to say losing her entity.
But Harry, there is no question but that the New Zealander is a long long
way the better soldier of the two. The Australian, is a dashing chap, but he
is not steadfast, and he will not or would not dig, work. He came here to kill
Turks, not to dig, and consequently, we have suffered. There are lots of good
men and good officers among them, but they are not disciplined or trained
like our men. In the landing fight, my Bn was sent to reinforce an Australian
Bn. The fighting was fierce and bloody. We lost (my Bn lost) over 200 out of
the 1st 450 men engaged, within a few hours, but within the same time I was
insisting to my Brigadier to have all the Australians taken away. They were
a source of weakness, and I was not content until I saw the last of them go
back into reserve. It was thro' them that the (our) particular casualties were
so heavy. It made me angry to so have to lose my splendid men. I am afraid
this particular experience has biased me, but still Quinn's Post is another

proof of their lob-sidedness,[43] tho' for some 8 days before my Bn took over, 2 other NZ Bns occupied it and might have squared it up.

All this comparison my dear Harry is strictly *entre nous*.[44]

[MSX 2553]

23/7/15
[second part of letter to Harry Penn started in MSX 2551]

The whole force any way has done a big thing. But we are by no means in possession of the Peninsula. The authorities quite misappreciated the situation, and the navy independent opening of the attack was a huge mistake. <u>We</u> are paying for it. Still we will see the things thro' and get thro' all right, but warfare is now <u>siege</u> warfare. The power of the pick and shovel is mighty. No huge walls and forts – trenches and trenches and trenches – machine guns and bombs. The day of big and numerous guns! Munitions of war, the great need.

NZ seems at last to <u>feel</u> what the war means. If she finds up to the 50000 men, spoken about, I hope that the people and Government will not forget that the NZ Army officers, now in the field, can supply better officers for higher command in the new Brigades, than the Imperial Army. We feel here that there has been and is too much altogether of the <u>Imperial</u> "so called" officers and with exceptions he is <u>not</u> as good as our own practical men.

I hear that some one in NZ has started a yarn that I have been promoted Brigadier. It is not so. I have been temporarily in command of our Inf Brigade, during illness of our Brigadier and I had command of a NZ detachment of 2 Bns and details at Suez under General Melliss. (Candidly I would like one of the new, NZ Brigades if formed, because I am just about fed up with our Brigadier and Brigade Major here, and tho' I should be very sorry to leave the Wellington Bn that I have trained, yet I often feel that I must get out of the Brigade. All this except that NZ might look to us New Zealand officers here to officer its new Brigades – *entre nous*.)

This is the kinematograph age all right. Yesterday Ashmead Bartlett (war correspondent) came to see Quinn's

Even at Quinn's Post, in awful conditions, Malone's stamp is seen in this officer wearing a tie. A still image from Ashmead Bartlett's film of Quinn's Post taken on 22 July 1915.

Australian War Memorial

Post with leave to take K – pictures of it. I showed him round and he took the pictures of the garrison and trench life, work and fighting. I gave him a thrill or rather two. We get a good few visitors, as the Post is an object of interest if not curiosity. I nearly always ask, would you like to see the Turks "trenches"? "Oh yes"! and then I walk them up a sidling,[45] in full rear of our trenches and only say 12 feet above where I now sit and write – halt them – turn them about and then say "see, those are the Turks trenches" – Full length view, distance about 350 yards. But say they "Can't they shoot us?" ["]Yes, and I think it is time we moved down again because they sometimes have a machine gun on to this track and these slopes". Thrills! and quick movement. The risk I know, is not a big one, because it is only in such state occasions or at night that anyone goes up the track and the odds are that no Turks or Germans is watching the place, but the Captain [author, deleted?] doesn't know that. But not being used to taking such chances, gets a thrill all right. Another thrill, is to take them into a tunnel trench (with the crown broken in) outside our fire trenches and within 20 yards of the Turks trenches on the same level and ask them to have a <u>look</u>. As soon as they put their heads thro', one of the holes in the crown of the tunnel and so above the ground surface, I make them duck it quickly, and then give them a periscope, so that they can safely see thro the same hole, the position of things. Then I tell them, some times the Turks throw bombs into these holes, or try to. Thrills – *exeunt omnes*![46] I first taking them to the end hole

A Wellington Battalion soldier at Quinn's Post using a periscope to observe the Turkish lines. A still image from Ashmead Bartlett's film of Quinn's Post shot on 22 July 1915. By this time some of the Wellington Battalion had gone back to wearing their lemon squeezer hats.

Australian War Memorial

and telling them that they are within 8 feet of some Turks, which they are! When it is all safely over as it has hither to been, they feel very pleased with themselves and the adventures. They will remember and recount them all their lives. . . .

With love to you all and Lucy and Charlie.

Yours affectly [affectionately]
W.G. Malone

———

The huge amount of work required to transform Quinn's Post took a great toll on those involved. Charles Saunders, the New Zealand engineer officer who worked with Malone at the post, for instance, told a medical board, after his health collapsed, that during all of July he estimated he had only slept for 90 hours. [Proceedings of medical board, 12 Nov 1915, Charles W. Saunders, PF, ANZ.]

Quinn's Post
Gallipoli Pa
23.7.15

My dear Hart

Yours of 28th Ulto to hand about 3 days ago.

I do so hope that you are all right again, and that I shall soon see you fit and well and in command of a Bn.

re D.S.O. I certainly specially mentioned you, for gallantry, and good service, but I had nothing to do with the D.S.O. There were 5 allotted to the Army Corps, but I don't know who allots them to individuals. We are all very proud of the fact that you got one. Salmondson [sic, Critchley-Salmonson] got another, the only 2 in our Brigade.

We are very busy here, expecting a big Turk attack tonight, 100,000 reinforcements said to have come to them. We are praying for their attack.

I am very fit and well.

Kindest regards

Yours sincerely
W.G. Malone.

[MSX 2553]

Quinn's Post
Gallipoli Pa
23.7.15

My very dear wife

I wrote you last on 17th/18th Inst and just as I was sending the letter away your little letter of 23rd June, arrived saying that you had posted a long letter the night before the 23rd June, but it had not come.

The next day 19th July, arrived your letter of 28th June and then a few hours later the missing one of 22nd June. Yesterday arrived yours of 1st July and just now that of 6th July. You can imagine my joy and delight at such a flow of letters, with such sweet expression of your love for me. My dearest I reciprocate every bit of it. I will refer to something in your last letter first – you say you dreamt I had come back, and that you were in my arms and that I held you so tightly, and then you wonder whether I am wounded or in danger and thinking about you and that you receive my thoughts, only if so the message was all wrong for I was so strong and happy. Well – sweetheart – the fact is every night before I go to sleep and every morning when I wake, I mentally take you in my arms and hold you to me so tightly and try and think that you are in them, so no wonder you have dreamt this. I haven't liked to say this before lest it might seem – not altogether nice – something not to write about but so it is. Your piece of poetry expresses too all that I feel about you and being away from you. It is lovely to read and to have you tell and repeat to me how much you love me, and it makes me long more than ever to be with you again. Tho' this war and my work must run their course first. You cannot love me or want me or long for me more than I do you and it will be heavenly "in the small compass of your clasping arms in reach and sight of your dear lips and eyes".

And now sweetheart to answer your dear letters. It is 5 pm – comparatively quiet. We have the last two nights and are expecting tonight a massed attack by the Turks. Large reinforcements are said to have reached them, and they are expected by their Govt to drive us into the sea, to commemorate their "Constitution Day" today. However, last night and today have been comparatively quiet. We have made every possible preparation to repel the attack and are fully confident that no better fate awaits the Turks than that of the occasion of their big May attack. We do so hope that they will come at us in mass and get slaughtered. We are calm and confident and I have some little time to spare before making a final round (for the day) of the Post.

First of all, thanks for the 3 silk h'chiefs they are lovely, useful and just right. I wear one, instead of a collar and … I have none of these with me, and don't want them, or anything else. We lately got 2 pr [pair] socks from a NZ committee so please don't send any shirts etc or anything except that muslin cage and, not that if it is weighty.

It was so disappointing, getting the short letter of 23rd June before the long one of 22nd Idem.[47] Still it has been lovely to get 5 letters within 5 days. I do so hope more got to you – spread like a … [illegible] and not all in a heap.

My darling, I do full well understand what you want me to feel about your love for me, but it is lovely to have you tell me again and again, but sweetheart, it sets up such a longing for you, and I am tempted to come to you at all hazards. But my work soon conquers the temptation and there is all the time some sound here to remind one of ones work.

Poor Terry has apparently got a turn for the worse, for he is being sent to England. He was being sent to NZ, but fixed up England instead. He will surely be all right and it will do him good to see you all again.

Edmond, has been wounded too, a bullet thro the leg, not serious. I saw him on the Hospital Ship *Sicilia* 3 days ago, and if all is well may get off for an hour or two to see him tomorrow. He is cheerful and will have no permanent injury.

I am glad that his engagement is off. Hope the girl won't take it hardly. Don't worry about me – 2 Malones out of 3 must fill the average bill of chances!

Yes when "he" comes for me, as you say, we will take those walks and river jaunts, and I will feast my eyes and lips.

I am glad that Miss Cox is so nice and capable. Keep on getting stronger. As for your confession about your hair – I cannot help smiling a little bit, because dearest I too was thinking and troubling about my grey hairs – nothing but water on them and the strain of things here made me think that probably I should be <u>white</u> by when I rejoined you. I dreaded, being too, too old for you. I am 56 yrs and 7 months, nearly 17 years older than you. But sweetheart, all that is pettiness. We know each other too well to really think that our love and happiness can depend on our hair or mere outward appearance. I love <u>you</u> not your hair or mere looks, and I believe you love <u>me</u> not only the outside of me. So we won't worry, or think anymore about such triviality. All the same dear one, I see in the photographs the line of you and the expression of you and the photos when they show me your beauty – don't lie. And these don't I know how you <u>blossom</u> out, with happiness. And it will be such a happiness, will it not, when we are reunited? If the strain of waiting for me makes its mark as no doubt it may, it will only be temporary and the mark will disappear as my arms go round you and as I kiss you when you meet me at the English wharf of my landing. It will be I that cannot so readily bloom and blossom. War makes hard lines at my age, and I am not fat, not an ounce too [sic] spare. Still I will chance your greeting – I may even try and look as worn as I can, because I believe, pity for a man whom a woman loves, makes her love, if possible all the greater. But dearest, I am so well and strong, and I know you don't like fat in a man. I hope your money from NZ turns up regularly, but in any case I expect the Bank will let you overdraw if needs be, on the guarantee I signed before I left NZ.

I am glad you liked the flowers. There are none I am sorry to say in this post. Too cut up and hacked about. Still I have a lovely look-out to sea and Imbros and so your answer, that I will have to make love to you again. Will you be hard to win? Answer that now.

I am so glad that your summer is perfect. Here too it is almost perpetual sunshine.

Give my love again to Aunt Agnes and thank her for her prayers. Phil Clemow is all right.[48] I see Genl Godley 2 or 3 times a week. He was up here yesterday. Lady Godley is in Egypt. This is no place for a woman. Impossible.

And so you liked the photo of me outside a dug out. I can't quite think which one it is. Probably Walkers Ridge when we fought our landing fight and dug trenches and held on, for 8 or 9 days, until relieved, to go to Cape Helles, for the Krithia battle.

Why shouldn't I pick flowers, even if we are fighting. A Commanding Officer if he organises his staff properly generally gets some time when he has apparently and actually nothing to do. Last night for instance, after a very long day, making every possible arrangement to repel the Turks expected massed attack and after going over everything with my Sub-commanders, I laid down and went to sleep, within 40 yards of where the attack might hit us, and tho' there were thro' the night one or two extra outbursts of fire, and a mine blown off, by the Turks, close to our trenches didn't get up until 5, this morning, only waking up once. If the Turks had come on I would have been awakened by my staff officer, a new one, Young Harston such a nice and capable lad, only 23. Capt Short, took the Taranaki Coy over on Brunt going sick with pneumonia.

9.45 pm

I have just come in after going round the post, and will finish this before I turn in. If the Turks come it will be we think after midnight. And so you got my letters up to and inclusive of June 3rd.

If the Turks use gas, we are prepared. We all carry night and day, a helmet of cloth soaked in some chemical solution with mica eyeglass.

Poor Terry's rifles (Turks) I had to give them up – a Divisional order was issued to do so, and I couldn't get special leave to keep them, though I tried hard. I still have the sword, it is here with me.

As to going back to The Farlands after the war, you are quite right I can't see myself going back to the office to work. I think I should like to get a soldiers job, as I do not think I could rest and do nothing. One thing – sure as perhaps it may be a long process – my love making or rather the winning of my love, who says yes! yes! yes! to my question, whether I shall have to make love to her. We may travel and see the world, in easy stages. There will be all the places to show you where I have been – Egypt, Imbros, Gallipoli Pa, etc. Time enough to think about "work". After all that as to staying at Caversham[49] all the winter or during the winter, would it not be nice for you to go to South of France and escape the English winter, which is rather dreadful, I think or go to Bournemouth or Weymouth or Torquay?

As to the papers, I think the New Zealanders, are being absorbed in the word Australasian and if not Australian. The Australians in this Army, are 3 to 1 New Zealander, but the New Zealander is a long way the better soldier, more steadfast, better disciplined and a worker. I don't like the <u>average</u> Australian a bit, in fact I dislike him.

As to shortness of munitions, it is quite true, we have been. I can say no more.

I am so glad you liked the Cairo presents. The Cashmere shawl no doubt got to NZ, after you left, and should be sent after you. Don't forget that I think it wants washing. And the dress is for your lover, eh? The wearing of it is to tell him that you are won!

You should know that I can never weary of reading your dear letters. I read and reread them. Why when I finish this, and turn in to bunk, I am going to reread the 5 last ones and go to sleep when I have finished them, had a last look at your photos and put my arms round you.

And dear Molly cuddled her Daddy photos up to her as she went to sleep the dear little soul, give her a good cuddle for me.

I am so sorry that your jaunt with the Pickerings was spoilt by the rain. You have not told me who they are except that they were on the *Rotorua* with you. I have the snapshot of you and the children, with them and others.

If you see the Hon T. Mackenzie our High Comr [Commissioner] give him a good hint – that NZ needn't go outside its own officers for the commands of the new Brigades etc.

It was good of you to get up, early to write to me, on July 6th. I have referred to your dream. I wish I could dream like that, tho' the disappointment of waking would be bitter. . . .

Oh! Nurse Harris (of *Rotorua*) sent me the other day a snapshot of the children, on the *Rotorua*, taken by a Nurse Young.[50] Such a good one. It was kind and thoughtful of Miss Harris to write and send the photo. She is at Alexandria. I wrote thanking her.

Ken Munro is here, all right, doing his work. I <u>don't</u> see much of him because the Wellington Bn goes out of this Post every 8 days, for a spell. I do wish it was in now, for the expected attack. The Canterbury Bn is in, and it is not up to the standard of the Wellington Bn, tho' not bad.

Yes dearie, "no news is good news".

I have just come to and reread the piece of poetry you send me, and with which you end your last letter. It is 10.45 pm. I shall turn in – read all the letters and go to sleep saying:

"In the small compass of your clasping arms
In reach and sight of your dear lips and eyes
There then for me the joy of Heaven here".

It sounds a bit Pagan, but God will forgive me, or rather know that I don't mean it so. With all my love

Your sweetheart and lover

[MSX 2546]

July 25th 1915, Sunday

13 weeks exactly from day of our landing.

The Turks did not attack last night. There was a good deal of shooting. We had 1 man killed and 3 wounded in this Post, about our average. One of our Mountain Battery guns plunged a shell into us this morning. No one hurt. When one is <u>under</u> gun fire, such accidents and premature bursts are inevitable.

Have made a discovery – small mesh wire netting at openings of shelter keep out most of the flies. They are adverse [sic, averse] to flying thro' it. I had noticed at Genl HQ the use of fishing net for the same purpose, so tried the wire. Result – cool passage of air and few flies. A great joy and relief.

[MSX 2553]

Quinn's Post
Gallipoli Pa
25.7.15

Sweetheart

I wrote you a long letter on 23rd Inst. This is just to let you know that all is well, and that so far the Turks have not come on in any strength and it does seem that their . . . proposed massed attack will not eventuate.

We are disappointed. On Saturday 25th April last we landed here, and today is Sunday 25th July, 13 weeks.

I have been having a clean up of odd papers etc in practice of "domestic virtues" and I think perhaps the enclosed may be of interest to you and Norah. The sketches will give you some idea of the country. . . . I may get off for an hour or two to see Edmond. I see the *Sicilia* is still at anchor, but I don't like leaving this Post in case the Turks come on in my absence.

This little note is also to tell you once more and how much I love long for, and want you. It is not easy making love by letter, but or perhaps, the winning of you may be a long process. The more love I make to you, as I go, the better. My love, I love you so – more than anything or anybody. With all my love for aye.

Your lover

[The next four pages of the letter book have been cut out.]

6

'My candle is all but burnt out'

Ordeal on Chunuk Bair, August 1915

[MSX 2546]

July 26th 1915

Another quiet night, but we hear that the Turks are still landing and massing troops. Got leave as all was quiet to go off to Hospital Ship and see Edmond. HQ said *Sicilia* was still here. On arrival at beach, found she had gone. Decided [to] have a swim and come back. As I was undressing Genl Birdwood passed, and asked me to have lunch with him. Very kind of him. Lunched and had quite a long chat with him. He told me to always look in and see him, when passing.

Awfully hot walking back to post at 1.30 pm. Only 1 man killed in trenches last night. He was firing <u>over</u> a loophole, instead of <u>thro</u>' it.

A Mr Schuler correspondent for *Melbourne Age* visited the Post and had a look round, stayed to dinner and seemed to enjoy himself.

July 27th 1915

Another quiet night for us. Full moon. Up at 2 am and 4 am, all in order. Post visited by Genl Monash and a Mr Wright some Australian newspaper correspondent who was very interested in the post, and took several snapshots. All the Brigade Commanders have been promoted to Brigadier

Genl. Very hot today. Turks still expected to attack – their Ramadan, or some such feast or fast ends today and they will be full of food and what not.

Visited by Genl Godley and Commodore – [Roger Keyes] Chief of Staff, to Admiral de Robeck. Turks got in a H.E. shell on us today. 1 casualty only. S.Sgt Major De Loree[1] [sic] by his prompt action saved the man's life. The man had been buried by earth, consequent on the explosion of the shell (a 6" one) which landed in a new sap in which de Loree and his party were working. The sap was partly filled up by the explosion. The Turks opened rifle fire on the place, and while de Loree and a Private Hughes[2] were digging to get the buried man out, they were partly under this fire. I have recommended de Loree and Hughes for special mention or distinction.

July 28th 1915

Another quiet night. By a ruse of sounding bugles, and cheering at 4 am this morning we drew a good deal of Turk fire, very little however from the fire trench immediately in front of us, showing as we thought, that the[y] don't like occupying it.

Wellington Bn came into the Post (Quinn's) today, and Canterbury Bn went out. I am of course better pleased.

July 29th 1915

Another fairly quiet night. The usual rifle, machine gun fire and bombing. Also some shelling. I have the base of the 6" shell which landed in the Post on 27th. I will try and get it home as a memento. It would make an interesting cigar ash tray tho' very heavy.

July 30th 1915

We got a surprise at 4 am. The Turks fired a huge mine about 10 yards in front of our fire trench, and beyond our defense mining gallery. The mine was about 12 yards long, and near the surface. It blew the earth above it, right over all our trenches, onto the terraces just above and in line with my shelter. It killed 4 men and wounded 8, that is the fall of the earth did large clumps. One smashed a wooden box seat just in front of my shelter. I thought from the horrendous explosion and the shower of earth etc that the Turks had got under our trenches and blown a section of them up and off the edge of the cliff. As it is, if only our men who were sleeping on the terraces had had overhead cover, no real damage would have been done to us. The Turks I think made a mistake or got nervous and thought that we would blow them up and so let go first. We had heard them mining and were waiting for them to come closer, and then we would have charged and blown up a mine underneath them. It is dreadful tho' to think that for want of the overhead cover which I have been begging and begging for, for the last 3 weeks, we have lost 4 lives and had 8 men injured. Perhaps now they will give me the timber and iron and nails. The want of supply of necessities is almost criminal. Still we must be thankful, that our losses were not greater.

The men and all of us expected an attack on top of the mine explosion and stood to arms, but no attack came off. The men were cool and very ready to give Mr Turk a hot reception.

Genl Birdwood came to see me, first visiting the men in the trenches. I made him a cup of tea and made him drink it. He always refuses. The reason being that he knew the difficulty of our water supply, and denies himself drink from us, in consequence. He is a splendid man, most loveable. So human and considerate. I get on with him splendidly as I do or have done with other Generals who are really good men. Yet I cannot get on with my Brigadier Genl Johnston late Col.

We have to organise "bomb" parties in our Bns but HQ sort of wash their hands of selection and supply of outfit, and say we must devise and make our own. I point out we have no materials or tools – no matter, HQ are not to be questioned! So it comes to this – a sandbag if we can get it, turned inside out, a piece of rope, if we can get it, to sling the sandbag, and then you have your up to date bomb carrying equipment!! Thus we go to war. "The joke war" as I have called it before. It is wrong all the same. There is not "a fair run for ones money". The British public I presume will get the truth some day and then wake up and give us every munition and equipment that we are entitled to. The blame, is to people like many of our Bn Cmdrs, and our Brigadier who will not tackle respective HQ and speak out. It is not popular and the best way of getting on to suggest let alone emphatically point out what HQ ought to do! I urged our Genl Johnston to urge Divn HQ to settle and make the best form of equipment (bomb carrying). He refused said as much that no one had any right to do so. Whatever HQ said was the last word. Such is the way of the Imperial army! I suppose! I spoke my mind. We met Bn Comdrs and the Brigadier, saw and discussed various ingenious "carriers", and then it was decided to adopt one of them: but no one had any material and the discussion became an absurdity. Even to make the sandbag carrier, we may have to use a horse shoe nail to sew it with string, i.e. if we can get the string. An officer solemnly suggested the nail saying he had some, but he couldn't suggest a substitute for sewing twine or string! What a poverty of organisation and supply!! As Major Hart says we, the British nation will begin this war <u>next summer</u>! But the lives lost in the meanwhile, the cost, who is responsible for them? I say the army officer or Departmental Head, who has obsequiously never questioned the ruling of his immediate chief, or dared to appeal, to insist on necessities. Weakness or corruption!

Commander England, H.M. Destroyer *Chelmar* visited the Post. I let him throw a bomb, he put it into the netting fronting the trench and it fell and exploded on the parapet. I managed to pull him right up against and under the parapet, and so we escaped injury. He was very apologetic. It <u>was</u> a rotten shot.

July 31st 1915

Another comparatively quiet night. I have been spelling "comparatively: with an i in 3rd syl [syllable] but have come to the correction that the i is wrong.

Another 6" H.E. shell landed on our front trench, missed a man by an inch or two, lodged in a traverse, and fortunately didn't explode. We dug it out, and it will go to NZ. I am keeping the brass detonator as a memento.

[MSX 2553]

Quinn's Post
Gallipoli Pa
31.7.15

My beloved

I wrote you letters on 23rd and 25th Inst and sent you a P. card about 28th Inst. Our mail closes tomorrow, so as I have some time to spare I start this letter to you. I received your very welcome letter of 8th July on 27th Inst, and it has set me querying over some . . . [illegible] of your question. "Can you guess what I mean?" And for my life I cannot. You have propounded complete mystery – you are going to <u>show</u> me that which you cannot <u>tell</u>. I thought I knew your every expectation. What is the speciality? Do my dear one tell me. I thought I knew the fullness of your love in every respect, but you have been keeping something back all these now nearly 10 years of married life! You told me in a recent letter that I am to make love to you (and I will do so, as I have always done) and I am when I meet[?] you to get a special reward or rather gift! I cannot imagine what it will be. Really I am puzzled – I thought you had given me all your gifts.

Father McMenamin has just been in. He is not looking very well. I took the opportunity of going to confession and will go to Crown [?] – Mass tomorrow. I think I shall be able to get off the post for Mass. I am very well indeed and <u>comfortable</u>. I have found out that flies do not like wire netting, and have put a piece across my window and another down my door. Then I get a current of air, and the flies which come thro are very few, and easily driven out, tho they do object to facing the wire. On the beach at HQ they have been using fish netting, with good results. Thinking it over and as I couldn't get good netting I tried the wire netting. We have it on the post to make bomb screens. It is a success.

Then I have had an <u>arm chair</u> made out of a biscuit box! I told the General the other day that Quinn's Post has got to the <u>arm chair</u> stage, and that it was a domestic virtue to have such chair. I sat him in it yesterday and made him have a cup of tea. He has always refused even a drink of water. Yesterday he confessed that he always refused because he knew how difficult it was for us to get water and what a shortage there was, and he would not as he called it "rob" us. Hitherto I have, in occidental fashion, always asked him if he would have a drink. This time I acted in oriental fashion. Had the tea made, and brought in, and put ready before him. He wouldn't take it at first, but I <u>made</u> "actually" <u>made</u> him take it saying I should feel hurt, and that I would fetch the tea away, if he didn't take it. He is an A/man and we all love him (Genl Birdwood), so kindly and considerate.

There is a lovely breeze blowing, and I am quite cool. Shorts, boots, and socks (no puttees[3]), silk shirt (no singlet) silk handkerchief for a neck tie and collar, sitting at my *escritoire* in my armchair, your plaid shawl over it, and a cushion of all my belongings. I must detail them to show what little one requires. Items: 2 singlets (in the wash 3) 1 pair socks, 1 pair thin riding breeches, 1 H'chief, *voilà tout* [French: that is all], my tunic, towels and hat hanging on the wall. My razor, soap etc etc are in my box side-board. The items enumerated are in a pillowslip, as a bag. The whole, a cushion by day, a pillow by night. As I wash I look out to and to sea and Imbros something like this: [see overleaf]

The big Turk attack, has not come off and it seems as if it wouldn't – we are sorry.

You will have heard from Terry and by now he is I expect in England. He went by the *Wanalla* about 20th Inst. Tell him I was glad to get his letter of 19th and so glad that he managed to get to England, and to hear, that in time he will be quite all right and not crippled. I don't think he will be, but he must help nature all he can. Edmond has gone I heard to Malta, and should be all right.

Ask Norah to tell me all about the Gaunts and her visit to them. I hope she <u>did</u> enjoy herself. I hope too to visit your aunt Lidderdale with you and am glad that she is mentally well, but it is very sad for her to be bodily helpless.

I sent the P. [picture] postcards to Nelson, to the boys thinking they were staying in NZ. You should get some letters, duplicates, I sent you addressed alternately to NZ and London. I hope that you soon got a letter from me and that you continue to get them. I wrote every week, since I am so sorry that

Sketch of Malone's dugout showing his view.

Alexander Turnbull Library

A – window frame of my shelter.

B – Terrace outside on it a table, at which I and young Harston, my staff officer sit and have our meals.

C – Timber posts supporting 2 brown blankets as an awning. Sand bags on left are of a shelter (occupied by the Engineer officer on the Post, one Captain Butler R.E.[4]) called by me "Fort Butler" because he got special leave from me to loophole it etc and hold it with a few of his men in case of a big Turk attack emerging over the crest of the hill which is at back – as part of four defensive works in rear. He is a red headed, blue eyed Irishman and was so delighted when I gave him the leave. He half expected I would pull the place down but it commands a couple of saps and so I could reasonably give him his wish.

D – a fire trench – the rest is the view, Hills, the sea Imbros, as I see looking thro' the window frame. With artists license I have left out a <u>pair of socks</u>, a silk <u>handkerchief</u> and a <u>silk shirt</u> which have been washed and are hanging out to dry, pinned to the edge of the awning and where the wind doesn't blow them up – blocking out most of the sea and Imbros!! I have left out the wire netting, as beyond my powers of drawing. The window frame is part of a bacon case! Bombs explode and rifles crack, but we don't worry.

E – is your photo – the original one I cut out of our double one that McAllister took. It is not to scale, I am afraid, as the window opening is only about 1'6" wide and the photo frame is 2½" wide still it will convey to you my *Mise en scene*.[5] I keep the photo on the window ledge now. The sea is more than a mile away from me, and Imbros about 13 miles away.

I forget about Denis['s] birthday but the watch and cake from you will have delighted him I suppose he and Barney will have quite long mid summer holidays. Here it is very hot in the camp but generally a breeze – always sunshine.

I am half expecting a letter from you today or tomorrow, as often the mail comes in on Saturday or Sunday. . . . I have been writing this with various interruptions and I must now leave off writing and go round the post and look into some special matters.

Back from my round – everything all right. An aeroplane (British) is flying round above us and has just dropped a bomb on the Turk trenches – such an explosion. The Turks are shelling it, and it is quite pretty, the blue sky the . . . buff semi-transparent looking aeroplane, the white puff-ball, bursts of the shells, one after another suddenly bursting into rows in the wake of the aeroplane. They never seem to get very near it. Then machine guns try and get on to it, no good tho – it sails and circles steadily on superior to everything however. I would so like a flight in one.

Sunday, 1st Aug 1915
Sweetheart it is 12.15 (afternoon) and I have just come in to finish and seal this which I must do by 12.45 pm. There was some extra special fighting all night last night, but we were not particularly interested, so we had a fairly quiet night. We let off a couple of mines, to smash up the Turks mining works about 9 of them.

I didn't get to Mass and communion this morning after all. I couldn't find the place. I walked for an hour, in the end I found it up a little side gully – Mass was just finishing as I got there. I was disappointed. Father McMenamin has promised to come and say Mass specially one morning on the Post for me. It will be quite an event. No letter from you, but no mail is in. I wonder what you are doing, not worrying I hope. We may get home to England soon for a complete rest and a refit. The 29th Divn is being withdrawn. They have had a very strenuous time. Our Brigade too has suffered such strain (2,500 casualties out of some 5,000) and the strain has been so heavy that really they could not do themselves justice in fresh hardwork. The food question too; is a big one. Bully beef (all worst beef) patty in this hot weather. Why on earth – dates and such cheap fruits cannot be supplied with rice beats me, the beef costs I am told 8d [pence] per lb. I put it at 4d. Dates at NZ prices retail are 4d. Here wholesale they should be say 1d. Theoretically we can exchange or have substituted jam for beef, anything for anything but in practice it is also likely[?] not so. More muddle, and more severe questioning by the Junior Officer of his superior. I spoke to Genl Birdwood about it two days ago. I have to wait for the supply people last night.[6] I meant to post [inform] him when I get the obvious . . . [illegible] truth, which apparently the British nation have not been told yet. There are a whole army of Heads who want sacking. I had three men killed and 8 men wounded two nights ago because my superior officer, would not back us up in allowance for a few sticks of timbers and some iron. I complained and complained and made myself a d-d [damned] nuisance, but I couldn't get the material. It was for what we could call head cover over a terrace when men had to lie down and sleep. It is almost criminal. Three fine young men killed and 8 wounded while sleeping. I almost cried not at their loss – we are used to that but at the "waste". Lives, valuable lives lost for nothing. We shall get the timber and iron now! But Dearie I mustn't bother you with this sort of thing. We are paying for England's unpreparedness and folly, and she is paying for the falsity of her rulers and their ... [illegible]

The postman [?] waits. With all my love, to the sweetest beloved and dearest sweetheart in the world.

Your lover

[MSX 2546]

August 1st 1915, Sunday

Time is beginning to fly. The Turks are evidently not going to come at us. We fired two mines under them last night, and the Australians, on the R [Right] flank went out and took a trench. They had allowed the Turks to dig close to them. We believe they are holding it all right. Wrote to Mater a long letter – by today's mail. There is to be a big move soon. I move too. A chap from Cape Helles says Achi Baba will be taken on 14th. So may it be.

Wellington Inf Bn casualties to date

	Officers	Others	Died of Sickness
Killed	7	124	3 men
Wounded	17	372	
Missing		28	

Totals 24 officers, 527 men.
The missing are almost certainly 'killed'.

[MSX 2547]

August 2nd 1915

Everything all right but we had a bad accident in the trenches. An Engineer Sergeant has contrived a new bomb mortar throwing a bomb of 4 slabs (15 oz each) [425 grams] gun cotton and had Headquarters leave to try it in the Post. The Turks had put up some new head cover and we wanted to smash it but the distance was a bit too far for our hand heavy Lobiniere[7] bombs so the Engineer asked to have a shot. I went up to observe. We cleared one trench just in front of where the Sergeant had his mortar, an observation place about 12 feet back. One of the two fuses used missed fire, and the bomb exploded in the mortar, killing a Sergeant [Robert Nairn][8] who was trying to pull the fuse out. He had his hand and forearm blown off and was so otherwise injured that he died within a short time. It was a bad explosion, 60 oz gun cotton. I thought the Turks had thrown a bomb at me observing so went on observing expecting the discharge of our mortar. Then I heard of the accident and went to the post.

August 3rd 1915

All well. We are to move out soon, round left flank. Went for a reconnaissance trip on HM Destroyer *Colne*. General Godley and General Shaw, 13 Division, came too. It was a pleasant trip but the beach and pier were shelled before we started. We go out and come in, in a picket (motor) boat to the Destroyer. As we wanted to land the Turks shelled the pier and us pretty persistently. One shell went just over us into the sea about 50 yards beyond. We circled about until a lull came and then went in and got ashore safely.

August 4th 1915

All well. Col Stoddart of 2nd Australian Light Horse is to relieve me as OC Post and I and the Wellington Battalion go to Happy Valley tomorrow night at 11.30 pm (2330) and stay there. No fires. No movement all day 6th and go out on night 6th with rest of Brigade to take Chunuk Bair in a big combined movement against 971, Koja Chemen Tepe. We are pleased to be moving but the men are run down and the reinforcement men are in a big majority so I am not too sanguine about what we can do. General Birdwood, it is reported, said the NZ Inf Bde had had so much hard work and had been so knocked about that it should not go out in the present move but our Brigadier wouldn't listen to that and insisted that we be given one of the toughest pieces of the job.[9] He is too airy for me and does not know the weakness of his Brigade. It really ought to have a long spell of absolute rest such as the 29th Division is getting. We'll do our best anyway but it is not altogether fair on the Brigade. My Battalion too has done extra work, has had no spell at Imbros as did the Canterbury and Otago Battalions and will go straight out of the trenches to fight again, climbing great hills. One thing the Brigade is getting credit for having <u>volunteered</u> for the job. We don't deserve it because we have had no say in it and "volunteers" were not asked for. If they had been I think we would have come forward all right. I do not like this ['rather dread' overwritten by WGM] job, it will be night work. We have to wait on the Maoris and our MR clearing some hills and trenches over or by which we have to tackle the high ridge and none of our troops are trained enough for night work in very rough country. We shall possibly mistake the Maoris for Turks and the confusion in the dark will be terrible. If we could only start fighting at dawn and have the day before us, we should have it a real good fight, artillery support and seeing what to do and when to go would be a treat. Still it is not for me to decide.

I and Col Young went up to Walker's Ridge and then on to No. 3 outpost at extreme left flank and had as good a look at the country as we could. If, and a big if, the Maoris and Mounted Rifles do their job properly then unless we get lost, ours ought to come off all right. And if too the Otago and Canterbury people do theirs. I wouldn't be surprised if the Wellington Battalion gets up alone the 1st and has to dig in and stick it out as at Walker's Ridge and Krithia respectively. I am feeling very fit and the prospect of action is inspiriting. But I do feel that the preparation as regards our Brigade anyway is not thorough. The Brigadier will not get down to bed rock. He seems to think that a night attack and the taking of entrenched positions without artillery preparation is like "kissing ones hand". Yesterday he burst forth "If there's any hitch I shall go right up and take the place myself". All as it were in a minute and on his own! He says "there's to be no delay". He is an extraordinary man. If it were not so serious it would be laughable. So far as I am concerned the men, my brave gallant men, shall have the best fighting chance I can give them or that can be got. No airy plunging and disregard of the rules and chances.

August 5th 1915

Col Stoddart took over at about 9 am. Conference with Army Corps Commander in Rest Gully at 2.30 pm. It is said that three new Divisions have landed and that the move is to be a big one. Apparently my plan of May last is to come off, in part anyway. But it is late now and it ought to be bigger and go as far as Mal Tepe.[10] Keep the Turks on the run, if we can shift him!

[MSX 2553]

Quinn's Post
2.8.15

My beloved.

This to begin my next letter. I am well and fit. Will you get a couple of copies of *The Sphere* of July 10th last and keep them for me. There is a double page picture of war position near Krithia and Achibaba [sic, Achi Baba], which is something like the facts, and as we (Wellington Bn) were in the Battle of 6, 7 and 8th May, it is and will be of special interest.

5.8.15
There has been no letter yet from you and it is not sure that tomorrow, when we expect the English mail to be in, that we shall be get at able [get-at-able] with the mail. I must finish this today. For there is a big move on and our NZ Inf Bde (including of course my Bn) takes an important part in it. We are all sanguine and expect to have a victory of such importance, that it will materially affect the whole position. By the time you get this it will be over and the result public. We shall have a lot of hard work. After this move I quite expect that our Brigade will be withdrawn for an absolute rest. The men are run down, 3 months fighting and work, big new strain[?], heavy casualties, not much rest, bring the best of men to a point, dangerously near that of breaking. I personally am not in need of a spell. I find I am one of the strongest men here and can stand anything. Always cool, calm and steady – most matter of course. I tell you this not out of boast, but to comfort you and prevent you from thinking me run down etc. As to the spell I shall most certainly welcome it because I think I shall be able to see you even if only for a short time. And that will be "Heaven". You know the poetry, you quoted. That is one big handicap to the Gallipoli campaign. We can't get off for weekends as do the officers and men in Flanders, and be able to run over to England, and then on longer spells of relief – stay there. Sweetheart I love you if it were possible, more and more than ever and do so long to be with you. You must not worry about me – if my letters don't arrive regularly, you will know that it is either the post or our shifting about that causes the delay.

I will always manage to write something. I have handed over the command of the Post to a Col Stoddart of the 2nd Australian Light Horse. In a way I am quite sorry to go. The Post is now one of the safest in the show, and I am very comfortable, everything going like clockwork. Still the feeling of the new move makes ones blood move quicker, and if I stayed here much longer I should be getting fat! Dear old Quinn's Post – you have been and are most interesting and are a monument to my gallant men. I have begun to soliloquise and not write to you and that is rude is it not dear one. I wonder what we shall be doing – this day next week. We shall have I expect 2 or 3 days really hard work, and rough time – and then get settled into something regular again.

I hope that Terry is all right. I have not heard further of Edmond, but he will be right I am sure.

Your dear letter of 13th July just came to my very great delight. But I must go off instanter to a conf [conference] with Army Commander, at 2.30 and I have only time to get there.

I hope to write another note this evening.

With all my love
Yr lover   x_____x_____x

Quinn's Post
8.10 pm 5/8/15

My Sweetheart,

In less than 2 Hours, we move off to a valley, where we will be up all night and tomorrow, in readiness for a big attack which will start tomorrow night. Everything promises well and victory should rest with us. God grant it so, and that our casualties will not be too heavy. I expect to go thro' all right but, dear wife, if anything untoward happens to me, you must not grieve too much, there are our dear children to be brought up. You know how I love and have loved you, and we have had many years of great happiness together. If at any time in the past I seemed absorbed in "affairs" it was that I might make proper provision for you and the children. That was due from me. It is true that perhaps I overdid it somewhat. I believe now that I did, but did not see it at the time. I regret very much now, that it was so and that I lost more happiness than I need have done. You must forgive me. Forgive also anything unkindly or hard that I may have done, or said in the past.

I have made a will and it is at the office at Stratford. I think it was justly drawn, anyway I intended it so to be. I hope and think that the provision for you and the children will keep you and them in ease and comfort. I know that you will never forget me, or let the dear children do so.

I am prepared for death, and hope that God will have forgiven me all my sins.

My desire for life, so that I may see and be with you again, could not be greater, but I have only done what every man was bound to do in our country's need. It has been a great consolation to me that you approved my action. The sacrifice was really yours. May you be consoled and rewarded by our dear Lord.

Your loving husband
W.G. MALONE

Quinn's Post
5/8/15
[about 10. pm]

Sweetheart,

I sent a letter off this afternoon, just after receipt of your of your so welcome letter of 13th Ulto. We move out of this Post in about an hour, so I write a little in answer to your letter, as probably I shall not have time, about Saturday or Sunday, when our next mail generally closes. We are in for a big move and everything promises well. The attack starts tomorrow night. You will have heard all about it, long before you get this. It was lovely getting your letter today, because things will be up side down for the next few days and mail delivery will be out of the question. I am so sorry that you were so long without letters from me. You will have got a big batch long ere now. Yours come now weekly or oftener – so mine ought to reach you in same way.

Yes I do want you. I long and long and am beginning to lose my enjoyment of this life, as it entails separation from you. You are, in all my spare time, in my thoughts, and I do so look forward to our *réunion*. I do think much and have time to do so every night and day.

And so you would like to be my orderly, "batman". You mean do you not? my body servant. The orderlies only run messages etc. Young Okey my batman from NZ to here is now with his Coy. My present man is a young

English lad only 20, Smart,[11] such nice boy and thorough in his work. But if you were my batman, you would get more than a "smile and a word". Would you not want a kiss now and again? But dearie this is no place for women. You must wait until I rejoin you.

I do know all your feelings and I reciprocate them, but do not be sad. All will be well and our future life together will be all the sweeter and better for this separation.

I am glad that Norah is enjoying herself at the Gaunts, in spite of the dog. I hope the Geo Vasey's visit passed off all right. I was so sorry to hear of Mr Standish's death and you did quite the right thing, as you always do, in writing to Mrs Standish as you did. And so "Bus" is coming to the war. He is not a bad chap. Give my regards to Miss Standish if occasion occurs. Major I. Standish[12] is on the Peninsula. I saw him at near Cape Helles, with his Battery, the evening before we went into the Battle of Krithia. He had been fighting his battery all day. We had a good chat. He is such a fine fellow.

I too hope to see your cousin's well ordered farm. It will be a great pleasure to visit him with you.

Yes we see newspapers, altho' they are a bit old. Mr G.H. Schofield [sic, Scholefield] NZ Press Representative, London sends me regularly the *Daily Mirror*, and *London Opinion*.[13] If you go to London, try and find him and give him my news.

Yes – more men and more munitions are wanted, right enough everywhere. Major Hart, who is in England wrote me that England will <u>begin</u> the war next summer! That people there are only now beginning to understand its magnitude and importance. Dear old England. She is a muddle right enough, but comes out all right in the end. And there is no country like her. If only we can knock a bit more thoroughness into her, as a matter of course it would help wonderfully.

My candle is all but burnt out and we will soon be moving. So good night, dearest one. With all my love.

Your lover and husband

x___x___x

Love to Norah and the little ones.

Postscript

August 5–8: Chunuk Bair

At 10.15 pm, a few minutes after he had finished his last letter to Ida, Malone led the Wellington Battalion, which had a strength of 23 officers and 828 other ranks, out of Quinn's Post. He had resumed command of the Battalion at mid-day on 5 August. Malone and his men marched to Happy Valley, a rest area, just north of Walker's Ridge that was concealed from Turkish observation. Earlier the men of the battalion had sewn white bands on the arms and a white patch on the back of their jackets to aid identification during the forthcoming night attack. They had to wear their jackets inside out while they rested in Happy Valley with the rest of the New Zealand Infantry Brigade. The New Zealand troops were not permitted to light any fires and hid in the valley's scrub to avoid detection by enemy reconnaissance aircraft.[1] With typical foresight, Malone had called a meeting of the regimental fund committee at Quinn's Post on 4 August and it had been agreed that £200 should be sent to Egypt to purchase comforts for the battalion's wounded and that the fund's books also be returned to Egypt for safekeeping. In the bloody aftermath of the August offensive, the fund, on which Malone placed such store, proved its worth helping wounded Wellington Battalion men to purchase essential personal items and small comforts.[2]

The Wellington Battalion and the rest of the New Zealand Infantry Brigade had been given a key role in the type of offensive to break the stalemate at Gallipoli that Malone and others had first considered in May. That Malone had appreciated after only a few weeks at Gallipoli that an offensive to the north represented the best and perhaps only way of breaking out of the beachhead demonstrates that he was a highly capable tactician. By August, even with the limited information available to him, Malone understood that such an operation was fraught with difficulties.[3] The main elements of the plan put forward by Birdwood and his staff and then finalised by Hamilton's headquarters and approved by him were:

- The secret landing of substantial reinforcements (13th Division and 29th Indian Brigade) at Anzac Cove between 4 and 6 August.

- Diversionary attacks at Helles and at Lone Pine in the southern part of the Anzac beachhead on 6 and 7 August.

- The landing of two British divisions at Suvla Bay, North of the Anzac area, late on the 6 August and early on 7 August.

- A 'left hook' launched from the Anzac area designed to seize the three key points on the Sari Bair range, Hill 971 (Koja Chemen Tepe), Hill Q and Chunuk Bair, which dominated the Anzac area. Possession of these high points would, it was thought, place the Allied forces in a good position to cut off the Turkish forces further south.

The forces involved in the offensive were organised into two attacking columns, each of which was to be assisted by a covering column. The Left Assaulting Column was commanded by Major-General H.V. Cox, and consisted of Monash's 4th Australian Infantry Brigade and Cox's 29th Indian Brigade. Its task was to move well to the north, advance up the Arghyl Dere valley and then to split into two parts to seize Hills 971 and Q. The left covering force consisted of two British infantry battalions and half a company

Men prepare for the start of the offensive against the Sari Bair range. The white patches stitched to their sleeves and backs are to aid identification in the dark. This photograph was probably taken in Happy Valley, just north of Walker's Ridge, late on 6 August 1915.

Laurie Smith Postcard Coll

of engineers, whose role was to clear the path of the assaulting column by seizing the lower ridges of the Sari Bair range. The Right Assaulting Column was commanded by Brigadier-General Francis Johnston and consisted of the New Zealand Infantry Brigade, most of an Indian mountain battery and a field company of New Zealand engineers. Its task was to advance up the Chailik Dere and Sazli Dere valleys, then to assault and capture Chunuk Bair. Once the New Zealanders were firmly established on Chunuk Bair they were to attack the Turkish positions on Battleship Hill from the rear. The right covering force, under the command of Brigadier-General Andrew Russell was made up of the New Zealand Mounted Rifle Brigade, the Otago Mounted Rifles, the Maori Contingent and a troop of New Zealand engineers. This force was to clear the way for Johnston's column by seizing, in a silent night attack, the foothills blocking the assaulting column's advance. The two assaulting column were to be in position to launch assaults on their final objectives at dawn on 7 August.

Major-General Godley was given command of this corps-sized force in what was bound to be a complicated and demanding operation. The small

Part of a map from C.F. Aspinall-Oglander, *Military Operations: Gallipoli, Vol. II*, which shows the opposing lines at Anzac on 6 August 1915 and the objectives of the Allied offensive.

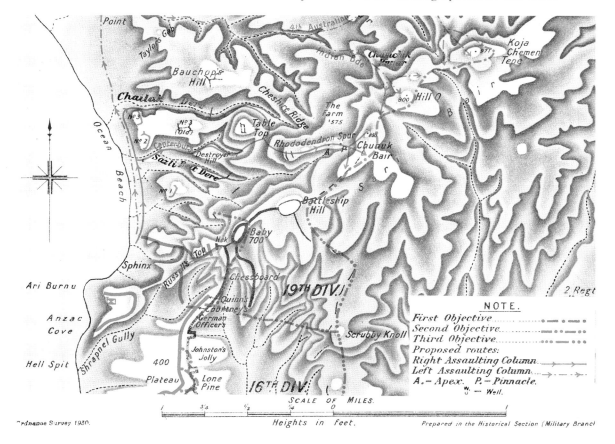

and inexperienced staff of his New Zealand and Australian Division was not capable of effectively directing the operations of Godley's force. The plan for the offensive was dependent on the troops involved keeping to a tight timetable. Before the offensive, the ground over which it was to be launched, was reconnoitred as well as possible. It is, however, now clear that those responsible for planning the offensive failed to take proper account of the difficulties involved in moving large forces over extremely rugged and confusing ground at night. The plan also involved unrealistic expectations of the physical capabilities of officers and men exhausted by months of combat and riddled with dysentery and other diseases.[4] The men of the Wellington Battalion were in the view of one man who survived the campaign, 'only shadows of what they had been when they landed. Probably half of them ought to have been in hospital.'[5] The strength of the Wellington Battalion's *esprit de corps* is demonstrated by the fact that when news of the planned attack reached sick men resting on Lemnos, many asked to return to Gallipoli to take part in the operation.[6] The situation of the Wellington Battalion was particularly serious because, unlike the other New Zealand infantry battalions, it had not had a short break on Lemnos and was committed to the offensive immediately after a strenuous period of work remodelling Quinn's Post.[7] Unlike the plan outlined by Malone in May, the planners of the August offensive, unfortunately, assigned key tasks to newly-arrived British units, which were fresh, but quite inexperienced.[8]

Johnston issued his final orders to Malone and the other battalion commanders while they waited at Happy Valley. Malone then convened a conference with his company commanders at which he issued and discussed with them his operations orders for the assault on Chunuk Bair. These orders set out the order in which the Battalion was to move off, stipulated that the head of the Battalion column had to be in the entrance to Otago Gully (near Outpost No. 3) at 9.30 pm on 6 August, and described the role each company would have in the attack. The orders also noted that the password for the night was 'Godley' and the countersign 'success'.[9] Malone would also almost certainly have taken this opportunity to brief his officers on the orders and instructions he and the other battalion commanders had received from brigade headquarters. These stressed the importance of speed and silence if the Brigade was to achieve its objectives, and noted the 'supreme importance of strict punctuality and accurate timing'. The instructions specifically warned against straggling when the troops moved along communication trenches or up gullies, and noted that any straggling 'must inevitably cause the troops in rear to be delayed and therefore not immediately available when wanted.'[10] He also took the opportunity to attend to some personal matters, despatching his batman, Private Smart, back to Quinn's Post to fetch his tunic and items for other officers.[11] Malone may also have gone with other officers to Outposts No. 2 and No. 3 to study through binoculars the ground over which they were to attack. Malone had a few days earlier embarked in a destroyer to observe from the sea the territory leading up to Chunuk Bair.[12]

The Wellington Battalion formed up in Happy Valley at 8.30 pm and then took its place, behind the Otago Battalion, in the assaulting column. For the operation each infantryman carried 120 rounds of ammunition, two empty sandbags, two water bottles, rations for 48 hours, a field dressing and his rifle and bayonet.[13] At the same time as the Right Assaulting Column was preparing to move out of Happy Valley, the New Zealand Mounted Rifles and the rest of the covering force began their silent attack with the bayonet to clear the foothills between the ANZAC perimeter and the Sari Bair range. Russell's men were well prepared for this task and after bitter, close quarter fighting achieved their objectives. It was, as the Australian official historian, C.E.W. Bean, later wrote a 'magnificent feat of arms, the brilliance of which was never surpassed, if indeed equalled, during the campaign'. Although the covering force had done great work, the whole operation was already beginning to fall behind its tight timetable.[14]

Johnston's orders called for the Right Assaulting Column to move to No. 2 Outpost; from there it was to move north following a route just inland from Ocean Beach. The whole force, apart from the Canterbury Battalion, was then to move east up Chailak Dere, the valley south of Bauchop's Hill. The Otago Battalion, which was to lead the column, would then take Rhododendron Ridge (also known as Rhododendron Spur) that led up to Chunuk Bair. The Wellington Battalion had the task of seizing Cheshire Ridge that was just to the north, and overlooked Aghyl Dere (the next Valley to the north) and the area known as 'The Farm'. The Auckland Battalion was to be in reserve. While the rest of the column advanced up Chailik Dere, the Canterbury Battalion was to move up Sazli Dere, the next valley to the south and occupy the southern side of Rhododendron Ridge. The column was then to attack and capture Chunuk Bair.

From the beginning of the advance it was clear that the Right Assaulting Column would be hard put to keep to its schedule. The Auckland and Canterbury Battalions became entangled and their progress was impeded. Later in the night, the Canterbury Battalion took the wrong route up Sazli Dere, and became lost and disorganised. Bauchop's Hill and Table Top, two key features on either side of Chailik Dere took longer to secure than had been anticipated. It was easy for troops to lose their way in the rugged country, and the valley itself was found to be blocked by barbed wire entanglements. Small parties of Turks in the area, who had been overlooked by the mounted rifles, also caused delays. As a result, the Wellington Battalion spent nearly two hours waiting at Outpost No. 2 before the way was clear for them to advance up Chailik Dere. It was clear to all involved that the operation was falling well behind schedule. Malone, who was in the head of his battalion, was acutely aware of the need to speed up the advance, but there was little he could do. Johnston ordered Malone's battalion to advance up the valley through the Otago Battalion, that had become dispersed during its actions to clear Chailik Dere and seize Table Top. Dawn, which was at 4.30 am, was approaching when Malone's troops got clear of the valley and began to advance onto Rhododendron Ridge near the position later known as the Apex; an area of sheltered ground near the intersection of Rhododendron and Cheshire Ridges below and about 500 metres from Chunuk Bair.[15] Just what took place at the Apex and later on Chunuk Bair, and why the New Zealand commanders made certain decisions is difficult to determine because of gaps in the available evidence and significant differences in the various primary sources covering the actions.[16]

Looking down Rhododendron Ridge (also known as Rhododendron Spur), which runs west from Chunuk Bair. The road that can be seen was built after the end of the campaign.

Australian War Memorial

Exactly when the Wellington Battalion reached the Apex is unclear, although the battalion war diary states that the position was in their hands by dawn, at 4.30 am. Other sources, however, indicate that the battalion was not in full possession of the Apex until significantly later in the morning, most probably at about 5.45 am or 6 am, and possibly not until shortly before 7 am.[17] The most probable explanation is that the leading elements of the battalion reached the Apex just before dawn, but that because the Wellingtons were strung out in a long column, it was not until later in the morning that Malone had his full unit at the position and would have been able to push on towards Chunuk Bair in some force.[18] This is a point of some importance because it has been alleged that Malone and the New Zealand Infantry Brigade as a whole missed an opportunity to push on and capture a lightly defended Chunuk Bair before or at dawn on 7 August.[19] It was, it seems, clear to Malone when he reached the Apex that any chance of taking Chunuk Bair at dawn, as originally planned, had gone. He immediately set about securing what was a valuable position that included the initial objective set for his battalion by Johnston. He sent the following message to Johnston: 'I am occupying a position nearly at the head of gully. As it is day and I am not sure of my position I am lining the crest of surrounding ridges so as to ensure reasonable safety. I am reconnoitring further and will act on further knowledge and report.'[20] Unfortunately, this message is not timed, but it must have been written before Johnston arrived at the Apex, at about 8.00 am. The Auckland Battalion joined Malone's battalion at the Apex and helped secure the position.[21] Turkish reserves were sent to Chunuk Bair on the morning of 7 August and by 8 am, it appears, that a force of about 250 men was holding the hill.[22]

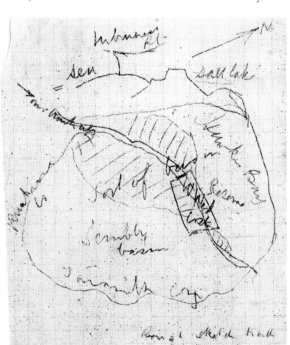

The crucial question that faced Malone and other New Zealand commanders on the morning of 7 August was whether they should press on and attack Chunuk Bair as soon as possible or secure their position at the Apex, before launching an assault. Bean, in the Australian official history, suggests that Temperley, Johnston's Brigade Major, advocated pressing on, but that Malone 'the most forcible of the New Zealand commanders, was against the attempt.'[23] Bean's view, is based at least in part on a discussion he had with Temperley in late 1918 or early 1919.[24] This position is supported by the Wellington Battalion history, the Gallipoli chapters of which were written by W.H. Cunningham, who was Malone's second in command.[25] An attempt to seize Chunuk Bair would certainly have been consistent with Birdwood's instructions to the commanders of units involved in the offensive, that they had to press on as quickly as possible.[26] It would, however, be in keeping with the views Malone expressed in his diaries and letters for him to oppose a quickly organised and risky attack. His lack of confidence in Johnston would also probably have influenced his position. By this time Johnston was in a very bad state of health and he may also have been drunk. In any case, he was by this time incapable of exercising effective command over his force.[27]

The British official historian of the Gallipoli campaign privately stated that it was 'a national calamity' that Johnston was not removed from his command before the offensive.[28] Temperley, however, states in his unpublished account of the battle that a pause and a period of consolidation seemed to be the most prudent approach. This was the course of action agreed at a conference between Malone, Robert Young, the Auckland Battalion commanding officer and Johnston, which took place at the Apex after the brigade commander arrived at about 8.00 am. This view was sent in a message to Godley, who responded by ordering Johnston to attack at once.

Johnston received this order at 9.30 am, Temperley stated later that he was so strongly opposed to this course of action that he recommended to Johnston that he disobey the order. Brigadier-General Johnston would not countenance such a course. He ordered the Auckland Battalion to attack along the 60-metre wide saddle linking the Apex with Chunuk Bair. Support was to be provided by the 2/10th Gurkhas from the Left Assaulting Column, which had become lost during the night advance and had agreed to cooperate with the New Zealand brigade. Lieutenant-Colonel Robert Young personally reconnoitred the ground over which his battalion would have to attack and was convinced that if the attack was to have any real chance of success, it should be delayed until after nightfall, but Johnston was adamant that Godley's order had to be obeyed. The attack at 11 am was a disaster. Because of the narrowness of the saddle, the Auckland Battalion had to attack with its companies arranged in echelon (one after another). The Aucklanders and Gurkhas were savaged by intense rifle and machine gun fire from Chunuk Bair, from the Turkish positions on Battleship Hill on their right flank, and from Hill Q on their left flank. A small force of Aucklanders managed to seize a Turkish trench about 100 metres along with saddle at a cost of some 300 men killed or wounded.[29]

After the failure of that attack, it appears that Johnston may have ordered the Wellington Battalion and the available element of the Canterbury Battalion to launch another hopeless assault. This attack did not eventuate, probably because of Malone's violent opposition to what would have been a useless waste of life. Many years later, Corporal Charles Clark of the Wellington Battalion recalled Malone arguing with two British officers (probably Johnston and Temperley). According to Clark, Malone refused to attack saying that he was 'not going to ask my men to commit suicide' and stating that his battalion would seize Chunuk Bair the next day, once it was dark.[30]

The New Zealand Infantry Brigade spent the rest of the day digging in at the Apex. They steadily lost men to enfilading fire from Battleship Hill, which appears to have caused many more losses than fire from Chunuk Bair. Three of the Brigade's four battalions were not immediately fit for further offensive operations. The Otago Battalion was being reorganised. The Auckland Battalion had been shattered and the Canterbury Battalion had suffered heavy losses when it was caught in the open by Turkish artillery firing from Hill Q. Most of the Allied troops involved in the attack were also exhausted and in need of a rest to recover their strength.[31]

The New Zealanders were much closer to the objective then their comrades in the Left Assault Column, which had become disorganised and disorientated in the steep hills and gullies leading to Hill 971 and Q. Monash, the Commander of the 4th Australian Brigade, seems to have lost his nerve and halted his brigade at dawn on 7 August, well short of his objective; Hill 971. The 29th Indian Brigade had pressed on more effectively and had halted only about 1000 metres from Hill Q.[32] Malone considered Monash's brigade to be a bad one, an opinion apparently shared by, at least, some Australians.[33] Although Monash went on to great achievements on the Western Front, he had a very mixed reputation at Gallipoli, where it appears he was known as the 'the dug-out king'.[34]

During the afternoon of 7 August, Godley reviewed the situation, and planned a new assault on the Sari Bair range for dawn the following day. The New Zealanders were to assault Chunuk Bair, the 29th Indian Brigade was to seize Hill Q and Monash's brigade was to renew its efforts to capture Hill 971. As part of this plan Godley reinforced the Indian brigade with a British brigade and dispatched two inexperienced battalions from 'Kitchener's New

The summit of Hill 971 from Chunuk Bair looking north, in early 1919. The road that can be seen did not exist in 1915.

Australian War Memorial

Army', the 7th Gloucesters and the 8th Welsh Pioneers to join the New Zealand Infantry Brigade. The Auckland Mounted Rifles and the Maori Contingent were also placed under Johnston's command as reserves for the new assault.

The New Zealand Infantry Brigade headquarters received orders from Godley for the new assault at 9.45 pm, but it appears that Malone whose battalion was to lead the attack was not given his orders until midnight or 1 am on the morning of 8 August. This delay may have been due to concerns Johnston and Temperley had about Malone's tactical judgement (see below), but the state of the other battalions of the brigade meant that the Wellington Battalion had to lead the attack. After returning from the brigade headquarters, Malone discussed the operation with his second in command, Major Cunningham. The necessary orders for the company commanders were prepared and Cunningham took these round while Malone returned to the brigade headquarters to ask for additional supplies of water and ammunition for his battalion. Malone apparently did not doubt that his men could capture Chunuk Bair, but was acutely aware that his battalion would need adequate supplies if it were to hold the hill against the inevitable Turkish counter-attacks. As a result of Malone's request, a party of men was sent back to Anzac Cove in an effort to obtain the necessary extra supplies.

During his visit to the brigade headquarters Malone also met with Captain Jesse Wallingford, the brigade machine gun officer, who promised to send forward four machine guns as soon as Chunuk Bair was secured. There was nothing more Malone could do and he returned to his bivouac where he apparently had a short, but sound sleep.[35]

At about 3 am Malone woke his batman, Private Benjamin Smart, and told him about the attack in which he was to lead his battalion. Smart later wrote in his diary that Malone 'gave me an address of his wife to write to in case he got hit. I thought he would pass out as he shook hands with me before he went over and said "good-bye"!'[36] Half an hour later, Malone and Cunningham went around the battalion rousing their men. At the same time a heavy and quite accurate bombardment of Chunuk Bair began. The Wellington Battalion formed up in four lines each of four platoons in the weak moonlight at the Apex. The Hawkes Bay Company was on the right, the Wellington West Coast Company on the left; they were supported by the Ruahine Company (on the left) and the Taranaki Company (on the right). At 4.15 am the bombardment ceased, and the Wellington Battalion with bayonets fixed moved across the narrow saddle connecting the Apex with Chunuk Bair in a solid column.[37]

Malone and his men could see Chunuk Bair in front of them, clearly and fatefully defined by the first rays of dawn as they crossed the saddle. The battalion then spread out over a frontage of about 200 metres on the

Lieutenant Allan Preston (on right), the Wellington Battalion machine gun officer, passes a trench on the Apex as soldiers of the 7th Gloucesters (left) wait to ascend Chunuk Bair to reinforce the Wellington Battalion, dawn, 8 August 1915. The New Zealand machine guns are on the ridge line firing on the Hill Q area. Preston was wounded just after this photograph was taken.

Hampton Coll, National Army Museum

open ground leading to the crest. They advanced at a steady pace, 'expecting every second to receive the full blast of rifle and machine-gunfire which greeted the Auckland Battalion's advance the day before. . . . tired and weary though the men had been when they started from the Apex, instinctively, the battalion seemed to feel that at last the great chance had come and that Chunuk Bair was to be its supreme test. The men in a few strides had recovered their old jaunty spirit of the training days of Egypt and, led by their gallant Colonel, they were in the right mood to tackle with cold steel any enemy that might stand to face them on the top.'[38] No blast of fire, however, greeted the Wellingtons as they advanced. Confused command arrangements for the Turkish troops on Chunuk Bair and the heavy and accurate artillery bombardment caused virtually all the Turkish defenders to flee the hill. Malone's troops captured a machine gun and its German crew, and occupied their objective at about 4.40 am; after meeting very little resistance.[39] The New Zealanders discovered that Chunuk Bair consisted of two crests about 200 metres apart, connected by a saddle. In front of them, towards the east, the land fell away fairly steeply until it reached some flatter ground where there were some vacant Turkish howitzer positions. Beyond these positions lay a valley. To the north, Chunuk Bair was dominated by Hill Q, which remained in Turkish hands. As it became light, the men of the Wellington Battalion could see the village of Boghali and the important

The Dardanelles from Chunuk Bair, looking southeast. Chanak (now Canakkale) on the far side of the Narrows is on the right, Boghali (now Canyayla) is on the extreme left centre. This photograph was taken in early 1919, from the position furthest inland reached by the New Zealanders on 8 August 1915. It is one of a series taken on the Gallipoli Peninsula by the Australian Historical Mission during the months of February and March 1919.

Australian War Memorial

north-south road that ran through it, and further east, catch a glimpse of the Dardanelles.[40]

Malone may have briefly considered taking advantage of the surprisingly easy capture of Chunuk Bair by pressing further forward. The size of his force, the strong position occupied by the Turks and his clear orders to secure Chunuk Bair and his lack of communications with his brigade headquarters all seemed to have combined to quickly convince him that the best course open to them was to dig in on the crest.[41]

Temperley would later allege that Malone hopelessly compromised the chances of a successful defence of Chunuk Bair by instructing his force to dig in on the reverse or western side of the ridge. In his unpublished memoirs, Temperley, who was no friend of Malone, suggested that the Wellington Battalion's commander was a dogmatic man with few ideas and little interest in or knowledge of tactics. He went on to allege that Malone was obsessed with the idea, set out in a booklet dealing with lessons learned on the Western Front, of occupying the reverse slopes of hills or ridges to reduce the effectiveness of enemy artillery fire.[42] As Brigade Major, Temperley was very well placed to influence official records of the battle and his unfair and inaccurate views on Malone's actions were widely accepted.[43] An official booklet, *Notes from the Front* (London, 1914) that sets out the advantages of holding a reverse slope position, with a covering force on the forward slope, was amongst Malone's effects.[44] Malone apparently supported the views set out in the booklet in an argument with Johnston and Temperley, who believed that because Turkish artillery at Gallipoli was comparatively weak the older idea of occupying forward or crest lines was still appropriate. According to Malone's adjutant, Captain (Later Major Sir) Ernest Harston, this question was still bothering Malone during the advance on Chunuk Bair and he decided to hold both the forward and the reverse slope. Each position was to be occupied by two of his companies and saps or trenches dug between the two as quickly as possible.

Harston's account is supported by other survivors of the battle for Chunuk Bair. It seems clear that Malone ordered two of his companies to occupy and expand the existing Turkish trenches on the crest of the ridge and the other two to dig a new support trench on the reverse slope. The two companies on the reverse slope were ordered to dig saps forward to connect the two trench lines, which were about 30 metres apart. The crest of Chunuk Bair was made up of extremely hard clay that made digging trenches a very slow and difficult proposition. A covering force of about 80 men was sent down the forward slope to establish outposts in and around the Turkish howitzer

emplacements. Its task was to prevent the Turks from surprising the troops digging in on the crest. These dispositions were sound and demonstrate Malone's tactical competence.[45]

Dawn was at 4.30 am, and half an hour later a haze that had concealed the capture of Chunuk Bair from the Turkish troops on Hill Q lifted. The Turkish response was immediate and deadly. Increasingly heavy rifle, machine gun and artillery fire swept over Chunuk Bair and the saddle leading to the Apex. The two leading companies of the 7th Gloucesters had by this time already crossed the saddle and had been ordered by Malone to deploy to the left (or north) of the Wellington Battalion and to extend the trenches the New Zealanders were digging. Their rear companies were caught by the Turkish fire crossing the saddle and suffered heavily. The 8th Welsh Pioneers were following the Gloucesters and lost most of their officers and men before they reached Chunuk Bair. They and some of the Gloucesters took up a position to the right (or south) of the Wellingtons.[46] The grievous losses inflicted on these units crossing the saddle clearly indicates how well the various Turkish positions could support each other and suggests that the size of the Turkish garrison holding Chunuk Bair on 7 August is not as an important an issue as some historians have claimed. The Turkish troops on Hill Q, which is slightly higher than Chunuk Bair, had a very good 'field of fire not only along the crest but also along the forward slope and over a considerable part of the reverse slope'. They were able to enfilade (fire down the length of) the old Turkish trenches and were able to inflict severe casualties on New Zealanders occupying them.[47] Fortunately some elements

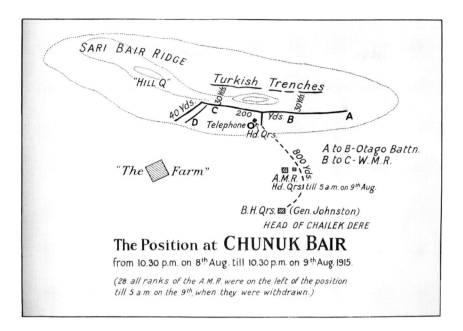

This sketch map from the *Official History of the Wellington Mounted Rifles* by
A. H. Wilkie shows the positions held by the New Zealand Mounted Rifles and the
Otago Battalion on 8–9 August. The troops under Malone's command essentially
occupied the same positions earlier on 8 August, after the Turkish forces had overrun
the covering force and driven the New Zealanders out of the Turkish trenches
on the crest of Chunuk Bair. The Wellington Battalion was in the middle the line
with two companies of the 7th Gloucesters on the left and a mixed group from the
7th Gloucesters and 8th Welsh Pioneers on the right. During Malone's period of
command on Chunuk Bair, it appears that the right rather than the left flank of the
Allied line was bent back; although it is possible that both flanks were in fact bent
back during the earlier fighting.

of the Wellington Battalion were sheltered from this fire 'by a small rise in the
ground.' Although the Allied troops on Chunuk Bair may well have received
fire from Battleship Hill, it seems clear that it was the fire from Hill Q that
was by far the most damaging. The slight rise that afforded Malone's men
some cover was, it appears, destroyed after the First World War; probably by
earthworks associated with the construction of the New Zealand Memorial.[48]

A small element of the Right Assaulting Column, led by the 1/6th
Gurkhas commanded by Major C.J.L. Allanson, attacked Hill Q on 8 August
and in a skilful and determined operation eventually succeeded getting to
within about 30 metres of the crest. The following day they briefly captured
Hill Q, but were then driven off the crest. The other elements of the column
achieved very little.[49]

At about 6 am the Turks launched the first of a series of strong counter-attacks. In severe fighting, the Wellington Battalion's covering force was practically annihilated after inflicting heavy losses on the enemy. A body of enemy troops also appeared along the ridge to the right and opened an enfilading fire on the Allied troops who were desperately trying to dig in. The trenches held by the New Zealanders were only between half and three quarters of a metre deep and provided very limited protection. The Turks then began to apply increasing pressure on the main forward slope line. They made extensive use of hand grenades, many of which were picked up by Malone's men and thrown back at the Turks before they could explode. The Turks attacked in dense masses. Charles Lepper, one of Malone's men, later wrote, 'we shot them down in fine style, like shooting at a haystack.' Dead and wounded men covered the forward slope of Chunuk Bair; the Wellington's trench became choked with casualties and was eventually overrun. Turkish soldiers then proceeded to kill most of the wounded New Zealanders they found there.[50] The Turkish attack on the forward slope trench line led to some panic amongst the 8th Welsh Pioneers and the 7th Gloucesters on the right of the line and they retreated from the crest and sheltered on the reverse slope. This withdrawal enabled the Turks to more effectively enfilade the New Zealanders from the right, and also nearly

Men of the 7th Gloucesters advancing from the Apex towards Chunuk Bair, 8 August 1915.

Hampton Coll, National Army Museum

caused a panic amongst Malone's men. The New Zealanders on the right of the line bent back so that they could, at least to a certain extent, cover the flank exposed by the flight of the British troops. It appears that after the initial Turkish counter-attack fewer than 100 men from the Gloucesters and the Welsh Pioneers were in the firing line. Throughout the day it was the Wellington Battalion that carried the main burden of the defence of Chunuk Bair. Such was the intensity of the fighting that by 7 am more than half of the Wellington Battalion's officers had either been killed and wounded.[51]

These sketch maps were drawn by Major Cunningham in February 1916. The top sketch shows the position of Malone's force before the first Turkish counter-attack, and the bottom sketch the position after the attack had led the British troops on the right flank of the New Zealanders to abandon their positions.

Alexander Turnbull Library

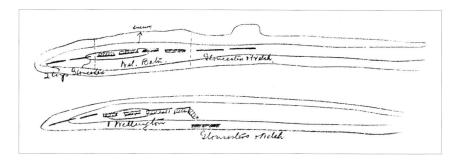

Malone and his small headquarters staff occupied a little trench just behind the main Wellington Battalion line on the reverse slope. He encouraged his men and calmly directed the defence of the hill. Throughout the day he was to demonstrate courage of the highest order. After they had seized the forward trench line, the Turks bombarded the remaining Allied positions on Chunuk Bair and then launched a series of attacks, which were preceded by showers of hand grenades. As agreed once Chunuk Bair had been seized, Wallingford ordered forward four machine gun teams, two each from the Wellington and Auckland Battalions. Only three gun teams advanced, because the commander of one gun claimed that he had not understood the order. It was now daylight and the machine gunners were met by a storm of Turkish fire as they advanced towards Chunuk Bair. Only one gun and its team reached Malone's position. The machine gun captured during the initial advance may also have been brought into service. The Turks concentrated their fire on the New Zealand machine guns, and by 10 am all the New Zealand machine gunners had become casualties and their guns damaged and put out of action. It has been suggested that the decision to delay sending the heavily-laden machine gunners forward until Chunuk Bair had been seized seriously compromised the defence of the position. That the machine guns on Chunuk Bair had to be placed in quite exposed positions and were quickly knocked out by the Turks suggests that the emplacement of additional machine guns would not have made a significant difference to the course of the fighting.[52] During the day the Wellington Battalion carried out several bayonet charges to clear the crest of the hill. On at least two occasions, when the situation was particularly critical, Malone personally led these attacks. Major W.H. Hastings, who had attached himself to the Wellington Battalion headquarters after he had become separated from his unit, later recalled how he and Malone 'joined the lads in front . . . I had my revolver and a handful of cartridges and Col M[alone] seized up a rifle and bayonet as he went. The Wellingtons seemed to rise up each time from nowhere, and the Turks were hurled back; in the first of these attacks the bayonet on Col M[alone]'s rifle was twisted by a bullet, . . . after this he kept it with him, as he said it was lucky.'[53] Half a century later a Wellington Battalion veteran Daniel Curham recalled how Malone 'was here and there, everywhere encouraging the troops, exposing himself to the enemy fire and showing tremendous courage.'[54]

It was a very hot day and supplies of water and ammunition soon began to run low. Efforts to carry supplies forward from Apex, which was itself subject to intense Turkish fire met with little success. Private Smart, Malone's batman, who had remained at the Apex, as part of the battalion's 46-strong rear party, was a member of a group of volunteers who tried to carry ammunition forward, but had to abandon the effort after lying under fire for three hours.[55]

There was no telephone line between Chunuk Bair and the brigade headquarters at the Apex, and Malone had to send messages back with wounded men. He could not be sure if these messages were getting through, so later in the morning (probably sometime after 8 am) he ordered Harston to return to the Apex and report on the situation to brigade headquarters. Harston found a signaller with a telephone on the saddle leading back to the Apex and used this to communicate with brigade headquarters. He had great difficulty convincing Johnston and Temperley that the situation on Chunuk Bair was critical and that the Wellington Battalion had already suffered catastrophic losses. Eventually he managed to do this and it was arranged that reinforcements would be sent up to Chunuk Bair. He also explained, before returning to Malone's headquarters, that fire from supporting warships was hitting the Allied troops on Chunuk Bair and as a result this fire was directed further inland.[56] Reinforcements in the form of a party from the Auckland Mounted Rifles succeeded at great cost in reaching Chunuk Bair in the early afternoon, but their experience made it clear that it would only be possible to move substantial reinforcements up to the hill after nightfall.[57]

By the afternoon, Chunuk Bair was an absolute charnel house, defenders used the bodies of fallen comrades or enemy soldiers for cover and fought on in a daze, losing all track of time.[58] Between about 2.30 pm and 5.30 pm the hard-pressed defenders of Chunuk Bair were subjected to a heavy bombardment by the Turks. During this time friendly artillery fire also inflicted many casualties. Artillery fire both from warships and from guns within the Anzac perimeter played a vital role in defeating the Turkish efforts to recapture Chunuk Bair. Unfortunately, as was to be expected in fighting at such close quarters, many Allied shells fell amongst the defenders. At about 5 pm a shell burst above the Wellington Battalion's headquarters trench, 'swish! swish! came the shrapnel and all except two in our little trench were killed or wounded'.[59] Malone was killed by one or two shrapnel balls that hit him in the head and he collapsed into the arms of either Cunningham or Harston.[60] Although the official history of the Wellington Regiment states that Malone was killed by Turkish artillery fire,[61] there is good evidence that he was killed by friendly gunfire, either from a Royal Navy destroyer as Harston believed[62] or by New Zealand artillery as Christopher Pugsley has concluded.[63] Not long before he was killed, Malone had received Holy Communion from Father McMenamin.[64]

Soon after Malone's death, Major Cunningham was wounded and command of the battalion passed from him to Captain Harston. Around dusk, the intensity of the enemy fire diminished and after nightfall reinforcements arrived: the Otago Battalion and two squadrons of the Wellington Mounted Rifles, a total of 583 men. Johnston intended that these men reinforce, but not relieve the troops on Chunuk Bair, but the terrible state of the defenders, who had survived a hellish day, demanded that they be withdrawn. Johnston's report on the struggle for Chunuk Bair and the brigade war diary, both of which were most probably prepared by Temperley, pointedly note that the Wellington Battalion 'withdrew without orders', and paid scant attention to the battalion's achievements and losses.[65]

Only between 50 and 70 unwounded or lightly wounded members of the Wellington Battalion walked off Chunuk Bair, fewer than one in ten of the 760 who had stormed up the hill in the morning. They were in a dreadful state: 'Their uniforms were torn, their knees broken. They had had no water since the morning; they could talk only in whispers; their eyes were sunken; their knees trembled; some broke down and cried like children.'[66] Charles Lepper was one of the survivors. He, along with the quartermaster sergeant and his assistant, who had not taken part in the fighting on Chunuk Bair, were the only men left in the Taranaki Company from the main body that had sailed from New Zealand in October 1914. With classic New Zealand understatement he remarked, 'so I suppose I have been very lucky.'[67] Another soldier who survived the battle simply stated that 8 August 1915 was the 'most awful day I ever spent'.[68] Amongst the Wellington Battalion dead were four pairs of brothers and the two youngest New Zealanders to lose their lives in the campaign, Privates Basil Ernest Mercer and Martin Andrew Persson, aged just 17.[69]

The 280-strong Fifth Reinforcements for the Wellington Battalion arrived at the front line on 8 August and were used to reinforce the Otago Battalion. They fought with that unit and the Wellington Mounted Rifles in their epic and costly defence of Chunuk Bair, that 'corner of Hell', on 9 August. Within 24 hours about half of the Wellington Battalion reinforcements become casualties. By the end of the day, the New Zealand troops on Chunuk Bair were exhausted and that evening they were relieved by two British battalions. These inexperienced battalions failed to prepare properly for renewed Turkish counter-attacks and were overwhelmed on 10 August. As well as driving the Allies from Chunuk Bair, the massive Turkish counter-attack recaptured the Farm area, and was only prevented from making further advances by devastating fire from the New Zealand machine guns at the Apex.[70] The Apex was thick with dead and wounded men. On 9 August Private Benjamin Smart noted in his diary: 'I never want to be in the midst of such a sickening and bloodcurdling sight again . . . the cries of the wounded nearly drove one mad'.[71] After these days of intense combat the seaward or

View of 'The Farm', a much fought over area below Chunuk Bair. This photograph was taken from the Turkish position on Chunuk Bair early in 1919.

Australian War Memorial

western side of Chunuk Bair was 'a most revolting sight, it is one solid mass of dead men'.[72]

After its withdrawal from Chunuk Bair the Wellington Battalion bivouacked on the side of Cheshire Ridge and spent periods in the front line on Rhododendron Ridge and at the Apex. During one of their periods of rest, on 21 August, a memorial service, attended by virtually every available member of Wellington Battalion, was held for William George Malone.[73] Sergeant George Bollinger noted in his diary at the end of the month that: 'bags upon bags of mail are arriving, but for every ten that arrive nine are returned "killed in action" "wounded" "missing" etc. It is hard to write this on all the letters.'[74] Five days after Malone's death, Private Smart gave Harston Malone's personal effects so that they could be sent to his widow.[75] On 14 September the Wellington Battalion and the other 'remnants of the New Zealand Infantry Brigade staggered down to Anzac Cove'.[76] The following day they sailed to Lemnos for a desperately needed rest.[77] In the August offensive the New Zealand Infantry Brigade has suffered 1714 casualties (killed, wounded or missing) of which 812 were from the Wellington Battalion.[78]

Before the battalion left Gallipoli, Johnston sent the unit a message of condolence over the death of Malone. Johnston and Godley also visited the battalion and praised its outstanding service in the battle.[79] Malone's inspiring leadership during the August offensive was recognised by a

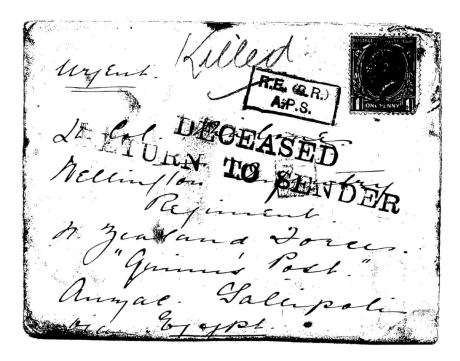

This letter from Ida arrived too late to reach Malone.

mention in despatches, his second. Because he had been killed there was effectively no honour or award that Malone could receive apart from a 'mention in despatches' or the Victoria Cross.[80] There was a strong undertone of bitterness within the Wellington Battalion after the battle at the lack of official recognition given to its achievements and sacrifices in General Hamilton's official despatch of 11 December 1915 and elsewhere. Within a few days of the battle, a member of the battalion, who had not taken part, wrote that: 'From what I can gather . . . there has [sic] been some very bad mistakes made, and we have lost far more heavily than we should have done.'[81] The traumatised survivors of the Wellington Battalion would have been even more disillusioned if they had known, as we know now, that the August offensive at Gallipoli had from the outset virtually no chance of achieving any sort of significant breakthrough. In particular, Chunuk Bair could not have been held as long as the rest of the Sari Bair range remained in Turkish hands.[82] Godley at least partially recognised this when he wrote in September 1915 that although the loss of Chunuk Bair 'was very disappointing . . . I console myself with the thought that I believe it is very questionable whether we could have stuck it out on this narrow razor backed ridge, exposed as we should have been [to the] concentrated fire of all the Turks' guns from Kilid Bahr, etc.'[83]

Conclusion

Tributes

Although Malone told his beloved Ida and others on many occasions that he was confident that he would survive the war, he told a friend just before he left New Zealand that: 'Something tells me I shan't come back here, that I will go out'.[1]

The death of Malone, who Charles Lepper described as 'one of the bravest men I ever saw',[2] was keenly felt within the battalion. It was to many in the Wellington Battalion emblematic of the destruction of their unit at Chunuk Bair.[3] Major-General Godley praised Malone both in public and in private. In one letter to an acquaintance in New Zealand he wrote: 'Poor Malone was the gallantest soul in action that ever walked, and his men would follow him anywhere. He was killed at the head of his battalion at the highest point which we attained, and literally in the very forefront of the battle, and lies now in a Turkish fort on Chunuk Bair, which he captured from the enemy – a more fitting restingplace [sic] for such a gallant soldier I cannot imagine.'[4] His wife Lady Louisa Godley also thought well of Malone. In a letter to her husband on 11 August, she remarked that 'Major Fitzherbert rang up to tell me that there had been a lot of casualties in the N.Z. force, and amongst them Colonel Malone killed. I am very sorry – he was a gallant fellow and was keen about his men and work. I know how you will miss him and the force will be the poorer of a good officer.'[5] After she learned of Malone's death Lady Godley wrote a letter of condolence to Ida.[6]

Ida Malone was devastated by the news of her husband's death, which she probably received in a telegram on 9 or 10 August.[7] She must have derived some comfort from the many condolence letters she received. One of the first was from Edward Harston, who wrote on behalf of the Wellington Battalion:

> I have a very difficult and painful duty to perform, all the more difficult because I knew and loved the Colonel so well. I wish to convey to you the very deepest sympathy of the whole Battalion in your great sorrow. We who knew him can realise how much his death must mean to you.

For to us it is irreparable. Colonel Malone made and kept his regiment through good times and bad always the best in the Brigade, which is the best in Gallipoli. Everything he did he made a crowning success. His holding and improving of Quinn's Post was the finest bit of work done in Anzac and his leading and care for his regiment was unequalled on the Peninsula. I say this because it is true, and any other officer will tell you the same. His regiment, rank and file loved him and trusted him implicitly with their lives. If the 'Old Man' ordered it, it was right, for we knew that he had first considered everything and that there was no better way of doing it.[8]

The sentiments in Harston's letter are also expressed in Birdwood's condolence letter, written only a day after Malone's death:

It is indeed with a sad heart that I write to you, for I well know how terribly grief-stricken you will be at the death of your husband, and though I know that nothing that I can say can be of any help to you in your great trouble, yet I feel that you will perhaps like to know that others are feeling for you in all you must be going through, and you may especially care to hear of this from one who was with your husband only the day before he was killed.

I had of course not met your husband until I arrived in Egypt and took over command of the Australian and New Zealand Army Corps in December, since when I had seen him fairly constantly in my frequent inspections of his regiment, while during the last three months in our fighting here I had come across him almost daily, and I want to tell you what a very high opinion indeed I had formed of him as an officer and a good leader of his men.

I always felt such complete confidence in him, and knew that while he was there all was going right in his regiment, for there was no detail [that] escaped his attention, and he was the life and soul of his regiment, being idolised by both officers and men.[9]

A few years later Birdwood told one of Malone's sons that his father was a 'matchless' battalion commander. Birdwood developed a high opinion of Malone and considerable affection for him. His work at Quinn's Post especially impressed Birdwood, who remarked that Malone 'thought out every necessary detail and by his determination and driving power saw that what he realised was necessary should be done'.[10]

Brigadier-General Johnston, with whom Malone had often clashed, wrote that he 'was such a thorough soldier and good comrade that he had endeared himself to all of us'.[11] Godley wrote, in a brief but clearly heartfelt letter, that 'He was the most valiant soul I think I have ever known . . . I would sooner have lost a battalion than him. . . . I cannot say how much I owe him personally. His loyalty and support to me both in New Zealand and here has been unfailing. I have lost one of my best friends and my sympathy for you is more than words can express.'[12] Sir Thomas Mackenzie, the New Zealand High Commissioner in London, whose son was blinded in August while serving with the Wellington Mounted Rifles, told Ida that her late husband had been 'one of the finest soldiers who ever fought for New Zealand'[13] and that he had 'left a great and honoured name behind him which will ever live in the memory of us New Zealanders'.[14] Included in the condolence letters from New Zealand was one from the Stratford Parish Committee which, like Johnston, remarked on Malone's strong Catholic beliefs, noting: 'As you know, Colonel Malone was one of the oldest and most highly esteemed of our parishioners and was both consistent and practical in his observance of the duties and obligations of our Faith, and, no less in his dying than in the manner of his living he was an inspiration to us all. . . . In cases like these we may repeat *Dulce et decorum est pro patria mori*.'[15]

Malone's death was announced in a casualty list released in New Zealand on 12 August.[16] This list was the first in a series of unprecedented size that made the full extent of the losses suffered by the NZEF in the August offensive clear to the New Zealand public. Prime Minister William Massey commented on the loss of so 'many of our brave men' which he described as:

> part of the price of Empire which we are being called upon to pay. The State (sic) again mourns for its dead, for those who have given their lives on Behalf (sic) of their fellow citizens, and the honour of the Nation, and our hearts go out in sympathy to the relatives and friends of those who have fallen . . . and whose remains lie to-day in graves of their comrades' making on the bleak hillsides of the Gallipoli Peninsula -- far from home and friends, it may be, but never to be forgotten by the people of this country.[17]

New Zealand newspapers widely reported Malone's death and many carried obituaries praising his achievements and noting his fine qualities as a soldier and a man.[18] Naturally, however, it was in Taranaki where his death was most keenly felt. The *Taranaki Herald* described him as 'one of the best known men in Taranaki' and noted that at Gallipoli 'he was making a mark as a leader, who, while willing to take every risk himself, was always careful not to expose his men to unnecessary risks. His loss will be keenly felt by the regiment, for it is certain that had he been spared he would have made a great name for himself as a soldier.' New Plymouth's newspaper concluded its lengthy and very positive obituary by stating that: 'The news of Colonel Malone's death in action caused quite a gloom locally when it became generally known this morning.'[19] Malone's demise was even more acutely felt in Stratford where the news was received via a telegram from Ida Malone. The *Stratford Evening Post* noted in a lengthy obituary that he had a 'wide circle of friends', described him as 'a true sport' who 'was brim full of enthusiasm, a keen soldier, a splendid disciplinarian, a magnificent organiser,' who was 'undoubtedly endowed with a thorough military genius'. In his civilian life the obituary stated he was a mainstay of a range of local organisations and activities. He was 'conscientious, painstaking and thorough'. Malone was said to possess 'exceptional abilities . . . As a farmer, a businessman, a lawyer, and a soldier, he filled the bill in every sense. Mr Malone proved himself a true gentleman, a loyal friend and honourable foe, and to those who were privileged to know him intimately for any length of time these characteristics were outstanding.'[20] Posthumously Malone's 'noble example' was used to encourage recruiting and to castigate those who shirked their duty.[21]

There is no doubt Malone was a formidable character, a 'rugged figure, a typical old New Zealand pioneer with a powerful jaw and an appearance of great strength and determination. He had a forcible character.' The Wellington Battalion 'was Malone's battalion and every man in it breathed the spirit of Malone and had been moulded according to his ideas.'[22] The strong foundations laid by Malone stood the Wellington Battalion and later the Wellington Infantry Regiment, which subsequently comprised up to three battalions, in good stead. Throughout its existence, the regiment exhibited the 'happy combination of a reasonable discipline – not enough to prejudice initiative, but sufficient to get the maximum team result.'[23] The officers and men who had served with the regiment commissioned a memorial plaque to Malone and the other battalion commander to lose his life in the war, Lieutenant-Colonel Charles Cook, DSO, in All Saints Church in Palmerston North. The regiment's colours had earlier been laid up at this church.[24]

The respect and affection the men of his battalion felt for their 'old' colonel is evident in the description of Malone in *The Arrower*'s [*The Arrower* was the magazine produced on board the *Arawa*] official Botanical Catalogue: 'Abies Malonia: A magnificent tree of the colonel species; very hardy and

of striking appearance; does best in clean sand and scrub.'[25] The special place Malone had in the memory of the Wellington Regiment veterans was demonstrated by the opening of the Malone Memorial Gates at the entrance to King Edward Park in Stratford on 8 August 1923. The gates are one of the most substantial memorials to an individual serviceman ever erected in New Zealand, and were paid for by former officers of the regiment and a variety of other supporters. At the well-attended opening ceremony, Lieutenant-Colonel Cunningham spoke about his old commanding officer, saying: 'in camp at Awapuni, . . . they soon found that he meant to make soldiers of them. They at first disliked him, but later learned to respect him, and finally came to love him for a man who could be relied on, although they knew he was determined to try out every man who came under him and remove the soft spots from them. He knew war would be a hard business, and made up his mind that the regiment would be fit when it had to take its part.'[26] It is a measure of the 'great respect and love' his men had for him that on the 50th anniversary of his death a former member of Malone's battalion remarked that he 'was the embodiment of the spirit of Anzac', that the efficiency of the unit and its military prowess were in large part due to his example, professionalism and leadership.[27]

Fred Waite's official history, *The New Zealanders at Gallipoli*, published in 1919, describes Malone as 'one of the striking characters in the New Zealand army' and praises his outstanding leadership.[28] Malone's contribution is well recognised in the regimental history, *The Wellington Regiment N.Z.E.F., 1914-1919*, which was published in 1928. Cunningham, who wrote the chapters dealing with the first year of the regiment's existence, had access to Malone's diaries.[29] Both Edmond Malone and his father are commemorated in Stratford's unique Hall of Remembrance, which contains photographs of the more than 180 men from the Stratford district who died in the Great War.[30] In November 2011, a life-size bronze statue of William Malone by Fridtjof Hanson was unveiled on the main street of Stratford. The erection of the statue was the product of years of work by a group of local people, the Malone Quest Committee.[31]

Impact on the Family

Throughout New Zealand, families were torn asunder by the Great War. In the case of the Malone family, the death of William George Malone and related events left the family scattered between England and New Zealand. Before August 1914 the Malone family had been one of the most prominent in the Stratford community. After that date, only Brian and Terry Malone seemed to have lived for any length of time at all in Stratford district. Ida and her three young children and Norah Malone remained in England, and only Denis ever returned to live in New Zealand. Norah visited New Zealand shortly after the end of the First World War and in the 1960s.[32]

Ida Malone mourned her much loved husband until her own death. She showed that she was in mourning by dressing exclusively in black and later grey clothes.[33] After Malone's death Ida made an effort to ensure that his life and achievements were remembered. Late in 1915 she corresponded with the Australian war correspondent, Ashmead-Bartlett, who had taken several photographs of Malone during his visit to Quinn's Post.[34] She was also in touch with William Whitlock of the *Hawkes Bay Herald-Tribune*, and provided him with copies of a number of letters she had received relating to Malone's service at Gallipoli. She probably got in touch with Whitlock through Brian Malone, who may have worked as a reporter on the *Herald-Tribune*. Whitlock suggested to the government that something should be done to commemorate Malone, stating that such an initiative 'would be very pleasing to the family and very acceptable to Taranaki where he was a soldier idolised.'[35] The suggestion was considered by the Cabinet on 22 December 1915, but no action was taken.[36]

In 1921, Ida sent some of William Malone's writings and photographs to Sir James Allen, New Zealand's High Commissioner in London. Allen, who had been Minister of Defence during the Great War and whose son had been killed at Gallipoli, wrote that: 'I cannot convey to you how deeply impressed I have been with all that I have read. Your late husband reveals himself in this correspondence as a noble man, an enthusiastic and lovable soldier, and I can well understand how those who were under his command came to like and trust him. You know how fully I sympathise with you in this great loss, and I realise how much our own country has suffered because Colonel Malone has gone from us.'[37]

Malone attached great importance to the financial security of his wife and family, and it is clear that on Gallipoli, particularly near the end of his life, took some solace from what he believed to be the sound provisions he had made for them. He left an estate valued at more than £25,000, the equivalent in today's terms of more than $3,400,000. The principal provisions of this will, which was prepared in August 1914, left Mater all his personal property, the right to live at 'The Farlands' and half the income from the estate for the rest of her life or until she remarried. The estate was then to be divided, with half being shared among his children from his first marriage and half among the children from his second marriage. Harry and Charles

Penn were the executors of the will and trustees of the estate.[38] Initially, Ida Malone received an income from the estate of between £150 and £240 a year, which combined with her war widow's pension from the New Zealand Government of £249.12, gave her an annual income of between £400 and £490. She found this inadequate and asked the trustees in 1922 for capital payments of £100 per annum for her two younger children.[39] New Zealand was affected by a severe economic recession after the end of the First World War that was caused by a collapse in agricultural prices. Efforts by the Penn brothers to recover money owed to the estate met with little success. The recession greatly reduced the income of the Malone estate, the major asset of which was farmland. The situation of the Malone estate was, it appears, made worse by the fact that Malone had personally guaranteed mortgages to people who became insolvent. By 1924 Ida Malone was receiving an allowance of only £40 each year from the estate. Ida Malone was placed in such a difficult financial position by these developments, that she was unable to purchase a home and lived a peripatetic existence in rented rooms or cottages. She was obliged to sell her jewellery and was unable, as she wished, to visit New Zealand.[40]

Ida Malone's situation was made even worse when she lost her personal effects. Norah Malone packed the effects during a visit to New Zealand in the 1920s and arranged with the Penn brothers for them to be sent to England. It appears Norah wrote to Ida telling her that the items were on their way, but this letter never seems to have reached Ida Malone and after sitting on the wharf in England for a year the personal effects were returned to New Zealand. Brian Malone then decided to sell the effects to recoup the shipping costs. This incident indicates the extent to which the English and New Zealand parts of the Malone family had by the 1920s become estranged from each other or had simply lost contact.[41] Ida faced her problems with considerable fortitude, and although she suffered from health problems, did her best for her children. She is remembered by her grandchildren as a generous, affectionate and cheerful woman whose life was blighted by her husband's death and her straitened circumstances. Before the Second World War, Ida Malone was allocated, much to her relief, a small cottage for war widows in Morden, Surrey. She died in 1946.[42]

Norah Malone was on very good terms with her stepmother and remained in the United Kingdom for most of the rest of her life. During the Great War she served as a Red Cross nurse. Norah Malone later married a British Army officer and died in Scotland in 1983. After her husband's death, Ida Malone was not in a position, because of ill health and financial concerns, to look

after her youngest child Molly who was sent to a convent at the age of five. Molly Malone later lived with her mother until her marriage in 1938 and again briefly during the Blitz on London. She died at the age of 69 in 1979. Barney and Denis Malone were sent to boarding schools and, like their sister, suffered from homesickness and a general feeling that their childhoods had been irretrievably damaged by the loss of their father.[43]

Edmond Malone, William George Malone's oldest son, was wounded in the leg on 20 July 1915. After being evacuated from Gallipoli, Edmond was sent to England for further treatment and then returned to Egypt and his unit, the Wellington Mounted Rifles, in January 1916. After William Malone's death, Brigadier-General Johnston apparently recommended that both Edmond and Terry receive commissions in their father's old unit. The severity of the wounds Terry received at Gallipoli ended his military service, but in March 1916 Edmond was commissioned as a second lieutenant and posted to the 1st Battalion of the Wellington Regiment. Between April and early June 1916 Edmond served with his battalion in France. He was then either taken ill or possibly wounded, and invalided back to England, where he remained until October 1916.[44] At this time Edmond was described by his commanding officer as a 'willing officer but without much experience'.[45] Sometime during his period in hospital in England, Edmond met and fell in love with a nurse, Mary 'Peter' Brocklehurst. They were married at Watford on 4 July 1917. In October 1917, by which time Edmond had been promoted to lieutenant, he suffered a severe gunshot wound to his right shoulder and was again sent to England for medical treatment. In November, Edmond was awarded the Military Cross for 'conspicuous gallantry and devotion to duty' while leading his platoon in an attack through 'heavy shell and machinegun fire. He set a splendid example of courage and energy to his men.'[46]

Edmond returned to his unit in France in February 1918. Late in the following month, during heavy fighting to halt the German Spring offensive, he suffered a grave wound to his left leg. A few days later, on 6 April 1918, Edmond Malone succumbed to this wound.[47] He was a popular and dedicated officer whose death was keenly felt by his comrades.[48] At the time of her husband's death, Mary 'Peter' Malone was pregnant with their daughter Elinor, who was always known as 'Petie'.

In 1945 after the end of the Second World War in Europe, one of Terry Malone's sons, Desmond Malone, who had been serving in the New Zealand forces in Italy, went to the United Kingdom on leave and decided to visit his aunt. Mary 'Peter' Malone had never remarried, and at her house she showed Desmond Malone his uncle's lemon squeezer hat and Military Cross, which were beside her bed, a position that they had occupied since 1918.[49]

Edmond Malone's lemon squeezer hat is now in the collection of Puke Ariki Museum in New Plymouth. It was donated to the museum in 2009 by Laurence and Ray Roebuck. They had been given it by Petie Malone's granddaughter, Mary Deighton. Laurence and Ray Roebuck are the sons of Robert Bryan (known as Bryan) Roebuck who was born in July 1912 and was, it appears, the illegitimate child of Edmond Malone and 19-year-old Gladys Roebuck. After his birth, Bryan Roebuck was adopted by his grandparents and bought up as their son. His real parentage remained a secret within the family for many years. Gladys Roebuck and Edmond Malone were, the family understand, briefly engaged, but the match was opposed by the Malone family because the Roebucks were Methodists.[50] This engagement may be the one William Malone refers to as having been broken off in his letter to Ida Malone of 23 July 1915. Bryan Roebuck was born in Okato on the coast south-west of New Plymouth where his mother, her family and Edmond Malone were living. Okato is a small settlement and it seems unlikely that Edmond Malone could have been ignorant of the fact that he had fathered a son. There is no evidence that William and Ida Malone knew of the existence of their grandson.[51] In 1999, the Okato Returned Services Association decided to mark Edmond Malone's death with a memorial plaque on the Okato War Memorial. The plaque was unveiled at a ceremony attended by members of the Malone family on 11 November 1999.[52]

EDMUND MALONE ('00-'05), wounded, July 20th   TERENCE MALONE ('01-'07), wounded, July 10th

COLONEL MALONE, killed in action, August 8th

BRIAN MALONE ('01-'10)   MAURICE MALONE ('09-'10)

Puke Ariki also has in its collection Edmond Malone's military compass. As with the lemon squeezer hat, there is an interesting story behind the museum's acquisition of this item. The compass was in a box of militaria purchased at an auction in 2009 by English art dealers David and Judith Cohen. They later noticed that it had 'EL Malone 1st WIB NZ Division' faintly inscribed on its leather case. The Cohens showed the compass to their friend Dr Christopher Pugsley, an eminent New Zealand military historian. Dr Pugsley's face apparently went white when he read the inscription on the compass. Once he explained the significance of the compass to the Cohens, they gave it to him. He at first intended passing the compass to Dr Judy Malone in Wellington. Dr Malone, however, felt strongly that the compass should go to Puke Ariki. Dr Pugsley agreed to this and donated it to the museum in 2010.[53]

Brian Malone had been working for his father as a clerk when he enlisted in the force dispatched in August 1914 to seize German Samoa. He returned from Samoa in November 1914 and was discharged from the New Zealand Expeditionary Force.[54] Not long after his father's death, Brian Malone noted that all four of William Malone's older sons were serving or were about to serve, in the NZEF, and that Norah was serving as a Red Cross nurse. He remarked that 'if there were more of us they'd be in it too'.[55] After returning from Samoa and while waiting to serve again in the NZEF, Brian worked as a journalist in Hamilton and later in Hawke's Bay. In January 1917, he was found to be unfit for service in the NZEF because of defective eyesight. Six months later, however, he passed a medical board and was re-enlisted in the NZEF. On this occasion he served in the New Zealand Medical Corps in New Zealand and on hospital ships returning wounded and sick NZEF personnel to New Zealand. He was discharged from the NZEF in October 1918 because of his defective vision.[56] Brian later became a lawyer in Te Awamutu. He died in Tauranga on 21 December 1967. One of his sons, the late Edmond 'Ted' Malone took a great interest in his grandfather's life. Ted Malone's widow, Dr Judy Malone, who like her late husband is an historian, has also undertaken extensive research into the Malone family.[57]

Terry Malone was evacuated from Gallipoli to Egypt after suffering multiple wounds to his right leg and arm on 1 June 1915. He spent a month in hospital there

Brian Malone in his medical corps uniform.

Malone Family Collection Wellington (now in ATL)

Maurice Malone (centre, marked with a cross) with other members of the machine gun corps. They are probably the men with whom he undertook his machine gun training course. The officer to the right of Maurice Malone was probably one of the course instructors.

Malone Family Collection Wellington (now in ATL)

before being sent to England for further treatment. In January 1916 Terry Malone returned to New Zealand and was discharged from the NZEF in April 1916 as being permanently unfit for further military service. Terry Malone's wounds left him partially disabled. He received a war pension and he suffered from the long-term effects of his wounds for the rest of his life. He greatly felt the loss of his brother Edmond and later Maurice. Terry Malone died in Wellington on 15 February 1963.[58]

Malone's youngest son from his first marriage, Maurice Patrick 'Mot' Malone, enlisted in the NZEF in April 1915. A few days after his father's death, Maurice sailed for Egypt as a reinforcement for the Wellington Mounted Rifles. He served with this unit in Egypt, before transferring, in July 1916, to the New Zealand Mounted Rifles Brigade's Machine Gun Squadron. On 14 November 1917, Maurice, who was by this time a sergeant, showed great initiative and courage during the New Zealand brigade's brilliant action at Ayun Kara, near Jaffa. After his commanding officer was wounded, Maurice took charge of his section of machine guns and showed inspiring leadership, particularly when his position was nearly overrun by a Turkish counter-attack. During this action, Maurice shot several of the leading Turks with his revolver and his bold action inspired his men. For his bravery and outstanding leadership at Ayun Kara, he was awarded the Distinguished Conduct Medal. Late in November, Maurice was wounded in the foot, and after months of medical treatment was invalided back to New Zealand in

August 1918. After further medical treatment, he was discharged from the NZEF on 8 January 1919, but continued to suffer from the effects of his wound.[59] Following his discharge, Maurice purchased, after being successful in a ballot, a small farm in the Ardkeen settlement for returned soldiers, near Wairoa. He died in Hastings on 16 January 1926 from an accidental overdose of an ointment containing morphia and belladonna, which he was taking to relieve the pain caused by piles. He left a widow and three-year-old daughter.[60]

Denis George Withers Malone worked for the National Bank of New Zealand in London and later joined the prison service. He was the assistant commissioner of prisons in Kenya during the Mau Mau insurgency, and later the Director of Prisons in Cyprus at the time of the EOKA terrorist campaign against British rule. Between 1960 and 1966 Denis Malone was a reforming governor of Dartmoor Prison. He then retired to New Zealand, living in Kerikeri until his death in 1983.[61]

Malone's youngest son, William Bernard Malone, who was always known in the family as Barney, also remained in the United Kingdom after his father's death. In 1930 he joined the British prison service and began to work in Borstals. Barney Malone quickly demonstrated an impressive mix of determination, intelligence, leadership and innovative thinking. During his time as second-in-command of the North Sea Camp near Boston he instigated a number of educational and other initiatives designed to improve the outlook for the youths sent to the institution. He more closely resembled his father than any of William Malone's other sons, and was, as a man who knew him wrote, 'marked out for death or glory'. Barney Malone had an 'ardent admiration for his father' and 'read and re-read' William Malone's war diaries. After war broke out in 1939 he was determined to serve and successfully petitioned for release from the prison service.[62] He was commissioned in the Scots Guards. In 1941 Barney was one of a group of Guards officers specially selected to watch over Rudolf Hess, at Camp Z, the secret prison, established to hold the Nazi leader. Captain Barney Malone was killed in action at Cassino in Italy on 7 December 1943.[63]

Rory Patrick Malone, Terry Malone's great-grandson, continued the family tradition of military service when he enlisted in the New Zealand Territorial Force in 2002. Three years later he transferred to the Regular Force. He was an

Second Lieutenant Barney Malone, Scots Guards.

Malone Family Collection Wellington (now in ATL)

Lance Corporal
Rory Malone

NZDF

exceptional soldier, heading his initial training course and being the top graduate on his infantry training course. Later after joining 2/1 Battalion of the Royal New Zealand Infantry Regiment as a rifleman he won the Top Soldier Competition. Rory Malone was intensely proud of his family's record of military service, although he rarely spoke about it. He was a popular, determined soldier who thoroughly enjoyed life in the Army. In 2006 and 2007 Rory Malone was deployed to East Timor. In 2012 he was posted to Afghanistan where as a Lance Corporal he served with Kiwi Company, an element of the New Zealand Provincial Reconstruction Team in Bamiyan Province. During the morning of 4 August 2012, Afghan National Directorate of Security personnel who had gone to the village of Dahane Baghak to detain suspected insurgents came under attack and suffered a number of casualties. Elements of Kiwi Company were dispatched to the scene to assist the Afghan forces. Early in the afternoon the Afghan and New Zealand forces came under fierce attack. Rory Malone was killed after bravely dragging his seriously wounded commanding officer behind cover.[64]

Malone's Reputation and Legacy

A great deal has been, and continues to be, written about the Gallipoli campaign. The campaign continues to attract particular attention in Australia and to a slightly lesser extent in New Zealand. Malone has perhaps attracted more attention than any other battalion or regimental commander at Gallipoli. There are, for example, references to Malone on 45 pages of *Bloody Gallipoli: The New Zealanders' Story* by Richard Stowers, whereas Lieutenant-Colonel Arthur Bauchop, the outstanding commander of the Otago Mounted Rifles, who was also killed in the August offensive, is mentioned on only five pages.[65] This can be attributed to a number of factors: firstly, Malone's strong personality and charismatic and idiosyncratic leadership of his battalion; secondly, the survival of his detailed, revealing diary and extensive collection of letters; and thirdly, to Malone and his battalion's involvement in three crucial actions during the campaign. These were securing Walker's Ridge and Russell's Top (the highest point on the ridge) during the opening days of a campaign, the transformation of Quinn's Post into a secure stronghold, and finally, and most importantly, the capture of Chunuk Bair in August 1915.

The desperate fighting by the Anzacs to seize and hold Walker's Ridge and Russell's Top between 25 and 28 April was absolutely vital to ensuring the security of the foothold gained by the Allied forces at Anzac Cove, and its importance was recognised at the time.[66] Lieutenant-Colonel Braund has been widely praised for organising and leading the defence of this vital area. The contribution made to the successful action by the Wellington Infantry Battalion and Malone is noted in the first volume of Bean's Australian official history,[67] and in the first volume of the British official history by C.F. Aspinall-Oglander.[68] Later, in 1936, after he had read Malone's account of the action, Aspinall-Oglander told Barney Malone that in his praise of Braund 'he had backed the wrong horse'.[69] Malone's strong criticisms of Braund and his men have generally been seen as being unduly harsh, although understandable given the circumstances.[70] In his recent well-researched and insightful account of the initial operations at Gallipoli, Chris Roberts has gone further and suggested that Malone's criticisms were 'unjustified, churlish and based on ignorance of the situation; the men who fought with Braund paid tribute to his courage and leadership.'[71] That Malone spoke to Braund and went up Walker's Ridge during the fighting points to him having a good knowledge of the situation there. It is also significant that Jesse Wallingford, who was in the thick of the action on Walker's Ridge is, if anything, more critical of Braund. Malone's allegation that Braund's tactics were not driven by the situation on the ground, but by a breakdown in discipline amongst his men due to inadequate training and leadership, is of particular interest.[72] There is evidence that discipline amongst Braund's men did falter, which should come as no surprise given that they were raw troops engaged in combat for the first time under the most trying of circumstances. It must, however, be admitted that Malone landed at Gallipoli prepared to think the worst of the Australians and his experiences on the peninsula did not substantially alter this negative opinion of them.[73]

Malone was quite properly very proud of the magnificent discipline and spirit shown by his battalion in the Second Battle of Krithia. He quickly realised, however, that the Wellington Battalion and the rest of the New Zealand Infantry Brigade had suffered terribly for no good reason in a botched attack that had no prospect of success.[74]

Malone was an outstanding commander whose superior organisational abilities and practical, determined approach to problems suited him particularly well for the task of completely reorganising the defences and tactics employed at Quinn's Post.[75] Waite's *The New Zealanders at Gallipoli* and Bean's encyclopaedic Australian official history both describe Malone's achievements, but provide little detail.[76] Peter Stanley's book, *Quinn's Post: Anzac, Gallipoli* details the work Malone and the New Zealanders and Australians who served under him at this vital point, and gives their efforts the prominence they deserve.[77]

For many years the controversy about the siting of the trenches on Chunuk Bair and to a lesser extent Malone's role in the decision to consolidate on the Apex rather than press on with an attack on 7 August overshadowed the achievements of the Wellington Battalion and its commander in the breakout from Anzac. These criticisms angered the Malone family and others closely associated with William Malone.[78] It was only with the publication of Robert Rhodes James' first-rate history of the campaign in 1965 that the inaccurate claims about the siting of the trenches on Chunuk Bair, which had been repeated in books by Sir Ian Hamilton and others, were effectively rebutted in a book published outside New Zealand.[79] Denis Malone gave Rhodes James access to his father's diaries, which Rhodes James recognised as being an important source. Major Sir Edward Harston also assisted Rhodes James in his research and was 'delighted' with the way in which the book corrected 'the stupid and inaccurate description which had been repeated at various times about how Chunuk Bair was held and what happened there.'[80] In New Zealand, the situation was somewhat different. Waite's official New Zealand history, which was published in 1919, contains a detailed defence of the siting of the trenches on Chunuk Bair, which concludes: 'The fact remains that the trenches on Chunuk Bair were the only possible ones for such a situation . . . what was done on Chunuk Bair could not have been done any better by anybody else; and there, for the present, the matter must

A watercolour sketch of Gallipoli at sunset on 17 May 1925. The artist is unknown, but was probably one of the New Zealanders who attended the unveiling of the New Zealand Memorial on Chunuk Bair on 12 May 1925. The memorial bears the inscription: In Honour of the Soldiers of the New Zealand Expeditionary Force 8th August 1915. 'From the Uttermost Ends of the Earth.'

Malone Family Collection Wellington (now in ATL)

stand.'[81] The Wellington Regiment official history that appeared nine years later contains an essentially accurate account of the dispositions and actions of the battalion at Chunuk Bair.[82]

In the 1980s there was a resurgence of interest in the Gallipoli campaign in general and in Malone and the struggle for Chunuk Bair in particular. This process effectively got underway with Maurice Shadbolt's 1982 play *Once on Chunuk Bair,* which was later adapted for the screen. Shadbolt was prompted to write the play by 'an emotionally numbing visit to Anzac Cove and Chunuk Bair'.[83] *Once on Chunuk Bair* is a work of literature that does not adhere rigidly to the historical facts. In the play Malone is renamed Connolly. Shadbolt did this because of the angry reaction by members of the Malone family to his brief, inaccurate and unflattering portrayal of Malone in his 1980 novel, *The Lovelock Version.*[84] It was not, however, until the publication of Christopher Pugsley's influential *Gallipoli: The New Zealand Story* in 1984 that Malone's actions on Chunuk Bair and the reasons for them became well known in New Zealand. Pugsley's book was produced in conjunction with an award-winning television documentary. Ted Malone greatly assisted Pugsley's research by providing him with access to William Malone's diaries, letters and associated papers.[85] Ted Malone was also one of the editors of the 1988 book, *The Great Adventure: New Zealand soldiers describe the First World War*, which included substantial extracts from William Malone's diary.[86]

Although there was an increasing interest in William Malone at this time, Ted Malone's efforts shortly before his death to interest an Australian publisher in producing an edition of his grandfather's diary were unsuccessful. The reader contracted by the publisher to review the manuscript considered that the diary was of limited interest, and found Malone to be 'narrow, fastidious, and irritating'.[87] This reader's report is rather unbalanced, but without reading his letters, especially those to Ida, it is not possible to get a good appreciation of all the aspects of Malone's character. When the full range of Malone's writings are examined, a much clearer and well-rounded picture of this complex man emerges.

Malone's Gallipoli diaries and letters have, especially since the 1980s, featured in discussions about the development of an appreciation of what it is to be a New Zealander. Malone's many references to his growing sense of national identity and pride have struck a receptive chord with an increasing number of New Zealanders.[88] Other aspects of Malone's thinking and writing, however, sit less well with New Zealanders of the twenty-first century because he was very much a man of his time. Malone was a firm believer in the concept of an heroic death in pursuit of a just cause, which had such a hold on men of his generation and background. The title of this book, *No Better Death*, is taken from comments made by Malone in his diary on 5 June 1915 about the death of a 'splendid young fellow'.[89] He was a great admirer of Ruskin and marked in a copy of *The Crown of Wild Olive* he gave to Godley the following passage:

> I found, in brief, that all great nations learned their truth of word, and strength of thought, in war: that they were nourished in war, and wasted by peace; taught by war, and deceived by peace; trained by war and betrayed by peace -- in a word, that they were born in war, and expired in peace.[90]

Although he was increasingly aware of the grim realities of war, Malone rather enjoyed the challenges of active service, writing in his diary as late as 4 August 1915 that 'the prospect of action is inspiriting'.

In the years preceding the 90th anniversary of Malone's death there was a campaign for him to receive some form of posthumous official recognition. In 2005 the anniversary of Malone's death was marked by a range of events that were attended by members of the Malone family from both New Zealand and the United Kingdom. In Wellington the Prime Minister unveiled a commemorative plaque in Parliament, a wreath-laying was held at the Wellington Cathedral of St Paul and the first edition of this book was launched.[91] Interest in the battle for Chunuk Bair and Malone remains strong in New Zealand.[92] Malone has always figured prominently in Taranaki's memory of the Great War, and each year on 8 August a ceremony is held at the Malone Gates in Stratford to commemorate a man who is now recognised as a national hero.[93]

William George Malone has no known grave and is commemorated along with more than 300 of his men on the New Zealand Memorial to the Missing on Chunuk Bair.[94] He, however, as General Sir Alexander Godley wrote, 'died at the head of the men who loved him well – a Happy Warrior – a glory to New Zealand and a shining light and example to the youth of the Dominion for all time.'[95]

On Anzac Day 2005 crosses were put up in Stratford for all the local war dead. To the left of the cross commemorating William Malone is a cross for Trooper Edward Sexton of the Wellington Mounted Rifles. Sexton was killed on Chunuk Bair on 9 August 1915; like Malone, he has no known grave.

Ian Maxwell

Notes

Preface

1 Diary 29 Nov 1914; William George Malone [WGM] to Ida Katherine Malone [IKM], 3 Jan 1915.

2 WGM to IKM 20 Oct 1914, 29 Nov 1914, diary, 23 Dec 1914.

3 WGM to IKM, 24 May 1915, 23 Jul 1915, WGM to Louie, 29 May 1915.

4 Diary, 23 Dec 1914, MSX 2543, Alexander Turnbull Library (ATL).

5 'Denis Malone' note by Dr Christopher Pugsley, encl. to email from Pugsley to editor,10 Dec 2013. Barney Malone also typed out a partial transcript of the diary. Email Anita Young to editor, 3 Mar 2014, NZDF 1325/11/4, HQ NZDF. Emails from David Colquhoun, ATL to the editor, 14 and 23 Feb 2005. The bound typescript copy of William Malone's diary with annotations in the Malone Family Collection Wellington (MFCW) is the copy given to Brian Malone, email Dr Judy Malone to editor 7 Mar 2014, NZDF 1325/11/4. Comments by Sir James Allen indicate that at least a partial transcript of the diary was in existence by August 1921. Allen to Ida Malone, 17 Aug 1921, Malone Family Collection London (MFCL) [copy, MS-Papers-9049-3, ATL].

6 *Otago Daily Times*, 20 Jul 1915, p. 6.

7 See for example the letter to the father of Corp Copeland, *Wanganui Chronicle*, 1 Jul 1915, p. 4.

8 'Denis Malone' note by Dr Christopher Pugsley, encl. to email from Pugsley to editor, 10 Dec 2013, NZDF 1325/11/4, HQ NZDF.

Introduction

1 WGM to IKM, 25 Sep 1914, MFCL.

2 WGM diary, 5 Jun 1915.

3 See for example, WGM's cousin Sister Teresa to WGM, 16 Apr 1915, MFCL.

4 Copy of birth certificate, dated 9 Jul 1993, WGM Dictionary of New Zealand Biography (DNZB) file, Ministry for Culture and Heritage (MCH), Wellington.

5 H.J.P. Arnold, *William Henry Fox Talbot: Pioneer of Photography and Man of Science* (London, 1977), pp. 151, 159–60; Louisa Sanders (WGM's sister) to Brian Malone, 1 May 1921, MS-Papers-11408-14, ATL.

6 Sanders to Brian Malone, 1 May 1921, MS-Papers-11408-14; Christopher Pugsley, 'William George Malone', *Dictionary of New Zealand Biography, Vol III, 1905–1920* (Auckland, 1996), p. 326.

7 WGM diary, 1 Oct 1914; 30 Nov 1914.

8 NZEF Statement of Service Form, William George Malone personal file (P/F), Archives New Zealand (ANZ); information provided by Dr Judy Malone.

9 WGM diary, 22 Oct 1914.

10 An anecdote told by Norah Crum (née Malone) to E.P. Malone in 1969, information provided by Dr Judy Malone; *Taranaki Herald*, 2 May 1907, p. 7.

11 Register No. 1, Armed Constabulary Description Book, pp. 131 and 183, P8/1, ANZ; obituary in the *Stratford Evening Post* of 12 Aug 1915; *Taranaki Herald*, 2 May 1907, p. 7; Sanders to Brian Malone, 1 May 1921, MS-Papers-11408-14; *A Return of Freeholders of New Zealand, October 1882* (Wellington, 1884), p. m6; *Carved from the Bush: Stratford, 1878–1928, The Town and District's Record of Effort* (New Plymouth, 1928), p. 16. WGM's mother died in August 1907, *Taranaki Herald*, 19 Aug 1907, p.2.

12 Rollo Arnold, *New Zealand's Burning: The*

Settlers' World in the Mid 1880s (Wellington, 1994), pp. 56, 287.

13 *Taranaki Herald*, 13 Dec 1889, p. 3, 20 Oct 1908, p. 3; *Stratford Press*, 18 Sep 1991.

14 Obituary, *Taranaki Herald*, 12 Aug 1915, p. 3.

15 James McLeod, *50 Years Rugby in Taranaki: 1885–1935* (New Plymouth, 1935), p. 5.

16 *Taranaki Herald*, 5 Dec 1889, p.3, 10 May 1897, p. 2; Ian Church, *The Stratford Inheritance: a History of Stratford and Whangamomona Counties* (Waikanae, 1990), p. 48; Alison Robinson, *Finnerty Road School and the Lowgarth District* (Lowgarth, 1992), p. 27.

17 *Taranaki Herald*, 2 Mar 1915, p. 2; email Debbie Sheehy (Austin's great-granddaughter) to editor, 21 Dec 2004.

18 WGM DNZB file, MCH; Bellini to editor, nd, but Nov 2004; Thomson to Judy Malone, 12 Aug 1991, MS-Papers-11408-19, ATL.

19 'Particulars of Children', History Sheet, W.G. Malone P/F; Terence, Brian and Maurice Malone History Sheets P/Fs, ANZ.

20 *Taranaki Herald*, 12 Aug 1915, p. 3.

21 *Taranaki Herald,* 9 Jun 1890, p. 4; *The Star Almanac Directory, Calendar and Diary 1887* (Hawera, 1887), pp. 216, 250; 1889 edition, pp. 164, 199; 1891 edition, p. 227; *Taranaki Herald*, 12 Aug 1915, p. 3; A.P.C. Bromley, *Hawera: An outline of the development of a New Zealand community* (Hawera, 1981), p. 84.

22 *Taranaki Herald,* 28 Feb 1900, p. 2, 21 Jun 1890, p. 3; Church, pp. 174–77, 200–7.

23 Lampen to Assistant Adjutant-General Wellington, 21 Apr 1911; Chaytor to HQ NZ Military Forces, 25 Apr 1911, AD1, 3/157, ANZ.

24 *New Zealand Gazette*, 1892, Vol. II, p. 1641.

25 *Taranaki Herald,* 6 Feb 1903, p. 6; *Taranaki District Law Society, 1879–1979: A brief history to mark the Centennial of the Taranaki District Law Society 1879–1979* (New Plymouth, 1979), p. 90; *Cyclopedia of New Zealand, Volume Six, Taranaki, Hawkes Bay and Wellington Provincial Districts* (Christchurch, 1908), p. 172; *Appendix to the Journals of the House of Representatives (AJHR)* 1905, C4,

pp. 1128–29. Supreme Court of New Zealand, Northern (Taranaki) District: Admission as a Solicitor, 19 Apr 1894; Admission as a Barrister, 22 Sep 1899, MS-Papers-11408-15, ATL.

26 Form V.-14, dated 16 Sep 1903, W.G. Malone P/F; J.A.B. Crawford, 'The Role and Structure of the New Zealand Volunteer Force 1885–1910', MA thesis in History, University of Canterbury, 1986, pp. 69–86, 183; *New Zealand Gazette*, no. 4, 1901. During the 1901–2 year WGM attended 30 parades. Stratford Rifle Volunteers, Nominal Capitation Roll for the Year Ending 28 Feb 1902, ARM41 69, 1910/4p, ANZ.

27 Obituary, *Taranaki Herald*; E.P. Malone typescript, 'Diary of Lt Col W.G. Malone 1914–15, New Zealand-Egypt-Gallipoli', pp. 9–10; Kathleen Laverty to Judy Malone, 11 Aug 1991, MS-Papers-11408-19; Murray Moorhead, *First and Strong: The Wellington West Coast and Taranaki Regimental Story* (Wanganui, 2002), p. 81.

28 Norah Crum (née Malone) to Denis Malone (copy), 7 Mar 1965, MS-Papers-11408-11, ATL.

29 *Taranaki Herald*, 14 Jan 1909, p. 7; E.P. Malone typescript, pp. 7, 12–13, MS-Papers-11408-28, ATL.

30 WGM to Officer Commanding 4th Battalion Wellington a Rifle Volunteers, 3 Sep 1903, Form V-14 (resignation), signed by Webb, 29 Sep 1903, W.G. Malone P/F.

31 Officer Commanding Taranaki Battalion to Officer commanding Wellington district, 26 Sep 1903, Form V-14 (appointment), signed by Webb, 29 Sep 1903, Appointment or Promotion of Volunteer Officer form, signed by Babington, 16 Nov 1904, W.G. Malone P/F.

32 Withers to Officer Commanding Wellington District, 3 Mar 1904, Pitt to Governor, 19 Mar 1904, Appointment or Promotion of Volunteer Officer form, signed by Babington, 16 Nov 1904 and marginalia on form, W.G. Malone P/F; *New Zealand Defence Forces Army List*

30th November 1905 (Wellington, 1905), cols 16, 28.

33 *Manawatu Times*, 18 Apr 1908, p. 5; *Evening Post*, 20 Apr 1908, p. 8.

34 *Taranaki Herald*, 18 Jun 1904, p. 4, 20 Jun 1904, p. 4; information provided by Dr Judy Malone.

35 Marriage certificate; *Hawera and Normanby Star*, 27 Sep 1905, p. 4; Clemow to Judy Malone, 12 Aug 1991, MS-Papers-11408-19, ATL; email Clare Lyons (daughter of Molly Malone) to editor, 2 Dec 2004.

36 Colleen Stevenson (née Malone, Terry Malone's daughter) notes on interview with Judy Malone, 28 May 1993 MS-Papers-11408-19; recollections of Norah Crum (née Malone) given to E.P. Malone, MS-Papers-11408-11, ATL; Edith Rogers to Denis Malone, 9 Aug 1977 and to E.P. Malone, 30 Oct 1983, MS-Papers-11408-21, ATL; 'The Family of LT. Col William Malone (England-NewZealand)', freepages.genealogy.rootsweb.ancestry.com/~kitwithers/malone/malone.html, accessed 18 Nov 2013; information provided by Penny Kidd.

37 WGM to IKM, 29 Nov 1914, 8.10 pm, 5 Aug 1915; WGM to Louie, 29 May 1915.

38 W.G. Malone history sheet, W.G. Malone P/F; Bellini to editor, nd, but Nov 2004.

39 WGM to IKM, 29 Nov 1914; Norah Crum (née Malone) to E.P. Malone, Dec 1979, MS-Papers-11408-11.

40 Clemow notes on interview with Judy Malone, 12 Aug 1991, MS-Papers-11408-19. Outline plan of the house drawn by Norah Crum (née Malone) and forwarded by Mr Richards to Judy Malone, 7 Dec 1990, MS-Papers-11408-17; recollections of Norah Crum (née Malone) given to E.P. Malone, MS-Papers-11408-11, ATL; information provided by Dr Judy Malone.

41 Report of Royal Commission on Land Settlement and Tenure, *AJHR*, C-4, 1905, minutes of evidence, p. 1126, para 291.

42 'Statement of Assets and Liabilities of W.G. Malone' as at 10 Aug 1914, MFCL; current value calculated using the Reserve Bank New Zealand CPI Inflation Calculator.

43 *AJHR* 1905, C-4, p. 1126, para 291; Jim McAloon, *No Idle Rich: The Wealthy in Canterbury and Otago 1840–1914* (Dunedin, 2002), pp. 52–54, 58, 60–62.

44 *AJHR* 1905, C4, p. 1126, para 295.

45 *AJHR* 1905, C4, p. 1127, para 295.

46 WGM to IKM, 11 Jul 1915.

47 Unidentified newspaper report on Malone's lecture attached to a poster advertising the lecture, MFCL; *Taranaki Herald*, 19 Sep 1907, p. 7; Miles Fairburn, *Nearly out of Heart and Hope: the Puzzle of a Colonial Labourer's Diary* (Auckland, 1995), pp. 163–77.

48 Notes by Thomas Malone on the endpapers of his copy of *The Public and Domestic Life of the Right Hon. Edmund Burke* (London, 1854) (copy) attached to 'Note on William G. Malone' by Dr Judy Malone, Oct 2012, MS-Papers-11408-18, ATL.

49 Tom Brooking, *Lands for the people? The highland Clearances and the Colonisation of New Zealand: A biography of John Mackenzie* (Dunedin, 1996), pp. 79–95.

50 *Taranaki Daily News*, 24 Apr 1907, p. 2 as quoted in Brian A.E. Bellringer, 'Conservatism and the Farmers: a Study in the Political Development of Taranaki-Wanganui between 1899 and 1925', MA thesis in History, University of Auckland, 1958, p. 156.

51 Ibid., p. 156; *Taranaki Herald*, 2 May 1907, p.7.

52 Bellringer, p. 161.

53 Ibid., p. 161; Guy H. Scholefield, ed. *New Zealand Parliamentary Record 1840–1949* (Wellington, 1950), p. 130.

54 *Taranaki Herald*, 2 May 1907, p. 7, 20 Oct 1908, p. 7; Letter by C.E. Major, *Auckland Star*, 30 Aug 1915, p. 8; Huddy Clemow to Judy Malone, 12 Aug 1991, MS-Papers-1408-19.

55 *Blue and White: The Magazine of St Patrick's College, Wellington*, Christmas 1915, p. 66; Norah Malone to WGM, 17 Aug 1913, MFCL; J.L. Jeffares ed. *St Joseph's Stratford 1897–1997* (Stratford, 1997), pp. 8–9.

56 Ward to Malone, 11 May 1910, W.G. Malone P/F.

57 Unidentified newspaper obituary dated Wellington, 12 Aug 1915, DNZB file; *The Star Almanac and West Coast Directory, 1910* (Hawera, 1909), p. 439 and 1911 edition (Hawera, 1910), p. 379; *Taranaki District Law Society 1879–1979*, p. 90.

58 Ian McGibbon, *The Path to Gallipoli: Defending New Zealand 1840–1915* (Wellington, 1991), pp. 181–93.

59 *Taranaki Herald*, 2 Nov 1908, p. 4, 12 Nov 1908, p. 7; Obituary, *Taranaki Herald*, 12 Aug 1915, p. 3.

60 Godley to IKM, 7 Jun 1932, MFCL; Statement of the Services of William George Malone, Malone P/F; *The Quarterly Army List of the New Zealand Forces for October 1911* (Wellington, 1911), column 76.

61 W.G. Malone military notebook dated 1909, MSX-9046, ATL.

62 Synopses of Course of Lectures on Military Tactics, 27 May, 10 Jun, 24 Jun, 8 Jul, 5 Aug and 19 Aug 1910, MFCL.

63 Ibid., Synopsis of the First Lecture, 27 May 1910.

64 Wellington District Report for the Year Ended 29 Feb 1912 by Colonel Edward Chaytor, AD19, 68/11, ANZ.

65 Ibid.; Colonel Tait to district headquarters, Palmerston North, 18 Apr 1913; Godley to IKM, 7 Jun 1932, MFCL.

66 'Remarks by O/C District (Wellington) Colonel Edward Chaytor Year 1913–1914, 16 Jul 1914, MFCL.

67 Ibid., 'Remarks by the Brigadier (Col R.W. Tate, W.I. Brigade, 19 Jun 1914).'

68 *The Quarterly Army List of the New Zealand Forces for April 1914* (Wellington, 1914), p. 82; Moorhead, p. 81.

69 W.S. Furby, 'The Beginning of the Lemon Squeezer Hat', *RSA Review*, Nov 1970, *RSA Review*, March 1957, p. 4; notes by G.T. Stagg, 14 May 1970, HQ NZDF Library.

70 Lampden to Wellington Infantry Brigade, 9 May 1913, Malone to OC Wellington Infantry Brigade, 13 May 1913, Collins to District Headquarters Palmerston North, 29 May and 2 Jul 1913, Malone to OC Wellington Infantry Brigade, 12 Jun 1913, AD19, 22/87, ANZ.

71 Court of inquiry evidence by Malone, Chaytor to HQ NZ Military Forces, 25 May 1914, AD 10, 2/11, ANZ; *New Zealand Freelance*, 20 Aug 1915, p. 4.

72 Telegram, Temperley to WGM, 8 Aug 1914, MFCL; Godley to IKM, 7 Jun 1932, MFCL; *New Zealand Freelance*, 20 Aug 1915, p. 4; McGibbon, *Path*, pp. 244–45; Christopher Pugsley, *Gallipoli: The New Zealand Story* (Reed, Auckland, 1998), pp. 50–52.

73 Peter Cooke and John Crawford, *The Territorials: The History of the Territorial and Volunteer Forces of New Zealand* (Auckland, 2011), pp. 195–96; Tim Shoebridge, 'Manawatu's First World War Camps, 1914–1919', *The Manawatu Journal of History*, No. 9, 2013, pp. 11–13.

74 Copy of will dated 11 Aug 1914 in Supreme Court probate file, MS-Papers-11408-15, ATL; WGM diary, 6–10 Aug 1914.

75 Attestation Forms. Brian, Edmond, Terence and Maurice Malone P/Fs, ANZ. Maurice Malone's History Sheet states he was born on 25 May 1894, a year earlier than his real birth date.

76 W.H. Cunningham, C.A.L. Treadwell and J.S. Hanna, *The Wellington Regiment NZEF, 1914–1919* (Wellington, 1928), pp. 1–2; Pugsley, *Gallipoli*, p. 46.

77 Certificate of Medical Examination, 31 Aug 1914, W.G. Malone P/F. The height recorded may be inaccurate as when he enlisted in the Armed Constabulary WGM was described as being 5 feet 9½ inches tall (1.76 m), Register No. 1, Armed Constabulary Description Book, p. 183, P8/1 and in 1900 as being 5 feet 10 inches tall (1.78 m), Stratford Rifle Volunteers, Nominal Capitation Roll for the Year Ending 28 Feb 1901, ARM41 69, 1910/4o, ANZ.

78 WGM to Laurenson, 26 Aug 1914; Clemow

to Judy Malone, 12 Aug 1991, MS-Papers-11408-19.

Chapter 1

1 Maj (later Lt-Col) Felix T. **Bellringer**, MBE; 5 Mar 1877 New Plymouth – 20 Jun 1965; married town clerk of New Plymouth 1902–53; OC 11th Taranaki Regt, medically unfit for service overseas; WWII OC Linton Camp.

2 Maj (later Lt-Col) William L. **Robinson**, NZSC, mid; 11 Nov 1881 Foxton – 1 Nov 1963; single soldier of Wellington; no. 39715, NZ Rifle Bde, DAAG NZ Div.

3 Maj (later Brig-Gen Sir) Herbert E. **Hart**, KBE CB CMG DSO mid(5) CG; 13 Oct 1882 Carterton – 5 Mar 1968; married solicitor of Carterton; 10/133 2i/c WIB, later OC WIB, OC 4NZIB, OC Sling Camp; WIA May 1915, 1918; SA War, WWII GHQ Mideast 1940–43. Hart kept a detailed diary throughout the First World War. John Crawford (ed.), *The Devil's Own War; the First World War Diary of Brigadier-General Herbert Hart* (Auckland, 2008).

4 Col (later Brig-Gen) F. Earl **Johnston**, CB mid(4) Kara; 1 Oct 1871 UK – 7 Aug 1917; single soldier of Palmerston North; 10/512A, OC NZ Inf Bde; KIA France.

5 Robinson 'lacks experience and knowledge. . . . He is of no real use to me'. Malone noted he was on good terms with Robinson and had told him he intended to ask for him to be replaced. WGM to Johnston, 18 Aug 1914, W.L. Robinson, P/F, ANZ.

6 Capt (later Maj) Michael **McDonnell**; 22 Jun 1873 Tuamarina – 25 Jul 1951; married soldier of New Plymouth; 10/1095, HQ WIB; soldier 1893–1921, Diamond Jubilee 1897, SA War 1901–02, NZEF 1914–16.

7 Penn – WGM's lawyers and his first wife's brothers.

8 Hon Capt & QM (later Capt) William J. **Shepherd**; 1 Nov 1885 Dunedin – 7 Nov 1946; married salesman of New Plymouth; 10/1094 QM HQ WIB.

9 Capt (later Lt-Col) George **Home**, NZMC, CBE OBE; 15 Feb 1870 USA – 7 Feb 1956; married doctor of New Plymouth; 10/1093 att WIB, later OC No. 3 NZ Gen Hosp.

10 Lt (later Maj) William E.S. **Furby**; 26 Sep 1887 Westport – 4 Apr 1981; single clerk of Stratford; 10/657 D Coy WIB. Furby seems to have been an unpopular officer. Oswald T. Meenken diary, 4–7 Jan 1915, Menken family.

11 Work lacking interest.

12 Mother of C.B. Lepper. Pte (later Lt) Charles B. **Lepper**, MC MM; 2 Mar 1893 New Plymouth – 20 Feb 1959; single farmer of Lepperton, Taranaki; 10/868,1st Refts WIB, later with 37th Refts; WIA Gallipoli; WWII HG 1940–42.

13 Georges **Clemenceau**, 28 Sep 1841 – 24 Nov 1929, leading French politician and premier from 1917 to 1920. He played a key role in the Allied war effort.

14 This comment and other material in two earlier letters suggest that Ida was perhaps not at first totally reconciled to her husband's decision to volunteer for the NZEF. WGM to IKM, 6 and 17 Sep 1914 (not published), MSX 2548, ATL.

15 In the NZEF embarkation orders dated 29 Aug 1914, Malone is named as the officer commanding troops on the *Arawa*. NZEF Embarkation Orders, 29 Aug 1914, MFCL. Colonel G.N. Johnston was later given this post, in part, it seems, because of Malone's complaints about the arrangements on the troopship. Telegrams QMG 149, 153, Device to F.E. Johnston, 14 Sep 1914, AD1, 25/19/20, ANZ.

16 Col Sir James **Allen**, 10 Feb 1855 – 28 Jul 1942, Minister of Defence 1912–20.

17 Fd Marshal Horatio Herbert **Kitchener**, KG KCB KCMG 1st Earl Kitchener of Khartoum, 24 Jun 1850 – 5 Jun 1916; British general and politician led the reconquest of the Sudan in 1896–98. Commanded British forces in South Africa 1900–1902, Secretary of State for War 1914–1916.

18 Spanish, we will see what we will see.

19 To pursue your own course.

20 This is the only mention by WGM of his first wife, Elinor, in his letters and diaries.
21 Capt (later Lt-Col) Norman C. **Hamilton**, RASC, DSO OBE mid(4); 2 Aug 1879 Wales – ?; single soldier of Palmerston North; 5/106, NZASC, later OC NZASC, served NZ 1913–17; SA War.
22 Brian Malone was serving with the Army Service Corps (ASC) component of the New Zealand force that had sailed on 15 Aug 1914 to seize German Samoa.
23 SS *Arawa* was one of three Shaw Savill & Albion's vessels requisitioned by the NZ Government on 10 Aug 1914. Built in 1906, the twin-screw steamship usually carried cargo and 220 passengers (in three classes) between NZ, Australia and the UK. For this voyage she was refitted for 49 officers, 1218 men and 200 horses. *Arawa* also conveyed the 30th Reinforcements in Oct 1917. S.D. Waters, *Shaw Savill Line: One Hundred Years of Trading* (Christchurch, 1961), p. 88.
24 Capt H. **Clayden** was master of *Arawa* from 1908 to 1919. He then became Shaw Savill & Albion's Marine Superintendent, South Island, and died in 1924. Waters, pp. 88, 106.
25 Lt-Col (later Brig-Gen) George N. **Johnston**, RA, CB CMG DSO mid(8) LH; 2 Aug 1867 Canada – 3 Apr 1947; married soldier of Wellington; 2/391, OC NZFA, later CRA NZ Div, GOC Admin NZEF.
26 Originally the convoy was to sail on 25 Sep, but concerns about the threat posed by the German Navy's East Asiatic Squadron led to its departure being delayed, McGibbon, *Path*, pp. 249–53.
27 Capt (later Lt-Col) Edward P. **Cox**, mid(2); 26 Oct 1886 Wanganui – 21 Jan 1959; single accountant of Hawera; 10/659 C-Coy WIB; WIA 1915; postwar OC 11th Regt, WWII OC ASC coy 1942.
28 Sgt-Maj (later temp Lt-Col) John B. **Parks**, MC mid; 25 Mar 1885 England – ?; married soldier of Wellington; 10/90 HQ WIB.
29 Col (later Maj-Gen Sir) Edward W.C. **Chaytor**, NZSC, KCMG KCVO CB CMG mid(7)Nile;

21 Jun 1868 Motueka – 15 Jun 1939; married soldier of Wellington; 15/6, AG HQ NZ Div, later OC NZMR Bde and Anzac Mounted Div, SA War, GOC NZ Military Forces 1919–24.
30 See Lady Liverpool to Mrs Malone, 16 Oct 1913, MFCL.
31 Attack verbally.
32 Allen shared some of Malone's concerns, see Telegram Device to F.E. Johnston, 14 Sep 1914 and Allen to QMG, 24 Sep 1914, AD1, 25/19/20, ANZ.
33 Now Sanson, 24 kilometres north-west of Palmerston North. In Jan 1914 WGM had purchased a new Buick touring car at a cost of £335. Invoice, 29 Jan 1914, MS-Papers-11408-22, ATL.
34 L/Sgt (later Sgt) George G. **Lowe**; 18 Apr 1890 Timaru – 17 Jan 1956; single PWD draughtsman of Stratford; 10/703 C-Coy WIB.
35 Alexander W. Reid, 1853–1938, developed the AWR milking machine and a prominent person in Stratford, Ron Lambert and Neil Henry, *Taranaki: An Illustrated History*, 2nd ed. (Auckland, 2000), pp. 125,137. Father of Pte Robert Reid, 10/713.
36 There was one other troopship not named by Malone, the *Ruapehu*.
37 Equal to 11 nautical miles an hour or 20 kilometres an hour.
38 To be recalcitrant.
39 John Ruskin, *The Crown of Wild Olive: four lectures on industry and war*, first published in 1888.
40 Lt (later Maj) James McD. **Richmond**, DSO MC mid(4); 17 Apr 1888 Wanganui – 27 Oct 1918; single soldier of Wellington; 2/311 NZFA, OC Bty, later Bde-Maj; KIA France.
41 Chaplain 4th Cl (later Brig) Alfred **Greene**, MC mid; 3 Nov 1872 Australia – 24 Nov 1950; married Salvation Army officer of Wellington; 10/206 NZ Chaplains Dept, NZEF 1914–20, army chaplain to 1935.
42 Men charged with cleaning the deck.
43 Sgt William F. **Southam**; 24 Apr 1882 England – 8 Jan 1963; single tailor of New Plymouth; 10/8 I/c Pioneer Sec WIB.

44 Sgt-Maj (later Capt) James T. **Dallinger**, MC; 6 Sep 1880 England – 22 Jun 1920; single soldier of Hawera; 10/162 QM-Sgt WIB; committed suicide.

45 Someone who has (or behaves as though they have) done something notable or are an expert at something.

46 Lt (later Major Sir) Ernest S. **Harston**, KBE, mid; 21 Aug 1891 Thames – 1975; single law student of Napier; 10/1074 B-Coy WIB; Coy Cmdr France, soldier 1909–26, League of Nations Secretariat, British Empire Service League.

47 L/Cpl Jack **Gilchrist**; 31 Feb 1884 Thornbury – 25 Oct 1914; single chemist of Gore; 3/323 NZMC att OIB; DOD at sea. A baseless rumour circulated through the convoy that Gilchrist had died as a result of the inoculations. Pugsley, *Gallipoli*, p. 66.

48 Maj John W. **Brunt**; 26 Feb 1862 UK – ?; married engineer of Hawera; 10/656 OC C-Coy WIB; later OC Codford Depot, OC Tauherenikau Camp, OC Featherston Camp; SA War, retired to South Africa.

49 Maj (later Lt-Col) Edward H. **Saunders**; 4 Jun 1873 England – 9 Oct 1948; married salesman of Featherston; 10/88 OC D-Coy WIB, later with 38th Refts 2nd draft, OC NZ Base Cairo.

50 Capt (later Lt-Col) Charles F.D. **Cook**, DSO mid(2); 23 Apr 1883 Christchurch – 2 May 1918; single lawyer of Marton; 10/543 B-Coy WIB, later OC WIR; DOD UK.

51 Maj (later Maj-Gen) William H. **Cunningham**, KBE CBE DSO mid(4) Stan; 24 Sep 1883 Wellington – 20 Apr 1959; single solicitor of Wanganui; 10/1085 OC WWC Coy WIB; OC 2nd WIB 1916, temp bde commands 1916–17, GOC Fiji 1940–42, WIR historian.

52 Lt-Col (later Maj Gen) Robert **Young**, CB CMG DSO mid(6) LH; 5 Jan 1877 UK – 25 Feb 1953; married dentist of Marton; 10/451 OC B-Coy WIB; later OC AIB, CIB then various bde commands; OC Southern Dist 1919–25, NZ Military Forces 1925–31; WWII OC HG 1940–44.

53 Maj-Gen (later Gen Sir) Alexander J. **Godley**, GCB KCMG mid(11) SSWar(4) LH(2) CG(2) WE Cour; 4 Feb 1867, England – 6 Mar 1957; married soldier of Wellington; 15/1 OC NZEF, GOC NZ Military Forces; soldier 1885–1928, serving NZ 1910–19.

54 Before.

55 Troopship magazine, six issues of 3–6 pages each, published between 24 Oct and 24 Nov 1914.

56 Pte (later Lt) Royden L. **Okey**, MC; 21 Feb 1893 New Plymouth – 30 Sep 1918; single clerk of Stratford; 10/761 HQ WIB, later with 35th Refts; KIA France.

57 Capt Frederick W. **Okey**, QM 11th Regt (Taranaki Rifles) and both related to Lt-Col E.N.L. Okey, VD, OC 11th Regt 1905–10.

58 Pte Arthur V. **Carbines**, mid; 19 May 1880 Auckland – 8 Aug 1915; single musician of New Plymouth; 10/706 C-Coy WIB; KIA Gallipoli.

59 Latin, by far the best.

60 This rumour sprang from the secret British offer to divert the Australian and New Zealand troops to South Africa to assist in quelling a Boer uprising. Timothy C. Winegard, *Indigenous Peoples of the British Dominions and the First World War* (Cambridge, 2012), pp.73–74.

61 2/Lt Harper M. **Lepper**, MC, single farmer of Lepperton, Taranaki; Direct Commission in 4th Middlesex Regt, British Army, 1914, died Mesopotamia, 9 Apr 1916; brother of Charles. One of five New Zealanders who had been granted commissions in the British Army travelling on the *Arawa*.

62 Cpl (later Sgt) Louis S. **Robertson**; 6 Apr 1881 Scotland – 9 Jun 1915; single builder of Ohura; 11/454 WMR; KIA Gallipoli; champion wrestler.

63 Pte Ernest W. **Hine**; 7 Nov 1891 Inglewood – 4 Dec 1957; married storeman of New Plymouth; 10/4 C-Coy WIB; WIA Gallipoli.

64 Battle of Coronel, off Chile, 1 Nov 1914, the German East Asiatic Squadron defeats a Royal Navy squadron.

65 Latin, make haste slowly. In his 1909 military notebook, WGM describes it as a good maxim for soldiers: 'especially in modern warfare'. WGM 1909 military notebook, MSX-9046, ATL.

66 The message was also picked up by the Australian troopship *Karoo*, Fred Waite, *The New Zealanders at Gallipoli* (Auckland, 1919), p. 20.

67 The *Emden's* collier *Buresk* was scuttled after HMAS *Sydney* caught up with her. C.E. Daw and L.J. Lind, *HMAS Sydney 1913–1929: The story of a Light Cruiser* (Garden Island, 1973), p. 37.

68 Capt (later Maj) Francis G. **Hume**; 17 Dec 1876 England – 5 Oct 1950; married soldier of Dunedin; 2/600 OC 11 Bty NZFA; SA War.

69 While there were four engagements at places with this name, WGM is most likely referring to the Battle of Driefontein (also known as Abraham's Kraal) on 10 Mar 1900, in the campaign to take Bloemfontein; during the South African War, 1899–1902. L.S. Amery, ed., *Times History of the War in South Africa*, vol. III, (London, 1905) pp. 572–86.

70 Under an ancient maritime custom, men on a ship who have not crossed the Equator before are called before 'King Neptune' and members of his court and are 'shaved' with paste or soapsuds and dunked in a pool. A.B. Campbell, *Customs and Traditions of the Royal Navy* (Aldershot, 1956), pp. 38–42.

71 Hugh Morrison was a prominent Wairarapa farmer and chairman of the Wairarapa Patriotic Committee.

72 Lt Ernest J.H. **Webb**; 14 Feb 1881 Dunedin – 17 Nov 1914; single doctor of Dunedin; 10/1021 NZMC att WIB; Died of Accident Colombo.

73 Pte Harry **McDowell**, 12/806, one of 20 Auckland Bn men on *Arawa*. An earlier case, Morrissy, had been left in Colombo. Pte (later Cpl) John W. **Morrissy**; 28 Sep 1892 England – 20 May 1920; single grocer's assistant of Takapau; 10/100 D Coy WIB, returned to NZ 29 Dec 1914, rejoined WIB with 3rd Refts;

Morrissy died 6 years later of complications from his appendicitis operation.

74 To shout or bellow.

75 Sgt-Maj Saxon W.B. **Foster**; 20 Apr 1890 Chatham islands – 21 May 1962; single soldier of Palmerston North; 10/526 D Coy WIB.

76 Edward M. **Smith**, known as 'Iron sand Smith' after the industry he advocated in Taranaki. He had come to New Plymouth in 1861 and with experience in the royal small arms factories became armourer in the NZ colonial forces. Later MP 1890–1907, as was his one of his seven sons S.G. Smith 1918–38. A.B. Scanlan, *Taranaki People and Places* (New Plymouth, 1985), p. 181.

77 Pte T. Douglas D. **Smith**; 30 Mar 1890 England – 3 Jul 1916; single dairy factory manager of Rahotu; 10/698 C-Coy WIB; KIA France.

78 Before sailing from Wellington WGM purchased 'two dozen' French novels, WGM to Mackay, nd, but Sep 1914, (not published) MSX 2548.

79 David **Lloyd George**, 17 Jan 1863 – 26 Mar 1945, British politician, Chancellor of the Exchequer 1908–15, Prime Minister 1916–22.

80 Fd Marshal Sir Frederick S. **Roberts**, 1st Earl Roberts, VC, 30 Sep 1832 – 1 Nov 1914; C-in-C India, Ireland, and of British forces in the South African War 1900, later head of the National Service League that campaigned for a system of compulsory military training like that adopted by New Zealand.

81 Hon Capt William D.H. **Baillie**, 22 Feb 1827 – 24 Feb 1922; MLC for Marlborough 1861–1922, Marl Superintendent, Chairman of Committees. Retired officer, late 24th Regt, politician of Wellington. Punjab Campaign 1849, Parihaka 1881.

82 Fatty.

83 WGM's number was actually 10/1039.

84 Papanui is a suburb of Christchurch.

85 Britain declared war on Turkey on 2 Nov 1914 after the expiry of an ultimatum about Turkish military operations against Russia.

86 Maj Charles **Shawe**; 15 Nov 1878 England –

?; single soldier of Wellington; 15/21 NZ Div
Censor, later GSO NZ&A Div, rejoined British
Army.

Chapter 2

1 A cousin of WGM's.
2 Don and Billy were WGM's horses, which he
  had brought from New Zealand after selling
  them to the NZEF.
3 Alexander Wemyss, 'A Short History of the
  Contingent Company of the Ceylon Planters',
  67/177/1, Imperial War Museum, London.
4 The German East Asiatic Squadron was
  destroyed in the Battle of the Falkland Islands,
  8 Dec 1914.
5 Thanks be to God.
6 On 18 Dec the Khedive Abbas was deposed
  and a British protectorate declared. The
  following day Hussein was proclaimed Sultan
  of Egypt. Waite, p. 326.
7 Chap 3rd Cl James J. **McMenamin**; 15 Aug
  1874 Wanganui – 9 Jun 1917; single chaplain
  of Petone; 6/1215 att CIB, later with 11th
  Refts, 2 NZ GH; KIA France.
8 Capt (later Maj) Francis H. **Lampen**, NZSC,
  DSO mid; 29 Oct 1879 India – 5 May 1950;
  married soldier of London, ex Nelson; 5/250A
  OC Br Sec NZEF, 2nd Refts OIB, later Bde Maj;
  WWII HG 1941–42.
9 To give a bad time.
10 Aged eight years.
11 Aged six years.
12 Real photograph postcards.
13 Maj-Gen (later Gen, Sir) John G. **Maxwell**,
  GCB KCMG CVO DSO mid(10) LH Nile WE;
  11 Jul 1859 England – 20 Feb 1929; married,
  soldier 1879–1922; OC Troops Egypt to 1916,
  later OC Ireland during Easter Rising; OC
  Northern Command; Sudan, SA War.
14 The time when the men were recalled to their
  quarters.
15 Godley had a more realistic approach to the
  threat posed by sexually transmitted diseases
  than most senior commanders, Jane Tolerton,
  Ettie: A Life of Ettie Rout (Auckland 1992),
  pp. 125–31; Pugsley, *Gallipoli*, pp. 76–78.

16 Maj-Gen (later Fd Marshal, 1st Baron of Anzac
  & Totnes, Sir) William R. **Birdwood**, GCMG
  KCB KCSI; 13 Sep 1865 India – 17 May 1951;
  married soldier of India; OC ANZAC, later OC
  AIF Admin, OC 5th Army, OC Indian Army;
  NW Frontier, SA War.
17 WGM's attitude towards flags is seen after the
  Union Jack that draped the coffin of Pte Albert
  Cooper on 31 Dec or 1 Jan was mislaid. In
  asking for its return in a notice, Malone said
  'the flag has value other than intrinsic'. This
  or a New Zealand flag had earlier been sent
  to him at Awapuni by a Mrs Keswick 'and
  the women of Taranaki' along with a plea
  for his soldiers to always give 'the courtesy
  and respect that is due to women'. NZEF
  War Diary 1915, Orders No. 108, 24 Mar
  1915; WGM to Keswick, 4 Sep 1914, (not
  published) MSX-2548, ATL.
18 The infantry of the NZEF was armed with the
  .303 Magazine Lee Enfield (MLE) (Long) Mark
  I, but after the Gallipoli campaign this rifle
  was replaced by the newer Short Magazine Lee
  Enfield (SMLE). Pugsley, *Gallipoli*, p. 45.
19 For the landing on Gallipoli the New Zealand
  troops replaced their distinctive headgear with
  peaked caps. Pugsley, *Gallipoli*, p. 120.
20 A devotional work, *The Imitation of Christ* by
  Thomas à Kempis; probably the edition with
  an introduction by H.C. Beeching.
21 Godley established a fairly demanding training
  regime for the NZEF, but clearly WGM
  considered that more training was necessary.
  Pugsley, *Gallipoli*, p. 78.
22 An Englishman who Malone had met on a
  tram on 24 Dec.
23 Referred to as the 'Muski' in Cunningham et
  al., *Wellington Regiment*, p. 16.
24 Maj (later Maj-Gen) Arthur C. **Temperley**, CB
  CMG DSO mid(5); 31 Aug 1877 UK – 7 Apr
  1940; married soldier of Palmerston North;
  10/1130, Bde-Maj, NZ Inf Bde; later GSO3
  NZ Div; SA War, NW Frontier, served NZ
  1913–17, attaché 1920–35. Temperley was
  Brigade Major of the NZ Infantry Bde; the bde
  commander's principal staff officer.

25 Capt (later Maj) John M. **Rose**, MC mid CG;
1 Aug 1868 Scotland – 12 Jun 1948; married
soldier of Palmerston North; 10/692 HQ WIB,
later 2i/c Conv Hosp.

26 Capt (Brevet Maj) R.E. **Coningham**, Indian
Army; joined the staff of HQ NZ&A Div as
GSO3 Jan 1915–Jan 1916; WIA 30 Jul 1915.

27 Maj-Gen Charles J. **Melliss**, VC KCB KCMG,
mid(8); 1862 – 6 Jun 1936; OC 30 Bde,
later Mesopotamia 1915–16, POW 1916–18;
married, soldier 1882–1916; E Africa NW
Frontier W Africa.

28 Pte William A. **Ham**; 14 Apr 1892 Ireland –
5 Feb 1915; single labourer of Pokororo,
Nelson; 6/246 CIB; DOW Egypt.

29 Arabic, a peasant, especially in Egypt.

30 A type of clover grown for forage in Egypt.

31 Lt (later Maj) Leopold G.D. **Acland**, OBE
MC mid(3); 2 Jul 1876 Christchurch – 7 Apr
1948; single sheep farmer of Christchurch;
14/97, NZASC, later DAAG NZEF; SA War.
Acland had lost an arm after he was mauled
by a tiger in India and was officially too old
to be commissioned, but because of a serious
shortage of ASC officers he was commissioned
in the New Zealand Military Forces and later
the NZEF. Smythe to HQ NZ military forces,
24 Mar 1914, L.G.D. Acland P/F, ANZ.

32 A village in the Sinai Peninsula 130 kilometres
east of the Suez Canal.

33 The wife of Captain Home who had travelled
to Egypt to serve as a nurse.

34 French, in company.

35 The New Zealand and Australian Division
under Godley was formally established on
18 Jan 1915. Birdwood's corps which was
to become the Australian and New Zealand
Army Corps (ANZAC) was formed in late Dec
1914, after he arrived in Egypt. C.E.W. Bean,
The Story of Anzac, vol. I (Sydney, 1921), pp.
117–25; Pugsley, *Gallipoli*, pp. 69–76, 360.

36 Viscount **Haldane**; 30 Jul 1856 – 19 Aug
1928; British Secretary of State for War
1905–12 directed extensive reforms of the
British Army including the establishment of a
volunteer Territorial Army.

37 Chaplain 4th Cl Patrick **Dore**, MC mid;
4 Feb 1886 Ireland – 15 Jul 1918; single RC
clergyman of Foxton; 13/655 att AMR; WIA
Gallipoli, DOW in NZ.

38 Chaplain 4th CI (later 3rd Cl) Rev Robert
Richards, MC SSWar; 9 Dec 1868 South
Africa – ?; single RC clergyman of Hawarden;
18/3 later 10/3A, 2nd Refts att WIB.

39 Chaplain 3rd Cl (later Chap 1st Cl) Rev John
A. **Luxford**, CMG mid(2) SSWar(2); 26 Mar
1854 Hutt Valley – 28 Jan 1921; Methodist
clergyman of Christchurch; 10/307A later
8/307A, NZEF 1914–20; WIA 1915;
SA War.

40 Value in 2014 over $106,000.

41 2/Lt (later Maj) William Francis **Tracy**, MC
mid; 8/496, OIB. Sometimes spelled Tracey in
official publications.

42 French, in order.

43 A young French boy whom Malone met in
January.

44 Capt (later Lt-Col) John L. **Short**, mid;
25 Apr 1887 Wellington – ?; single solicitor
of Taumarunui; 10/146 WIB, later with 12th
Refts, OC 3WIB.

45 French, a smacking kiss.

46 Conceit or pretentiousness.

47 An oppressive, hot south or south-easterly
wind that frequently blows across Egypt
between March and May.

48 A tip or gratuity.

49 Col (later Maj-Gen Sir) Andrew 'Guy' H.
Russell, KCB KCMG mid(9) CG(2) WE Dan
Leo; 23 Feb 1868 Napier – 29 Nov 1960;
married farmer of Hastings; 11/257 OC NZMR
Bde.

50 WGM wrote to Madame Thomas once and her
daughter twice (in French) while he was at
Gallipoli (letters not published).

51 Sister Teresa [Vasey[, Sisters of Charity,
Spennymore, England; a cousin of WGM.

52 Killed on 19 Feb 1915, *Taranaki Herald*, 2 Mar
1915, p. 2. WGM appears to have written to
his brother once after joining the NZEF. WGM
to Austin Malone, 4 Sep 1914 (not published),
MSX 2548, ATL.

53 The 3rd Reinforcements (total strength 2230) had sailed from Wellington on 14 Feb 1915.

54 Capt John R. **Henderson**, NZSC; 1 Oct 1875 Scotland – 19 Sep 1944; married soldier of Wellington; 15/9 and 18541, to Admiralty 1918. In August 1915 Henderson was convicted of stealing money given to him for official purposes in 1913 and sentenced to 12 months' imprisonment. He had resigned from the NZSC shortly before he went on trial and after his release from prison re-enlisted in the NZEF as a private. In 1917 he was commissioned as a 2/Lt in the NZEF. *New Zealand Truth*, 21 Aug 1915, p.7; History Sheet Henderson P/F, ANZ. Robinson's promotion to Major was confirmed, in large part, to assuage his feelings after being sacked as adjutant of the WIB. Telegram Godley to Robin, 20 Aug 1914, W.G. Robinson P/F, ANZ.

55 French, That she is pretty and clever.

56 Russia offered in March to provide a corps of 40,000 men to co-operate with the assault on the Dardanelles from the Black Sea end of the Bosporus once the Turkish fleet had been destroyed and the Allied fleet had entered in Sea of Marmara; C.F. Aspinall-Oglander, *Military Operations: Gallipoli*, vol. 1 (London, 1929), pp. 82–83, 87, 124–25.

57 Gen Sir Ian S.M. **Hamilton**, GCMG GCB DSO; 16 Jan 1853 Corfu – 1947; OC Medit Exp Force (the Allied force formed for the Gallipoli operation) until recalled 17 Oct 1915; married, soldier since 1872, visited NZ 1914 as Inspector General Overseas Forces; Afghan Egypt Burma India SA Russo-Jap War Sudan. WGM had met Hamilton in May 1914 when he visited New Zealand. Menu with annotations for a dinner in honour of Sir Ian Hamilton organised by the Taranaki Club, New Plymouth, 20 May 1914, MFCL.

58 Capt (later Maj) Arthur C.B. **Critchley-Salmonson**, DSO mid(2) Nile; 27 Apr 1886 England – 14 Oct 1930; single soldier of Christchurch; 6/1173 HQ CIB to Dec 1915; WIA 1915; served NZ 1911–16, Egyptian Army 1917–20.

59 Wife of Ramasses II.

60 A large Nile river-boat.

61 Maj (later Lt-Col) Alfred H. **Herbert**, DSO mid(2); 4 Oct 1870 England – 14 May 1946; married merchant of Eketahuna; 11/1079, 3rd Refts WMR, OC Maori Cont, later OC ADOS corps level.

62 This must have been a story going around the force, but it is not correct. Lemnos Island had been Turkey's until taken by Greece in Oct 1912, in the second Balkan War. The Greek Prime Minister E. Venizelos was keen to let the Allies have use of it and its huge harbour at Mudros for an advanced base for their operations in the Dardanelles, but he had to do so without compromising Greece's neutrality. So Venizelos arranged to merely withdraw the Greek garrison (leaving intact the fixed defences), thus allowing the Allies to occupy it (and Imbros) as enemy territory. J.S. Corbett, *Naval Operations*, vol. II (London, 2nd ed., 1929), p. 123.

63 Short for, Latin, *Deo Volente*, God willing.

64 Pte John A. **Campbell**; 15 Nov 1888 Dunedin – 14 Dec 1914; single horse driver of Napier; 10/1028 Transport Driver WIB; DOD Egypt. Pte Albert G. **Cooper**; 27 Aug 1891 Hastings – 26 Dec 1914; single painter of Wairoa; 10/380A B-Coy WIB; DOD Egypt. Pte Bethel J. **Simpson**; 26 Aug 1884 Amberley – 17 Mar 1915; single lineman of Napier; 10/941 WIB; Died during operation, Egypt; SA War.

Chapter 3

1 Behave in a stingy way.

2 Luxford who disliked WGM was happy to transfer. Luxford diary, 2–3 Apr 1915; MS-papers 6454/2, ATL.

3 A city on the west coast of Turkey, now Izmir. WGM is mistaken. The attack he refers to was carried out by a Turkish torpedo boat. Corbett, vol. II, pp. 300–1.

4 East Indian seamen serving on British ships.

5 HMS *Ocean*, a pre-dreadnaught type battleship, was sunk by gunfire and a mine on 18 Mar 1915. Corbett, vol. II, pp. 221–22.

6 Latin, nothing but good. By this Malone meant that an officer should, at least in public, say only positive things about more senior officers.

7 HMS *Queen Elizabeth* was of the modern 'dreadnought' configuration, multiple turrets with eight 15-inch guns, and turbine driven. She was also twice the displacement of pre-dreadnought types, at 27,500 tons, and much larger at 645 ft long. Served 1915–1948.

8 Brig-Gen (later Lt-Gen, Sir) John **Monash**, GCMG KCB mid(5); 27 Jun 1865 Vict — 8 Oct 1931; married engineer of Melbourne; OC 4 Aust Bde, later OC 3 Aust Div, OC corps.

9 Worthless.

10 Settled their accounts, i.e. undertaken confession and absolution. Father Maples was the parish priest in Stratford.

11 A small case for needles and thread, etc.

12 A concentrated drug-preparation.

13 The area at the toe of the Gallipoli Peninsula where the main British landings took place.

14 The sea between the east coast of the Gallipoli Peninsula and the Turkish mainland.

15 The plan for the landings called for the Australians to push inland quickly.

16 A village inland from Anzac Cove where the Turkish Army had a major headquarters.

17 Col (later Brig-Gen) William G. **Braithwaite**, CB CMG DSO mid(6 WWI, 3 SA) WE; 20 Oct 1870 England – 15 Oct 1937; single soldier of Wellington; 15/4, HQ NZ Div; SA War 1899–1902, regular soldier, served NZ 1911–18.

18 WGM appears to be making a joke by referring to the phrase 'lo and behold' meaning, here is a surprising fact.

19 Brig-Gen (later Lt-Gen, Sir) Harold B. 'Hooky' **Walker**, KCB KCMG DSO mid(9); 26 Apr 1862 England – 5 Nov 1934; Chief of Staff Anzac Corps, temp OC NZ Inf Bde from 11 am 25 Apr, later OC 1 Aust Bde, 1 Aust Div; WIA Gallipoli; SA War.

20 Lt-Col George F. **Braund**; 13 Jul 1866 England – 4 May 1915; OC 2 Bn, NSW Member of Parliament; KIA Gallipoli.

21 Lt Edmund R. **Wilson**, mid; 15 May 1882 Ireland – 27 Apr 1915; single dentist of Masterton; 10/75 MG Officer WIB; KIA Gallipoli.

22 Maj (later Brig) Norris S. **Falla**, CMG DSO mid(5); 3 May 1883 Westport – 6 Nov 1945; married Union Steamship Co Asst Traffic Manager of Dunedin; 2/996 4 How Bty NZFA; later OC DAC, OC NZFA bde cmds, temp CRA, OC NZ Arty Reserve Depot. TF to 1929. WWII 1940–41; died at sea.

23 WGM sent Falla a personal note thanking him for his assistance. WGM to O/C Howitzer Battery, 30 Apr 1915, WA 73/3, item 3A, ANZ.

24 Sgt-Maj Archibald J.M. **Bonar;** 24 Aug 1876 Hokitika – 28 Apr 1915; single soldier of Stratford; 10/1116 C-Coy WIB; KIA Gallipoli; Lt in SA War.

25 Sgt-Maj Matthew **McGlade**; 8 Oct 1880 Ireland – 26 Apr 1915; single soldier of New Plymouth; 10/1115 CSM C-Coy WIB; KIA Gallipoli.

26 Lt Laurence W.A. **Hugo**; 28 Mar 1885 Napier – 27 Apr 1915; single compositor of Wellington, 10/7 D-Coy WIB; KIA Gallipoli.

27 Lt (later Col) Leonard H. **Jardine**, DSO(2) MC mid; 18 Jul 1890 Napier – 15 May 1969; single surveyor of Napier; 10/1049 B-Coy WIB, later OC 3WIB; WIA; WWII OC Taranaki Regt 1925–30, 1939–40.

28 Lt (later Capt) Alexander B. **McColl**, mid; 28 May 1892 Wellington – 2 Jul 1916; single surveyor of Taumarunui; 10/18, WIB, later Adj; KIA France.

29 Lt (later Lt-Col) Frank K. **Turnbull**, DSO MC mid(3); 3 Jan 1885 Nelson – 22 Nov 1946; single solicitor of Wanganui; 10/131 A-Coy WIB; WIA; later OC 1WIB; WWII OC Papakura Camp 1941–44.

30 Lt Douglas I.C. **Bryan**; 28 Sep 1892 – 28 Jul 1968; single soldier of Royal Military College, Duntroon, ex-Westport; 10/976 A-Coy WIB; WIA Gallipoli.

31 More commonly called Lala Baba, the highest ground between Nibrunesi Point and the salt lake.

32 Cpl William J. **Copeland**; 23 Jan 1890 Wanganui – 2 May 1915; single motor mechanic of New Plymouth; 10/666 C-Coy WIB; KIA Gallipoli. In a condolence letter to Copeland's father, Malone noted that he was killed directing the fire of the battalion machine guns and praised Copeland as 'one of the best of the splendid soldiers under my command'. *Auckland Star*, 3 Jul 1915, p. 5.

33 Fit of nervousness.

34 Booklets produced by the British Imperial General Staff that summarised lessons learned from operations.

35 The page of the manuscript in the Alexander Turnbull Library containing the text down to 'a muddler' is missing, but is in the old diary transcript and this version has been inserted to complete the text.

36 Bugler George F. McG. **Bissett**; 1 Dec 1894 Normanby – 27 Apr 1915; single joiner of Feilding; 10/304 A-Coy WIB; KIA Gallipoli.

37 Pte Sydney **Roberts**; 1 Jun 1882 England – 27 Apr 1915; single labourer of Wanganui; 10/503 WIB, MIA/KIA Gallipoli.

38 Lt Charles B.S. **Menteath**; 5 Mar 1892 Wellington – 8 May 1915; single farmer of Hunterville; 10/1082 A-Coy WIB; KIA Gallipoli.

39 Cpl (later Sgt) Gerald **Sievers**; 31 Jul 1891 Clareville – 8 Aug 1915; single treemonger of Tiraumea; 10/87, D Coy WIB; KIA Gallipoli.

40 Lt-Col Edmund G. **Evelegh**, Royal Marine Light Infantry. The Nelson Bn formed part of the Royal Naval Division.

41 Heliograph – signalling device using flashes of sunlight reflected from a movable mirror.

42 Tekke Burnu and Sedd el Bahr are at the south-western tip of the Gallipoli Peninsula where the British forces landed. This area was generally referred to as Helles, after Cape Helles.

Chapter 4

1 Naval term for ratings without any naval training.

2 Allied casualties in the second Battle of Krithia, 6–8 May 1915, were in fact about 6,500, Aspinall-Oglander, vol. I, p. 347.

3 Lt-Col Alexander B. **Charters**, CMG DSO mid(4); 30 Jun 1876 Christchurch – 10 May 1948; married school inspector of Wellington; 10/1168, 2nd Refts WIB; OC Base Depot Alexandria, OC 1OIB; SA War.

4 1st Bn Royal Inniskilling Fusiliers.

5 Hampshire Regiment.

6 Essex Regiment.

7 Latin, thanks be to God.

8 Lt George W. **Tayler**; 4 Feb 1890 Eltham – 8 Aug 1915; married solicitor of Eltham; 10/1681 3rd Refts WIB; KIA GAllipoli. Lt (later Capt) Frank L. **Hartnell**; 26 Apr 1875 Auckland – 19 Jan 1939; married carpenter of New Plymouth; 10/1517 3rd Refts WIB, later with 21st Refts as coy cmdr WIB.

9 Brig-Gen (later Lt-Gen, Sir) William R. **Marshall**, GCMG KCB KCSI; 29 Oct 1865 England – 29 May 1939; OC 87 Bde 29 Div and OC X Beach Landing, soon temp OC 29 Div, later OC divs, corps, Mesopotamia Expeditionary Force; married, soldier 1885–1924; SA War.

10 2/Lt Alan H. **Preston,** MC mid; 28 Nov 1890 England – 7 Jun 1917; single station hand of Makauri; 10/910 MG-Sec WIB, later NZ MG Corps; KIA France.

11 Lt-Col Athelstan **Moore**, CMG DSO mid(3); 9 Jul 1879 England – 14 Oct 1918; married soldier of Dunedin; 8/1155, OC OIB; DOW France; SA War.

12 French, let us return to the subject.

13 WGM also refers to this in his letters to Maj Sandford of 17 May 1915 and Madame Thomas of 23 May 1915 (not published).

14 A plentiful supply.

15 A makeshift shelter.

16 Pte (later QM-Sgt) David G. **Whitmore**; 22 Jan 1879 Christchurch – 26 Jul 1950; single carpenter of Feilding; 10/561 A-Coy WIB, later with 24th Refts; WIA Gallipoli.

17 Lt-Col (later Maj-Gen Sir) George S. **Richardson**, KBE CB CMG mid(3) SSWar(3) LH, CG; 14 Nov 1868 England – 11 Jun 1938;

single soldier seconded to London; AA&QMG Royal Naval Div, later 12 Corps, 15/209 OC Admin NZEF; Administrator Western Samoa, Dep Mayor Auckland.

18 The 100-strong New Zealand Staff Corps consisted of the regular officers that provided the professional core of the Dominion's military forces.

19 Maj-Gen (later Sir) Archibald **Paris**, KCB mid(8); 9 Nov 1861 England – 30 Oct 1937; OC RN Div; married, WIA France.

20 A Roman Catholic religious order active in Turkey before the Great War.

21 Capt (acting Maj) Fred W. **Sandford**, VD; Christchurch Rifle Volunteers 1885–91, Christchurch City Guards 1894–1904, Unattached List 1904–07, Active List to 1911. Commanded and umpired Taranaki's Cadet units under WGM after moving to New Plymouth 1907.

22 Hill 971 (elevation in feet) or Koja Chemen Tepe the highest point in the ridge that runs roughly North to South, which includes Chunuk Bair, and dominates the Anzac Cove area.

23 The southern cape of Suvla Bay.

24 A map reference for Baby 700, a Turkish position between the Nek and Battleship Hill.

25 The village of Biyuk Anafarta (Great Anafarta) inland from Suvla Bay.

26 A small hill inland from the coast just south of Anzac Cove.

27 Point on east coast.

28 The first large hill north of the toe of the peninsula; the location of the village of Krithia; the objective of repeated Allied attacks.

29 Subalterns, officers below the rank of captain, especially second lieutenants.

30 Gaba Tepe the headland about two kilometres south of Anzac Cove; presumably WGM means the Walker's Ridge area.

31 Lt-Col (later temp Col) Arthur **Plugge**, CMG mid(3); 17 Feb 1878 England – 1 Jul 1934; single schoolmaster of Auckland; 12/1 OC AIB, later OC Div Trg.

32 A type of explosive.

33 WGM could be referring to a line in *Don Quixote* by Cervantes, 'Hunger is the best sauce in the world'.

34 This could be Malone's off-hand acknowledgement of having been formerly in conflict with his bandsmen. At Awapuni he had stopped them playing in honour of one of their own, who died in New Plymouth before attesting, and did so again when the Main Body of the NZEF sailed from Wellington. Similar tensions arose after the battalion's Bandmaster, Pte Bethel Simpson, died in Mar 1915, and Malone chose his replacement against the wishes of the bandsmen. Pte Laurie E. Smith 10/609, interviewed by Murray Moorhead in the 1980s, pers com 24 Feb 2005; *NZ Freelance*, 27 Mar 1915, p. 5.

35 A loyal, dependable person.

36 Latin, To die for fatherland is a sweet thing. Probably a contraction of a quotation from Horace.

37 When the New Zealand Infantry Brigade and the 2nd Australian Infantry Brigade arrived at Cape Helles they were formed into a composite division with a brigade from the Royal Naval Division. Waite, p. 121.

38 Midshipmen.

39 Lt (later Capt) Bruce H. **Morison**, MC mid; 12 Nov 1888 Wellington – 22 Feb 1924; single law student of Wellington; 10/663, B-Coy WIB.

40 This dry water course, just north of Walker's Ridge, became known as Malone's Gully and is between Happy Valley and No. 1 Post and leads up to Baby 700.

41 L/Cpl (later 2/Lt) Philip H.G. **Bennett**, DCM mid; 28 Sep 1891 – 15 Jan 1962; single journalist of Wanganui; 10/274 A-Coy WIB; later with 36th Refts, 1918. Pte Horace E. **Hayden**, mid; 10 Jan 1890 England – 26 Apr 1915; single upholsterer of New Plymouth; 10/723 C-Coy WIB; KIA Gallipoli. The Pte Swan is probably Pte (later Cpl) James W. **Swan**, DCM mid; 23 Dec 1884 Mosgiel – 16 Sep 1916, single, miner of Gisborne; 10/1674 3rd Refts; KIA France.

42 S-Sgt (later Cpl) Beaumont W. **Woodhead**; 22 May 1880 – 30 Apr 1936; married soldier of Wanganui; 10/1118 A-Coy WIB.

43 Gen Otto **Liman Von Sanders**; 17 Feb 1855 – 22 Aug 1929. In 1913 he led the German military mission reorganising the Turkish Army. Late in 1914 he commanded Turkish forces in the Caucasus and was then moved to command the Fifth Army in the Dardenelles. He later commanded the Turkish forces in Palestine and Syria.

44 Capt Jesse A. **Wallingford**, NZSC, MC mid; 25 Jan 1872 England – 6 Jun 1944; married soldier of Auckland; 12/1125 HQ AIB, later Bde MG Officer. Shooting champion.

45 Maj (later Lt-Col) James H. **Whyte**, NZSC, DSO(2) DCM mid(7); 17 Dec 1876 Clevedon – 3 Nov 1951; single soldier of Palmerston North; 11/698 WMR, later OC WMR, OC CMR, Bde-Maj 2ALH Bde; SA War; WWII OC Troopships 1940–45.

46 Lt-Col (temp Brig-Gen) William **Meldrum**, CB CMG DSO mid(6) WE; 28 Jul 1865 Kamo – 13 Feb 1964; single farmer of Hunterville; 11/675, OC WMR, later OC NZMR Bde; WWII HG 1940–42.

47 Maj-Gen Sir William T. **Bridges**, KCB CMG; 18 Feb 1861 Scotland — 18 May 1915; married soldier; OC 1 Aust Div; former OC RMC, SA War, Insp Gen, IGS; DOW Gallipoli.

48 WGM was mentioned in dispatches twice in the supplements to the *London Gazettes* of 3 Aug 1915 and 28 Jan 1916. History Sheet, WGM P/F, ANZ. Because the DSO is an order it cannot be given posthumously. It is probable that WGM's DSO never eventuated because he was killed before the necessary administrative work had been completed.

49 Italy declared war on Austria-Hungary on 23 May 1915, on Turkey on 21 Aug 1915 and on Germany on 28 Aug 1915.

50 Maj William F. **Levin**; 6 Dec 1879 Wellington – 25 Dec 1915; married farmer of Greatford, Rangitikei; 11/787 2nd Refts WMR, later Beachmaster; DOW Egypt; SA War.

51 Originally Ida planned to leave Denis and Barney in New Zealand.

52 HMS *Triumph* was torpedoed and sunk by a German submarine, *U-21*, off Gaba Tepe. Casualties were 73 out of a complement of 800. Malone did not note that another battleship, HMS *Goliath*, was sunk on 13 May by a Turkish torpedo boat. Corbett, vol. II, pp. 407–408, vol. III (London, 1923), pp. 29–30.

53 A member of a Russian Trio, the Cherniavsky Brothers, who were touring New Zealand, *Auckland Star*, 11 Aug 1915, p. 9.

54 Capt (later Maj) William J. **Hardham**, VC; 31 Jul 1876 Wellington – 13 Apr 1928; single blacksmith of Petone; 11/661 WMR; later with 35th Refts NZMR and OC 2 Sqn WMR; WIA; NZ's only SA War VC winner.

55 Hamilton was a British observer with the Japanese Army during the war and wrote a popular book, *A Staff Officer's Scrap-Book: During the Russo-Japanese War* (London, 1905), which WGM had read. 1909 military notebook, notes on Russo-Japanese war actions.

56 HMS *Majestic* was torpedoed by U-21 off W Beach. Of her crew of 672 about 40 drowned, entangled in her torpedo nets which were deployed at the time. Corbett, vol. III, p. 31.

57 French, as it should be.

58 This group were the first New Zealand Army Nursing Service personnel to be sent overseas. Anna Rogers, *While You're Away: New Zealand Nurses at War 1899–1948* (Auckland, 2003), pp. 50–59.

59 Tire out.

60 Louisa Sanders [née Malone], WMG's sister, known as Louie.

61 Jessie Malone's (née Trimble) family.

62 French, very troublesome, irksome.

Chapter 5

1 Sgt Hugh M. **Parrington**; 31 Jan 1894 Hawera – 25 Aug 1915; single engineer of Hawera; 10/785 Orderly WIB; DOD Egypt.

2 Col (later Gen, Sir) Henry 'Harry' G. **Chauvel**, GCMG KCB mid(10) CG Nile; 16 Apr 1865

NSW – 4 Mar 1945; married soldier; OC 1 ALH, later OC Div and OC corps, Australian CGS 1923–30.

3 Well-designed mortar which fired a large high explosive bomb, Bean, vol. I, p. 614.

4 Page 52 (containing part of the entries for 1 and 2 June) of the manuscript in the Alexander Turnbull is missing, but the passage is in the old diary transcript and this version is inserted here to complete the text.

5 The sniping party established by WGM was commanded by a noted marksman, 2/Lt Thomas 'Army' Grace. The Wellington Battalion squad was first properly organised and highly effective response to the threat posed by Turkish snipers. C.E.W. Bean, *The Story of ANZAC, Volume II, from 4 May 1915, to the Evacuation of the Gallipoli Peninsula* (Sydney, 1924), pp. 248–49; Pugsley, *Gallipoli*, pp. 237–40.

6 A town at the northern end of the Gallipoli Peninsula.

7 Lt (later Capt) Leslie S. **McLernon**; 7 Sep 1891 Gisborne – 8 Aug 1915; single clerk of Napier; 10/1079 B-Coy WIB; KIA Gallipoli.

8 2/Lt James R. **Cargo**; 12 Feb 1892 Auckland – 3 Jun 1915; single bank clerk of New Plymouth; 10/740 C-Coy WIB; KIA Gallipoli; former 11th Regt.

9 Chaplain 4th Cl (later 3rd Cl) Rev Charles J. **Bush-King**, VD; 3 Mar 1875 Wellington – 1 Nov 1950; single curate of Dunedin; 2/626, att NZFA, later with 9th, 35th and 41st Refts. Long-term TF chaplain.

10 4th Reinforcements, left NZ 17 Apr, 2260 men.

11 Maj (later Lt-Col) John 'Jackie' G. **Hughes**, NZSC, CMG DSO mid(2); 12 Mar 1866 Bluff – 23 Jul 1954; married soldier of Wellington; 15/2, OC CIB, later Asst Mil Sec; SA War.

12 Capt (later temp Brig-Gen) Charles H.J. **Brown**, NZSC, DSO mid(3); 8 May 1872 Christchurch – 8 Jun 1917; married soldier of Greymouth; 15/14, Asst Provost Marshall, HQ NZ Div, OC CIB, AIB; KIA France.

13 Rabbit, rock hyrax or dupe.

14 Maj-Gen A.E.de L. **Joly de Lotbinière**, CB CSI CIE, Chief Engineer ANZAC.

15 Lt Godfrey C. **Wells**; 27 Oct 1890 Wellington – 21 Dec 1965; single farmer of Taringamutu; 10/608 C-Coy WIB; WIA July 1915. Lt (later Maj) A. Hugh **Carrington**, mid CG; 28 Jul 1895 England – 1947; single soldier of Christchurch; 10/2386 4th Refts WIB; WIA Gallipoli.

16 Now Ayduncik.

17 Vice-Adm (later Adm of Fleet, Sir) John M. **de Robeck**, Bt, GCB GCMG; 10 Jun 1862 Ireland – 20 Jan 1928; married, sailor 1875–1924; i/c RN Dardanelles in HMS *Queen Elizabeth*, later 2nd Battle Sqn, CinC Mediterranean Fleet, Atlantic Fleet; previously Capt HMS *Pyramus*.

18 Henry Nevinson, author of *The Dardenelles Campaign* (London, 1918).

19 23 July.

20 Lt Kenneth **Munro**; 7 Jul 1891 Patea – 3 Jul 1916; single law clerk of Stratford (in Malone's employ); 10/1930, 4th Refts WIB; KIA France.

21 Probably the memo referred to as 'most insubordinate', see WGM to Richardson, 19 Jun 1915, p. 248.

22 L/Cpl Francis A. **Haynes**; 16 May 1894 Pleasant Pt – 2 Jan 1988; single mechanic of Timaru; 6/471 CIB.

23 On 7 May the liner *Lusitania* was sunk in the Atlantic with great loss of life, by a German submarine.

24 Bulgaria entered the war in October 1915 on the side of the Central Powers (Germany, Austria-Hungary and Turkey).

25 Probably referring to memorandum reproduced on pp. 243–44.

26 Hart's DSO was officially announced in the *London Gazette* of 3 Jun 1915.

27 Hart and Saunders appear to have spent money in England helping WIB wounded.

28 'It is magnificent, but it is not war.' Maréchal Bosquet referring to the charge of the Light Brigade.

29 The pro-Allied Prime Minister of Greece.

30 French, a writing desk with drawers.

31 Mrs George Vasey? A relative of WGM's.

32 Latin, in person.

33 WGM was the most senior of the New Zealand battalion commanders. *Gradation List: New Zealand Expeditionary Force, 1914.*

34 Advantage or influence.

35 WGM is referring to the withdrawal of the British Army units in New Zealand during the later stages of the New Zealand Wars and their replacement with locally raised units.

36 A rag gatherer.

37 Bridport, a market town in Devon.

38 Sunbury-on-Thames, 24 kilometres south-west of London.

39 An idler.

40 L/Cpl Adrian **Winter**; 18 Aug 1886 England — 29 Apr 1915; single bushman of Wanganui; 10/541 A-Coy WIB; KIA Gallipoli.

41 Extracts from this letter and another he sent to Harry Penn on 24 Jul, despite stating that the contents were 'strictly entre nous [between us]', appeared in the *Wanganui Herald* on 22 Sep 1915, p. 6. The 'letter' published in *The Dominion* on 20 Jul, said to be sent by Malone to Harry Penn and describing events from 25 Apr to 12 Jun, appears not to have survived or is a montage of comments from other letters to him, or possibly diary entries.

42 Admitted defeat?

43 Clumsiness or unbalancedness.

44 French, between ourselves (private).

45 A variant spelling of 'sideling', a slope especially one along the side of which a track runs.

46 Latin, all leave the stage.

47 Same word, i.e. June.

48 Driver (later Gunner) Philip C. **Clemow**; 2 Mar 1894 Stratford – 21 Oct 1920; single clerk of Stratford; 11/537, WMR; WIA Gallipoli, Invalided 1918, DOW in NZ. The Clemow family were neighbours of the Malones in Stratford.

49 A village near Reading where Ida Malone had rented a house.

50 Staff Nurse (later Sister) Elizabeth B. **Young**, ARRC mid SSWar Sam; 28 Apr 1882 – 3 Feb 1969; single nurse of New Plymouth; 22/93 NZ Army Nursing Service 1915–19.

Chapter 6

1 QM-Sgt Peter A. **de Loree**; 4 Jun 1877 Kumara – 3 Mar 1939; married soldier of Taihape; 15/34 HQ NZ Div; Invalided 1916.

2 Pte William C. **Hughes**; 11 Jul 1884 Dunedin – 12 Jul 1961; single engine driver of Taumaru; 10/405 C-Coy WIB.

3 Long strips of material wound from ankle to just below the knee for protection and support. Part of the NZEF's uniform.

4 Hon 2/Lt (later temp Lt) Robert T.R.P. **Butler**, RE, MC mid; 4 Oct 1883 UK – ?; single British soldier; att No.1 Fd Coy, later Adj NZE.

5 French, the setting or surroundings of an event or action.

6 The rations issued to the Allied troops at Gallipoli were it appears seriously nutritionally deficient and undermined their health. Nick Wilson, Nhung Ngheim, Jennifer A. Summers, Mary-Ann Carter, Glyn Harper, 'A Nutritional Analysis of New Zealand Military Food Rations at Gallipoli in 1915: likely contribution to scurvy and other nutrient deficiency disorders', *New Zealand Medical Journal*, 19 Apr 2013, pp. 12–29.

7 'Lobiniere' is probably a play on the name of Maj-Gen Joly de Lotbiniére, the ANZAC Chief Engineer who had designed one model of hand grenade.

8 Sgt Robert R. **Nairn**; 21 Jan 1891 Auckland – 2 Aug 1915; single farmer of Auckland; 4/654 4th Refts NZE; Accidentally killed Gallipoli. *Official History of the New Zealand Engineers During the Great War 1914–1919* (Wanganui, 1927), p. 34.

9 I have not found any documentary evidence that supports this comment by WGM.

10 A small hill inland from Gaba Tepe.

11 Pte (later Lt-Col) Benjamin W.H. **Smart**, MBE; 1 Mar 1896, England – 24 Nov 1959; single clerk of Palmerston North; 10/1659, 3rd Refts, WIB.

12 Maj (later Lt-Col) Ivon T. **Standish**, CMG DSO mid(3); 31 Feb 1883 New Plymouth – 11 Sep 1967; married soldier of Palmerston

North; 2/283 NZFA, later OC 3Bty, OC 3Bde NZFA, postwar OC CMD; SA War.

13 The *London Opinion*, a humorous weekly publication.

Postscript

1 Wellington Infantry Battalion (WIB) War Diary, 5–6 Aug 1915, Appendix 128, operation orders, No. 128, 5 Aug 1915, WA 73/1, ANZ; Benjamin Smart diary, 5–6 Aug 1915, 1989.369, KMARL; Pugsley, *Gallipoli*, p. 270.

2 Minutes of the Regimental Fund Committee Meeting, 4 Aug 1915, WA 73/3 item 1, ANZ; Watson to Hughes, 15 Aug 1915, NZC15/10/14, Lovegrove papers, Wanganui District Library.

3 WGM diary, 14 May, 4 and 5 Aug 1915; Tim Travers, *Gallipoli 1915* (Stroud, 2001), p. 114.

4 Robert Rhodes James, *Gallipoli* (first published 1965, Pimlico ed., 1999), pp. 235–58; Travers, pp. 114–117; Pugsley, *Gallipoli*, pp. 268–69; Robin Prior, *Gallipoli: The End of the Myth* (New Haven, 2009), pp. 160–68.

5 Recollections of Cpl Leonard Leary, recorded 6 Oct 1960, MS papers 4022, ATL; Smart diary, 10 Jul 1915; Cunningham et al., p. 62.

6 Cunningham et al., pp. 62–63.

7 Pugsley, *Gallipoli*, p. 263; Peter Stanley, 'Whom at first We did not like . . . Australians and New Zealanders at Quinn's Post, Gallipoli', in John Crawford and Ian McGibbon eds, *New Zealand's Great War: New Zealand, the Allies and the First World War* (Auckland, 2007), p. 192.

8 WGM diary, 14 May 1915; Pugsley, *Gallipoli*, p. 264; Waite, pp. 187–88.

9 WIB War Diary, operations orders No. 2 (No. 129), 6 Aug 1915, Appendix 129, WA73/1, ANZ; Cunningham et al., p. 62.

10 Instructions signed by Temperley, nd, appendix number 130, WIB War Diary Aug 1915, WA 73/1, ANZ; Pugsley, *Gallipoli*, p. 275.

11 WGM to O/C Guard Happy Valley, 6 Aug 1915, (not published) MSX 2553, ATL; Smart diary, 6 August 1915.

12 WGM diary, 4 Aug 1915; Smart diary, 3 Aug 1915; Pugsley, *Gallipoli*, p. 270.

13 Cunningham et al., p. 63; Pugsley, *Gallipoli*, p. 270.

14 C.E.W. Bean, *The Story of ANZAC, Volume II, from 4 May 1915, to the Evacuation of the Gallipoli Peninsula* (Sydney, 1924), p. 576; Pugsley, *Gallipoli*, pp. 271–75.

15 New Zealand Infantry Brigade (NZIB) War Diary 6–7 Aug 1915, WA 70/1, ANZ; 'The August Battle for Chunuk Bair as seen by a Subaltern' by Gibson Bishop, 76-095, ATL; Cunningham et al., pp. 63–64; A.C. Temperley, 'A Personal Narrative of the Battle of Chunuk Bair, Aug 6th–10th 1915', pp. 1–4, 95/16/1, Imperial War Museum, London; Pugsley, *Gallipoli*, pp. 275–77.

16 Pugsley, *Gallipoli*, p. 277.

17 WIB War Diary, 7 Aug 1915, WA 73/1, ANZ; 'Draft History of the Wellington Infantry Battalion New Zealand Expeditionary Force', p. 24, WA 1/3 item 11, ANZ; Johnston to HQ NZ and A Div, 10 Aug 1915; WA20/5 box 2, ANZ; Godley, 'Report on the Operations against the Sari Bair position 6th–10th August 1915 of the Force under the command of Major-General Sir A.J. Godley, KCMG, CB, Commanding New Zealand and Australian Division', 16 Aug 1915, WA1, 1 box 1, ANZ; Smart diary, 7 Aug 1915; Ernest Mayo diary, 7 Aug 1915, MS-Papers-2641, ATL; Temperley, p. 5.

18 Cunningham et al., pp. 64–65.

19 See for example, John North, *Gallipoli: The Fading Vision* (London, 1936), p. 111.

20 WGM to OC NZ Inf Bde, 7 Aug 1915, MS-Papers-11408-03, ATL; Rhodes James, p. 288; Pugsley, *Gallipoli*, p. 277.

21 O.E. Burton, *The Auckland Regiment: Being an account of the doings on active service of the first, second and third Battalions of the Auckland Regiment* (Auckland, 1922), p. 58; Pugsley, *Gallipoli*, pp. 277–78.

22 Hans Kannengiesser, *The Gallipoli Campaign* (English Edition, London, 1927), pp. 206–10; Travers, p. 127.

23 Bean, vol II, p. 637.

24 Temperley, p. 1.

25 Cunningham et al., p. 67.

26 Pugsley, *Gallipoli*, p. 278.

27 Temperley, p. 18; Pugsley, *Gallipoli*, p. 278; Howe to Denis Malone, 19 Sep 1964, MS-11408-09, ATL.

28 Aspinall-Oglander to W.B. Malone, 3 December 1936, MS-Papers-11408-07, ATL.

29 Temperley, pp. 6–7; Burton, pp. 59–60; Pugsley, *Gallipoli*, pp. 282–83.

30 Charles Clark interview transcript, 1999. 2888, KMARL; Smart diary, 7 Aug 1915; David Ferguson, *The History of the Canterbury Regiment, NZEF 1914–1919* (Auckland, 1921), p. 61.

31 Mayo diary, 7 Aug 1915, MS-Papers-2641, ATL; Charles Lepper to his parents, nd but 1915, H.D. Skinner collection, c2001-122, Puke Ariki, New Plymouth; Cunningham et al., pp. 67–68; Cecil Malthus, *Anzac: A Retrospect* (Christchurch, 1965), pp. 117–18; Pugsley, *Gallipoli*, p. 284; Travers, p. 126.

32 Travers, p. 127; Bean, vol II, pp. 634–35.

33 WGM diary, 8 Jun 1915.

34 Harston to Denis Malone, 9 Mar 1965, MS-Papers-11408-09; C.E.W. Bean, *Gallipoli Mission* (Canberra, 1948), p. 208.

35 Johnston to NZ and A Division, 10 Aug 1915, WA 20/5 box 2, ANZ; Wallingford to son, 6 Sep 1915, Wallingford Family Collection Wellington (WFCW); Cunningham to Hughes (copy), 23 Feb 1916, MS-Papers-4192, ATL; Temperley, p. 13; Cunningham et al., pp. 68–69; Pugsley, *Gallipoli*, p. 284.

36 Smart diary, 8 Aug 1915.

37 'Report of Fighting on Chunuk Bair, 8 August 1915', unnumbered appendix, WIB War Diary, Aug 1915, WA 73/1; draft history of WIB, WA 73/3 item 11.

38 Cunningham et al., pp. 69–70.

39 'Report of fighting on Chunuk Bair', WA 73/1; Cunningham to Hughes, 23 Feb 1916, MS-Papers-4192; Travers, pp. 127–28.

40 Pugsley, *Gallipoli*, p. 286.

41 Cunningham et al., p. 71.

42 Temperley, pp. 11–12.

43 Pugsley, *Gallipoli*, pp. 287–88.

44 *Notes from the Front: Collated by the General Staff* (London, 1914), MFCL. This booklet has been widely distributed among NZEF officers, *NZEF War Diary 1914*, p. 245.

45 Harston to W.B. Malone, 5 Mar 1942 and to Denis Malone, 9 Mar 1965, MS Papers-11408-09 Cunningham et al., p. 70; Pugsley, *Gallipoli*, p. 288.

46 Cunningham to Hughes, 23 Feb 1916 (copy), MS-Papers-4192; Pugsley, *Gallipoli*, p. 289.

47 Harston to W.B. Malone, 5 Mar 1942, MS-Papers-11408-09.

48 Ibid.; 'Contour Plan of Chunuk Bair, 31 May 1921, WO 32/5867, The National Archives, London; Cunningham et al., p. 73.

49 C.F. Aspinall-Oglander, *Military Operations Gallipoli: Volume II, May 1915 to the Evacuation* (London, 1932), pp. 209–12, 217–20; Travers, pp. 131–32.

50 Lepper letter, H.D. Skinner collection, c2001-122, Puke Ariki, New Plymouth; Account of the fighting on Chunuk Bair by Lieutenant-Colonel W.H. Hastings, 5 Feb 1929, MS-Papers-11408-09; 'Report of Fighting on Chunuk Bair', WA 73/1; Statement by Private R.J. Davie (a former prisoner of war), 19 Jan 1919, WA 10/3, box 3, ANZ; Clark Interview Transcript, 1999.2888, KMARL; Cunningham et al., pp. 7–73; Pugsley, *Gallipoli*, pp. 291–93.

51 Cunningham to Hughes, 23 Feb 1916, MS-Papers-4192; 'Report of Fighting on Chunuk Bair', WA 73/1; Harston to W.B. Malone, 5 Mar 1942, MS-Papers-11408-09; Pugsley, *Gallipoli*, p. 295.

52 Wallingford to son, 6 Sep 1915, WFCW; W.D. Curham diary, 8 Aug 1915, Acc 1988-2165, KMARL; Hastings account, MS-Papers-11408-09; Accounts of the fighting on Chunuk Bair differ on how many guns were brought into action and how long they were in action for, but it is clear that only one or two guns were brought into action and that they were put out of action relatively quickly.

53 Hastings account, MS-Papers-11408-09; 'Report of Fighting on Chunuk Bair', WA 73/1.

54 W.D. Curham interview, 8 Aug 1965, ID247159, Sound Archives, Christchurch.

55 Smart diary, 8 Aug 1915; WIB War Diary 8 Aug 1915, WA 73/1, 'Report of Fighting on Chunuk Bair', WA 73/1; Pugsley, *Gallipoli*, p. 285.

56 Harston to W.B. Malone, 5 Mar 1942; Hastings account, MS-Papers-11408-09; 'Report of Fighting on Chunuk Bair', WA 73/1; Cunningham et al., p. 75, states that Harston was sent to brigade headquarters at 3 pm and returned to Chunuk Bair within an hour, but Harston's account and the sequence of events make the morning more likely.

57 'Report of Fighting on Chunuk Bair', WA73/1; 'Draft History of the WIB', pp. 25–26, WA 73/3, item 11; C.G. Nicol, *The Story of Two Campaigns: Official War History of the Auckland Mounted Rifles Regiment, 1914–1919* (Auckland, 1921), p. 72; Pugsley, *Gallipoli*, pp. 297–98.

58 Nicol, p. 73; Pugsley, *Gallipoli*, pp. 295–98.

59 Hastings account, MS-Papers-11408-09.

60 Some sources suggest Malone was killed an hour or two later, but about 5 pm seems most likely. *Grey River Argus*, 28 Oct 1915, p. 5; *Otago Witness*, 3 Nov 1915, p. 50; Watson to Hughes, 15 Aug 1915, NZC 15/10/14 Lovegrove papers, Wanganui District Library; Cunningham et al., p. 74; Hastings account, MS-Papers-11408-09.

61 Cunningham et al., p. 74.

62 Harston to Denis Malone, 23 Mar 1965, MS-Papers-11408-09; Lepper letter, c2001-122.

63 Christopher Pugsley, *The ANZAC Experience: New Zealand, Australia and Empire in the First World War* (Auckland, 2004), p. 106, note 36, p. 319.

64 Unidentified newspaper clipping quoting letter dated 25 Aug 1915 by McMenamin, MFCL.

65 NZIB War Diary, 8 Aug 1915, WA 70/1, Johnston to NZ and A Div, 10 Aug 1915, WA 20/5 box 2.

66 Bean, vol. II, p. 679; 'Report of Fighting on Chunuk Bair', WA 73/1.

67 Lepper letter, c2001-122.

68 Daniel Curham diary, 8 Aug 1915, 1988.2165, KMARL.

69 Richard Stowers, *Bloody Gallipoli: The New Zealanders' Story* (Auckland, 2005), p. 182; Commonwealth War Graves Commission Website data.

70 Harry Ernest Browne diary, 'Chunuk Bair', MS-Papers-3519, ATL; 'Report of Fighting on Chunuk Bair', WA70/1; Smart diary, 11 Aug 1915; A.H. Wilkie, *Official War History of the Wellington Mounted Rifles Regiment, 1914–1919* (Auckland, 1924), pp. 51–59; A.E. Byrne, *Official History of the Otago Regiment, NZEF in the Great War 1914–1918* (Dunedin, 1921), pp. 56–63; Pugsley, *Gallipoli*, pp. 301–10; Pugsley, *ANZAC Experience*, pp. 109–13; Travers, pp. 133–34.

71 Smart diary, 9 Aug 1915.

72 Tahu Rhodes diary, 17 Aug 1915, MS-1691, ATL.

73 Bollinger diary, 21 Aug 1915, MS Papers-1469, ATL; Smart diary, 21 Aug 1915, 1989.369; WIB War Diary, 8 Aug–14 Sep 1915, WA 73/1, ANZ.

74 Bollinger diary, 31 Aug 1915, MS Papers-1469, ATL.

75 Smart diary, 13 Aug 1915.

76 Cunningham et al., p. 78.

77 Cunningham et al., p. 79.

78 Pugsley, *Gallipoli*, p. 312.

79 Smart diary, 12 Aug 1915.

80 Cunningham to Hughes, 23 Feb 1916; Graham to IKM, 11 May 1916, MFCL; Howe to Denis Malone, 12 May 1964, MS-Papers-11408-10; Pugsley, *Gallipoli*, pp. 310–12.

81 Watson to Hughes, 15 Aug 1915, NZC 15/10/14; *Hawera and Normanby Star*, 23 Oct 1915, p. 4.

82 Prior, *Myth*, pp. 185–89; Robin Prior, 'A ridge too far: the obstacles to Allied victory', in Ashley Ekins ed., *Gallipoli: A Ridge too Far* (Wollombi, 2013), pp. 76–105.

83 Godley to Sclater, 9 Sep 1915, WA 252/6, ANZ.

Conclusion

1 'A Fearless Leader, Work of Colonel Malone, Creation of a Battalion, Training in Egypt', MFCL. The author of this paper is not identified, but clearly knew WGM well.

2 Lepper letter, c 2001-122, Puke Ariki.

3 Cunningham to Hughes (copy), 23 Feb 1916, MS Papers-4192.

4 Godley to Hughes, 31 Aug 1915, MS-Papers-3871-3/1, ATL.

5 Lady Godley to Godley, 11 Aug 1915, post-script (copy), see also Godley to Lady Godley, 12 Aug 1915 (copy), WA 252/12, ANZ.

6 Lady Godley to IKM, 22 Aug 1915; Godley to IKM, 14 Aug 1915, MFCL.

7 Telegram, Godley to IKM, 9 Aug 1915; Mackenzie to IKM, 12 Aug 1915, MFCL.

8 Harston to IKM, 13 Aug 1915 (copy), MFCL.

9 Birdwood to IKM, 9 Aug 1915, MFCL. Birdwood mentions only two New Zealand battalion or regimental commanders in his autobiography. The 'most admirable' Malone and the 'great-hearted' Arthur Bauchop. Lord Birdwood, *Khaki and Gown: An Autobiography* (London, 1941), p. 275.

10 Birdwood to one of WGM's sons, nd (copy), Malone/1, Peter Liddle Collection, Brotherton Library, University of Leeds.

11 Johnston to IKM, Aug 1915, MFCL.

12 Godley to IKM, 14 Aug 1915, MFCL.

13 Mackenzie to IKM, 12 Aug 1915, 3 Sep 1915, MFCL.

14 Mackenzie to IKM, 30 Aug 1915, MFCL.

15 Coleman to IKM, 23 Dec 1915, MFCL. It is, however, odd that the committee did not write to Ida Malone until more than four months after WGM's death.

16 *Evening Post*, 12 Aug 1915, p. 7.

17 *Evening Post*, 12 Aug 1915, p. 8.

18 See for example, *Auckland Star*, 12 Aug 1915, p. 2; *Dominion*, 12 Aug 1915, p. 6.

19 *Taranaki Herald*, 12 Aug 1915, p. 3.

20 *Stratford Evening Post*, 12 Aug 1915.

21 *Evening Post*, 22 Oct 1915, p. 3; *Hawera and Normanby Star,* 4 Nov 1915, p. 4.

22 Temperley, p. 11.

23 Cunningham et al., p. vi; 'A Fearless Leader', MFCL.

24 W. Fraser, 'The Colours of All Saints Church', 99-221 R3B453, Wairarapa Archive, Masterton.

25 *The Arrower*, vol. I, No. 6, 24 Nov 1914, p. 5.

26 *Taranaki Herald*, 9 Aug 1923; Chris Maclean and Jock Phillips, *The Sorrow and the Pride: New Zealand War Memorials*, (Wellington, 1990), pp. 68, 88.

27 W.D. Curham interview, 8 Aug 1965, ID247159, Sound Archives, Christchurch.

28 Fred Waite, *The New Zealanders at Gallipoli* (Auckland, 1919), pp. 221, xii–xiii.

29 *Taranaki Herald*, 9 Aug 1923; Cunningham et al., p. v.

30 Graham Hucker, 'A Hall of Remembrance and its Narrative of the Great War', paper presented at the Professional Historians Association of New Zealand Aotearoa conference, Wellington, 3 Sep 2000; David Walter, *Stratford: Shakespearean Town under the Mountain: A History* (Stratford, 2005), p. 39.

31 *Stratford Press*, 25 Nov 2011.

32 Clare Lyons to editor, email, 2 Dec 2004; information provided by Dr Judy Malone.

33 Lyons email, 2 Dec 2004; information provided by Tessa Keegan, email Lyons to editor, 19 Feb 2014, NZDF 1325/11/4.

34 Ashmead-Bartlett to IKM, 6 Nov 1915, MFCL.

35 McNab to Prime Minister, quoting Whitlock, 20 Dec 1915, W.G. Malone P/F; Attestation Form 11 and 17 Jan 1917, Brian Malone P/F.

36 Marginalia on McNab to Prime Minister, 20 Dec 1915; Prime Minister's office note, nd and attachment, 29 May 1916; W.G. Malone P/F.

37 Allen to IKM, 17 Aug 1921, MFCL.

38 Copy of will dated 11 Aug 1914 in Supreme Court probate file, MS-Papers-11408-15, ATL; information provided by Dr Judy Malone.

39 IKM to the District Trustee Hawera, 7 Dec 1922 (Copy), MFCL.

40 Papers relating to Thomas Harry Penn and Charles Penn v. Samuel Kindberg and Andrew Kindberg, (1919). ARC2013-1200, Puke

Ariki; .District Public Trust Hawera to IKM, 11 Oct 1922, 30 Nov 1923 and 2 May 1924, MFCL; Clare Lyons email, 2 Dec 2004.

41 Clare Lyons email, 2 Dec 2004.

42 District Public Trustee Hawera to IKM, 6 Dec 1929, MFCL; Clare Lyon email, 2 Dec 2004.

43 *Auckland Weekly News*, 19 Aug 1915, p. 64; Clare Lyons email, 2 Dec 2004, 18 Feb 2014, NZDF 1325/11/4, HQ NZDF; Ida Malone to District Public Trustee Hawera, 7 Dec 1922 (copy); Desmond Malone telephone interview, 9 Dec 2004; Extract from the Scottish register of deaths, Norah Crum (née Malone), 23 Mar 1983, copy provided by Penny Kidd.

44 Johnstone to IKM, Aug 1915, MFCL; History Sheet and Statement of Service, Edmond Leo Malone P/F, ANZ; Cunningham et al., pp. 89–101.

45 Cook to 1st New Zealand Infantry Brigade, 28 Dec 1916, Edmond Malone P/F.

46 History Sheet, Edmond Malone P/F; Cunningham et al., p. 226.

47 History Sheet, Edmond Malone, P/F; Cunningham et al., pp. 247–53; Glyn Harper, *Spring Offensive: New Zealand and the Second Battle of the Somme* (Auckland, 2003), pp. 96–132.

48 *Blue and White: The Magazine of St Patrick's College*, Dec 1918, pp. 12–13.

49 Telephone interview with Desmond Malone, 9 Dec 2004; information provided by Dr Judy Malone.

50 Email Mr Ray Roebuck to editor, 1 Oct 2013; Notes on telephone interview with Ray Roebuck, 14 Oct 2013, NZDF 1325/11/4; *Dominion Post*, 15 Jul 2009, p. A11; Andrew Moffat, *Flashback: Tales and Treasures of Taranaki* (Wellington, 2012), p. 87–89.

51 Copy of duplicate birth certificate Robert Bryan Roebuck [the original birth certificate is sealed], 22 Apr 1921, copy of marriage certificate of Gladys Geraldine Roebuck, 22 Aug 1918 provided by Penny Kidd, email to editor, 14 Oct 2013; Ray Roebuck telephone interview, 14 Oct 2013, NZDF 1325/11/4.

52 'Remembrance Day Service and Unveiling of Memorial Programme,' 11 Nov 1999 and associated papers, Edmond Malone P/F.

53 Pugsley to Puke Ariki, 13 Mar 2010, copy in editor's possession; information provided by Dr Judy Malone and Dr Christopher Pugsley; Moffat, p. 89.

54 Attestation Forms, 13 Aug 1914 and 31 Jul 1917, Certificate of Discharge, dated 22 Oct 1918, Brian Malone P/F, ANZ.

55 *Auckland Weekly News*, 19 Aug 1915, p. 64.

56 History Sheet, attestation forms, 11 and Jan 1917, 31 Jul 1917, Brian Malone P/F.

57 Notification of death, 18 Jan 1968, Brian Malone P/F; Bellringer, p. 161; information provided by Dr Judy Malone. Dr Malone has recently donated her substantial collection of Malone family material to the Alexander Turnbull Library and Puke Ariki.

58 History Sheet, Casualty Form-Active Service, Proceedings of Medical Board, 27 Mar 1916, notification of death, 18 Mar 1963, Terence Joseph Malone P/F; Terry Malone probate file, AAOM W3265 0217/63, ANZ; Desmond Malone telephone interview.

59 History Sheet, Maurice Patrick Malone P/F, ANZ; J.H. Luxford, *With the Machine Gunners in France and Palestine: the Official History of the New Zealand Machine Corps in the Great War 1914–1918* (Auckland, 1923), pp. 208–11; Desmond Malone telephone interview.

60 Copy of death registration provided by the Department of Internal Affairs; Coroner's court proceedings and related papers, Feb 1926, J46, 221/1926, ANZ; information provided by Dr Ashley Gould.

61 Draft letter to Public Trustee Hawera, enclosure to Willis to IKM, 1 Dec 1922, MFCL; *New Zealand Herald*, 25 Oct 1983; Tom Tullet, *Inside Dartmoor* (London, 1966), pp. 186–87, 197–201; Hugh Foot, *A Start in Freedom* (London, 1964), pp. 179–80.

62 Obituary *The Times*, 6 Jan 1944, p. 6.

63 David Irving, *Hess: the Missing Years 1941–1945* (London, 1987), pp. 101–02; David Erskine, *The Scots Guards 1919–1955* (London, 1956),

pp. 64–65, 187; Commonwealth War Graves Commission Web Site data.

64 'Summary NZ Army Court of Inquiry Baghak Contact, Bamiyan Province 4 August 2012 and Improvised Explosive Device Attack, Bamiyan Province 19 August 2012 (Afghan Court of Inquiry)', copy in editor's possession; Note on telephone interview with Mr Denis Malone (the father of Rory Malone), 23 Aug 2013, NZDF 1325/11/4; *Dominion Post*, 7 Aug 2012, p. A4; *Army News*, Aug 2012 pp. 6–9.

65 Richard Stowers, *Bloody Gallipoli: The New Zealanders' Story* (Auckland, 2005). Similarly there are 20 references to Malone in Les Carlyon's popular general history, *Gallipoli* (Sydney, 2001), but only one to Lieutenant-Colonel Arthur Bauchop, the outstanding commander of the Otago Mounted Rifles who was also killed in August 1915.

66 *Dominion*, 16 Jul 1915, p. 6.

67 Bean, vol. I, pp. 509–15.

68 Aspinall-Oglander, vol. I, pp. 296–98.

69 Aspinall-Oglander to W.B. Malone, 3 Dec 1936, MS-Papers-11408-07.

70 Pugsley, *Gallipoli*, pp. 163–71.

71 Chris Roberts, *The Landing at ANZAC: 1915* (Canberra, 2013), p. 145.

72 Malone's views are supported by material in the WIB War Dairy, 27–28 Apr 1915, WA 73/1, ANZ.

73 WGM diary, 14 May 1915; Howe to Denis Malone, 12 May 1964, MS Papers-11408-10.

74 WGM to IKM, 23 Jul 1915; Pugsley, *Gallipoli*, pp. 192–206.

75 John Crawford, 'War as the Cultivation of Domestic Virtues: William Malone and the New Zealand Experience at Gallipoli' in A. Mete Tuncoku ed., *Gallipoli in Retrospect 90 Years On* (Canakkale, 2005), pp. 113–38.

76 Waite, p. 177; Bean vol. II, pp. 250–53.

77 Peter Stanley, *Quinn's Post: Anzac, Gallipoli* (Crows Nest, 2005), pp. 100–10.

78 Harston to W.B. Malone, 5 Mar 1942, Denis Malone to Harston, 1 Mar 1965, MS-Papers-11408-09; Howe to Denis Malone, 26 Jun 1965, MS-Papers-11408-10.

79 Ian Hamilton, *Gallipoli Diary*, Vol II (London, 1920), p. 86; Rhodes James, p. 285.

80 Rhodes James to Denis Malone, 18 Nov 1963, Denis Malone to Rhodes James, 3 Dec 1963 (copy), MS-Papers-9049-1, ATL; *RSA Review*, Aug 1965, p. 16; Rhodes James, p. 359.

81 Waite, p. 238.

82 Cunningham et al., p.70.

83 Author's note, Maurice Shadbolt with photographs by Brian Brake, *Once on Chunuk Bair* (Auckland, 1982); 'Chunuk Bair', Avalon NFU studios and Daybreak Pictures, 1991; *Evening Post*, 25 Jul 1991, p. 24; James Bennett, 'Man Alone and Men Together: Maurice Shadbolt, William Malone and Chunuk Bair', *Journal of New Zealand Studies*, NS13 (2012), pp. 46–61.

84 Clipping Edmond P. Malone letter to the editor, *Listener,* 7 Jun 1980 and related papers, MS-Papers-8752-197, ATL; Maurice Shadbolt with photographs by Brian Brake, *Once on Chunuk Bair* (Auckland, 1982); 'Chunuk Bair', Avalon NFU studios and Daybreak Pictures, 1991; *Evening Post,* 25 Jul 1991, p. 24; information provided by Dr Christopher Pugsley.

85 Pugsley, *Gallipoli*, pp. 6, 378; information provided by Dr Judy Malone.

86 Jock Phillips, Nicholas Boyack and E.P. Malone eds, *The Great Adventure: New Zealand soldiers describe the First World War* (Wellington, 1988), pp. 16–68. A poem about Malone and his battalion on Chunuk Bair was included in the 1999 collection *Gallipoli and Other Poems* by leading New Zealand poet Alistair Te Ariki Campbell. 'Lt-Colonel W. G. Malone: Wellington Battalion, 8 August 1915', Alastair Te Ariki Campbell, *Gallipoli & Other Poems* (Wellington, 1999), pp. 18–19.

87 Readers Report enclosed with Iremonger to Malone, 15 Aug 1989, Williams to Malone, 18 Sep 1986, MS-Papers-11408-28, ATL.

88 See for example O.E. Burton, *The Silent Division: New Zealanders at the Front: 1914–1919* (Sydney, 1935), 120; Michael Neill, 'Introduction: Getting Out From Under', in

Shadbolt, *Chunuk Bair*, pp. 11–16; Pugsley, *Gallipoli*, pp. 354–57.

89 Christopher Moore-Bick, *Playing the Game: The British Junior Infantry Officer on the Western Front 1914–18* (Solihull, 2011), pp. 250–52.

90 Note by Godley, 7 Jun 1932, MS-Papers-11408-06, ATL.

91 Jim Anderton, *Unsung Heroes: Portraits of Inspiring New Zealanders* (Auckland, 1999), pp. 15–34; *Sunday Star Times*, 23 Apr 2000, pp. B1, B9; *Dominion*, 2 May 2000; *Dominion Post,* 9 Aug 2005; 'William "Molly" Malone's Life Celebrated', 5 Aug 2005, www.scoop.co.nz.

92 Speech by Hon Sir Anand Satyanand, Governor-General of New Zealand, Chunuk Bair service, 25 Apr 2009, MS-Papers-9314, ATL; *Dominion Post*, 23 Apr 2010, p. A2. The suggestion in this article that Malone was mistakenly shot by one of his own men is not supported by the available eyewitness evidence.

93 Murray Moorhead, 'Town pays tribute to great soldier' and other newspaper clipping in W.G. Malone biography file Defence Library, HQ NZDF.

94 Ian McGibbon, *Gallipoli: A Guide to New Zealand Battlefields and Memorials* (Auckland, 2004), pp. 98–99.

95 Note by Godley, 7 Jun 1932, MSPapers-11408-06.

Select Bibliography

Primary sources
Unpublished

Alexander Turnbull Library, National Library of New Zealand, Wellington (ATL)
  Lt Gibson Bishop [8/1406]. 'The August Battle for Chunuk Bair as seen by a Subaltern', 76-095
  Diary of Cpl George Bollinger [10/1024], MS Papers 2350
  Harry Ernest Browne diary, 'Chunuk Bair', MS Papers 3519
  Diary of Pte Harry Burton [10/958], MS Papers 5432
  Hughes Coll, MS Papers-4192
  Recollections of Cpl Leonard Leary [10/188]1, MS Papers 4022
  Diary of Capt John Luxford [10/307A], MS Papers 4453
  Macfarlane Coll, Ms Papers 3871
  Diary of Pte Ernest Mayo [10/984], MS Papers 2841
  Diary of Capt A Tahu Rhodes [15/3], qMS1690-1691
  Pte Aubrey Tronson [10/492]. 'A Soldiers Book of Life', MS Papers 2393

Archives NZ, Wellington (ANZ)
  Armed Constabulary Description Book, P8/1
  Army Inquiries papers, AD19 Series 22
  Army Personnel papers, AD10 Series 2
  Buildings – Stratford Drill Hall. AD1, 3/157
  Godley Papers, WA 252
  Miscellaneous Reports and Papers relating to the NZEF, WA1
  Reports & Summaries AD19 Series 68
  Stratford Rifle Volunteers Capitation Roll. ARM41 1910/4 O
  Transport No.10 NZEF, SS *Arawa*. AD1, 25/19/20

Wellington Infantry Battalion War Diary and miscellaneous records. WA 70/3

Brotherton Library, University of Leeds
  Malone/1, Peter Liddle Collection
  Memorial book compiled from the letters and diaries of L/Cpl Claude Comyns, Peter Liddle Collection

Imperial War Museum, London
  Colonel A.C. Temperley, 'A Personal Narrative of the Battle of Chunuk Bair – August 6th–10th, 1915', 95/16/1
  Alexander Wemyss, 'A Short History of the Contingent Company of the Ceylon Planters', 67/177/1

Kippenberger Military Archives and Research Library, Waiouru (KMARL)
  Interview Transcript Cpl Charles Clark [10/20], Acc1999.2888
  Diary of Pte Daniel Curham [10/300], Acc1988.2165
  Diary of Sgt Saxon Foster [10/526], Acc1998.2648
  Diary of Pte Ben Smart [10/1659], Acc1989.369
  Diary of Pte Peter Sutherland [10/1673], Acc1998.1737
  Diary of Pte James Swan DCM [10/1674], Acc1999.1086
  Diary of Pte Arthur Swayne [10/1019], Acc1992.50

Malone family Collection London (MFCL). Copies of virtually all the material referred to from this collection are now held by the Alexander Turnbull Library.

Puke Ariki, New Plymouth
    Letter of Pte CH Lepper, HD Skinner Coll,
    ARC2002.122
    Papers relating to Thomas Harry Penn and
    Charles Penn V. Samuel Kindberg and Andrew
    Kindberg, (1919). ARC2013-1200
    11th (Taranaki Rifles) Regimental Coll,
    ARC2003.858

Wairarapa Archive
    Wally Fraser, 'The Colours of All Saints Church',
    99-221 R3B453

Wallingford family collection, Wellington
Wanganui District Library
    Papers of Pte Cecil Lovegrove 10/410, NZC15

Other sources
Desmond Malone, Telephone Interview
    9 December 2004
Diary of Pte Oswald Meenken 10/185, Menken
    family, Palmerston North

Published
*Appendices to the Journals of the House of
    Representatives,* various years
The Arrower. Troopship Magazine HMNZT No.10.
    q940.484 ATL
Auckland Weekly News, various issues
Auckland Weekly News – Roll of Honour. Auckland,
    1915
Blue & White. St Patrick's College, Vol 7 No 2,
    Christmas 1915
*Cyclopedia of New Zealand, Vol 6, Taranaki,
    Hawkes Bay & Wellington Provincial Districts.*
    Christchurch, 1908
Newspapers – *Auckland Star, The Dominion,
    Evening Post, Manawatu Evening Standard,
    NZ Freelance, NZ Herald, Taranaki Almanac,
    Taranaki Daily News, Taranaki Herald, Wanganui
    Herald*
*New Zealand at the Dardanelles – Special War
    Number of The Weekly Press.* Vol 1, Christchurch,
    1915

*New Zealand Expeditionary Force (Europe), 1914.
    War Diary.* Wellington, 1915
New Zealand Expeditionary Force Embarkation Rolls,
    Vol 1. Wellington, 1916
New Zealand Gazette, various issues
Notes from the Front – Collated by the General
    Staff, London, 1914
Our Boys at the Front, NZ 1914-15. Wellington,
    1915
RSA Review, various issues
The Quarterly Army List of the NZ Forces.
    Wellington, various issues

Secondary sources
Aspinall-Oglander, C. F., *Military Operations:
    Gallipoli* Vol. I (London, 1929), Vol. II (London,
    1932).
Bean, C. E. W., *The Story of Anzac* Vol. 1, (Sydney,
    1921), Vol II (Sydney, 1924).
Corbett, J. S., *Naval Operations*, 2nd ed. (London,
    1929).
Cunningham, W. H., Treadwell, C. A. L. and
    Hanna, J. S., *The Wellington Regiment NZEF,
    1914–1919* (Wellington, 1928).
McGibbon, I., *The Path to Gallipoli: Defending New
    Zealand, 1850–1915* (Wellington, 1991).
Moorhead, Murray, *First and Strong: The
    Wellington, West Coast and Taranaki Regimental
    Story* (Wanganui, 2002).
Prior, R., *Gallipoli: The End of the Myth* (New
    Haven, 2009).
Pugsley, C., *Gallipoli: The New Zealand Story* (Reed,
    Auckland, 1998).
Rhodes James, R., *Gallipoli* (1965; Pimlico edition
    1999).
Shadbolt, Maurice, *Once on Chunuk Bair*
    (Auckland, 1982).
Stowers, Richard, *Bloody Gallipoli: The New
    Zealanders' Story*, (Auckland, 2005).
Travers, T., *Gallipoli 1915* (Stroud, 2001).
Waite, F., *The New Zealanders at Gallipoli*
    (Auckland, 1919).
Waters, S. D., *Shaw Savill Line: One Hundred Years
    of Trading* (Christchurch, 1961).

Index

Ranks mentioned are only those relevant to the period covered by the diaries.